Life-Span Developmental Psychology

Nonnormative Life Events

CONTRIBUTORS

BERNARD L. BLOOM
WILLIAM S. BRASTED
ROBERT L. BURGESS
ROBERT A. CALDWELL
EDWARD J. CALLAHAN
ROSALYN BENJAMIN DARLING
NANCY DATAN
BERNICE T. EIDUSON
ALAN B. FORSYTHE
JAMES GARBARINO
BONNIE GILSTRAP
JUAN L. GRANADOS
WILLIAM F. HODGES

JIM KILLARNEY
DEAN G. KILPATRICK
JON E. KRAPFL
KATHLEEN A. McCLUSKEY
DENNIS R. PAPINI
HAYNE W. REESE
JOHN W. SANTROCK
RICHARD J. SEIME
MICHAEL A. SMYER
LOIS J. VERONEN
RICHARD A. WARSHAK
JEFFREY ZIMMERMAN

LIFE-SPAN DEVELOPMENTAL PSYCHOLOGY

NONNORMATIVE LIFE EVENTS

Edited by

EDWARD J. CALLAHAN   and   KATHLEEN A. McCLUSKEY

Department of Psychology
West Virginia University
Morgantown, West Virginia

Department of Psychology
West Virginia University
Morgantown, West Virginia

 1983

ACADEMIC PRESS

A Subsidiary of Harcourt Brace Jovanovich, Publishers

New York   London
Paris   San Diego   San Francisco   São Paulo   Sydney   Tokyo   Toronto

ACADEMIC PRESS, INC.
111 Fifth Avenue, New York, New York 10003

United Kingdom Edition published by
ACADEMIC PRESS, INC. (LONDON) LTD.
24/28 Oval Road, London NW1 7DX

Library of Congress Cataloging in Publication Data
Main entry under title:

Life-span developmental psychology.

Proceedings of the 7th West Virginia University
Life-Span Conference, held in Morgantown, W. Va.,
in May 1980.
  Includes bibliographies and index.
  1. Developmental psychology--Congresses.
2. Family--Mental health--Congresses. 3. Social
problems--Congresses. I. Callahan, Edward J.
II. McCluskey, Kathleen A. III. West Virginia
University Conference on Life-Span Developmental
Psychology (7th : 1980) [DNLM: 1. Psychology--
Congresses. W3 LI442]
BF712.5.L53 1983   155.9   82-22784
ISBN 0-12-155140-7

PRINTED IN THE UNITED STATES OF AMERICA

83 84 85 86   9 8 7 6 5 4 3 2 1

To our parents, Jim and Mary, Merrill and Vivienne
and our children, Becky, Josh, Shavahn, and John

Contents

4. Adolescent Pregnancy and Parenthood: Implications for Development
Kathleen A. McCluskey, Jim Killarney, and Dennis R. Papini

5. The Birth Defective Child and the Crisis of Parenthood: Redefining the Situation
Rosalyn Benjamin Darling

6. Fetal Loss and Sudden Infant Death: Grieving and Adjustment for Families
Edward J. Callahan, William S. Brasted, and Juan L. Granados

7. Rape: A Precursor of Change
Lois J. Veronen and Dean G. Kilpatrick

8. Violence to the Family
Robert L. Burgess, James Garbarino, and Bonnie Gilstrap

9. Marital Separation: The First Eight Months
Bernard L. Bloom, William F. Hodges, and Robert A. Caldwell

10. Children of Divorce: Impact of Custody Disposition on Social Development
Richard A. Warshak and John W. Santrock

11. Traumatic Injury in Midlife
Jon E. Krapfl

12. Dialysis: A Unique Challenge?
Richard J. Seime and Jeffrey Zimmerman

Epilogue

Contributors

Numbers in parentheses indicate the pages on which the authors' contributions begin.

BERNARD L. BLOOM (217), Department of Psychology, University of Colorado, Boulder, Colorado 80309

WILLIAM S. BRASTED[1] (145), Department of Psychology, West Virginia University, Morgantown, West Virginia 26506

ROBERT L. BURGESS (193), College of Human Development, The Pennsylvania State University, University Park, Pennsylvania 16802

ROBERT A. CALDWELL[2] (217), Department of Psychology, University of Colorado, Boulder, Colorado 80309

EDWARD J. CALLAHAN (145), Department of Psychology, West Virginia University, Morgantown, West Virginia 26506

ROSALYN BENJAMIN DARLING[3] (115), Division of Social Sciences, University of Pittsburgh at Johnstown, Johnstown, Pennsylvania 15904

NANCY DATAN (35), Department of Psychology, West Virginia University, Morgantown, West Virginia 26506

BERNICE T. EIDUSON (45), Department of Psychiatry and Biobehavioral Sciences, University of California, Los Angeles, Los Angeles, California 90024

ALAN B. FORSYTHE (45), Department of Biomathematics, University of California, Los Angeles, Los Angeles, California 90024

JAMES GARBARINO (193), College of Human Development, The Pennsylvania State University, University Park, Pennsylvania 16802

BONNIE GILSTRAP (193), College of Human Development, The Pennsylvania State University, University Park, Pennsylvania 16802

---

[1]PRESENT ADDRESS: Department of Psychiatry and Behavioral Sciences, Medical University of South Carolina, Charleston, South Carolina 29403

[2]PRESENT ADDRESS: Department of Psychology, Michigan State University, East Lansing, Michigan 48824

[3]PRESENT ADDRESS: In-Home Services, City–County Clinic, Johnstown, Pennsylvania 15901

JUAN L. GRANADOS (145), Department of Obstetrics and Gynecology, West Virginia University, Morgantown, West Virginia 26505

WILLIAM F. HODGES (217), Department of Psychology, University of Colorado, Boulder, Colorado 80309

JIM KILLARNEY[1] (69), Department of Psychology, West Virginia University, Morgantown, West Virginia 26506

DEAN G. KILPATRICK (167), Department of Psychiatry and Behavioral Sciences, Medical University of South Carolina, Charleston, South Carolina 29425

JON E. KRAPFL[2] (265), Department of Psychology, West Virginia University, Morgantown, West Virginia 26506

KATHLEEN A. McCLUSKEY (69), Department of Psychology, West Virginia University, Morgantown, West Virginia 26506

DENNIS R. PAPINI (69), Department of Psychology, West Virginia University, Morgantown, West Virginia 26506

HAYNE W. REESE (1), Department of Psychology, West Virginia University, Morgantown, West Virginia 26506

JOHN W. SANTROCK (241), Department of Psychology, University of Texas at Dallas, Richardson, Texas 75080

RICHARD J. SEIME (281), Department of Behavioral Medicine and Psychiatry, West Virginia University Medical Center, Morgantown, West Virginia 26506

MICHAEL A. SMYER (1), College of Human Development, The Pennsylvania State University, University Park, Pennsylvania 16802

LOIS J. VERONEN (167), Department of Psychiatry and Behavioral Sciences, Medical University of South Carolina, Charleston, South Carolina 29425

RICHARD A. WARSHAK[3] (241), Department of Psychiatry, Division of Psychology, University of Texas Health Science Center, Richardson, Texas 75235

JEFFREY ZIMMERMAN[4] (281), Department of Behavioral Medicine, West Virginia University, Morgantown, West Virginia 26506

---

[1]PRESENT ADDRESS: Aroostook Mental Health Center, Madawaska, Maine 04756

[2]PRESENT ADDRESS: COBA, Inc., 2215 York Road #202, Oakbrook, Illinois 60521

[3]PRESENT ADDRESS: 5735 Brushy Creek Trail, Dallas, Texas 75252.

[4]PRESENT ADDRESS: Rehabilitation Medicine, Mt. Sinai Hospital, Hartford, Connecticut 06112

Preface

The topic of the Seventh West Virginia University Life-Span volume was chosen to complement the content of the fourth Life-Span volume published in 1975. That volume on Normative Life Crises (Datan & Ginsberg, 1975) was the first to break with the strictly academic tradition of the previous volumes to " ... create an interface between academic and applied perspectives on the life cycle ... " (Datan & Ginsberg, 1975, p. xiii). The contributors to that volume analyzed the effects of normative life crises, those events which occur to most members of a specific culture or group (Baltes, Reese, & Lipsitt, 1980) on four levels: academic and applied perspectives, individual development, the family life cycle, and the social system. In contrast, we chose to focus the seventh volume on the effects of nonnormative life crises, those which occur to only certain individuals within a specific culture or group and are for the most part considered to be disruptive to the normal life course.

This issue of disruptiveness is critical, though. The ancient Chinese characters for "crisis" consisted of two parts: problem and opportunity. A subtheme of this volume, then, was to examine not only the problematic aspects of nonnormative life events, but the opportunity aspects as well. We thought it advantageous to go beyond the traditional life-span academicians in inviting chapters for this book.

Contributors were invited from a number of orientations and academic disciplines, ranging from traditional life-span psychologists to practicing clinical psychologists. The dynamic interplay of these diverse approaches results in a very exciting level of intellectual and practical stimulation which we feel is reflected in the chapters of this volume. The chapters are grouped topically to mirror the pairings of the conference presentations. Two papers originally presented at the conference, one by Noel McIntosh, Rosalind Parkinson, and Ann Dacey entitled "Adolescent Pregnancy" and another by David Rigler entitled "The Terminally Ill Child" have been replaced by the chapters by McCluskey, Killarney, and Papini

(Chapter 4), and Callahan, Brasted, and Granados (Chapter 6). The contributions of Rigler and McIntosh *et al.* were significant to the quality of the conference, and we hope that they find in these replacements some of their influence.

References

Baltes, P. B., Reese, H. W., & Lipsitt, L. P. Life-span developmental psychology. In M. R. Rosenzweig & L. W. Porter (Eds.), *Annual Review of Psychology.* Palo Alto, California: Annual Reviews, Inc., 1980.

Datan, N., & Ginsberg, L. H. (Eds.), *Life-span developmental psychology: Normative life crises.* New York: Academic Press, 1975.

Acknowledgments

The success of the Seventh West Virginia University Life-Span Developmental Psychology Conference was made possible by the cooperative efforts of many individuals. Special thanks are given to Ray Koppelman, Vice President for Energy Studies, Graduate Programs, and Research, an active supporter and procuror of funds for this and many previous Life-Span Conferences. Our chairman, Jon Krapfl, provided us with additional funds and departmental resources which were essential to our success. Hayne Reese and Nancy Datan lent us their guidance based on long-standing histories in this conference's tradition. We are also grateful to those individuals who served as discussants for the paper sessions: Robert Pawlicki, Reba Thurmond, and Karen Connors. Their comments and insights contributed significantly to the vital atmosphere of this conference. Philip Comer deserves special recognition for the stirring keynote address delivered at the conference. Special thanks are in order for the graduate students, whose help, as usual, was invaluable: Nancy Croghan, Carol Giesen, Jim Killarney, Bonnie Kwiatkowski, Gale Richardson, Dean Rodeheaver, J. R. Simons, and Jeanne Thomas.

CHAPTER 1

The Dimensionalization of Life Events

HAYNE W. REESE
WEST VIRGINIA UNIVERSITY
MORGANTOWN, WEST VIRGINIA

MICHAEL A. SMYER
THE PENNSYLVANIA STATE UNIVERSITY
UNIVERSITY PARK, PENNSYLVANIA

I. Introduction

The life course is like the act of writing an essay, beginning with promises about goals to be reached, continuing with development toward these goals, and ending with variable success in attaining the goals. In the writing, the essay is divided into sections by major transitions and into subsections and paragraphs by lesser transitions, sometimes with footnoted digressions but always punctuated by pauses, stops, and starts. Like essays, lives vary in content, organization, length, and style; they vary in meaning and merit. But let us limit our attention to the analogues of punctuating and sectioning, lest we be beguiled by possible analogues to the typewriter or the Great Copyeditor in the Sky.

Our analogy implies, aptly, that the life course is formed by major and minor transitions. Most relevant research has been concerned with the major transitions, which are stressful and disruptive of customary behavior patterns (Danish, Smyer, & Nowak, 1980; Hultsch & Plemons, 1979; Lieberman, 1975). Appropriately, these major transitions are usually called life *crises*. The word *crisis* comes from the Greek *krinein*, "to separate," and means a

LIFE-SPAN DEVELOPMENTAL PSYCHOLOGY
Nonnormative Life Events

decisive moment, turning point, or crucial time. In medicine, it refers to the turning point in a disease, the outcome of which will be recovery or death. This "pathological and often fatalistic [Riegel, 1975, p. 100]" implication seems to be commonly associated with the term. To avoid this dire implication, some writers use the word *event*, which in its broadest sense merely means something that happens, and therefore more clearly can refer to positive "crises" such as graduating, marrying, and being promoted, as well as to negative crises such as failing, divorcing, and being fired.

In its broadest sense, *event* has a very mild connotation. Having a drink of water, for example, is an event, but in most circumstances it is unlikely to have a noteworthy effect on the life course. Nevertheless, it must have some effect, however small and transient, and therefore a decision to ignore it would be arbitrary. Events vary in impact, with no large, naturally given gap separating noteworthy from trivial ones. But the arbitrary decision must be made to keep the research field tractable. We will therefore limit our discussion to *noteworthy* life events. We mean by *life events* possible happenings during the life course, and by *noteworthy* we mean that they have been discussed in the relevant literature.

The relevant literature is complicated for at least three reasons. First, it comes from several disciplines, including medicine, psychiatry, psychology, social work, and sociology, which offer different perspectives on life events and different theories about the mechanisms underlying their effects. Also, the total number of life events that have been identified is very large; for the analysis we shall present later, we used about 350 items. Finally, the taxonomic classification, or dimensionalization, of life events is chaotic, perhaps because of the variety of theoretical orientations of life-event researchers and the large number and variety of life events that have been considered noteworthy. In this chapter we shall review the life-event dimensions that have been identified and explore the implications of proposed classification systems. We begin with an examination of two very general approaches to life events.

II. Life Events as Processes and as Markers

Danish *et al.* (1980) identified two general conceptualizations of life events: as processes and as markers. Viewed as *processes*, events have antecedents, durations, contexts, and outcomes. They are also called *transitions* (e.g., Brim, 1976), although they can be conceptualized as causes of transitions, or causes of *becoming* (Overton & Reese, 1973). Viewed as *markers*, events signal that a transition has occurred or is impending. Danish *et al.* (1980) cited as examples retirement, as a marker of "the transition from an active work career to a life of leisure [p. 342]," and "becoming pregnant," as "a marker in the course of one's family development [p. 342]." Markers have causal status, but as causes of *being* rather than as causes of becoming or change. Becoming pregnant is a cause of change—and is a process—and therefore Danish *et al.* should have cited "being pregnant" rather than "becoming pregnant" as the marker. Retirement, or being retired, is an apt example, because it is a marker or product of the process of retiring, which begins before retirement and includes expectations about postretirement life.

The distinction between events as processes and as markers or products is usually not clear in the literature. For example, some investigators have studied life events as dependent variables, sometimes using age, birth cohort, and time of measurement (Schaie, 1965), or pairs of these, as independent variables. (In the sociological literature, time of measurement is usually called *period*.) A problem with the approach is that the life events investigated are *treated* as outcomes rather than as processes regardless of how they are *conceptualized*.

Another example of the process–product confusion is that life events have usually been labeled with nouns and noun phrases rather than with gerunds. Havighurst (1953) used gerunds, such as "learning to walk," but Holmes and Rahe (1967) and Paykel (1973) used noun phrases. Sarason, Johnson, and Siegel (1978) used mostly noun phrases, and the gerunds they used, such as "leaving home for the first time" and "failing a course," seem to refer more to products than to processes. Of course, nouns can be used to label processes; but gerunds label them less ambiguously because by definition a *gerund* is the name of an action.

The process–product confusion may reflect a difference between deeply held convictions or presuppositions. In mechanistic thought, time is conceptualized as atomistic, consisting of discrete elements, and process is conceptualized as a succession of cross-sections. In the fundamental type of law, called a *process law* (Bergmann, 1957), instantaneous assessment of a system is used to predict future states of the system, or to postdict past states. The concept of process therefore tends to blur into a concept of product—concrete, material, and discrete. In dialectical thought, in contrast, time is conceptualized as a continuous range, area, or spread, which includes the immediate "past" as well as the immediate "future" (Reese, Note 1; see also Kvale, 1974, 1977; Riegel, 1977; 1979, Chap. 8). In dialectical thought, therefore, process is conceptualized as an ongoing activity in a context that includes a spread of time. The Mbuti, who are an African pygmy people, conceptualize the life process dialectically: A person moves through life in a space–time sphere (Turnbull, 1978; if the movement is too violent or too sudden, the person may break out of the sphere and become "wazi-wazi"—

'disoriented and unpredictable' [p. 166]). Such a process can be said to have antecedents and consequences only if these words are put in quotation marks to indicate that they are a part of a unitary whole and can be distinguished from it only analytically. This way of thinking about process may be less familiar than the mechanistic way to many researchers who study life events. If so, their concept of process might tend toward stasis; that is, it might tend to acquire an implication of product instead of retaining the dynamic implication of process.

III. Dimensions of Life Events

The *dimensions* of life events are their "structural characteristics" (Danish *et al.*, 1980), "properties" (Brim & Ryff, 1980), or "attributes" (Hultsch & Plemons, 1979). Life events are obviously multidimensional, but some researchers believe that a single dimension is so salient in importance that life events can be treated as functionally unidimensional. Other researchers disagree and treat life events as functionally multidimensional. The "unidimensional" group includes, for example, Holmes and his colleagues (e.g., Holmes & Masuda, 1973; Holmes & Rahe, 1967), for whom the salient dimension is impact or stressfulness. The Holmes and Rahe (1967) Social Readjustment Rating Scale includes 43 events, each of which has a mean impact rating. The scale is used by asking a person to indicate which events have occurred in some specified period of life, then summing the rated impacts of the events indicated. The scale includes both desirable and undesirable events, such as "marriage," "vacation," "Christmas," "divorce," "foreclosure of mortgage or loan," and "minor violations of the law." However, the desirability of the events is disregarded in the scoring because both kinds of events are stressful. Thus, the sum is interpreted to reflect the amount of stress the person experienced in the specified period.

The "unidimensional" group also includes Lieberman (1975), at least with respect to life *crises*. He conceptualized life crises as involving three elements—a loss or disruption of some kind, a demand for behavioral change, and a particular meaning attached to the event. However, despite this multidimensional conception of life crises, he concluded that the central element is the degree of behavioral change demanded, making life crises *functionally* unidimensional.

The other group, taking a multidimensional approach, is not unanimous about the number of life-event dimensions, as might be expected, or even about the nature of the dimensions, as will be seen later. They have identified a total of at least 35 different dimensions. Some of these have a theoretical basis and some have an empirical basis in factor analyses, but most seem to have been derived from speculation or intuition. A further complication is that relatively little systematic research has been done on the significance of most of these dimensions and on their interrelations (Hultsch & Plemons, 1979).

Some order can be introduced into this chaos by using a classification system proposed by Brim and Ryff (1980). They noted that some dimensions (or "properties," as they said) refer to the *effects* of events, others refer to the affected person's *perceptions* of events, and still others refer to *event properties*—characteristics of the events themselves independent of the effects of the events and perceptions of them. We used this system, in an a priori way, to classify the 35 dimensions of life events we found in our survey, which was by no means exhaustive. (For example, we have omitted Cobb's [1974] model because it is explicitly limited to the relationship of life events to illness. He separated *objective stress, subjective stress*, and *strain* and identified several dimensions of subjective stress and strain. He also emphasized the moderating effect of the social context in which an event occurs, as did Brown [1974b].) Table 1.1 shows our classification. Within each type the dimensions are alphabetized for ease of reference. As can be seen, the "event" dimensions are more numerous than the "perception" dimensions, and both are more numerous than the "effect" dimensions (about 54%, 29%, and 17% of the total, respectively). *Event* dimensions are by definition objective, and *perception* dimensions subjective, perhaps accounting for the difference in their frequency—reflecting not only the differential ease of studying these respective types of dimensions but also the objectivity of mainstream American gerontology, psychology, and sociology, which account for the majority of the relevant research. The effect dimensions are the least numerous, perhaps because of a conceptual difficulty. *Effect* dimensions refer explicitly to the effects of life events; hence they implicate the conceptualization of life events as processes, or causes. However, effect dimensions actually refer to properties of outcomes, obviously, rather than to properties of causes, and therefore they may seem inappropriate for analyzing life events conceptualized as processes.

All but six of the dimensions included in Table 1.1 are quantifiable; the six exceptions are qualitative. The qualitative dimensions are *domain* and *focus*, which are effect dimensions; *meaning*, which is a perception dimension; and *context, source*, and *type*, which are event dimensions. One of the qualitative dimensions—*focus*—and all of the quantitative dimensions seem to be straightforward and in need of no further explication than that given in the table. The other five qualitative dimensions need explication, but *meaning* is entirely subjective and is too complicated to be explicated in this chapter (for

TABLE 1.1

Classification of Several Dimensions of Life Events[a]

Dimension	Definition
"Effect" dimensions	
Contextual purity	Extent to which one event influences the resolution or outcome of concurrent events.
Direction of impact	Enhancement or debilitation of the life course in response to the event.
Direction of movement	Entering or leaving a role or social field as a result of the event.
Domain	Type of functioning affected (e.g., biological, social). (Also called *context, life area.*)
Focus	Person directly affected by the event (self or other).
Impact	Amount of behavioral change in response to the event; or amount of stress engendered by the event. (Also called *severity, stressfulness.*)
"Perception" dimensions	
Control	Belief that the event was chosen versus imposed, or under personal control versus uncontrolled.
Desirability	Perception of the event as desirable versus undesirable, or good versus bad.
Expectation	Extent to which the event was expected or anticipated.
Familiarity	Familiarity with an event through prior experience versus novelty of the event.
Long-range threat	Perceived severity of the negative *impact* over a long period.
Meaning	The person's interpretation of the event (e.g., accident versus will of God).
Perceived gain or loss	Perceived amount of gain or loss resulting from the event.
Social desirability	Perceived evaluation of the event by society at large or by smaller reference group.
Stress	Perceived stressfulness of the event.
Timeliness	Belief that the event occurred on time or off time.
"Event" dimensions	
Age congruity	Typical amount of overlap in the *spreads* of two or more specified events. Age congruity is independent of *contextual purity*, because an event can influence other events whether or not they are congruous in age, and events can be congruous in age without influencing one another.
Age relatedness	Strength of correlation with age. (Also called *age grading, temporal predictability.*) Note that *spread* and *timing* can be computed even if *age relatedness* is weak.
Adequacy of functioning	Extent to which event reflects inferior or superior functioning of the individual (e.g., divorce might reflect inferior functioning).
Breadth of setting	Extent to which event is limited to or is independent of particular settings.

Continued

TABLE 1.1 *(continued)*
Classification of Several Dimensions of Life Events[a]

Dimension	Definition
"Event" dimensions (continued)	
Cohort specificity	Extent to which the nature of an event depends on the individual's cohort, or generation.
Context	Area of the "life space" in which the event occurs (e.g., family, work). (Also called *domain*.)
Duration	Amount of time required for the event to transpire. (Also called *chronicity*; chronic versus acute.)
Integration	Extent to which the occurrence of one event depends on the occurrence of another. Integrated events may or may not exhibit *age congruity*.
Likelihood of occurrence	The probability that the event will occur for a given person (e.g., the *prevalence* of having Huntington's chorea is low in the population, but its likelihood is high in the offspring of an affected individual).
Onset	The suddenness or gradualness of the onset of the event.
Order	The sequence in which events typically occur.
Prevalence	The number of individuals who experience a given event, proportionate to the number of individuals in the population. (Also called *extensiveness of occurrence, generality, social distribution.*)
Recency	The amount of time passed since the occurrence of the event.
Reversibility	The degree to which a transition is reversible (e.g., entering the job market is reversible; but marrying is irreversible, because if a marriage is broken by death, for example, the survivor is a widow or widower, not a spinster or bachelor).
Sequencing	The sequence in which events occur in an individual case.
Source	The cause of an event, or the domain of the cause (e.g., heredity, physical environment). (Also called *domain*).
Spread	The age range within which an event typically occurs.
Type	The nature or domain of an event (e.g., biological processes, physical–environmental events). (Also called *domain.*)
Timing	The average age at which an event occurs. (Also called *age grading.*)

[a]The sources of these dimensions are Beeson & Lowenthal, 1975; Brim & Ryff, 1980; Brown, 1974a; Danish *et al.*, 1980; B. S. Dohrenwend, 1973; Dohrenwend *et al.*, 1978; Fairbank & Hough, 1979; Horowitz, Schaefer, & Cooney, 1974; Lieberman, 1975; Lowenthal & Chiriboga, 1973; Modell, Furstenberg, & Hershberg, 1976; Neugarten, 1969; Paykel, 1973; Pearlin & Schooler, 1978; Rabkin, 1980; Ruch, 1977; Sarason *et al.*, 1978; Gatz, Note 2; George, Note 3; and our own additions.

a brief discussion, see Brown, 1974b). *Context, domain, source,* and *type* are complicated, but can be explicated within the confines of this chapter. We turn to this explication in the next section.

IV. Categories of Life Events

A. *Contexts of Life Events*

As indicated in Table 1.1, we are using *context* to refer to the area of the "life space" in which an event occurs. Hultsch and Plemons (1979) identified four contexts of life events: community and society, family, occupation and career, and primary friendship network. Pearlin and Schooler (1978) also identified four contexts: occupation, which is also in Hultsch and Plemons's list; and household economics, marriage, and parenting, which Hultsch and Plemons might include under "family." Similarly, George (Note 3) identified four contexts overlapping only slightly with the lists of Hultsch and Plemons and Pearlin and Schooler. George's contexts were family and occupation, which are in the other lists, and health and self, which the others omitted. Danish *et al.* (1980) also identified four contexts: biological functions, family, occupation, and psychosocial functions. Again, the overlap with other lists is incomplete. Paykel (1974) identified five contexts: employment, family, health, and marital—which overlap with the other lists—and legal, which is not in the other lists.

Dohrenwend, Krasnoff, Askenasy, and Dohrenwend (1978) offered a list with 11 contexts: crime and legal matters, family, finances, having children, health, love and marriage, residence, school, social activities, work, and "miscellaneous." Despite its length, their list does not include three of the specific contexts identified in the other lists (friendship network, household economics, self).

Combining these lists and eliminating overlap yields the 14 contexts listed in Table 1.2. We have arranged them roughly into five superordinate sets, but these sets are for convenience of reference and do not have any theoretical basis.

Flanagan (1978) identified 15 contexts of "critical incidents" (life events), divided into 5 superordinate sets. The differences between Flanagan's contexts and those in our Table 1.2 are, roughly: (*a*) Flanagan's "material well-being and financial security" includes (most of) our "residence" and "finances"; (*b*) Flanagan's "intellectual development" includes our "school" and some of our "self"; (*c*) our "self" includes five of Flanagan's contexts— "intellectual development, personal understanding and planning, creativity

TABLE 1.2
A Sample of Contexts of Life Events[a]

Superordinate set	Context	Comments
Family	1. Family	Context is family of origin; parents, siblings, etc.
	2. Love and marriage	Context involves date or mate.
	3. Parenting	Context refers to children, or having and rearing children.
	4. Residence	Context refers to dwelling place.
Self	5. Health	Context is own health and biological functions.
	6. Self	Predominant reference of event is to the self.
Social relations	7. Community	Context involves community relations and functions.
	8. Friendships	Reference is to close friends, primary friendship network.
	9. Social relations	Context refers to psychosocial relations.
Work	10. Finances	Includes all contexts related to money (including household economics).
	11. School	Context is schooling, education, training.
	12. Work	Context is related to occupation and career.
Miscellaneous	13. Law	Reference is to crime and legal matters: perpetration of crime; legal consequences (for victim of crime, context is classified elsewhere).
	14. Miscellaneous	Contexts that do not fit elsewhere in the list.

[a]The sources of these contexts are Danish *et al.*, 1980; Dohrenwend *et al.*, 1978; Hultsch & Plemons, 1979; Paykel, 1974; Pearlin & Schooler, 1978; George, Note 3.

and personal expression, passive and observational recreational activities, and active and participatory recreational activities"; (*d*) our "community" includes Flanagan's "activities related to helping or encouraging other people" and "activities relating to local and national governments"; (*e*) our "law" and "miscellaneous" are not in Flanagan's list; and (*f*) our superordinate sets overlap minimally with Flanagan's.

B. Domains, Sources, and Types of Life Events

As defined in Table 1.1, the *domain* of a life event is the area of functioning affected. However, the literature on the domains of life events is complicated by an inconsistency in terms. "Context" (or "area") is sometimes used to refer to what we and others call "domain"; and "domain" is sometimes used to refer to what we and others call "context." (George, Note 3, used both of these terms and essentially reversed the definitions we use.) As indicated in Table 1.1, "domain" has also been used to refer to what we are calling "source" and "type" of events. Indeed, some writers seem to use "domain" to refer to a muddle of all three dimensions—domain, source, and type—but often with source and type implicitly given more emphasis.

The typologies based on domains in the broad, inclusive sense usually contain three or four categories (e.g., those of Brim & Ryff, 1980; Escalona, 1954; Havighurst, 1953; Piaget, 1967; Riegel, 1975; 1979, Chap. 8). The categories are (a) biological, hereditary, or maturational; (b) personal, individual, organismic, self-determined, or psychological; (c) physical–environmental; and (d) social, cultural, or historical. When only three categories are used, the physical–environmental category is likely to be omitted. Of course, the labels and specific definitions of the categories vary somewhat across the typologies, but the following examples from Riegel (1975; 1979, Chap. 8) are characteristic—"biological: having an accident or illness"; "individual: choosing a career, selecting a marriage partner"; "physical: being in an earthquake or a flood"; and "social: marrying, rearing children."

Hultsch and Plemons (1979) used only two categories of events—cultural and individual. Their cultural category seems to be the same as the physical category, and their individual category seems to include the biological and social categories as well as the individual category. Discussing Hultsch and Plemons's categories, Danish et al. (1980) said that individual life events can include biological events, such as being ill and being pregnant, and socialization-related events, such as being promoted and marrying. However, Hultsch and Plemons said, "The occurrence of some of these events is based, in part, on biological capacity and social norms [p. 19]," which can be interpreted to mean that the categories refer to biological and social *sources* of events rather than to biological and social *types* of events.

Havighurst (1953) included three categories—biological, psychological, and social, omitting anything like the physical category—but he explicitly referred them to *sources* of events—physical maturation, self-determination, and the culture—rather than to types of events, or "developmental tasks" as he called them. Riegel's (1975) position is unclear, in that he referred to the four categories as dimensions, levels, and sequences of events, but Brim and Ryff (1980) explicitly referred the four categories both to sources of events and to types of events.

It seems obvious that the nomenclatural procedure that has been used is faulty. We would suggest that typologies based on combinations of dimensions are likely to produce confusion rather than clarity unless the dimensions are explicitly separated and then combined in a systematic way, defining the categories by the intersections of the dimensions. Two examples of the latter procedure are considered in the next subsection.

C. Categories as Dimension Intersections

Brim and Ryff (1980) defined eight categories of life events by the intersections of three dichotomized "event" dimensions: age relatedness, likelihood of occurrence in a given individual, and prevalence in a given population. Examples of events that are high on all three dimensions include entering the work force for the first time, having a Bar Mitzvah, marrying, retiring, and a sibling's being born; examples of events that are low on all three dimensions include being blacklisted in Hollywood in the 1940s, being cured of alcoholism, being the first black female lawyer in the South, being a victim of rape, and winning a lottery. Brim and Ryff did not label the eight categories, and appropriate names are not readily apparent.

Baltes and his colleagues (e.g., Baltes, 1979; Baltes, Cornelius, & Nesselroade, 1978; Baltes, Reese, & Lipsitt, 1980; Baltes & Willis, 1979) divided life events into age-graded, history-graded, and nonnormative categories, which are partially dimensionalizable on age relatedness and cohort specificity, as shown in Table 1.3. Prevalence might seem to be relevant, given that Baltes and his colleagues have sometimes referred to the age- and history-graded categories as *normative* (e.g., Baltes, 1979; Baltes *et al.*, 1980). However, the range of prevalence is actually from low to high in all three categories. For example, having Huntington's chorea and beginning puberty are both age graded, but the first is low in prevalence and

TABLE 1.3
A Dimensionalization of Baltes's
Age-Graded, History-Graded, and Nonnormative Categories

	Dimensions	
Category	Age relatedness	Cohort specificity
Age-graded	High	Low
History-graded	Low to high[a]	High
Nonnormative	Low	Low

[a]For example, the bombing of Berlin and of London in World War II probably affected all age groups; the Great Depression apparently affected young adults more than other age groups.

the second is high in prevalence; being in the first class of women admitted to Yale University and being in the Black Death plague in fourteenth-century Europe and Asia (Russell, 1948; Ziegler, 1969) are both history graded, but the first was low in prevalence and the second was high in prevalence; and winning a lottery and losing a friend are both nonnormative, but the first is low in prevalence and the second is high in prevalence.

The normative–nonnormative distinction does not actually refer to a basic dimension of life events, and therefore it should be derivable from an intersection of basic dimensions. It seems to be incompletely derivable, as we have shown, and therefore its potential usefulness seems to be limited. The problem is that the distinction is ambiguous, for at least four reasons that we shall discuss even though we suspect that the labels "normative" and "nonnormative" have become too firmly established in the literature to be dispossessed. To begin with our conclusion, the ambiguities would be avoided if *desirability* (or *social desirability*), *prevalence*, *age relatedness*, and *cohort specificity* were substituted for the *normative–nonnormative* distinction.

1. The normative–nonnormative distinction is ambiguous because *normative* has two different meanings. It is used loosely to mean *normal*, which means usual or average; but in strict usage it means establishing or setting up a norm. The word *norm*—from the Latin *norma*, a rule or pattern—means a model, pattern, standard, or type, that is, an ideal. Strictly, then, a normative life event would be one that should occur, and a normal life event would be one that does occur. Leach (1968) used the terms in their strict senses when he said, "in anthropology, customs and jural rules are *normative*, not *normal* [p. 340]." In the strict sense, an event can be normative no matter how rare it is, or it can be nonnormative no matter how ordinary. This sense seems to be intended in some of the relevant literature, but the sense of being normal seems to be more prevalent. These senses of normative, referring to the ideal and to the actual, are conveyed more unambiguously by the dimensions of *desirability*, or perhaps *social desirability* (as defined in Table 1.1), to refer to the ideal, and *prevalence* to refer to the actual.

2. The normative–nonnormative distinction is also ambiguous because *normative* is a relative term in both of its senses discussed in the preceding paragraph. That is, an event is normative if it is the ideal or is prevalent in some specific reference group. Perhaps the only event that is entirely culture-free is dying, although its timing and prevalent causes vary across cultures and other reference groups. It seems likely that all life events exhibit cross-cultural differences in some of their dimensions. For example, the timing of weaning varies from about 1 year of age for the Alorese, who inhabit an East Indian island, to about 4.5 years of age for the Ainu of Japan

(Munroe & Munroe, 1975). Another example is having Huntington's chorea, which has a low probability in the population at large but has a probability of .50 in the subpopulation who have a parent with the disorder. A final example is being unemployed, which has a low probability in the population at large but is normative (i.e., high in prevalence) for the subpopulation of black adolescents. The point is that an event can be normative (in either sense) only with respect to some specific population, which is usually smaller than the total human population, and even the most clearly nonnormative event is normative for some group. Thus, the designation of an event as nonnormative must be based on an explicit or implicit selection of a reference population, and this selection seems generally to be arbitrary. If the reference population is defined by age or cohort, the problem is avoided by the use of *age relatedness* or *cohort specificity* instead of the normative–nonnormative distinction. For other reference populations, however, the problem can be avoided only by explicitly restricting the reference population or by introducing some kind of dimension not included in Table 1.1.

3. A third problem with the distinction is that events that are non-normative in the sense referring to prevalence can be age- or history-graded. For example, being physically abused recurrently by another member of the family is nonnormative and is at least moderately age graded in that the abused individual is apparently more likely to be a child than an adult or an elder, although the prevalences for the latter two groups are not well established (Block & Sinnott, Note 4). An example of a nonnormative history-graded event is an accident's occurring at a nuclear power plant, which may affect individuals of all ages in a small geographical region. Thus, the normative–nonnormative distinction inappropriately implies a distinction between events that are graded by age or history and events that are not graded by age or history. This problem would obviously be avoided if *age relatedness* (age grading) and *cohort specificity* (history grading) were used with *prevalence* rather than with the normative–nonnormative distinction.

4. Finally, the normative–nonnormative distinction is ambiguous because an event can be normative (in either sense) on some dimensions, non-normative on others, and neither normative nor nonnormative on still others. For example, a parent's dying is "normative" in likelihood and prevalence, but it is believed to be nonnormative in age grading (i.e., low in age related-ness; Brim & Ryff, 1980), and it is probably neither in duration and recency.

V. A New Taxonomy of Life Events

Among the various schemes for categorizing life events, the best seem to be those in which categories are defined by intersections of dimensions. The number of dimensions that can be used is limited, in practice, because the number of possible cells increases so rapidly. For example, if each of the 10 "perception" dimensions in Table 1.1 were dichotomized, their combination would yield 1024 cells, which is more than the number of life events that have been discussed in the literature. However, the necessity to restrict the number of dimensions used in a taxonomy immediately raises the question of how the dimensions are to be selected. The basis can be theoretical, empirical, or pragmatic; but the available theories are not sufficiently detailed, the available empirical evidence is fragmentary, and the available pragmatic considerations vary markedly across disciplines and across investigators within a discipline. (We are using "pragmatic" in the sense that includes usefulness as well as practicability.) Another possible basis is the "scholarly guess," or informed conjecture, which is the basis we used to develop the suggestions discussed in the present section.

For many purposes, a taxonomy should include the contexts and domains of life events, except, obviously, when these dimensions are dependent variables or when the research is limited to a single context or domain. We initially selected the five superordinate sets of contexts listed in Table 1.2, but a preliminary test suggested that these sets are too broad to be useful for a taxonomy. We had anticipated that use of all 14 of the contexts in Table 1.2 would be difficult because of vague definitions, but we found that the classification of life events into these contexts was fairly reliable (on an informal test–retest basis).

The conceptualization of domains, as noted earlier, often includes three separable notions, referring to *domains* as defined in Table 1.1 (area of functioning affected), *sources* of life events, and *types* of life events. As defined in Table 1.1, the *domain* dimension could be dichotomized into personal and interpersonal areas of functioning. The personal area could be further dichotomized into physiological and psychological personal areas, and the interpersonal area could be further dichotomized into community and social interpersonal areas. However, most events probably affect more than one area of functioning, and therefore an a priori identification of *the* domain affected is likely to be arbitrary and misleading. Furthermore, the outcome of an event can be an event causing another outcome, etc. (Nowak, Note 5). We therefore omitted this kind of dimension from our taxonomy.

Four kinds of *sources* of life events can also be identified—heredity, physical environment, social–cultural environment, and self. However, events are generally produced by interactions among the various kinds of sources, as Havighurst (1953), Piaget (1967), and Riegel (1975) noted, and therefore the sources of life events do not provide a clear-cut dimension for categorizing life events.

Four *types* of life events can be identified—biological, personal–psychological, physical–environmental, and social–cultural. The biological type refers to physiological functions, pregnancy, accidents, illness, and death. The personal–psychological type includes self-determined events, such as choosing a career and selecting a mate. The physical–environmental type refers to physical objects found or lost, natural disasters, and the like. The social–cultural type includes interpersonal events such as being promoted, as well as more direct social events such as marrying and childrearing. We used these four types of events and the 14 contexts in Table 1.2 to form a two-dimensional taxonomy.

To test the practicality of this taxonomy, we categorized 355 life events that we found in a sample of the relevant literature (cited in the first note to Table 1.4). The results are shown in Table 1.4. Only 3.7% of the events were associated with "miscellaneous" contexts, implying that the other contexts included in the taxonomy are almost exhaustive and thus supporting the construct validity of the taxonomy. However, two contexts—friendships (2.3%) and community (2.5%)—were less well represented than the miscellaneous category, perhaps suggesting that some of the categories are too finely drawn. Other contexts may be defined too broadly in that almost half of the events (48.8%) were related to only four contexts: family (15.5%), work (13.3%), health (10.4%), and love and marriage (9.6%). However, the disproportionate distribution of events in the various contexts may be merely a reflection of the interests of the investigators we sampled. These interests seem likely to have also determined the distribution of events among the *types*: the best represented were the social–cultural (48.0%) and personal–psychological (31.9%), and the least represented were the biological (16.1%) and physical–environmental (4.0%).

To illustrate the use of our taxonomy, we selected 20 events, 2 each from 10 contexts, and rated them on 10 dimensions. The dimensions selected were focus and impact, which are "effect" dimensions; control, desirability, and expectation, which are "perception" dimensions; and age relatedness, likelihood of occurrence, prevalence, reversibility, and timing, which are "event" dimensions. (The 2:3:5 ratio reflects the ratio of percentages of these dimensions in Table 1.1—17:29:54.) We selected these specific dimensions because they seemed hospitable to intuitive rating, although of course in practice empirical rating would be desirable for all of the dimensions—and indeed would be *required* for some. The results are shown in Table 1.5.

In an empirical study, of course, the selection of events and dimensions to be included would not be arbitrary, but rather would be based on theory or hunch. A possible use of the taxonomy is to provide a framework for studying the significance of the various dimensions and interrelations among them. As

TABLE 1.4
A Sample of Life Events Classified
by Type and Context[a]

Type	Context	Event
Biological	Family	Baby sibling's being born
		New birth(s) occurring in family
		Father's improving in health
		Mother's improving in health
		Family member's being ill
		Close family member's being seriously ill or injured
		Father's worsening in health
		Mother's worsening in health
		Father's having severe illness or accident
		Mother's having severe illness or accident
		Sibling's dying
		Close family member's dying
		Father's dying
		Mother's dying
	Love and marriage	Wife's experiencing menopause (male)
		Husband's experiencing testosterone decline (female)
		Wife's becoming pregnant (male)
		Wife's having abortion (male)
		Wife's having miscarriage or stillbirth (male)
		Spouse's dying
		Ex-spouse's dying
	Parenting	First child's being born
		Second or later child's being born
		Defective child's being born
		Leaving childbearing stage
		Child's having severe illness or accident
		Son's dying
		Daughter's dying
	Residence	(None)
	Health	Achieving physiological stability
		Having an operation
		Changing in reproductive and related body parts
		Declining in testosterone production (males)
		Going through menopause (females)
		Becoming pregnant accidentally (females)
		Having wanted pregnancy (females)
		Having unwanted pregnancy (females)
		Having abortion (females)
		Having miscarriage or stillbirth (females)
		Being injured
		Being disabled
		Being disfigured
		Losing limb in auto accident
		Having minor personal illness

Continued

TABLE 1.4 *(continued)*
*A Sample of Life Events Classified
by Type and Context[a]*

Type	Context	Event
		Having major personal illness
		Having a venereal disease
		Having a heart attack
		Having spina bifida
		Going blind
		Improving in physical health
		Being cured of alcoholism
	Self	(None)
	Community	(None)
	Friendships	Close friend's being seriously ill or injured
		Close friend's dying
	Social relations	Being unable to get treatment for an illness or injury
		Having sex difficulties
	Finances	(None)
	School	(None)
	Work	Having work disability
		Having pro football injury
	Law	(None)
	Miscellaneous	Pet's dying
Personal– psychological	Family	Succeeding father in family business
		Experiencing guilt about a family member
		Achieving emotional independence of parents
		Leaving home for the first time
	Love and marriage	Preparing for marriage and family life
		Selecting a mate
		Learning to live with a marriage partner
		Adjusting to death of spouse
	Parenting	Starting a family
		Finding out that cannot have children
		Redefining parenting role
	Residence	Establishing satisfactory physical living arrangements
		Managing a home
		Building a home or having one built
		Being unable to move after expecting to be able to move
	Health	Learning to take solid foods
		Accomplishing toilet training
		Experiencing change in body image
		Walking for first time
		Learning to walk
		Accepting own physique and learning to use the body effectively
		Changing in activity level
		Changing in perceptions of sexuality

TABLE 1.4 *(continued)*
A Sample of Life Events Classified
by Type and Context[a]

Type	Context	Event
	Self	Changing in eating habits
		Changing in sleeping habits
		Accepting and adjusting to the physiological changes of middle age
		Adjusting to decreasing physical strength and health
		Becoming aware of own mortality
		Experiencing mitigation of events or circumstances formerly thought stressful
		Developing wholesome attitudes toward oneself as a growing organism
		Having changed perceptions of self-worth and esteem
		Changing self-definition
		Experiencing identity crisis
		Losing skill functioning
		Taking up a new craft, hobby, sport, or recreational activity
		Dropping a craft, hobby, sport, or recreational activity
		Developing adult leisure-time activities
		Experiencing change in leisure opportunities
		Taking a vacation
		Being unable to take a planned vacation
		Learning to talk
		Revising personal habits
		Having a scary dream
		Getting lost
	Community	Learning to distinguish right from wrong and developing a conscience
		Developing morality and a scale of values
		Acquiring a set of values and an ethical system as a guide to behavior
		Forming simple concepts of social and physical reality
		Developing intellectual skills and concepts necessary for civic competence
		Taking on civic responsibility
	Friendships	Developing capacity for intimacy and/or perspective taking
	Social relations	Learning sex differences and sexual modesty
		Learning an appropriate masculine or feminine social role
		Developing attitudes toward social groups and institutions
		Learning to get along with age-mates
		Learning physical skills necessary for ordinary games

Continued

TABLE 1.4 *(continued)*
A Sample of Life Events Classified
by Type and Context[a]

Type	Context	Event
	Finances	Achieving personal independence
		Having outstanding personal achievement
		Establishing and maintaining an economic standard of living
		Going on welfare
		Going off welfare
		Having financial problems concerning school (in danger of not having sufficient money to continue)
	School	Developing fundamental skills in reading, writing, and calculating
		Having problems in school or in training program
		Taking an important exam
		Not getting a perfect score on an exam
		Failing an important exam
		Being ridiculed in class
		Wetting in class
		Failing a course
		Dropping a course
		Changing a major
		Graduating from school or training program
		Not graduating from school or training program
		Starting school or training program after not going to school for a long time
		Changing to a new school at same academic level (undergraduate, graduate, etc.)
		Changing schools or training programs
		Beginning a new school experience at a higher academic level (beginning nursery school, elementary school, college, professional school, etc.)
		Ceasing education
	Work	Selecting and preparing for an occupation
		Getting started in an occupation
		Having first job
		Having second job
		Changing jobs for a better one
		Changing jobs for a worse one
		Changing jobs for an equivalent one
		Having significant success at work
		Experiencing change in self as a result of societal value placed on work
		Learning not going to be promoted at work
		Experiencing change in commitment to work
		Taking a trip other than a vacation

TABLE 1.4 *(continued)*
A Sample of Life Events Classified
by Type and Context[a]

Type	Context	Event
		Having work load sharply reduced
		Taking on greatly increased work load
		Having reduction in work hours
		Having increase in work hours
		Stopping working for an extended period (not retiring)
		Being unemployed
		Returning to work after not working for a long time
		Adjusting to retirement and reduced income
		Ending postcareer work activity
		Entering the Armed Services
		Leaving the Armed Services
		Starting a business or profession
		Expanding business or professional practice
		Acceding to empty throne at 18
	Law	Violating the law in minor ways
		Embezzling
		Receiving a jail sentence
		Serving a jail term
		Not getting out of jail when expected
	Miscellaneous	Acquiring a pet
		Developing concepts necessary for everyday living
		Having an expectable event fail to occur
		Not experiencing change
Physical– environmental	Family	(None)
	Love and marriage	(None)
	Parenting	(None)
	Residence	Moving into first home
		Moving into second home
		Experiencing change in physical setting
		Experiencing major change in living conditions of family (building new home; remodeling; home, neighborhood, etc., deteriorating)
		Losing home through fire, flood, or other disaster
	Health	(None)
	Self	Losing drivers license
		Losing personally valuable object
	Community	Being in earthquake
		Being exposed to polio epidemic
		Being exposed to plague
		Being in a disaster
	Friendships	(None)

Continued

TABLE 1.4 *(continued)*
A Sample of Life Events Classified
by Type and Context[a]

Type	Context	Event
	Social relations	(None)
	Finances	Winning a lottery
		Having car, furniture, or other item bought on installment plan repossessed
	School	(None)
	Work	(None)
	Law	(None)
	Miscellaneous	Being involved in accident in which no one was injured
Social–cultural	Family	Learning to relate emotionally to parents, siblings
		Coming into a large estate with other heirs
		Family receiving public acclaim
		Competing with sibling
		Sibling's dropping or flunking out of school
		Sibling's having trouble because of drugs
		Sibling's being arrested
		Parents' having a fight
		Having conflict with family member
		Having serious family argument other than with spouse
		Having increased arguments with family member
		Having argument with nonresident family member
		Having markedly closer relations with family members
		Having marked deterioration of relations with family members
		Having more family get-togethers
		Having fewer family get-togethers
		Spending more time in family context
		Interacting less frequently with family
		Family member's (not child) leaving home
		Any sibling's leaving the family household
		Person's moving out of the household
		Someone's staying on in the household after he or she was expected to leave
		Parent's separating
		Parents' divorcing
		Father's remarrying
		Mother's remarrying
		Adjusting to aging parents
		Father's worsening in moods and feelings about life in general
		Mother's worsening in moods and feelings about life in general
		Father's improving in moods and feelings about life in general

TABLE 1.4 *(continued)*
A Sample of Life Events Classified
by Type and Context[a]

Type	Context	Event
		Mother's improving in moods and feelings about life in general
		Father's being in therapy
		Mother's being in therapy
		Sibling's being in therapy
		Father's being institutionalized
		Mother's being institutionalized
		Sibling's being institutionalized
	Love and marriage[b]	Having reconciliation with boyfriend/girlfriend
		Starting a love affair
		Becoming engaged
		Marrying (first marriage)
		Marrying (second or later marriage)
		Spouse's beginning work
		Ceasing steady dating
		Breaking up with boyfriend/girlfriend
		Breaking engagement
		Spouse's stopping work
		Being unfaithful
		Spouse's being unfaithful
		Being separated from spouse (due to work, travel, etc.)
		Separating maritally from spouse
		Having marital reconciliation
		Being divorced
		Learning to relate to spouse as a person
		Having improved relations with spouse
		Having worsened relations with spouse, without separation or divorce
		Having increased arguments with fiance
		Having markedly fewer arguments with spouse
		Having markedly more arguments with spouse
		Having trouble with in-laws
	Parenting	Adopting a child
		Rearing children
		Assisting teen-age children to become responsible and happy adults
		Your being unemployed made it hard to feel warm and loving to child
		Spouse's being unemployed made it hard for him or her to feel warm and loving to child
		Child's leaving home
		Grown children's returning home to live
		Son's being drafted for military service

Continued

TABLE 1.4 *(continued)*
A Sample of Life Events Classified
by Type and Context[a]

Type	Context	Event
		Last child's leaving home (empty nest)
		Child's becoming engaged to marry
		Child's marrying (approved)
		Child's marrying (not approved)
		Last child's marrying
		Child's being a victim of violence (mugging, rape, robbery)
		Children's being in preschool
		Children's being in school
		Child's changing schools
		Child's failing in school
	Residence	Family's having to move
		Moving to a better residence or neighborhood
		Moving to a worse residence or neighborhood
		Moving to an equivalent residence or neighborhood
		Migrating from the South
		Moving in same city
		Moving to another city
		Moving to another country
		Being institutionalized
	Health	Going to dentist
		Experiencing change in physical dependence
	Self	(None)
	Finances	Getting a large raise, without a promotion
		Not getting an expected wage or salary increase
		Taking a cut in wage or salary without a demotion
		Undergoing change in financial resources (better or worse)
		Undergoing small change in financial status (better or worse)
		Undergoing marked change in financial status (better or worse)
		Having moderate financial difficulties
		Having major financial difficulties
		Achieving assurance of economic independence
		Starting purchase of a car, furniture, or other high-priced item on the installment plan
		Borrowing moderately large sum (for car, TV, school loan, etc.)
		Borrowing large sum (for house, business, etc.)
		Having mortgage or loan foreclosed
		Suffering a financial loss or loss of property not related to work

TABLE 1.4 *(continued)*
A Sample of Life Events Classified
by Type and Context[a]

Type	Context	Event
		Having financial improvement not related to work
	School	Giving a report in class
		Being sent to the principal
		Getting a poor report card
		Not being promoted
		Being put on academic probation
		Failing in school
		Being dismissed from dormitory or other residence
		Being in first class of women at Yale
	Work	Being promoted
		"Topping out" in work career
		Being demoted
		Being fired
		Being blacklisted in Hollywood in 1940s
		Going on strike
		Being unemployed due to recession or depression
		Ending role as member of the paid labor force
		Retiring
		Finding conditions at work have improved (excluding physical setting, promotion)
		Finding conditions at work have worsened (excluding physical setting, demotion, and trouble with boss)
		Having trouble with boss
		Having conflict with co-worker
		Experiencing change in contact with colleagues/ co-workers
		Being the first black female lawyer in the South
		Receiving a public award
		Holding office
		Undergoing business readjustment
		Failing in business
	Community	Meeting social and civic obligations
		Having confirmation, Bar Mitzvah, or Bat Mitzvah
		Being in combat
	Friendships	Learning to relate emotionally to others (nonfamily)
		Making new friends
		Having conflict with friends
		Breaking up with a friend
		Separating from significant person (nonfamily)
		Experiencing teenage unpopularity
	Social relations	Achieving socially responsible behavior
		Finding a congenial social group
		Establishing an explicit affiliation with own age group

(continued)

TABLE 1.4 *(continued)*
A Sample of Life Events Classified
by Type and Context[a]

Type	Context	Event
		Achieving new and more mature relations with age-mates of both sexes
		Experiencing change in social network or reference group
		Experiencing major change in social activities such as movie-going, partying, visiting (increased or decreased frequency)
		Having marked change in church or synagogue activities (e.g., increase or decrease in attending)
		New person's (not family) moving into household
		Joining a fraternity/sorority
		Not being pledged by favorite fraternity/sorority
		Being picked last to be on a team
		Losing a game
		Being robbed
		Being assaulted
		Being victim of rape
		Being victim of homosexual rape
	Law	Being involved in a law suit
		Getting involved in a court case
		Having a court appearance
		Being suspected of lying
		Being caught in theft
		Being arrested
		Being accused of something for which a person could be sent to jail
		Being acquitted of a crime
		Being convicted of a crime
		Being detained in jail or comparable institution
		Being released from jail
	Miscellaneous	Christmas's occurring
		Being in the Great Depression
		Nation's being at war

[a]We used gerunds to label the life events even though some may be conceptualized as products more aptly than as processes. We used the technically correct possessive throughout, even when awkward. The life events are adapted from Beeson & Lowenthal, 1975; Brim, 1976; Brim & Ryff, 1980; Danish *et al.*, 1980; B. P. Dohrenwend, 1974; B. S. Dohrenwend, 1973; Dohrenwend *et al.*, 1978; Gersten, Langer, Eisenberg, & Simcha-Fagan, 1977; Glick, 1977; Havighurst, 1953; Holmes & Rahe, 1967; Lieberman, 1975; Myers, Lidenthal, & Pepper, 1974; Paykel, 1973, 1974; Plato, *Laws* VI; Riegel, 1975; Sarason *et al.*, 1978; Yamamoto, 1979; George, Note 3; and our own additions.

[b]In the context of love and marriage, the personal–psychological and social–cultural types of events differ in that the former directly involves only the self and the latter directly involves another person (e.g., selecting a mate is personal; wooing a mate is social).

TABLE 1.5

*A Priori Ratings of a Sample of Life Events
on Selected Dimensions[a]*

Type of event	Context of event	Event	Focus	Impact	Control
Biological	Family	Father's dying	Other	High	Imposed
	Parenting	First child's being born	Other	High	Controlle‹
	Work	Having pro football injury	Self	High	Imposed
Personal– psychological	Family	Achieving emotional independence	Self	High	Controlle‹
	Love and marriage	Selecting a mate	Self	High	Controlle
	Health	Adjusting to decreasing health	Self	High	Imposed
	Social relations	Learning sex differences and modesty	Self	Low	Controlle‹
	School	Dropping a course	Self	Low	Controlle
	Law	Embezzling	Self	High	Controlle‹
Physical– environmental	Finances	Winning a lottery	Self	High	Imposed
	Miscellaneous	Being in earthquake	Self and other	High	Imposed
Social–cultural	Love and marriage	Marrying (first marriage)	Self	High	Controlle‹
	Parenting	Last child's leaving home (empty nest)	Self	High	Imposed
	Health	Going to dentist	Self	Low	Controlle‹
	Social relations	Being a victim of rape	Self	High	Imposed
	Finances	Getting a large raise	Self	High	Imposed
	School	Being in first class of women at Yale	Self	High	Controlle‹
	Work	Having trouble with boss	Self	Low	Either
	Law	Being arrested	Self	High	Imposed
	Miscellaneous	Christmas's occurring	Self	Low	Imposed

[a]All dimensions are dichotomized, except for *type, context,* and *timing.*

[b]For *timing,* 0 = any age or all ages; 1 = infant (0-2 years); 2 = child (2-13); 3 = adolescent (13-20‹
4 = young adult (20–40); 5 = middle-aged adult (40–60); 6 = old adult (60 on).

[c]Likelihood and prevalence are low in the population at large, but high in the population of profession‹

TABLE 1.5 *(continued)*
*A Priori Ratings of a Sample of Life Events
on Selected Dimensions*[a]

Dimension						
Desirability	Expectation	Age relatedness	Likelihood	Prevalence	Reversibility	Timing[b]
Negative	Varies	Weak	High	High	Irreversible	4–5
Positive	Expected	Strong	High	High	Irreversible	4
Negative	Unexpected	Strong	—[c]	—[c]	Varies	4
Positive	Varies	Strong	High	High	Reversible	3
Positive	Expected	Strong	High	High	Reversible	4
Negative	Expected	Strong	High	High	Reversible	6
Positive	Unexpected	Strong	High	High	Reversible	2
Negative	Varies	Strong	Low	High	Reversible	3
Negative	Expected	Weak	Low	Low	Reversible	5–6
Positive	Unexpected	Weak	Low	Low	Reversible	3–6
Negative	Unexpected	Weak	High	Low	Reversible[d]	0
Positive	Expected	Strong	High	High	Irreversible[e]	4
Generally negative	Expected	Strong	High	High	Reversible	5
Negative	Expected	Weak	High	High	Reversible	2–6
Negative	Unexpected	Weak	Low	Low	Irreversible	3–4
Positive	Varies	Weak	Low	High	Reversible	4–5
Positive	Expected	Strong	Low	Low	Irreversible	3
Negative	Varies	Weak	Low	High	Reversible	4–5
Negative	Varies	Weak	Low	Low	Reversible[f]	3–6
Positive	Expected	Weak	High	High	Reversible	0

football players.
[d]Damage can be repaired.
[e]Marrying is irreversible, as explained in Table 1.1.
[f]Being arrested is reversed by being freed.

mentioned in the section in this chapter on dimensions of life events, Hultsch and Plemons (1979) have noted that such research is scarce. Such research might indicate that some dimensions can be eliminated because they exhibit little or no variance, or because they are highly correlated with other dimensions. Or, the research might indicate that certain dimensions can be combined to yield meaningful superordinate scores.

A second possible use of the taxonomy is to investigate differences in the dimensional values of life events as a function of, for example, age, sex, culture, history, or moderating variables such as the nature and extent of support networks. Such research has been done, but not on the scale we envision. For example, effects of support networks are discussed in several chapters in this volume (e.g., Seime & Zimmerman, Chapter 6; Eiduson & Forsythe, Chapter 9). Another example is a study by Schwarz, Burkhart, and Green (1978) in which the *meaning* of drinking was found to vary with age. For young adults, drinking was related to sensation-seeking needs; for older adults, it was a mechanism for coping with anxiety and stress.

A more complex example is a study by Modell, Furstenberg, and Hershberg (1976) on age, sex, and cohort differences in the *age congruity, integration, prevalence, spread,* and *timing* of five components of the transition to adulthood. The components studied were leaving school (personal–psychological type, school context), entering the work force (personal–psychological type, work context), leaving the household of origin (personal–psychological type, family context), marrying (social–cultural type, context of love and marriage), and establishing own household (personal–psychological context, context of residence). In other words, Modell *et al.* used age, sex, and cohort as independent variables and five dimensions of five life events as dependent variables. The results suggested that the transition to adulthood had become more closely age graded between the two times of observation that were investigated, 1880 and 1970. This study clearly illustrates the usefulness of the approach. However, researchers who use it should be aware of a problem mentioned in our discussion of the process–product distinction: When life events are treated as dependent variables they are being treated as products, even if they are conceptualized as processes in the relevant theory.

A third possible use of the taxonomy—and the last one we shall mention— is to study differences in the dimensionalization of life events as a function of variables such as those just mentioned. For example, the timeliness (on-time/ off-time) of an event may moderate the impact of the event in adulthood but not in childhood. Baltes and his colleagues (e.g., Baltes, 1979; Baltes *et al.,* 1978; Baltes *et al.,* 1980; Baltes & Willis, 1979) hypothesized that the relative importance or impact of age-graded, history-graded, and nonnormative life events varies with age period—age-graded events most important in childhood, history-graded events in adolescence and early adulthood, and nonnormative events in old age. This hypothesis implies that the dimensionalization of life events may change with age.

VI. Summary

During the last several years, the area of life events has received increasing attention in a number of disciplines. As yet, however, no single approach to nomenclature has emerged as universally accepted. In this chapter, we have reviewed several attempts at categorizing and dimensionalizing life events. We have argued that previous attempts have been marred by a lack of clarity regarding terminology and a limited applicability to the broad range of events in the life-event literature. From our perspective, the most useful approach to a taxonomy of life events is in defining categories by the intersections of dimensions. In this chapter, we have outlined such an approach.

Defining event categories by the intersection of event dimensions requires clarity regarding the dimensionalization of events. We have adopted Brim and Ryff's (1980) classification system focusing on the *effects* of events, the affected person's *perceptions* of events, and the *event properties* or characteristics of the events themselves. Using this division, we sorted 35 dimensions of life events identified in a selective search of the relevant literature. Of the 35, only 6 are qualitative in nature. In the second half of the chapter, we focused on 4 of the qualitative dimensions: context, source, and type (event dimensions), and domain (an effect dimension).

We use the term *context* to refer to the area of the life space in which an event occurs. Not surprisingly, there have been several approaches to specifying the salient contexts of life events (e.g., Dohrenwend *et al.*, 1978; Hultsch and Plemons, 1979; George, Note 3). A synthesis of previous attempts yields the 14 contexts of life events presented in Table 1.2.

When one focuses on domain, source, and type of event, the literature is extremely confusing. These terms are often used interchangeably and the lack of theoretical clarity is apparent. We have argued that typologies based on combinations of dimensions require an initial delineation of the dimensions. Once this is done, dimensions can be combined in an orderly fashion.

Other colleagues have attempted to define categories of life events by the intersection of event dimensions. Brim and Ryff (1980), for example, have developed eight categories of events, based on the intersections of three dichotomized event dimensions: age relatedness, likelihood of occurrence in a given individual, and prevalence in a given population. Similarly, Baltes and his colleagues (e.g., Baltes, 1979; Baltes *et al.*, 1980) have suggested a division of events into age-graded, history-graded, and nonnormative categories. Each of these approaches, however, has been hampered by ambiguity.

We have proposed a taxonomy based on the intersection of two event dimensions: type and context. Four types of events can be identified: biological, personal–psychological, physical–environmental, and social–cultural. Using these four types and the 14 contexts listed in Table 1.2, we have presented a two-dimensional taxonomy for life events in Table 1.4.

As an informal test of the taxonomy, we categorized 355 life events. Only 3.5% of the events were associated with "miscellaneous" contexts, implying that the other contexts included in the taxonomy are almost exhaustive and thus supporting the construct validity of the taxonomy.

As an illustration of the utility of the taxonomy, we selected 20 events, 2 each from 10 contexts, and rated them on 10 dimensions. The results were presented in Table 1.5.

The proposed taxonomy may have several uses. For example, it could provide a framework for studying the significance of various dimensions and the interrelations among them. Similarly, the taxonomy may be used to investigate differences in the dimensional values of life events as a function of age, sex, or other moderating variables. It is our hope that the taxonomy offers an initial step toward greater clarity in the dimensionalizing and categorizing of life events.

Reference Notes

1. Reese, H. W. *Dialectics in theory and educational practice.* Paper presented at the meeting of the American Psychological Association, Toronto, September 1978.
2. Gatz, M. *Ready or not: Solicited and unsolicited life events.* Paper presented at the meeting of the Gerontological Society, Washington, D.C., November 1979.
3. George, L. K. *Dimensions of events: Diamonds in the rough.* Unpublished paper, Duke University Medical Center, 1979.
4. Block, M. R., & Sinnott, J. D. (Eds.). *The battered elder syndrome: An exploratory study.* Mimeographed report, Center on Aging, University of Maryland, November 1979.
5. Nowak, C. *Life events research: Conceptual consideration.* Unpublished manuscript, Pennsylvania State University, 1979.

References

Baltes, P. B. Life-span developmental psychology: Some converging observations on history and theory. In P. B. Baltes & O. G. Brim, Jr. (Eds.), *Life-span development and behavior* (Vol. 2). New York: Academic Press, 1979.

Baltes, P. B., Cornelius, S. W., & Nesselroade, J. R. Cohort effects in behavioral development: Theoretical and methodological perspectives. In W. A. Collins (Ed.), *Minnesota symposia on child psychology* (Vol. 11). Hillsdale, N.J.: Lawrence Erlbaum Associates, 1978.

Baltes, P. B., Reese, H. W., & Lipsitt, L. P. Life-span developmental psychology. *Annual Review of Psychology*, 1980, *31*, 65–110.

Baltes, P. B., & Willis, S. L. The critical importance of appropriate methodology in the study of aging: The sample case of psychometric intelligence. In F. Hoffmeister & C. Müller (Eds.), *Brain functions in old age*. Heidelberg: Springer, 1979.

Beeson, D., & Lowenthal, M. J. Perceived stress across life course. In M. F. Lowenthal, M. Thurnher, D. Chiriboga, & Associates, *Four stages of life: A comparative study of women and men facing transitions*. San Francisco: Jossey-Bass, 1975.

Bergmann, G. *Philosophy of science*. Madison: University of Wisconsin Press, 1957.

Brim, O. G., Jr. Theories of male mid-life crisis. *Counseling Psychologist*, 1976, *6*, 2–9.

Brim, O. G., Jr., & Ryff, C. D. On the properties of life events. In P. B. Baltes & O. G. Brim, Jr. (Eds.), *Life-span development and behavior* (Vol. 3). New York: Academic Press, 1980.

Brown, G. W. Life-events and the onset of depressive and schizophrenic conditions. In E. K. E. Gunderson & R. H. Rahe (Eds.), *Life stress and illness*. Springfield, Ill.: Charles C Thomas, 1974. (a)

Brown, G. W. Meaning, measurement, and stress of life events. In B. S. Dohrenwend and B. P. Dohrenwend (Eds.), *Stressful life events: Their nature and effects*. New York: Wiley, 1974. (b)

Cobb, S. A model for life events and their consequences. In B. S. Dohrenwend & B. P. Dohrenwend (Eds.), *Stressful life events: Their nature and effects*. New York: Wiley, 1974.

Danish, S. J., Smyer, M. A., & Nowak, C. A. Developmental intervention: Enhancing life-event processes. In P. B. Baltes & O. G. Brim, Jr. (Eds.), *Life-span development and behavior* (Vol. 3). New York: Academic Press, 1980.

Dohrenwend, B. P. Problems in defining and sampling the relevant population of stressful life events. In B. S. Dohrenwend & B. P. Dohrenwend (Eds.), *Stressful life events: Their nature and effects*. New York: Wiley, 1974.

Dohrenwend, B. S. Life events as stressors: A methodological inquiry. *Journal of Health and Social Behavior*, 1973, *14*, 167–175.

Dohrenwend, B. S., Krasnoff, L., Askenasy, A. P., & Dohrenwend, B. P. Exemplification of a method for scaling life events: The PERI Life Events Scale. *Journal of Health and Social Behavior*, 1978, *19*, 205–229.

Escalona, S. The influence of topological and vector psychology upon current research in child development: An addendum. In L. Carmichael (Ed.), *Manual of child psychology* (2nd ed.). New York: Wiley, 1954.

Fairbank, D. T., & Hough, R. L. Life event classifications and the event–illness relationship. *Journal of Human Stress*. 1979, 5(3), 41–47.

Flanagan, J. C. A research approach to improving our quality of life. *American Psychologist*, 1978, *33*, 138–147.

Gersten, J. C., Langner, T. S., Eisenberg, J. G., & Simcha-Fagan, O. An evaluation of the etiologic role of stressful life-change events in psychological disorders. *Journal of Health and Social Behavior*, 1977, *18*, 228–244.

Glick, P. C. Updating the life cycle of the family. *Journal of Marriage and the Family*, 1977, *39*, 5–13.

Havighurst, R. J. *Human development and education*. New York: Longmans, Green, 1953.

Holmes, T. H., & Masuda, M. Life change and illness susceptibility. In J. P. Scott & E. C. Senay (Eds.), *Separation and depression: Clinical and research aspects* (AAAS Publ. No. 94). Washington, D.C.: American Association for the Advancement of Science, 1973.

Holmes, T. H., & Rahe, R. H. The social readjustment rating scale. *Journal of Psychosomatic Research*, 1967, *11*, 213–218.

Horowitz, M. J., Schaefer, C., & Cooney, P. Life event scaling for recency of experience. In E. K. E. Gunderson & R. H. Rahe (Eds.), *Life stress and illness*. Springfield, Ill.: Charles C Thomas, 1974.

Hultsch, D. F., & Plemons, J. K. Life events and life-span development. In P. B. Baltes & O. G. Brim, Jr. (Eds.), *Life-span development and behavior* (Vol. 2). New York: Academic Press, 1979.

Kvale, S. The temporality of memory. *Journal of Phenomenological Psychology*, 1974, *5*, 7–31.

Kvale, S. Dialectics and research on remembering. In N. Datan & H. W. Reese (Eds.), *Life-span developmental psychology: Dialectical perspectives on experimental research*. New York: Academic Press, 1977.

Leach, E. R. The comparative method in anthropology. In D. L. Sills (Ed.), *International encyclopedia of the social sciences* (Vol. 1). New York: Macmillan and Free Press, 1968.

Lieberman, M. A. Adaptive processes in late life. In N. Datan & L. H. Ginsberg (Eds.), *Life-span developmental psychology: Normative life crises*. New York: Academic Press, 1975.

Lowenthal, M. F., & Chiriboga, D. Social stress and adaptation: Toward a life-course perspective. In C. Eisdorfer & M. P. Lawton (Eds.), *The psychology of adult development and aging*. Washington, D.C.: American Psychological Association, 1973.

Modell, J., Furstenberg, F. F., Jr., & Hershberg, T. Social change and transitions to adulthood in historical perspective. *Journal of Family History*, 1976, *1*, 7–32.

Munroe, R. L., & Munroe, R. H. *Cross-cultural human development*. Monterey, Calif.: Brooks/Cole, 1975.

Myers, J. K., Lidenthal, J. J., & Pepper, M. P. Social class, life events, and psychiatric symptoms: A longitudinal study. In B. S. Dohrenwend & B. P. Dohrenwend (Eds.), *Stressful life events: Their nature and effects*. New York: Wiley, 1974.

Neugarten, B. L. Continuities and discontinuities of psychological issues into adult life. *Human Development*, 1969, *12*, 121–130.

Overton, W. F., & Reese, H. W. Models of development: Methodological implications. In J. R. Nesselroade & H. W. Reese (Eds.), *Life-span developmental psychology: Methodological issues*. New York: Academic Press, 1973.

Paykel, E. S. Life events and acute depression. In J. P. Scott & E. C. Senay (Eds.), *Separation and depression: Clinical and research aspects* (AAAS Publ. No. 94). Washington, D.C.: American Association for the Advancement of Science, 1973.

Paykel, E. S. Life stress and psychiatric disorder. In B. S. Dohrenwend & B. P. Dohrenwend (Eds.), *Stressful life events: Their nature and effects*. New York: Wiley, 1974.

Pearlin, L. I., & Schooler, C. The structure of coping. *Journal of Health and Social Behavior*, 1978, *19*, 2–21.

Piaget, J. *Six psychological studies* (A. Tenzer, trans; D. Elkind, Ed.). New York: Random House, 1967.

Plato. *Laws*. In *The dialogues of Plato* (B. Jowett, trans.). In R. M. Hutchins (Ed.), *Great books of the Western world* (Vol. 7). Chicago: Encyclopædia Britannica, 1952.

Rabkin, J. G. Stressful life events and schizophrenia: A review of the research literature. *Psychological Bulletin*, 1980, *87*, 408–425.

Reigel, K. F. Adult life-crises: A dialectical interpretation of development. In N. Datan & L. H. Ginsberg (Eds.), *Life-span developmental psychology: Normative life crises.* New York: Academic Press, 1975.

Riegel, K. F. The dialectics of time. In N. Datan & H. W. Reese (Eds.), *Life-span developmental psychology: Dialectical perspectives on experimental research.* New York: Academic Press, 1977.

Riegel, K. F. *Foundations of dialectical psychology.* New York: Academic Press, 1979.

Ruch, L. O. A multidimensional analysis of the concept of life change. *Journal of Health and Social Behavior*, 1977, *18*, 71–83.

Russell, J. C. *British medieval population.* Albuquerque: University of New Mexico Press, 1948.

Sarason, I. G., Johnson, J. H., & Siegel, J. M. Assessing the impact of life changes: Development of the Life Experiences Survey. *Journal of Consulting and Clinical Psychology*, 1978, *46*, 932–946.

Schaie, K. W. A general model for the study of developmental problems. *Psychological Bulletin*, 1965, *64*, 92–107.

Schwarz, R. M., Burkhart, B. R., & Green, S. B. Turning on or turning off: Sensation seeking or tension reduction as motivational determinants of alcohol use. *Journal of Consulting and Clinical Psychology*, 1978, *46*, 1144–1145.

Turnbull, C. M. The politics of non-aggression. In A. Montagu (Ed.), *Learning non-aggression: The experience of non-literate societies.* New York: Oxford University Press, 1978.

Yamamoto, K. Children's ratings of the stressfulness of experiences. *Developmental Psychology*, 1979, *15*, 581–582.

Ziegler, P. *The Black Death.* New York: John Day, 1969.

CHAPTER 2

Normative or Not?
Confessions of a Fallen Epistemologist

NANCY DATAN

WEST VIRGINIA UNIVERSITY
MORGANTOWN, WEST VIRGINIA

I came to psychology by such a peculiar route that a fair portion of my career has been spent trying to invent some sort of nonrandom significance which might be imposed over my intellectual odyssey. The theme of this volume, nonnormative life events, and my own role as co-creator of the companion volume, *Normative Life Crises* (Datan & Ginsberg, 1975) conspire to provide exactly the juxtaposition of purposes I require.

I came to psychology from philosophy, physics, cultural anthropology, and evolutionary biology. In this chapter, I shall trace some of the contributions made by these older sciences to our present understanding of norms, normative life crises, the nonnormative life event in life-span developmental psychology, and the consequences of this understanding for the development of the individual as well as the development of the field.

My philosophical inheritance may be obvious from my attention to intellectual migration; it will soon become even more obvious, for I shall begin with a definition of *nonnormative* through the negation of normative. Such a beginning betrays my mathematical origins, and these will become clearer as I develop a hybrid definition with a peculiar pedigree: by Bertrand Russell out of Francis Bacon.

LIFE-SPAN DEVELOPMENTAL PSYCHOLOGY
Nonnormative Life Events

Only a mathematician would propose to define a concept by negation and consider the definition complete. But I shall start at this point and consider what can be learned. I shall begin with "pure" mathematics, some distance away from the nonnormative events of the human life cycle discussed in the chapters of this volume. It has been said that the following toast was once proposed over dinner in Cambridge: "Here's to pure mathematics, and may it never be of any use to anyone!" Apocryphal or not, the wish reflects the world of pure mathematics, where there are no norms at all—though a sociologist of science might argue the existence of intellectual norms—but only definitions, relations among definitions, and a resulting rigor and apparent lack of ambiguity that social scientists frequently envy and sometimes seek to imitate.

The social scientist's own pretensions at mathematical rigor come by way of applied mathematics, specifically from statistics and the stochastic model of human behavior. This model has its intellectual roots in physics where we encounter our first approximation of the concept of "norm," graced by an appropriately rigorous constellation of axioms. For the purposes of this discussion, the most important of these axioms is one of the most elemental: that one electron is equivalent to any other.

The relevance of this axiom to a consideration of nonnormative life events may not be immediately apparent. But this and equivalent propositions are at the heart of a physical model of the universe that derives order out of a combination of random events and probability. I "know," as a fallen physicist, when I light the fire under the teakettle, that there is a chance—infinitesimal but not zero—that random events at the molecular level might result in ice cubes rather than hot tea. I am never surprised when the water boils. Indeed, I would be astonished if it froze. But if in fact the water did freeze, my physical epistemology would force me to declare that I had witnessed an event of extremely low probability, but one within the bounds of physical theory.

This familiar example from high school physics illustrates the physical equivalent of norms: probabilistic statements based on induction and the assumption of random individual events. These have the force of causal statements for most of us most of the time: No one I know has ever tried to make ice cubes by turning the fire on under the teakettle. However, the causal beliefs of physicists, disguised as probabilistic statements, are under constant inductive review: For example, no one in the community of atomic scientists was completely prepared to believe that mass could be transformed into energy until the atomic bomb went off. It is my personal belief that social scientists who are most deeply attached to the stochastic model of behavior are not seeking the scientific rigor of physics but its flash.

Since physics seems to provide a Platonic ideal against which to measure the social scientist's definition of normative, it is of some interest to note that physicists have also provided a definition of *nonnormative*. James Clerk Maxwell, a generally sober physicist whose principal contribution was electromagnetic field theory, has also given us the concept of Maxwell's Demon. If the teakettle freezes, Maxwell's Demon has made it freeze by flitting from molecule to molecule, personally arresting the transfer of kinetic–molecular energy. Physicists are considerably less embarrassed by the prospect of a demonic violation of their laws than are social scientists; perhaps this, too, is a consequence of the fact that we cannot produce as big a bang for the bucks.

The physicist's definition of the normative event is one with surprisingly wide currency among social scientists—surprising when we consider that statistical probability for the atomic scientist rests on the assumption of random individual events, whereas the human individual has historically been described as a creature of purpose, a description congruent with the personal self-image of most of us. The application of statistical techniques to the study of human behavior, however, reverses the explanatory processes of physicists: Whereas physical probability depends on the assumption of random atomic events, a statement with "statistical significance" to the social scientist is one that statistical distribution shows is unlikely to be random. It is a statement about collections of events, or individuals, or behaviors that have a measure of regularity shown that exceeds a probability distribution that would suggest the regularity was a consequence of chance.

Like the physical definition of *normative*, the statistical definition of norms employed by social scientists overlooks the individual in order to describe the group. Although this definition of normative has proven useful, as the chapter by Reese and Smyer (Chapter 7) has shown, it appears that a large measure of the attractiveness of the stochastical model of human behavior lies in its close approximation to the physical model of the world and to the rigor of mathematics. The statistical definition of *normative* excludes not only the individual but the vital.

If we proceed from physics to biology, we discover that the probabilistic definition of *normative* retains its force in such fields as population genetics. But the familiar statistical, descriptive meaning has been supplemented by a new, prescriptive definition. Normative development for the biologist includes imperatives that derive from the nonprobabilistic properties of organic life.

I shall illustrate this point with a thought experiment, the biological equivalent of the frozen teakettle. A hypothetical volunteer's left ventricle is pierced by a hatpin, an action destroying a small, statistically negligible number of cells. Although for the purposes of physics one electron is as good as any other, for the purpose of this volunteer, who has died for science, some cells are more equal than others: a consequence of the hierarchical organization of living matter that is not represented by the stochastical model of physics. The infrequent is unimportant in a probability model; in a hierarchical model, the infrequent may be vital.

Epigenetic models of psychological development, based on the epigenetic model of prenatal human development, reflect a recognition of the vital as normative. The Freudian concept of psychosexual stages of development and Erikson's description of critical periods are based on a biological model in which each organ system has a critical period of ascendancy, of rapid growth, and differentiation, in which the system is vulnerable to disruption by factors that might otherwise have a trivial effect or none at all. The hierarchical nature of development recalls biology; the importance of timing has social implications as well, as we shall see.

The biologist may refer not only to the vital processes of development but also to the distinction between health and disease. *Nonnormative* may mean not something unusual, but something *wrong*. Death by plague in the small towns of fourteenth-century Europe was statistically "normative"—proof by example that demonstrates the shortcomings of an exclusively mathematical definition of norm. *Nonnormative* may mean for the biologist not *scarce* but *sick*. This distinction is recognized in the social sciences in discussions of delinquency and psychopathology, where no claim of scarcity is offered in support of the definition of deviance or abnormality. However, as I shall suggest and as the contributors to this volume illustrate, in fact there is an interaction between the uncommon event in human life and the equation of "nonnormative" with abnormal.

For the cultural anthropologist, norms are both descriptive and prescriptive: What *is* done may also be what *should* be done. A final illustration, this time a personal experience, will convey the double meaning of social norms, used prescriptively in the hope that prescription will take on causal powers. I was seventeen when I first read about the Israeli kibbutz, and I reported one of my most interesting discoveries to my mother: that kibbutz adolescents had sexual relationships. My mother's response was to declare, "That's not Jewish!"

With hindsight, I am certain that neither I nor my mother was attempting a statistical critique of these normative observations. In fact, from my newly enlightened perspective as the mother of a 17-year-old daughter, I am prepared to admit that our use of the normative exceeded its usual boundaries, not only descriptive but prescriptive. I now believe that each of us was invoking the normative and hoping to achieve causality. In so doing, we were attempting in innocence to employ social norms as a form of social control, as is done in all well-regulated social organizations. "That's not done!" has more than descriptive force, because social consensus may be implemented through a range of sanctions from personal scorn to legal action.

My own concern with the normative as prescriptive lies somewhere between these two extremes, in the gray realm where frequency is equated with health. The contributions to this volume unite the unusual and the traumatic: In human development this is a legitimate synthesis of statistics and values. However, as I shall suggest, and as many of these contributors illustrate, that which is non-normative today may represent adaptive radiation in a changing world, and hence a healthy option for tomorrow.

I have considered separately the biological and the cultural, which in human development are intimately linked, and which in the study of human development are bound up in the dialectical tension between nature and nurture, as well as in the political debates that proceed from a consideration of this tension—ranging from the politics of IQ (Kamin, 1974) to the politics of the Equal Rights Amendment (Datan, Antonovsky, & Maoz, 1981) and well beyond. As I shall illustrate, what we "know" of human nature is what we have seen of the human experience, and the norms of any culture are necessarily tied to the present and the past.

As a student of anthropology, I have been deeply impressed by the variability of human "nature," and almost equally impressed by the general inability of individuals to see beyond the bounds of their own culture. I cannot claim that I am particularly farsighted myself, but I was fortunate to acquire in the space of a single year a copy of Dr. Spock's *Baby and Child Care* (First Edition, 1946)—a free gift from a local diaper service—and Whiting and Child's *Child Training and Personality* (1953), a comparative study of childrearing practices and their consequences in 75 primitive cultures.

Thanks to the temporal proximity of a graduate class in cultural anthropology and the birth of my first child, when the wise, friendly voice of Benjamin Spock instructed me not to rock and cuddle my baby lest the baby become lastingly dependent on constant maternal contact, I could place Dr. Spock's advice on a scale measuring tolerance for dependency across 76 cultures—he ranked very low—and follow my own preferences in child-rearing with the assurance that I was well within the bounds of human tolerance, if slightly outside the bounds of American middle-class norms. The baby gave up cuddling with me and went to college, while I became and remain a skeptic regarding cultural norms as guides for individual adaptation.

For, finally, it is the question of adaptive value, for the culture and species as well as the individual, that must be answered when a behavior, a social institution, or a cultural pattern is questioned as nonnormative. The insidious tendency of the usual to be seen as the healthful has some paradoxical consequences for human social organization: As a species, we are distinguished by behavioral plasticity, whereas as individuals we spend our long childhood learning the normative patterns of our culture.

The social value of stability is never more obvious than when it is threatened by change; the very notion of nonnormative life events is suggestive of trauma. Yet—as an evolutionary perspective will confirm—the nonnormative life event is not only expressive of the individual behavioral plasticity that characterizes our species but may also be the forerunner of social change, and thus of adaptive radiation—the biologist's term for diversification that maximizes a species's chances for survival in a changing environment.

The family—the social institution at the interface between individual development and the social context—is the most useful illustration of the tension between stability and change, the normative and the nonnormative, the usual and the unusual, the conventional and the deviant, yes, even the tension between nature and nurture. It is hardly surprising that in this volume nonnormative life events are almost invariably seen in the context of the family life cycle, for the family is the social institution that most sensitively measures social change, since it is also the social institution that is pivotal in transmitting social norms.

For decades, American sociologists have "known" that the normal, normative nuclear family consists of a working father, a homemaking mother, and a couple of children. This model, proposed by Talcott Parsons and painted by Norman Rockwell, was communicated to schoolchildren in the form of primers that expressed these norms in elementary English and thus transmitted these expectations to the next generation.

In the meantime, however, outside the pages of sociological journals and elementary primers, change was taking place. Beginning with the "quickening" of the family life cycle—fewer children spaced more closely, and an extended life expectancy, bringing with it a prolonged postparental period— women who had grown up expecting a lifetime of motherhood found themselves out of a job with most of their lives yet ahead of them. It is tempting to impose logic on social history and to suggest that participation of women in the labor force in increasing numbers has been the logical outcome of this and other changes in the family life cycle. It is more correct, however, to recall that the family has always been an economic unit, and that women have always played an active part in the economy whether as farm wives, mothers, or professional career women.

Nevertheless, the widespread participation of women in the industrial labor force is a comparatively new phenomenon, as is the presence of women as a political force. A Florida bumper sticker that appeared during the controversy over women's suffrage posed the question of what is "natural" in fundamental terms: "Would you marry a woman who votes?" The answer, eventually, was yes: But it is worth pausing to recall that 1920, when our mothers' mothers were young, was a year when a woman's vote had just been transformed from an act of civil disobedience—Susan B. Anthony was threatened with jail for casting a vote—into law and, of course, into a "natural" act.

Economic, demographic, and behavioral changes have legitimated new roles for women that were once nonnormative if not illegal. Elizabeth Mann Borghese, daughter of the Nobel Laureate Thomas Mann, was once advised by a psychiatrist that she would have to choose between the satisfactions of a career and the satisfactions of a family. "Why?" she replied. "Why should I have to choose? Nobody made my father choose [Olsen, 1978, p. 31]." Such a declaration of independence, farsighted and courageous at the time, has come to seem self-evident—or at least an attainable ideal. Equally important, the psychiatrist's advice would now be seen not only as unsound but unhealthful. However, as recently as 1972, Pauline Bart pointed out that psychiatric treatment often "adjusted" the individual to the needs of the group, notwithstanding what she termed "the myth of a value-free psychotherapy." In other words, frequency and value interact more often than we realize; yet when the nonnormative is not merely statistically deviant but adaptive, the burden of proof is on the deviant. Nevertheless, eventually adaptive variation may become the norm. How does such a transformation occur?

The heart of this transformation is that of the quantitatively insignificant into the qualitatively new and important. For although, as I have suggested, statistically based and value-based norms are in theory independent in origin, in everyday life they are interdependent. Thus, the exceptional becomes the scarce, the scarce becomes the infrequent, the infrequent becomes the acceptable, and finally the acceptable becomes the norm. Just as physicists understand the concept of critical mass, the quantity necessary for a self-sustaining nuclear reaction, so also in the human community we might argue for a critical mass by which new patterns of human interaction become self-sustaining and a quantitative increase becomes a qualitative change. An evolutionary biologist would be inclined to view recent changes in sex roles, family structure, and childrearing practices as examples of adaptive radiation, differentiation into new ecological niches representing new behavior patterns that may soon become dominant. And far from signaling the end of the nuclear family, these changes reflect an adaptive response to a changing community.

However, art—even the art of seeing the world through the eyes of an evolutionary biologist—is proverbially long, and the life of the individual caught in the process of social change is relatively short. Piaget has argued that behavioral change precedes cognitive awareness in the normal course of cognitive development. I propose a similar lag in social processes: I suggest that behavioral change precedes change in social institutions, social policy, and the social sciences. Although I cannot offer definitive support for this sweeping assertion, I can illustrate each of these claims, and the reader will find further support for these claims throughout this volume.

The family, I would argue, is the most effective illustration of the process by which behavioral change leads to a change in a social institution; many of the most dramatic recent changes, perhaps most notably the widespread "alterative life styles," illustrate behavior change that has newly found a label. An increase in single parenthood, whether by choice or through divorce early in the family life cycle, has created awareness of the need for day care, although the role of government is still a matter of debate; midlife divorce has created awareness of the newly economically handicapped, the displaced homemaker.

Finally, our concept of normality affects the process of science, which, as Merton has shown (1973), has its own norms and values that affect not only recognition but the very process of discovery. I shall illustrate this final point with one more brief excursion into my own history. Aaron Antonovsky, Benjamin Maoz, and I have shown that women in middle age, regardless of variation in childbearing history, which may range from as many as 25 pregnancies to only 1 or 2 planned children, may look back on the past with some desire to have borne more children, but they do not wish in middle age to care for infants (Datan et al., 1981). This finding, particularly since it is constant across five very different Israeli subcultures, suggests a developmental transition in the lives of middle-aged women. What about the men?

The answer, unfortunately, is that we have no idea at all. In 1969 we proposed a study of our subjects' husbands—feasible, with a population that was 98% married, but unfunded, due to the rapidly changing attitude toward support for basic research overseas. Yet American researchers working independently of us on studies of career development with homogeneous populations of white, middle-class, American men found that themes of stagnation, rebirth, renewal, and often remarriage were frequently found in middle age (Gould, 1978; Levinson, 1978; Osherson, 1980; Sarason, 1977). Seeking personal development, these researchers found midlife to be a time of crisis for men; seeking crisis, we found middle age to be a time to reap for women. The next generation of researchers, proceeding from what we have shown to be "normal," may discover how the lives of women and men interact in middle age. Yet these investigations were sparked by a sense of the unusual: ours by cultural differences in depression in middle age, Gould's by recurrent themes encountered in psychotherapy, and so on. In other words, the apparent regularities in adult developmental processes suggested by recent studies of middle age grew out of investigations of apparent abnormalities.

I conclude, then, on a cautionary note. Psychotherapy, claims Bart (1972), instills group values into the individual in the service of adjustment; social science, claims Merton (1973), is no more value-free than psychotherapy, and is subject to the blinders of a sociology of science. From the individual to social policy, changes seem to proceed not only by small steps but through a recognition of what is initially viewed as nonnormative. If this general rule applies in the present case, this volume may be seen as a first step toward a new developmental psychology of the life cycle.

References

Bart, P. B. The myth of a value-free psychotherapy. In W. Bell and J. A. Mau (Eds.), *Sociology and the future*. New York: Basic Books, 1972.

Datan, N., Antonovsky, A., and Maoz, B. *A time to reap: The middle age of women in five Israeli subcultures*. Baltimore: The Johns Hopkins University Press, 1981.

Datan, N., and Ginsberg, L. H. (Eds.). *Life-span developmental psychology: Normative life crises*. New York: Academic Press, 1975.

Gould, R. L. *Transformations: Growth and change in adult life*. New York: Simon and Schuster, 1978.

Kamin, L. J. *The science and politics of IQ*. Hillsdale, N.J.: Lawrence Erlbaum Associates, 1974.

Levinson, D. *The seasons of a man's life*. New York: Alfred A. Knopf, 1978.

Merton, R. K. *The sociology of science: Theoretical and empirical investigations*. Chicago: The University of Chicago Press, 1973.

Olsen, T. *Silences*. New York: Delacorte Press, 1978.

Osherson, S. D. *Holding on or letting go: Men and career change at midlife*. New York: The Free Press, 1980.

Sarason, S. B. *Work, aging, and social change: Professionals and the one-life one-career imperative*. New York: The Free Press, 1977.

Spock, B. *Baby and child care*. First Edition. New York: Pocket Books, 1946.

Whiting, J. W. M., and Child, I. L. *Child training and personality*. New Haven: Yale University Press, 1953.

CHAPTER 3

Life-Change Events in Alternative Family Styles[1]

BERNICE T. EIDUSON
ALAN B. FORSYTHE
UNIVERSITY OF CALIFORNIA AT LOS ANGELES
LOS ANGELES, CALIFORNIA

I. Introduction

A. Background

The University of California at Los Angeles interdisciplinary study of 200 families and children is examining socialization to which children are exposed in some of the family forms extant in contemporary America. Under investigation are single-mother households of never-married women, living-group or commune families, cohabiting or social-contract families, as well as the traditional, married, two-parent nuclear units. Each of these households

[1]This chapter was supported in part by the National Institutes of Mental Health Research Scientist Career Award No. 5KO5 MH 70541-08/09 to Bernice T. Eiduson, by the United States Public Health Service Grant No. 1 R06-07 MH 24947, and by The Carnegie Corporation Grant B3970. The Family Styles Project, from which the data were drawn, is co-directed by Bernice T. Eiduson. Senior investigators are Thomas S. Weisner, Jannette Alexander, Irla Lee Zimmerman, and M. R. Mickey.

LIFE-SPAN DEVELOPMENTAL PSYCHOLOGY
Nonnormative Life Events

has a target child, whose parents first entered the study when the mother was in the third trimester of pregnancy. During the past 6 years of the child's life, the family and child have been subjects of close study. Data on parent values, attitudes, childrearing practices, and family experiences, as well as data on the child's physical, cognitive, and socioemotional development have been gathered using baby books, in-depth interviews, naturalistic home observations, and a variety of field techniques, such as maps, daily routines, environment questionnaires, and psychological tests (Eiduson & Weisner, 1978).

Our interest was in the groups of families that depart from the two-parent nuclear structure, stimulated by the desire of some young adults of childbearing age to restructure the family unit into one that they believed more appropriate to contemporary values. Alternative family forms emerged in the late 1960s and early 1970s in increasing numbers, as young people throughout the Western world looked for ways of living that expressed a humanistic orientation, as well as their desires for closeness and intimacy, and a feeling of being one with the environment. These were attitudes they thought could not be fostered in the traditional nuclear family. In their daily lives, they sought to replace competitive strivings, disaffection, and alienation among individuals in mainstream society by a more emotionally meaningful, warm, empathic family relationship, one more consonant to their desires to recast traditional family roles and practices. The family forms in our longitudinal study represent the units that were viable after the heyday of the counter-culture, which have since stabilized, and though not as common as the traditional nuclear family, may be presaging changes in adult values in childrearing attitudes and practices, and in infant and child behaviors, that are already diffusing into the mainstream nuclear family (Eiduson, Cohen, & Alexander, 1973).

The 200 participating parents do not differ significantly among life-style groups in demographic characteristics or family background. Mothers range from 18 to 35 years of age, with an average age of 25.4 ± 3.8 years; fathers are 27.9 ± 4.9 years of age, with a range from 19 to 49 years. At project inception, all resided in California: 50% in Los Angeles and environs, 25% in the San Diego area, and 25% in northern California. Eighty-three percent of the families resided in urban settings, with the remainder in semirural settings.

Both parents had an average of slightly more than three siblings. Mothers were most often second-oldest children, while 50% of the fathers were eldest children. Data about the socioeconomic status (SES) of mothers' families (Hollingshead–Redlich classification using criteria of fathers' education and occupation) showed that 16% were upper class, 18% upper middle class, 31% middle class, 27% lower middle class, and 7% lower class. Fathers' families showed a similar SES distribution (16% upper class, 12% upper middle class, 33% middle class, 32% lower middle class, and 8% lower class). The SES of parents at the time of entry into the study was very different because the nontraditional families, by and large, had become downwardly mobile, whereas the traditional families were more on a par with their previous backgrounds (Cohen & Eiduson, 1975).

B. Descriptions of Families

To understand the parents' motivations for entering into the various types of families, a large number of demographic and social background variables, such as place of birth, birth order, years of education completed, and present perception of past relationships with families were studied. In general, our data supported findings by other investigators that showed that young people who had opted for variations from the nuclear family were, in the main, not different from their peers in similar social classes (Keniston, 1965).

We found relatively few background variables and attitudes that seemed to differentiate the traditional and nontraditional life-style groups. However, the significant differences added to our understanding of the motivations of those seeking an alternative family. Alternative-family parents had moved from one residence to another as children much more frequently than the traditional-family parents. Also, their parents had remarried significantly more often. As would be expected from the literature on young adults attracted to the counter-culture movement in the late 1960s, the alternative group interrupted their education more frequently than the traditional group; nevertheless, differences in years of education completed were not significant (Cohen & Eiduson, 1975).

There was a significantly greater tendency for the alternative group to view their early childhoods as unhappy; by contrast, the traditional group more frequently perceived this period as happy. Traditional parents tended to maintain a better relationship with their own parents throughout childhood and adolescence than persons who chose alternative life-styles. Mothers who were currently living in groups and in social-contract marriages appeared to have had the most difficulty with their own parents. Among the alternative groups, the single mother seemed to have maintained the best relationship with her parents in the growing-up years.

The data presented suggest a few commonalities in early background features that differentiate those persons who entered alternative families from those who chose two-parent nuclear units. Studies of ideologies and value systems in the third trimester of pregnancy suggest that there were notable differences between the groups in attitudes. The differences included valued achievement and success, reliance on rationality and intellect, problem solving, goal setting, and planning for the future and use of established educational and medical institutions. The traditionally married sample was significantly different as a group from the nontraditional participants. Within each of the four life styles, however, there was a range of perspectives and values among the participants (Rocheford, Cohen, & Weisner, Note 1).

1. Social-Contract Families

Living together in a social-contract rather than a legal marriage involves an ideological commitment that the relationship should be viable only as long as it is emotionally meaningful. Having a marriage license is perceived as encouraging a relaxation of the dedication to working at the relationship.

The social contracts in our populations were sufficiently committed to each other to have a child together. Their life style was distinguished by distributed parenting, sex-egalitarian caregiving roles, and a relaxed work ethic (Alexander, 1978). Income remained significantly lower than in the other two-parent family unit, the traditionally married, because many fathers worked only as needed. Mothers remained at home and involved themselves more in child care than mothers from any other family unit. The social contracts emphasized personal closeness in the family unit, so that the child tended to accompany parents everywhere, be less frequently exposed to babysitters, and thus more a part of the entire family's experiences.

2. Single Mothers

Single-mother families were composed of women who opted to keep their babies, although the option of abortion was available. Some had selected men for the purpose of fathering the child and providing a suitable genetic background; others were in temporary relationships when pregnancy occurred and decided to have the baby without marrying. In this family group, three subsets of families emerged upon analysis of motivational and background data: (a) "nestbuilders," the slightly older (28–32 years) woman, usually identified with the women's movement, well educated and professionally trained, and living alone in an apartment. By 6 months postpartum, all had returned to work and used day care facilities or home babysitters for child care; (b) "post-hoc adaptors," a less well educated and vocationally competent group who anticipated that marriage might result at a later point, and who shared apartments with other women, often living on Aid to Families with Dependent Children (AFDC) until they returned to work; and (c) a small group of "unwed mothers," psychologically and sociologically like the unwed mothers of yesterday: young, dependent on their own parents and relatives for support, and overwhelmed by their new role of family head, with its increased need for economic support and social stability (Kornfein, Weisner, & Martin, 1976). As a group, more single mothers were in the work force or in school by the 18-month postpartum period than in any other family group; this remained the pattern throughout the child's early years. For hours worked, however, they brought in less income than did the traditional mothers because of their more limited training (Eiduson, 1980).

3. Living-Group Families or Communities

Living-group families were of two kinds: creedal or domestic. The former designates the religious-headed community or the charismatic leader group, usually large hierarchically structured entities in which roles are ascribed and adhered to, and authority relationships carefully delineated (Eiduson, 1979). In some, children remained with parents throughout the early years, with the family entity nested in the larger community with its common and shared norms, rules, and regulations. In others, children after infancy lived as a group, with 24-hour caretakers providing the main nurture, supervision, and home-learning experiences. Involvement with parents was usually controlled by the group, although parents were generally physically in the same setting. By contrast, the domestic living group was less rigidly structured, being composed of people who shared social or political philosophies, artistic or craft interests, rural propensities, and who wanted to have the sense of extended family with nonbiologically related people (Weisner & Martin, 1979). Group living provided social, personal, as well as child care resources: three triadic marriages and one eight-person group marriage were included here.

4. Traditional, Married Nuclear Families

The three alternative family groupings were a network or "snowball" sample, obtained by contracts with Lamaze teachers, ecology centers, etc. The comparison group of traditional, married nuclear families was a random sample obtained from contacting obstetricians in the California Medical Association directory and having them nominate one mother from their practice who met sampling criteria of age, ethnicity, marital status and middle-class background. Generally, these families lived in urban apartments or houses and practiced traditional family roles; mothers were primary or sole child caretakers in infancy while fathers were employed in blue- or white-collar occupations. These couples had known each other significantly longer prior to marriage, and their relationship stability was coupled with a more scheduled and organized home life for both parents and child. The SES of this group was the highest of the four groups; more mothers worked on a part-time or full-time basis by the 18-month postpartum period than mothers in any family group except for the single mothers. Closer relationships with grandparents led to their playing a larger role in babysitting than in other family units (Eiduson, 1978).

C. The Importance of Change in Alternative Life Styles

As we examined variables in the family environment that are likely to impact on the psychological development of children, the frequency of changes in the parents' and children's lives was noted. Detailed studies of mobility patterns in each family revealed that alternative populations are significantly more likely to change life styles, residences, and household members than are traditional married families. As illustration: In the first 18 months after the birth of the child the alternatives were more than three times as likely to make multiple changes in their lives than were traditionals; 50% of the alternatives made three or more changes as compared to only 14% of traditionals, and this trend continued for 3 years: 39% of alternatives made multiple changes compared to 12% of traditionals.

Such data around family changes however, have to be considered together with the value placed by many alternatives on change. These family groups came into existence because the young adults in these groups wanted to express and to be identified with social change. They had an experimental flair and viewed change as both a useful way of expressing dissatisfaction and an appropriate way of resolving conflicting or troubling situations. They had little sympathy with enduring frustrations if some change in family life style, relationship, or work could produce a more personally gratifying condition, or provide more quality in their lives.

Their perspective and their family histories in regard to change since the birth of the child were of interest, especially in the light of the work of others on life-change events, which has suggested that change can be a stress or trauma that might precipitate or at least be correlated with the incidence of mental and physical pathology (Rahe, 1968; Dohrenwend & Dohrenwend, 1974). The original work of Holmes and Rahe (1967) had shown that, if life changes were quantified and scaled, estimates of the magnitude of stress could be discerned from the total life-change units "to which an individual had been subjected in a given period; in turn, these summed or total scores could be predictive of the occurrence of illness [p. 215]." Coddington

(1972a, 1972b) had extended this work to childhood, holding out the possibility of identifying a systematic and reliable way of predicting children "at risk" in their early years and identifying the environmental events that put them at jeopardy.

With this work in mind, we thought it appropriate to examine whether family life-change events in normal populations would invariably serve as an index of potential jeopardy in the young child. Would the same rationale hold within our sample? Our sample differed in their casualness and comfort with change. Could this make the fact of change a more routine chapter in a young child's life?

These questions oriented our studies to the following issues: Do children growing up in certain family life styles experience more life-change events than the children in other life styles? Is the child in the traditional, married nuclear unit more protected from change events than the child in an alternative family? Do life-change experiences influence the developmental outcome of the child? If there is an impact on outcome, is the impact related to the family style of the child? Or to the age of the child? Or to interaction between life style and age? Is there any evidence to show that if parents place a premium on change and experimentation in their own value system that their perspective mitigates the impact of family-change events on children's outcome scores?

These questions initiated our studies of family events and their impact on child development. This chapter deals with differences in life-stress events among family styles. It also relates total life-change events to three-year child-development outcome scores, especially in the cognitive area. Subsequent publications will present events in terms of conceptually related categories. Later analyses will also focus on emotional and social outcome scores at the end of the 3-year period.

II. Methodology

A. Data Collection of Change Events

The data used to empirically derive the list of change events were notes dictated by staff members after each contact with the child or family. Such notes were dictated following each interview, test, home observation, or telephone call according to a semistructured format that emphasized the appearance and manner of the participant, a description of the current life style, and any unusual events that had transpired during the contact that were

TABLE 3.1
Family Change Events (Ages: Birth–3 Years)

Event	Rank Order	Weighted scores (6 judges)
Marriage of parent	38	24
Divorce of parents	16	65
Parents separate	10	69
Death of grandparent–close relative	23	45
Death of biological parent	1	98
Change of residence	45	1
Mother reunites with father or former socially adoptive father after a separation	41	18
Mother has a new mate who lives in the family home	35	29
Adult moves in or out of family residence	42	12
New sibling	27	43
Mother goes to work full-time	28	43
Mother works nights	36	29
Parent unemployed though wants to be	37	29
Severe financial stresses	19	52
Jail term or parent arrested	17	56
Environment reported as containing source of physical danger	34	34
Absence of toys, books, stimulating objects	40	19
Parental–marital conflict	18	55
Observer reports mother as having hard time with child	29	41
Mother or primary caretaker has physical illness or disability that affects her caretaking of child	4	78
Mother hospitalized for medical problems or illness	7	72
Family member living with child or living-group member has a serious physical illness	33	36
Parent reported emotionally disturbed	8	71
Mother hospitalized for mental illness	5	74
Regular or heavy usage of alcohol or drugs by parents	14	67
Child given drugs or alcohol	2	86
Macrobiotic diet	22	46
Serious illness regarding hospitalization of child	3	83
Accident involving emergency room	24	45
Exposure to sexual behavior of parents or other adults	25	45
Sexual abuse by an adult	9	70
Adoption of child	26	44
Child is reported as being unscheduled	44	3
Observer reports mother or primary caretaker openly rejecting the child	11	69
Family member living with child or household member other than parent	30	41
Observer reports child ignored, neglected	12	68
Observer reports child's environment and/or parents caretaking style as overstimulating	32	39

Continued

TABLE 3.1 *(Continued)*
Family Change Events (Ages: Birth–3 Years)

Event	Rank Order	Weighted scores (6 judges)
Observer reports mother or primary caretaker insensitive and/or overprotective with child	31	41
Conflict between mother and child reported as intense	15	67
Physical punishment repeatedly used on child	13	68
Parent–child separation for more than 2 weeks, and child living with grandparents, friends, etc.	21	48
Congenital illness	20	50
Child acquiring a visible deformity	6	74
Child starts school	39	22
Child stops ongoing school experience	43	11

not captured in formal data collection. From these dictated notes a summary was prepared for each case. The purpose of these summaries was to organize the information chronologically and to eliminate anecdotal and other material not directly relevant to the child under study. Preparation of the summaries also provided a means for verifying dates and cross-checking the validity of information. The case abstractors were trained to make lists of experiences or events that might change or disrupt the family life of the infant and young child. Cumulative lists of change events were checked by clinicians for agreement that the change listed was likely to be a notable one in a child's experience. The list of change events derived empirically by this summarization process can be seen in Table 3.1.

B. Establishing Weights for Events Using Social Consensus

Using the Coddington model, a social-consensus scaling model was adapted to assign weights to each event on the basis of the extent of readjustment each life change demanded (Coddington, 1972a). Consensus by groups of diversely trained experts served to provide appropriate rankings of these events.

The list of change events that are believed to have a potential impact on the young child was submitted to an expert panel of judges who ranked the items from 1 to 45. The six judges, who are currently active and employed, had the following professional training and experience:

1. M.D., child psychiatrist, board certified, with over 7 years clinical experience
2. Ph.D. psychologist, American Board of Examiners in Professional Psychology (ABPP), over 25 years clinical experience with adults and children, strong research background
3. Ph.D. in clinical social work, over 25 years in clinical social work, supervision, and training
4. Ph.D. in developmental psychology, with internships in child and adult clinical psychology, postdoctoral training in social psychology and personality development, 1 year clinical experience
5. Ph.D. in early childhood education, minor in clinical psychology, 7 years clinical experience with children and adults
6. Ph.D. in clinical psychology, 10 years experience in clinical practice, training, and supervision

C. Derivation of Change Scores

A chart was prepared for each case that tabulated occurrences of changes. The rows of the chart represented the events. The columns represented 6-month periods from birth to age 3. Scorers transferred the change information from the summaries to the charts, which were periodically checked for consistency and to reconcile differences in order to maintain quality control. If the summary indicated that a given change event occurred during a 6-month period, the child received the full score for that stress for that period; no additional points were given for multiple occurrences during one 6-month period. Each chart contained an area in which the scorer could list any change events described in the summaries to which none of the changes in the list readily applied. Overall, there was a good correspondence between the events detailed in the summaries and those contained in the change list, and very few family-change events could not be scored.

Cumulative change scores were derived in a number of ways:

1. Total weighted change scores were determined for the periods birth–1 year, 1–2 years, 2–3 years, and birth–3 years by adding all weighted scores for all changes entered on the charts, including repeated occurrences of the same stress.
2. To avoid chronic events from being underscored (since if an event occurred in each 6-month period within 1 year, it received two weighted scores), an alternate set of scores was prepared that gives an event one weighted score per 1-year period, thus ignoring all repeated occurrences during that year.

3. There is a total that gives one weighted score for each event that occurs during the total 3 years; this score is given no additional points for repeated events.
4. Other scores have been created that indicate the number of occurrences of change events by 1-year periods, as well as the number of different events by years and for the entire 3-year span.
5. A chronicity score gives the total number of occurrences minus the number of different events (i.e., the number of repeated change events). The purpose of devising such diverse scoring techniques is to examine the differential impact of severe change (a few major events) and chronic change (many different events, or much repetition of the same event).
6. The 45 events can be grouped into a few broad categories: (*a*) changes in life style; (*b*) parent psychological variables; (*c*) parent–child interaction variables; and (*d*) changes in which the child was directly involved (health, environment, etc.). Subscores (based on the original weights) by 1-year periods have now been determined for each of the four categories.

The total weighted change scores noted in (1) form the basis for the analyses in this chapter.

D. Developmental Outcome Scores as Dependent Variables

The extent to which developmental outcome data are related to the incidence of change events was investigated by analyzing psychological test scores obtained when the child was tested at 1 year and 3 years of age. The choice was made to focus initially on cognitive scores, since during the first 3 years these provide the most robust measures of development, although obviously the word *robust* is generous. Developmental outcome scores in the cognitive area were considered least likely to be affected by change events; thus results of interest in this area would encourage further examination in the area of emotional and social development variables. The latter are more ambiguous and difficult to measure precisely at this age period. Our work has assessed personality growth through parents' reports of personality and behaviors in questionnaires and interviews, as well as in test data obtained on the Ainsworth Strange Situation Test (Ainsworth, Blehar, Waters, and Wall, 1978) administered at 1 year and 3 years, on the Vineland Social Maturity Scale at 3 years, the Minnesota Child Development (Ireton) administered at 18 months, 2 years, and 2 years 9 months, and on tests of frustration toleration, freedom of fantasy, aggression, distractibility, and measures of competency at 3 years.

In this chapter, data presentation is limited to scores on the following outcome variables:

1. Newborn Neurological Examination Score (NNE)

   An index providing baseline data on the health of children at birth based on an examination done on the infants by a trained pediatrician or nurse, according to a manual and coding scheme developed for the procedure (Parmalee & Michaelis, 1971).

2. Obstetrical Complication Scale, Adjusted (OCS–a)

   A measure based on the occurrence of any complicating factors in the maternal medical history and the birth process. These data are obtained from medical, hospital, and maternal reports (Parmalee & Littman, Note 2).

3. Two scores on the 1-year Bayley Scales of Infant Development: Mental Development Index (MDI 1) and Performance Development Index (PDI 1)

4. Stanford–Binet IQ score (at 3 years)

5. Risk score

A score of 1, 2, 3, or 4 was assigned by examining the actual scores attained on the Stanford–Binet Test and on the Peabody Picture Vocabulary Test (PPVT), a linguistic competency measure. Cases receiving scores that were 1 standard deviation (SD) below the mean on both of the latter tests given at 3 years were identified as "high risk" cases and given a score of 4; those with scores below 1 SD on the Binet, a 3; those below 1 SD on the Peabody, a 2; and cases receiving scores above 1 SD on both tests received a score of 1.

III. Event Scores for Each Life Style at Various Time Periods

Table 3.2 presents the event scores (mean) for each family life style. The top chart presents these data by the family life style to which each case was assigned at the beginning of the study. It is evident that the mean of change events is significantly lower for the traditional group than for the alternatives. The single-mother and social-contract groups have the highest event scores, but the living group appears close to the mean for all groups. All have sizable dispersions in scores, the traditionals having the greatest spread, but not significantly more than the other groups.

TABLE 3.2
Total Weighted Event Statistics by Life Style (Years 1–3)

Statistic	Social-contract	Single-mother	Traditional married	Living-group	All groups
		By original life style[a]			
Mean	413	419	290	326	362
Standard error of the mean (SEM)	45	37	40	35	20
Maximum	1642	1262	1712	1335	1712
Minimum	73	22	0	22	0
N	54	50	51	54	209
		By life style at 18 months[b]			
Mean	399	457	311	321	363
SEM	42	51	32	36	20
Maximum	1112	1712	1642	1081	1712
Minimum	85	22	0	22	0
N	41	46	79	42	208
		By life style at 3 years[c]			
Mean	389	452	305	332	360
SEM	46	48	30	36	20
Maximum	1262	1712	1642	1081	1712
Minimum	90	22	0	22	0
N	40	47	81	39	207

[a]ANOVA: $p = .530$; $SD = .3260$ (Levene).
[b]ANOVA: $p = .0307$: $SD = .4924$ (Levene).
[c]ANOVA: $p = .0345$; $SD = .6027$ (Levene).

The living-group data are interesting when families that have changed their life style at one year are compared with those in the original life styles. Note that there has been a departure from living-group status for 12 families (primarily domestic groups), and 13 social-contract families have left the original group and moved into other groups—with the move being toward the traditional marrieds. When event scores are looked at in terms of life style at 18 months, mean event scores still show significant differences, with the single-mother sample now having the highest mean event scores. Scores of the other alternative groups remain about the same, with the traditional sample's scores reflecting the number of alternatives moving into the traditional group.

It also appears from these data that a few single cases with high event change scores may be skewing the traditional and single-parent populations data (note high maximum scores throughout).

A. Relationship between Event Scores and Outcome Scores for All Subjects

Results indicate that Stanford–Binet scores are inversely correlated with event scores for the total population. That is, the greater the change event scores, the lower the Stanford–Binet scores. This is the case for the event scores for each year of life and for the first 3 years as a whole: All relationships are weak but significant.

A child identified as "at risk" by scores on both the Binet and the PPVT at 3 years is likely to have higher event change scores during years 2 and years 3 than nonflagged children. Again, correlations are low but significant.

A low score on the Obstetrical Complications Scale (OCS) at birth is also positively associated with higher event scores at 2 and at 3 years of age, and with a high total event score. This post-hoc relationship may mean that certain birth conditions are likely to set the stage for future event changes for the child; however, a more plausible implication is that poor birth conditions may point to families who are likely to be unstable, and who subsequently subject the child to more event changes in his or her life. Further analyses should elucidate the meaning of the data.

TABLE 3.3

Correlations between Event Scores and Outcome Scores ($N = 209$)[a]

	Event scores			
Outcome variable	1-year	2-year	3-year	Total
NNE	−.11*	.04	−.01	−.03
OCS	−.10	−.13*	−.22**	−.18**
MDI 1	.00	−.06	−.11	−.07
PDI 1	.00	−.10	−.09	−.08
Stanford–Binet	−.15*	−.19**	−.14*	−.20**
Risk	.15*	.18**	.17**	.21**

[a]Correlations among event scores of life style at 1 year ($N = 209$), life style at 18 months ($N = 209$), and life style at 3 years ($N = 208$) are not substantially different from those on this table.

*$p \leq .05$.

**$p \leq .01$.

Essentially the same relationships between event and outcome test scores are found when the families are grouped by the life style in which they are at 1 year, at 18 months, or at 3 years. Correlations cited remain low, but significant.

B. Relationship between Event Scores and Outcome Scores for the Various Life Styles

1. Traditional Married Populations

Very respectable correlations between Stanford–Binet and summary event scores at 2 years, at 3 years, and for the total 3-year period, emerge for persons who were traditional marrieds at the onset of the study (from −.26 to −.38 from Table 3.4).

Risk summary scores correlate with events at an even higher level (.45–.56) and are in the direction that suggest that a child flagged as intellectually at risk at 3 years is likely to have experienced many change events at 2 and 3 years, and during the whole first 3 years of life. For this group, a low Bayley MDI Score at 1 year is also related to significantly higher event change scores in years 2, 3, and over the total period. This suggests that the low score may flag children whose poor performance is part of a gestalt in which many family changes and intellectual inadequacies at 1 year are also related to significantly higher event change scores in years 2, 3, and over the total period. The low score may flag children whose poor performance is part of a total picture in which stresses and cognitive weaknesses go hand in hand.

By 1 year, the traditional married sample size has been enhanced by participants' shift to this life style. The same effects as just stated are seen for this enlarged population, although to a slightly smaller, but still significant, extent.

The traditional married group at 18 months consists of 80 participants. This enlargement by persons not originally traditionally married reduces the association of changes with Binet scores, except for year 2 (which has proved to be a developmentally important period) and over the total period. However the risk score remains significantly correlated even with the enlarged traditional married population. This group also increases slightly in the third year to 82 participants. Again, change events at year 2 (and over the total period) are negatively correlated with Binet scores. Also, the risk scores remain positively correlated with change scores at each year and over the total period.

TABLE 3.4

Correlations between Event Scores and Outcome Scores for the Traditional Married Group

	Event scores			
Outcome variable	1-year	2-year	3-year	Total
Original life style (*N* = 51)				
NNE	−.04	−.02	−.02	−.03
OCS	.20	−.06	−.09	.02
MDI 1	−.17	−.22	−.26*	−.26*
PDI 1	−.06	−.12	.01	−.07
Stanford–Binet	.02	−.38**	−.34**	−.29*
Risk	.22	.56**	.45**	.50**
Life style at 1 year (*N* = 73)				
NNE	−.04	−.08	−.14	−.10
OCS	.00	−.11	−.26**	−.14
MDI 1	−.16	−.19	−.28**	−.24*
PDI 1	−.16	−.17	−.16	−.19*
Stanford–Binet	−.05	−.32**	−.34**	−.29**
Risk	.17	.36**	.36**	.36**
Life style at 18 months (*N* = 80)				
NNE	−.08	−.04	−.16	−.11
OCS	−.06	−.21*	−.26**	−.22*
MDI 1	−.07	−.12	−.11	−.12
PDI 1	−.08	−.12	−.11	−.12
Stanford–Binet	−.16	−.26**	−.17	−.24*
Risk	.33**	.31**	.27**	.37**
Life style at 3 years (*N* = 82)				
NNE	−.05	−.02	−.10	−.07
OCS	−.10	−.12	−.29**	−.21*
MDI 1	−.09	−.07	−.05	−.08
PDI 1	−.04	−.05	.00	−.03
Stanford–Binet	−.24*	−.22*	−.13	−.24*
Risk	.46**	.42**	.30**	.48**

*$p \leq .05$.
**$p \leq .01$.

2. Alternative Families

a. Social-Contract Families. For this group, change scores at 1 year predict high risk scores. The size of the correlation is substantial (.28).

A high score on the Newborn Neurological Examination (NNE) showed a surprising negative relationship to change event scores at 1 and 3 years.

TABLE 3.5

Correlations between Event Scores and Outcome Scores for the Social-Contract Group

Outcome variable	Event scores			
	1-year	2-year	3-year	Total
Original life style (*N* = 54)				
NNE	−.25*	.07	−.23	−.17
OCS	.04	−.04	−.14	−.06
MDI 1	.02	−.08	−.05	−.04
PDI 1	.19	.15	−.02	.13
Stanford–Binet	−.20	−.10	−.11	−.16
Risk	.28*	.04	.16	.19
Life style at 1 year (*N* = 49)				
NNE	−.17	.22	−.08	.01
OCS	−.14	−.19	−.16	−.22
MDI 1	.04	−.17	−.14	−.13
PDI 1	.23	.10	.05	.16
Stanford–Binet	−.19	−.05	−.02	−.10
Risk	.31*	.09	.08	.20
Life style at 18 months (*N* = 41)				
NNE	−.27*	.06	−.09	−.11
OCS	−.07	−.15	−.24	−.19
MDI 1	.08	−.13	−.26*	−.12
PDI 1	.33*	.15	−.05	.19
Stanford–Binet	−.04	.00	−.22	−.09
Risk	.06	.01	.26*	.12
Life style at 3 years (*N* = 40)				
NNE	−.36**	−.13	−.28*	−.30*
OCS	−.06	−.16	−.14	−.15
MDI 1	.14	−.10	−.25	−.07
PDI 1	.28*	.08	−.01	.15
Stanford–Binet	−.20	−.16	−.25	−.24
Risk	.12	−.02	.10	.07

*$p \leq .05$.
**$p \leq .01$.

However, by 1 year there are no significant relationships between event scores and outcome measures except a positive correlation between change score and risk score at 1 year. As the group was constituted at 18 months, some of the same relationships seen originally emerged between change and NNE at 1 year and risk at 3 years, although the relationships were in the same direction; the relationship with NNE was stronger while the relationship with risk was weaker. As constituted at 3 years, the social contracts with elevated stress score at both 1- and 3-year periods and over all periods showed significantly higher NNE scores.

   b. Single-Mother Families. For the single-mother group, the Stanford–Binet scores were significantly and negatively related to change events, as measured by summary scores. Correlations ranged from −.30 to −.40, so

TABLE 3.6

Correlations between Event Scores and Outcome Scores for the Single-Mother Group

Outcome variable	Event scores			
	1-year	2-year	3-year	Total
Original life style (N = 50)				
NNE	−.12	−.21	−.10	−.18
OCS	−.18	−.36**	−.35**	−.36**
MDI 1	−.15	−.26*	−.34**	−.30*
PDI 1	−.04	−.16	−.23	−.18
Stanford–Binet	−.35**	−.34**	−.30*	−.40**
Risk	.03	.11	.12	.11
Life style at 1 year (N = 50)				
NNE	−.20	.02	−.01	−.08
OCS	−.08	−.21	−.18	−.18
MDI 1	.05	.02	−.05	.01
PDI 1	.04	−.07	−.05	−.03
Stanford–Binet	−.34**	−.30*	−.29*	−.36**
Risk	.11	.10	.19	.16
Life style at 18 months (N = 46)				
NNE	−.06	.07	.07	.04
OCS	−.10	−.14	−.12	−.15
MDI 1	.00	−.10	−.08	−.08
PDI 1	−.02	−.14	.07	−.05
Stanford–Binet	−.30*	−.40**	−.18	−.35*
Risk	.10	.32*	.14	.24
Life style at 3 years (N = 47)				
NNE	.05	.18	.03	.12
OCS	−.01	−.16	−.13	−.13
MDI 1	.04	−.06	−.06	−.04
PDI 1	−.07	−.06	−.03	−.06
Stanford–Binet	−.01	−.25*	−.18	−.20
Risk	−.16	.16	.11	.07

*$p \le .05$.
**$p \le .01$.

they are rather substantial, and all are in the same direction, showing that the relationship holds for stresses at each age period and for the total score.

The OCS score is also related negatively to change for the original single-mother group, for events experienced at 2 and 3 years, and for the total score. The Bayley MDI score correlations at 2 years are in the same direction as the 3-year Binet and total score, with the latter two scores of slightly greater magnitude.

For those families in the single-mother population at 1 year ($N = 50$), the Binet relationship holds at about the same level. This persists as women who are single mothers at 18 months are studied (with the exception of a nonsignificant relationship at 3 years).

A significant relationship between change score and risk score at 2 years appears. The Binet relationship is also significant for those women who are single mothers at 3 years, when their stress scores at 2 years are examined.

Figure 3.1 shows the inverse relationship of Binet scores and change event scores for the single-mother life style. The change event score for year 2 is presented with the Binet score at age 3, putting the relationship in some meaningful temporal order. Illustrated for one life-style, the findings noted here are common to all life-styles.

c. Living-Group Families. For living-group families, the birth measures and 1-year tests are correlated with change. Correlations as high as .41 emerge between the NNE and change, but the direction is different from what was found with the social-contract group; for the living group, a high NNE score predicts a high change score. This relationship remains potent despite changes in the living group's membership. This unexpected finding is also noted with Bayley MDI scores at 1 year, where higher scores are related to greater extent of change at 1 and 2 years, and for total score. Interestingly, neither Binet nor risk scores were significantly related to change scores, as had been found with the other groups, and for the total sample.

The significant associations for Bayley MDI scores decrease slightly for the living-group families at 1 year and at 18 months. In both periods there has been substantial membership change, with the total number of families in the life style being reduced disproportionately in the domestic living groups as compared to the creedal groups.

For 18-month living-group participants however, the Binet scores line up with those found in other populations; significantly higher change events are found in children with lower Binet scores. These results did not reach significance but do indicate a trend. At 3 years, the significant relationships lie with the NNE and the Bayley PDI scores at 2 and 3 years, and the overall score.

TABLE 3.7

Correlations between Event Scores and Outcome Scores for the Living Group

	Event scores			
Outcome variable	1-year	2-year	3-year	Total
Original life style (N = 54)				
NNE	.02	.33**	.41**	.34**
OCS	−.35**	−.09	−.26*	−.27*
MDI 1	.26*	.30**	.11	.28*
PDI 1	−.16	−.26*	−.20	−.26*
Stanford–Binet	−.08	.00	.06	.00
Risk	.01	.02	.05	.03
Life style at 1 year (N = 37)				
NNE	.11	.23	.41**	.34*
OCS	−.22	.03	−.28*	−.18
MDI 1	.17	.27*	.08	.22
PDI 1	−.21	−.27**	−.22	−.30*
Stanford–Binet	−.06	−.01	.17	.06
Risk	.01	.05	.00	.03
Life style at 18 months (N = 42)				
NNE	−.10	.17	.30	.20
OCS	−.20	.08	−.22	−.13
MDI 1	.11	.27*	.03	.18
PDI 1	−.18	−.28*	−.28*	−.33*
Stanford–Binet	−.16	−.05	.00	−.08
Risk	−.01	.05	.03	.04
Life style at 3 years (N = 39)				
NNE	.02	.26	.41**	.33*
OCS	−.26*	−.09	−.28*	−.27*
MDI 1	.11	.20	−.04	.10
PDI 1	−.15	−.45**	−.31*	−.40**
Stanford–Binet	−.01	−.11	−.01	−.06
Risk	−.07	.11	.12	.09

$*p \leq .05$.
$**p \leq .01$.

IV. Summary

Findings emerging from the current pilot studies implicate certain socialization features as bearing directly on the child's cognitive functioning as measured by Stanford–Binet at 3 years of age:

1. The child who has experienced an elevated level of change (as measured by life-change events) in his life by age 3 is likely to have

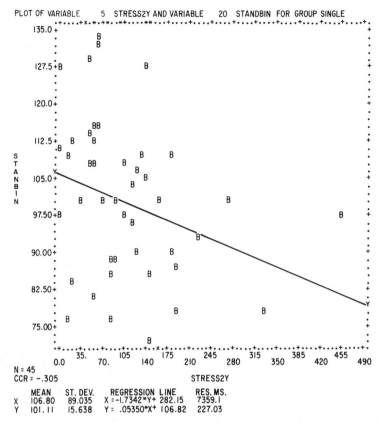

FIGURE 3.1. Plot of weighted event scores at 3 years with Stanford–Binet scores at 3 years (Single-mother group).

lower Stanford–Binet scores. This finding holds for the sample considered as a whole and is also found within each family life style. Children who have been exposed to such events as frequent moves, breakup of marriage or family, who grow up in a family where parents are heavy alcohol or drug users, etc, are likely to be functioning at a lower level by the age of 3 than are children whose lives have been less eventful and have not included such negative events.

2. There is also significant association of event scores and a composite cognitive risk score based upon the Stanford–Binet and the Peabody Picture Vocabulary Test.

3. The inverse relationship between change and the Binet score as an index of cognitive functioning was first noted when events occurring

during the first year were tabulated. The relationship found at that time persisted when change events for the second and for the third years of a child's life were tabulated separately. However, for the child who was flagged "at risk" on the basis of poor performance on 3-year cognitive tests, the family change event score did not seem to show up as significantly associated until the second year of life.

4. The correlations between life-change events scores and cognitive performance were in the vicinity of .2, which, while not strong, was significant for the total sample.

5. Further, and important for this study of alternative life styles, as life styles are looked at separately, the findings relating life events to Stanford–Binet scores at 3 years holds for the single-mother and the traditionally married populations, but not as strongly for the two most alternative groups, the social-contract and the living groups.

This is of interest because, in studies of perspectives and values espoused by the study population, the single mother and the traditional parent held similar values in about half of the dimensions that composed the alternative philosophy, whereas the groups considered to show the most alternative life styles, the living-group and social-contract populations, were like each other. This was the case for the dimensions of achievement orientation, future planning, natural-organic perspective, and attitudes toward authority, and to a less than significant extent, for the value of humanism. In the latter, adherence to humanitarian values was found common to all family styles, but the extent of affiliation saw a similar distribution in single-parent and traditional groups.

It should be noted that 3-year life-event data included in these preliminary analyses were not as complete as were data from years 1 and 2. As data are more thoroughly examined for the 3-year period, their significance for Binet scores for the different family groups will be reanalyzed, when events are classified into groups in terms of more generic areas to which they refer (i.e., change in life style; psychological factors in the parents, such as depression, hospitalization; parent–child interaction factors; or direct child stresses, such as acquiring a visible deformity, or hospitalization). It appears from preliminary analyses that the changes that are grouped in the category, parent–child interaction, tend to be most highly correlated in an inverse direction with Stanford–Binet scores. While total change event scores show a $-.22$ correlation with Binet scores for the total population (significant at the .01 level), the parent–child relationship score suggests an even higher level of association ($-.31$). These findings are of particular interest, since Rutter (1973), Hetherington *et al.* (1978), Bowlby (1973), and the other investigators who are currently exploring some of the determinants of stress in children have conceptualized and found that in some limited populations of preschool and elementary school children there exist interactional and relationship problems that affect parent contacts and which are likely to be sources of elevated stress.

It is of interest that the events that are postulated by other investigators and by ourselves as likely to produce a need for readjustment by the child involve some change in psychological or social status or relationships. As we have noted in our discussions of our alternative families, the notion of change seems more ego-syntonic to them than to traditional populations. From the child's youngest years, the "experimental flair" of some parents have led to changing residences, mates, and jobs in line with their philosophy of not staying with situations that are troublesome and of maximizing personal opportunities and satisfactions. One foremost issue in this study has been whether parental practices counter to prevailing thinking about influence on child growth can in fact prove to have a salutory effect if valued by parents and sanctioned by them and their immediate surroundings. The preliminary data on changes and cognitive scores suggest that, though perhaps valued by parents, events demanding readjustment can be stressful for a young child and effect cognitive growth in measurable ways. It will be very important to see if these data are supported as the study continues into the preschool and elementary school years, for the results will be relevant to this all-important issue in child development.

Acknowledgments

Randolph Pitts was instrumental in abstracting life-change event data from case record material and Joyce McLarty provided the computer work.

Reference Notes

1. Rocheford, B., Cohen, J., & Weisner, T. S. Family values in traditional and alternative life styles. In J. Alexander (Chair), *Characteristics of alternative families and their children: Implications for mental health.* Symposium presented at the meeting of the American Orthopsychiatric Association, San Francisco, March 1978.
2. Parmalee, A. H., & Littman, R. *Obstetrical complications scale.* Mimeographed report, University of California at Los Angeles, 1977.

References

Ainsworth, M.D.S., Blehar, M. C., Waters, E., & Wall, S. *Patterns of attachment: A psychological study of the strange situation.* Hillsdale, N.J.: Lawrence Erlbaum Associates, 1978.

Alexander, J. *Marriages without weddings: Changes in the American family.* Unpublished doctoral dissertation, Institute for Clinical Social Work, Los Angeles, 1978.

Bowlby, J. *Attachment and loss: Separation and anger* (Vol. 2.) New York: Basic Books, 1973.

Coddington, R. D. The significance of life events as etiologic factors in the diseases of children. I. A survey of professional workers. *Journal of Psychosomatic Research*, 1972, *16*, 7–18. (a)

Coddington, R. D. The significance of life events as etiologic factors in the diseases of children. II. A study of a normal population. *Journal of Psychosomatic Research*, 1972, *16*, 205–213. (b)

Cohen, J., & Eiduson, B. T. Changing patterns of child rearing in alternative life styles: Implications for development. In A. Davids (Ed.), *Child personality and psychopathology: Current topics.* New York: Wiley, 1975.

Dohrenwend, B. S. & Dohrenwend, B. P. *Stressful life events: Their nature and effects.* New York: Wiley, 1974.

Eiduson, B. T. Emergent families of the 1970's: Values, practices, and impact on children. In D. Reiss and H. Hoffman (Eds.), *The family: Dying or developing.* New York: Plenum, 1978.

Eiduson, B. T. The commune-reared child. In J. Noshpitz (Ed.), *Basic handbook of child psychiatry* (Vol. 1). New York: Basic Books, 1979.

Eiduson, B. T. Contemporary single mothers as parents. In L. G. Katz (Ed.), *Current topics in early childhood education* (Vol. 3). Norwood, N.J.: Ablex, 1980.

Eiduson, B. T., Cohen, J., & Alexander, J. W. Alternatives in child rearing in the 1970's. *American Journal of Orthopsychiatry*, 1973, *43*, 720–731. [Also reprinted in J. Clarke (Ed.), *Intimacy, marriage, and the family.* New York: Allyn & Bacon, 1975. Also reprinted in J. T. Gibson & P. Blumberg (Eds.), *Readings for child psychology.* Reading, Mass.: Addison-Wesley, 1976.]

Eiduson, B. T., & Weisner, T. S. Alternative socialization settings for infants and young children. In J. H. Stevens & M. Mathews (Eds.), *Mother/child, father/child relationships.* Washington, D.C.: National Association for the Education of Young Children, 1978.

Hetherington, E. M., Cox, M., & Cox, R. The aftermath of divorce. In J. H. Stevens & M. Mathews (Eds.), *Mother/child, father/child relationships.* Washington, D.C.: National Association for Education of Young Children, 1978.

Holmes, T. H., & Rahe, R. H. The social readjustment rating scale. *Journal of Psychosomatic Research*, 1967, *11*, 213–218.

Keniston, K. *The uncommitted: Alienated youth in American society* (3rd ed.). New York: Dell, 1965.

Kornfein, M., Weisner, T. S., & Martin, J. C. Women into mothers: Experimental family lifestyles. In J. R. Chapman & M. J. Cages (Eds.), *Women into wives: Sage annual of women's policy studies* (Vol. 2). Beverly Hills, Calif.: Sage, 1976.

Parmalee, A. H., & Michaelis, R. Neurological examination of the newborn. In J. Hellmuth (Ed.), *Exceptional infant. Studies in abnormalities.* New York: Bruner/Mazel, 1971.

Rahe, R. H. Life-change measurement as a predictor of illness. *Proceedings of the Royal Society of Medicine*, 1968, *61*, 1124–1128.

Rutter, M. Maternal deprivation reconsidered. In S. Chess & A. Thomas (Eds.), *Annual progress in child psychiatry and child development.* New York: Bruner/Mazel, 1973.

Weisner, T. S., & Martin, J. C. Learning environments for infants: Communes and conventionally married families in California. *Alternative Lifestyles*, 1979, *2*, 201–241.

CHAPTER 4

Adolescent Pregnancy and Parenthood: Implications for Development

KATHLEEN A. McCLUSKEY
JIM KILLARNEY
DENNIS R. PAPINI
WEST VIRGINIA UNIVERSITY
MORGANTOWN, WEST VIRGINIA

I. Introduction

Adolescence is frequently perceived as a period fraught with disruptive events; yet most of these events can be viewed as normative crises—the rites of passage that admit the child to the adult world. One of the most common nonnormative events of adolescence that accelerates this transitional passage for teenage girls and, to a lesser extent, boys, is pregnancy. No matter what circumstances surround the pregnancy—planned or unplanned, single or wed, terminated or carried to term—the adolescent is thrust into a crisis situation that has serious implications and ramifications for herself, her partner, their child, their families, and society at large.

Although pregnancy and birth are cited by many authors (see Reese & Smyer, Chapter 1, this volume) as one of the most common nonnormative life events, pregnancy during adolescence is considered nonnormative because of its occurrence early in the life cycle. Statistically, adolescent pregnancy is also nonnormative. The annual incidence of teenage pregnancy in the United States is approximately 1 million, with 600,000 of these resulting in live births. While this number is alarmingly large, it represents

LIFE-SPAN DEVELOPMENTAL PSYCHOLOGY
Nonnormative Life Events

only 6% of the population 12–19 years of age (Alan Guttmacher Institute, 1976), therefore making it a relatively uncommon event. Adolescent pregnancy is also typically characterized as a life crisis. The majority of the pregnancies are unplanned and unwanted, leading to a crisis situation for the adolescents and their families.

The pregnant adolescent has been investigated along a variety of dimensions: theoretical, medical, the pregnancy resolution, the social and economic correlates, and the adolescent as parent. This chapter is an integrative review of these areas.

II. Theoretical Perspectives

Several studies (Baizerman, Sheehan, Ellison, & Schlesinger, 1974; McKenry, Walters, & Johnson, 1979; and Plionis, 1975) are unanimous in condemning the lack of adequate theoretical and empirical bases for the interpretation of data concerning adolescent pregnancy. McKenry *et al.* (1979) note that "the lack of development of theoretical models concerning the etiology of adolescent pregnancy and the behavior of pregnant adolescents has resulted in a lack of cumulative findings [p. 17]." Baizerman *et al.* (1974) suggest the need for both theory and theoretical models in the examination of adolescent pregnancies. Finally, Plionis (1975) contends that this lack of a theoretical base has resulted in loose terminology, the unlikelihood of formulating and testing hypotheses, and the impossibility of establishing cause-and-effect relationships. Her last statement is especially troublesome in attempts to identify the etiology of adolescent pregnancy. The difficulty that arises is in determining whether adolescent pregnancy is a response to, or product of, the unfavorable economic, educational, socio-cultural, psychological, and biological conditions that have traditionally been associated with the pregnant teenager. In an initial search for an etiology, four developmental theories, the psychodynamic theories of Freud and Erikson, and the cognitive theories of Piaget and Elkind will be analyzed, focusing on their views of adolescence with specific focus on the life crisis of pregnancy.

A. Psychodynamic Theories

Sigmund Freud conceived of adolescence as a period in the life span during which the biological changes associated with puberty revive the unresolved psychic conflicts of earlier childhood (1953). To Freud, adolescence in and of itself was not a particularly interesting phase of development for the very reason that no new psychosexual crises were experienced. According to Anna Freud (1958) puberty was described as "the time when the changes set in which give infantile sexual life its final shape. Subordination of the erotogenic zones to the primacy of the genital zone, the setting up of new sexual aims, different for males and females, and the finding of new sexual objects outside the family were listed as the main events [p. 256]." Thus, the normal course of development for the adolescent consists of changing the objects of cathexis from the same-sex parent to an outside love object.

Virtually all of the literature on psychodynamic explanations of adolescent pregnancy focus on illegitimacy as a pathology caused by unresolved Oedipal conflicts (Babikian & Goldman, 1971) and/or poor mother–daughter relations (Babikian & Goldman, 1971; Barglow Bornstein, Exum, Wright, & Visotsky, 1968; Friedman, 1966). It is the contention of all of these authors that pregnancy during adolescence brings about the conflict between being mothered and mothering.

Babikian and Goldman (1971) defined the problems of adolescent motherhood as consisting of obstetrical risks, psychological and social stress at home, lost opportunity for education, and enhanced fertility. The subjects in this study were 15 adolescents who were at least 20 weeks pregnant and under 17 years of age. An additional 15 adolescents served as controls. These authors found three predominant patterns in their sample. First, there were psychodynamic factors associated with the relationship of the adolescent to the mother. These factors consisted of dependency, separation, and individuation. These relationships were evidenced by a need to comply with the adolescent's mother's wish for a baby, identification with the adolescent's mother through out-of-wedlock pregnancy, or as a form of competition with the mother. The second pattern was associated with the relationship or absence of the adolescent's father and was conceptualized as a response to a strong unresolved Oedipal complex. These factors have been identified as important variables by other researchers as well (Abernathy, 1974; Gottschalk, Titchener, Piker, & Stewart, 1964; Schaffer & Pine, 1972). The final pattern involved social and peer influences on the adolescent and was conceptualized as the need to prove oneself as an undamaged woman in comparison to and through identification with peers.

An investigation of these adolescents' adaptation to their pregnancies indicated that 22 out of the 30 subjects had intense dependency needs due to poor ego functions. The findings were consistent in that there was a preponderance of broken homes, and the formative years (2 to 5 years of age) were characterized by chaotic homes with little consistency in behavioral limitations and no constancy against which to test reality. These findings indicate poor ego functioning. These adolescents also revealed a marked deficit in moral reasoning.

Other contemporary psychoanalytic literature tends to focus on more positive aspects of adolescent pregnancy (Youngs & Niebyl, 1975). Bibring and Valerstein (1976) state that pregnancy is a time when major psychological and biological changes represent major developmental tasks. At this time, earlier unresolved conflicts reappear. The new emphasis, however, is placed on the assertion that these crises are normal, time limited, and precipitated by the stress of pregnancy. In his exploration of psychodynamic focus in married adolescents' pregnancies, La Barre (1968) cites optimism, courage, and adaptability as positive forces within the dynamic family.

Erikson (1950, 1968), unlike Sigmund Freud, views adolescence as a particularly important and significant stage in human development. Erikson broke with traditional Freudian psychoanalytic theory because of the severe restrictions placed on theorists by the concept of infantile sexuality. In *Childhood and Society* (1950), Erikson established the basis for a psychosocial theory of human development based on Freudian conceptualizations. Erikson conceives of adolescence as the period of the lifespan during which the individual must establish a personal identity in order to begin a productive adult life.

Erikson (1950) defines identity as "the accrued confidence that the inner sameness and continuity prepared in the past are matched by the sameness and continuity of one's meaning for others [p. 261]." If the adolescent does not form this identity, role confusion will result. Role confusion is characterized by self-doubt as to one's personality and sexual identity, and frequently results in delinquent and antisocial behavior. The adolescent pregnancy is viewed by Erikson as occurring because of severe role confusion. A study by Konopka (1967) examined psychodynamic and life-situational factors in the pregnancies of young married adolescents. She found that females who become pregnant in early adolescence face the concurrent crises of adolescence, pregnancy, and oftentimes marriage. In Eriksonian terms, the nuclear conflicts would consist of identity, intimacy, and generativity. Konopka concluded that such a life situation is a family cultural pattern that provides a socially approved sexual outlet for adolescents. In addition, she found that these concurrent crises strengthened the girl's identification with her mother, sisters, and peers, and provided a pattern of feminine identity, role, and status for the adolescent. Motherhood established an identity for the adolescent, allowing her to avoid developing a personal identity separate from her socially prescribed role.

One of the major problems of a psychodynamic approach to understanding adolescent pregnancies is that both Freud and Erikson advance theories that are decidedly male oriented. As Gallatin (1980) explains: "If we examine our own culture, we discover that the adolescent male experiences strong pressures to define himself. He is expected to achieve a sense of self-certainty, to decide upon a line of work, and to initiate sexual relationships. His destiny depends on himself, but I wonder if this model applies as well to the adolescent female [p. 50]?" Additional support for Gallatin's argument is provided by Gilligan and Notman (Note 1) who suggest that there are sex differences in the sequence of development in Eriksonian theory. In men the usual sequence is autonomy, identity, and intimacy. The suggestion here is that female identity is, in part, determined by intimacy. Thus the argument persists that the psychodynamic account of adolescents may be sex specific and inappropriate for an analysis of adolescent pregnancy, a distinctly female phenomenon.

In sum, the traditional psychoanalytic profile of a pregnant adolescent is of a girl suffering from abnormal relationships with either or both parents who seeks to resolve her identity diffusion by an accelerated role transition to motherhood. Let us turn now to an examination of cognitive theories.

B. Cognitive-developmental Theories

Jean Piaget (1972) and David Elkind (1967), the most prominent of the cognitive-developmental theorists, view the individual's stage of intellectual development as the major mediating variable governing all other aspects of behavior. Unwanted pregnancy occurs during adolescence because of the discrepancy in the rates of maturation between physical and cognitive development, making the girl reproductively capable but incapable of fully understanding the ramifications of her sexual activity. In addition, certain characteristics of adolescent thought processes prevent the teenager from realistically evaluating the consequences of her behavior. Also, the increasing social pressure to engage in sexual intercourse during early adolescence increases pressure on immature cognitive systems, increasing the risk of pregnancy.

In Piagetian theory (1972), adolescence is characterized by the stage of formal operations from whence logical, abstract, adult thought processes emerge. The individual who is formally operating is capable of formulating systematic and complex solutions to hypothetical problems. This mode of thought also allows for the analysis of one's own thought. This metacognition

(Flavell, 1979) gives the individual the flexibility to evaluate motivations and potential consequences of thoughts and action critically.

Given these sophisticated thought processes theorized by Piaget to occur during early adolescence, it would seem that adolescents would be capable of either controlling their sexual behavior or engaging in effective modes of contraception. Numerous investigations validating Piagetian theory, however, have demonstrated that formal operations are often content specific and are typically not achieved until late adolescence or early adulthood. In fact, the vast majority of adolescents are cognitively functioning at the concrete operational stage (Piaget, 1972). Concrete thought is characterized by the individual's ability to think only about concrete, real things (Flavell, 1963). The concrete thinker is incapable of simultaneously evaluating the future outcomes of current activity. It is impossible for the adolescent in this stage of cognitive functioning to understand fully the consequences of sexual behavior and take the precautions necessary for prevention of pregnancy.

Two studies (Cobliner, 1974; Cobliner, Schulman, & Romney, 1973) illustrate this relationship between cognitive level and contraception. Cobliner *et al*. (1973) interviewed 100 young adolescents (18 and younger) and the same number of 19- and 20-year-olds. They found that the majority of the younger women were operating at the concrete not the formal level of reasoning. The subjects' thinking was also marked by a predominance of concern with the immediate effects of an activity rather than its future consequences. In a companion study, Cobliner (1974) interviewed 200 teenagers pregnant for the first time and 50 teenagers who had been successfully practicing birth control for at least 6 months. The interview was focused primarily on the girl's knowledge and understanding of contraception. For the majority of the pregnant teenagers, pregnancy had been an unanticipated outcome of sexual activity. Also, virtually all forms of birth control require some degree of formal thought for successful, long-term use. The constraints of concrete thought may interfere with effective contraception in the majority of adolescents.

Two other characteristics of adolescent thought have been postulated by Elkind (1967). The resurgence of egocentrism in a new form occurs during this developmental stage. This is marked by intense preoccupation with the self (Hamachek, 1980). The adolescent believes that no one before has ever thought as deeply, felt as strongly, or loved so purely. This egocentrism is related to the other characteristic of adolescent thought, the personal fable (Elkind, 1967). The adolescent constructs a tale of personal uniqueness about herself, particularly her invulnerability to harm. The egocentric adolescent may have a strong, personal belief that she will not become pregnant, that pregnancies may happen to others, but not to her. This feeling of invincibility can make the adolescent careless about contraception or controlling her sexual behavior. This combination of self-preoccupation and sense of personal uniqueness and freedom from harm can be volatile.

In sum, the cognitive developmental explanation of adolescent pregnancy is that the majority of adolescents are incapable of intellectually understanding the long-term ramifications of their sexual behavior. They are also incapable of believing this can happen to them. But, as we shall see, it most certainly does. When it does occur, pregnancy for the adolescent has special medical ramifications.

III. Medical Considerations

Adolescent pregnancy can be a medically risky condition for both the mother and infant. Very young mothers (those under 16 years of age) and mothers receiving little or no prenatal care are at especially high risk for infantile and maternal morbidity and mortality.

Malnutrition, frequently in combination with anemia and folic-acid deficiency, is one of the more common conditions of adolescent females in general. The malnourished adolescent who becomes pregnant puts her developing child at increased risk for fetal and neonatal death (Marinoff & Schonholz, 1972), as well as at increased risk for prematurity and low birth weight, mental deficiency, rickets, and cerebral palsy (Annis, 1978). Further, venereal diseases such as syphilis, gonorrhea, and *Herpes simplex* prevalent in sexually active adolescents may have devastating, even fatal effects on the infant (Marinoff & Schonholz, 1972).

In addition, other pregnancy complications that are more frequent in adolescent mothers than in older women are preeclampsia, eclampsia, and toxemia (Duenhoelter, Jimenez, & Baumann, 1975; Marinoff & Schonholz, 1972), a set of conditions involving serious hypertension. These conditions can cause premature onset of labor, fetal distress, and maternal and infant death.

In addition, complications found in labor and delivery, particularly in mothers less than 16 years of age, are also frequent. The single most common problem in this age group is cephalopelvic disproportion, a condition in which the baby's head is too large for safe delivery through the mother's pelvis. The growth of the female pelvis is incomplete for the majority of women until 16 or 17 (Aiman, 1976), making an uncomplicated vaginal delivery less likely. This disproportion is the primary reason for the higher rates of midforceps and Cesarean section deliveries in young adolescents

(Duenhoelter *et al.*, 1975); these delivery methods themselves involve risk for both mother and infant.

The key to lowering mortality and morbidity for both infants and mothers is good prenatal care. In studies comparing the pregnancies of adolescents with good prenatal care with those where prenatal care was inadequate or nonexistent, the results clearly demonstrate that prenatal care improves pregnancy outcome (Dwyer, 1974). Pregnant adolescents who seek prenatal care early in the first trimester and comply with advice on nutrition, and on such things as nicotine, alcohol, and drug use, are at no higher risk for negative outcomes than are women in their 20s (Fielding, 1978). It is critical for the optimal development of the 600,000 babies born annually to adolescent mothers that prenatal and obstetrical care be made readily available. Early diagnosis of the pregnancy and high-quality medical counselling will alleviate many of the medical and subsequent psychological risk factors adversely affecting these mothers and their babies. However, other psychological issues must be resolved regardless of the quality of medical care.

IV. The Pregnancy Resolution

The majority of conceptions that occur during adolescence are unplanned and unwanted. The adolescent is faced with two choices: She can either carry the baby to term (marry and assume care for the baby, remain single and assume total care for the infant, let a significant other assume the major caregiving role, or put the baby up for adoption) or she can terminate the pregnancy. The choice to abort is considered a viable alternative for many teenagers. Of the approximately 1 million adolescent pregnancies annually, approximately 350,000 adolescents choose abortion. In fact, women 17 years and younger composed one-third of all women terminating their pregnancies (Hale, 1978). A number of factors including family and peer relationships, economic conditions, educational variables, and age have all been suggested as influential in the decision-making process. However, as Olson (1980) cautions, "The decision to abort or carry to term is highly complex and involves an interplay of often conflicting feelings, attitudes, beliefs and intentions [p. 437]."

A. *Family and Peer Relationships*

In her review of the family structures of pregnant adolescents, Olson (1980) has suggested several differences in adolescents who choose to abort in comparison with those who do not. She found that teens who terminate are more likely to come from intact families with fewer siblings than adolescents carrying to term. Those adolescents who carry to term typically come from large single-parent families. In addition, adolescents who terminate their pregnancies are more independent of family than term adolescents. Thus, it may be that the adolescents' decision to terminate their pregnancies is facilitated by active, supportive family networks.

Boyce and Benoit (1975) conducted a study to determine the personal and familial characteristics of 250 unmarried, sexually active adolescents. It was reported that both of the parents cohabited in less than one-third of the homes and that the mother was the head of the household in one-half of the homes. Thus, not only does adolescent pregnancy appear to be related to disrupted family relations, but the pregnancy resolution decision is also influenced by the family situation.

In a 1975 study, Fischman employed 299 13- to 18-year-old black adolescents from the Baltimore area to compare the resolution decisions of girls who terminate versus those who deliver. Sixty-six percent of the sample chose to deliver and the remaining 34% opted for termination. Differences in family relationships were discovered between the two groups. Those adolescents who chose to terminate their pregnancies possessed good family relations but experienced some conflict in mother–daughter relations. Adolescents who chose to deliver had significantly better mother–daughter relations. However, these better relations may possibly be the consequences of decisions rather than the antecedent causes.

The results also revealed that one-half of both groups of teenagers were fatherless, either because of death or divorce. The fatherless girls choosing to terminate were fatherless due to divorce or separation. The implication is that the girls who choose to deliver still possess more potential family support sources than do those who terminate.

The relationship with the baby's father also has an effect on the decision-making process. Fischman (1977) found that girls who delivered reported a longer and more stable relationship with the father of the child than girls who chose to deliver and the remaining 34% opted for termination. Differences in older when girls chose to deliver and were also more likely to be working full-time. The partners of adolescents who elected to terminate their pregnancy were usually younger and were either students or working only part-time. In any case, it is clear that in relationships of longer duration and greater intimacy, the adolescent is less likely to seek an abortion.

B. Economic Conditions

Economic conditions on a microlevel refer to the relationship between the pregnant adolescent and her financial bond to her parents and to the father.

Previous studies have found that employment among fathers is related to the pregnancy resolution decisions of adolescents (Fischman, 1977). The relationship of the adolescent to the macroeconomic background also exerts an influence on the pregnancy decision, although SES distinctions are difficult to separate from their social, psychological, and educational correlates.

Olson (1980) reports that adolescents who have aborted their pregnancies exhibit greater financial independence from their parents than do adolescents who carry to term. However, she reports some SES trends that may serve to dispel many stereotypes. The first such finding is that women of lower SES were more likely to deliver than were women of higher SES. In addition, women who sought termination tended to have higher educational and vocational goals than did those adolescents who carried to term. This last finding is probably explainable by the fact that parents of adolescents seeking termination are better educated, are of higher social status, hold higher paying jobs, and have the financial resources for more easily arranging the termination.

Fischman (1975, 1977) suggests that the decision of an adolescent to terminate her pregnancy is related to SES as well. The fact that those adolescents who seek termination come from higher SES lends credence to the notion that these girls are achievers who opt for social and educational mobility rather than babies. Conversely, the fact that adolescents of lower SES choose to deliver may be attributed to the real or perceived lack of opportunity for social or educational mobility. In effect, the lower SES adolescent may achieve her identity by having babies, whereas the higher SES adolescent achieves identity through social and educational channels.

Evans, Selstad, and Welcher (1976) compared the economic dependence of 333 unwed but pregnant adolescents aged 13 to 19 years. At the time of conception those adolescents who terminated their pregnancies were earning various amounts of income. At a 6-month follow-up the most conspicuous change involved those unmarried adolescents who chose to deliver. The results showed that far fewer of these adolescents lived at home with their parents. There is an appropriate cause for concern when it is known that these women were less likely to be working before they became pregnant. This study also provides evidence for the notion that those adolescents who terminate their pregnancies may be achievers. In any event, these authors conclude that economic conditions play a decreasingly important role among married but pregnant adolescents.

C. Educational Performance

In general, the educational performance of adolescents who become pregnant has been shown to play an important role in the subsequent resolution decision. Evans *et al*. (1976) reported that those adolescents who decided to terminate their pregnancies performed well in school both before and after the pregnancy. Adolescents who carried their pregnancy to term evidenced some difficulties in school before the pregnancy and usually dropped out of school afterwards. Those adolescents who did return to school after delivery typically performed quite well.

Fischman (1975, 1977) reports that adolescents who terminate their pregnancies are more likely to continue their educations. Adolescents who decide to deliver are more likely to discontinue their educations, sometimes even before the pregnancy occurred. It remains unclear whether this discontinuation is enforced by school authorities, or whether it results from peer pressure or the demands of caregiving. Childrearing may even substitute for the social acceptance found in school.

Boyce and Benoit (1975) found that most of the adolescents planned to return to school. However, these authors employed verbal reports, and it is unclear how many of the 250 subjects actually did return to school. Of the 100 mothers who chose to deliver in this sample, 30% had not completed the elementary grades in school. Thus, either the majority of respondents who said that they would return to school came from those who had terminated and those who were not pregnant but sexually active, or the adolescents who chose to deliver had unrealistic estimates of the time constraints of caregiving.

D. Age

Olson (1980) points to a number of age-related trends in decision making that are characteristic of the pregnant adolescent. She found that unmarried adolescents are more likely to terminate their pregnancy during the early (less than 15 years of age) and late teens (18–19 years of age) but less frequently between these ages. For those girls who carry to term, the greatest number are between the ages of 16 and 17. However, the average adolescent who terminates her pregnancy is older than the average adolescent who delivers.

Additional support for these age trends has been reported by Evans *et al*. (1976) and Fischman (1975). In the Evans *et al*. study, three age groups were compared to detect age-related differences in pregnancy-resolution decisions. In the 18- to 19-year-old group the decision to terminate the pregnancy was adopted by 50% of the sample. The 16- to 17-year-old group decided by more than a majority of the sample to deliver the baby (53%). Fischman's study revealed that 50% of the adolescents 13 years old and 64% of the adolescents 14 years old decided to terminate their pregnancies. Conversely, a majority of those adolescents aged 16 decided to deliver

(74%). It is likely that in the younger age groups, parents and health professionals were more influential in making the decision to terminate, and that in the older group, the women themselves were more realistic concerning the potential difficulties in carrying the infant to term. The 16- to 17-year-old group was probably less affected by family input and less realistic about the outcome of their decisions.

E. The Aftermath of Adolescent Abortion

A number of studies examining adolescents who terminated their pregnancies have yielded some general trends. Martin (1973) found that the role of the family becomes more pronounced following the termination. Perez-Reyez and Falk (1973), in a 6-month follow-up study, also found that favorable outcomes for 41 early adolescents were dependent on positive support from parents, caretakers, and society. In another follow-up study Cvejic et al. (1977) found that the adolescents did not regret their pregnancy-resolution decisions 2 years later. However, when asked if they would "do it again," most responded that they would neither terminate the pregnancy nor put the infant up for adoption. In addition, most of the teens remained on the job or in school (84%) and maintained good relationships with their parents (92%). The relationship with the adolescent father also underwent significant changes. Immediately following termination, 37% of the adolescents broke off relations with the father despite the fact that 32% of these relationships had durations exceeding 1 year. One year following the termination, 45% of the relationships had been severed.

F. Summary

The majority of pregnant teenagers carry their babies to term, but the number who choose termination through abortion is quite large. It would be a gross oversimplification to attempt to describe these young women as a homogeneous sample. Women who do choose abortion, however, do appear to share some common characteristics. The majority are teenagers who have become pregnant in relationships of relatively short duration. An absence of a strong bond to the baby's father appears central to the decision-making process. It may be that the prospect of forced marriage to such a partner, or of raising the child alone, holds no attraction for these women. It also may be the case that they feel less attachment to the child they are carrying because of their lack of intimate attachment to the father.

A supportive familial environment is also conducive to the decision to abort. One of the primary reasons for this may be the earlier diagnosis of pregnancy in these families. Women who feel sufficiently secure in their relationships with their parents are less likely to try to conceal the pregnancy from them. Abortion after the first trimester is medically risky and, in some states, illegal. After this stage neither the parents nor the teenagers have much choice in the pregnancy resolution—time has made the decision for them. The primary concern of the supportive family may also be the adolescent rather than the fetus. Many parents view pregnancy as a major obstacle to their daughter's future educational, economic, and social success. In these homes, termination is the most viable option.

These parents and girls appear to be correct in their view that abortion is likely to lead to more positive life circumstances. The reports reviewed here indicate a much brighter future both educationally and economically for adolescents who terminate their pregnancies when contrasted with those who do not. Whereas the aftermath of abortion appears positive, there is still a need for further investigation of the short- and long-term consequences of adolescent abortion, particularly on measures of life satisfaction, educational attainment, and emotional adjustment. Until these factors are more widely investigated, firm conclusions cannot be drawn. Having compared the teenager who chooses to abort with her counterpart who carries the infant to term, let us now look more closely at the developmental sequelae for the teenager who becomes a parent.

V. The Social and Economic Correlates of Adolescent Pregnancy

Unanimously, investigators have maintained that becoming a parent during adolescence may affect the life situation of the individuals involved both negatively and permanently. This section reviews the life circumstances of adolescents who carry their infants to term, focusing on marriage and marital stability, educational achievement, income and assets, and fertility.

A. *Marriage and Marital Stability*

Teenagers are less likely to marry in response to pregnancy than are women over 20. Based on a sample of 408 urban, black and white women from varied socioeconomic backgrounds, Presser (1974) found that as age decreased, the percentages of out-of-wedlock as well as unplanned births increased. For women aged 24–29, 9% of births occurred out of wedlock and

30% of these were unplanned. For 20- to 23-year-olds, 15% of births occurred out of wedlock, with 60% unplanned, whereas for 15- to 19-year-old women, 60% of the births were out of wedlock, with over 80% unplanned. Furstenberg (1976b, 1976c) interviewed 323 predominantly black, low-SES pregnant women from Baltimore, along with a control group of classmates, and found that only 3% were married at conception. By the time of delivery, approximately 25% had married, with 94% of these marriages occurring to the natural father. According to statistics compiled by the Alan Guttmacher Institute (1976), of the 6% of U.S. teenagers who give birth, one-third of the pregnancies are conceived out of wedlock, one-third marry during pregnancy, and one-third give birth out of wedlock.

Racial differences for out-of-wedlock pregnancy and birth are also apparent (McCarthy & Menken, 1979; Zelnik & Kantner, 1974, 1978). Zelnik and Kantner (1974) reported that 17% of births to white 15- to 19-year-old women were illegitimate compared with 61% of births to nonwhite women. However, though blacks are more likely than whites to be unmarried when they deliver, this difference appears to be diminishing, based on a comparison of statistics from 1971 and 1976 (Zelnik & Kantner, 1978). In addition, reported race differences may be largely accounted for by a higher likelihood of white women aborting as well as a higher tolerance for illegitimacy in black communities (Furstenberg, 1976c).

Overall, based on Zelnik and Kantner's (1978) comparison of first pregnancies to women aged 15–19, the likelihood of marriage as a resolution to pregnancy has declined, even despite the finding that fewer live births were reported to be unintended. This decreasing tendency for marriage as a resolution to pregnancy is apparently characteristic of the pattern of teenage family formation subsequent to World War II. From 1940 to the late 1960s, early childbearing has been occurring increasingly outside the institution of marriage (Sklar & Berkov, 1974).

Trends in marriage after pregnancy and birth are evidenced in a sample of 162 predominantly black girls, aged 12 to 17, attending a prenatal clinic and followed for 2 years postpartum (Lorenzi, Klerman, & Jekel, 1977). Seven percent were married within 3 months following delivery; this increased to 17% by 15 months and 27% by 26 months. Of those who did eventually marry, 73% married the natural father. In Presser's (1980) analysis of 69 women—predominantly black, under 20, and unmarried at the time of birth—28% reported that they married within 45 months after birth, with approximately two-thirds of the marriages to the natural father. Furstenberg (1976b) interviewed the mothers in his Baltimore sample during pregnancy and at 1, 3, and 5 years after birth. Though only 3% were married at conception and one-third by delivery, three-fifths were married by the end of

1 year and only 36% remained single at the 5-year follow-up. Of the marriages that did occur, 70% were to the child's father. Using data from a national sample, McCarthy and Menken (1979) found that teenagers, though more likely to be unmarried at the time of birth, were more likely than women 20 years of age and older to marry within one year following delivery.

The decision to marry is determined by a number of factors. Furstenberg (1976c) found that the younger the mother, the less likely marriage was to occur; 10% of girls under 15 in his sample married before delivery, whereas one-third of the girls over 17 married before delivery. The father's age was also relevant to the decision to marry, probably because of the relationship between paternal age and economic position. The majority of girls in the study had affirmed their desire to marry the father if and when they thought he would be able to support the family (Furstenberg, 1976b, 1976c). This feeling was also held by the girl's family, with financial and child care assistance often contingent on her remaining at home unmarried. The greater tolerance of black families for illegitimacy, then, appears to be mediated by the families' intolerance for their daughters marrying into an unfavorable economic position. Educational ambitions and educational performance also appeared to be influential in the decision to marry (Furstenberg, 1976a); the more ambitious and able the young women, the less likely they were to marry. Finally, Stack (1974) has implicated the welfare system as influential in marriage decisions; welfare payments may be available only if the couple does not live together.

To summarize, adolescent births are typically unplanned and out of wedlock. There is a tendency for adolescent parents to marry within the first 2 years following delivery, most frequently because of an improved economic position of the father. However, if marriage to the father does not occur within these 2 years following birth, it probably will not occur at all. The chance of marriage to a person other than the child's father increases with the length of time following birth (Furstenberg, 1976c).

Teenage marriages show a high rate of instability (Barglow et al., 1968; Bartz & Nye, 1970; Card & Wise, 1978; Furstenberg, 1976a, 1976b, 1976c; Kruger, 1973), the rate of instability being two to three times that for marriages to women aged 20 and older (Alan Guttmacher Institute, 1976; Baldwin & Cain, 1980; Nakashima, 1977). This pattern of instability is evidenced in results from Furstenberg's (1976a, 1976b, 1976c) Baltimore sample. One-fifth of the marriages broke up in 1 year, one-third by 2 years, more than one-half by 4 years, and three-fifths had ended by 6 years.

McCarthy and Menken (1979) have found that the separation rate among black couples is higher than among whites and that blacks are more likely to separate within the first 7 months after birth. Blacks, however, are less likely to obtain legal divorces. Both black and white marriages occurring after birth are more likely to disband than marriages occurring before birth. For all women, marriages after an out-of-wedlock birth have a 50% dissolution rate within 15 years compared with approximately a 17% dissolution rate for marriages with births within wedlock.

A number of reasons for the high rate of marital instability found among adolesents has been suggested, including individual and/or cultural pre-dispositions (Chilman, 1966), inadequate preparation for married life (Christensen, 1960), accelerated role transition and family formation (Furstenberg, 1976a), and heightened stress due to a nonnormative ordering of life events (Bacon, 1974; Coombs & Freedman, 1970; Furstenberg, 1976c; Hogan, 1978).

Regarding the notion that early marriage and childbearing cuts short one's preparation for married life and parenting, Furstenberg (1976c) has found that the rate of separation was one-half as high for couples who had had frequent and intensive contact with each other when compared to individuals who married with less intensive contact. However, the rate of marriage dissolution for couples with long-standing exclusive relationships was still high. It is more likely that inadequate preparation combined with the stresses experienced by early marriage and childbearing offers a more viable explanation for adolescent marriage instability.

The most viable explanation for instability deals with potential stress-producing factors associated with a nonnormative ordering of events in the life cycle. It has been suggested by Neugarten, Moore, and Lowe (1968) that the ordering of events is important in the individual's life cycle. Our social institutions are built on a normative sequence of life events for individuals. Therefore, nonnormative events such as early marriage and childbearing may be incompatible with a socially prescribed course for individuals (Hogan, 1978). Because of variation from this prescribed course, individuals may experience heightened stress in their transition from one social role or status to another (Bacon, 1974).

Because adolescent parents usually enter marriage educationally and financially unprepared, additional stresses occur in the relationship. In addition, the family of origin may indirectly contribute to the observed marriage instability. Once marriage occurs, economic support and child care from families usually diminish, making educational achievement and financial security more difficult to achieve for the young couple (Furstenberg, 1980). This enhances stress in their transition to family life.

In adjusting to adolescent pregnancy and birth, it is apparent from this review that lasting familial stability is infrequently achieved through marriage. Additional information regarding factors associated with the life circumstances of adolescent parents will be discussed in the following sections.

B. Education

A strong negative relationship exists between both the educational achievement of adolescent parents and the factors associated with early childbearing and/or marriage (Bacon, 1974; Bartz & Nye, 1970; Card & Wise, 1978; Freedman & Coombs, 1966; Furstenberg, 1976a, 1976b, 1976c; Hogan, 1978; Kerckhoff & Parrow, 1979; Klein, 1974; Moore & Waite, 1977; Presser, 1977, 1980; Trussell, 1976). Women are particularly disadvantaged in continuing their education. There are prevailing social expectations for women to assume child care responsibility. When combined with the time involved in and the cost of arranging child care, it is often enough to inhibit further education for both married and unmarried women. This seems to be true for all but the most educationally ambitious young mothers.

Reasons for the educational deficits of adolescent parents have been conceptualized in two ways: as a result of individual or motivational factors and as a response to a role transition out of synchrony with a normative life course. School failure due to personality or motivational factors has been discussed by both Furstenberg (1976c) and Moore and Waite (1977). The assumption is made that less competent and less ambitious students use pregnancy as an excuse to drop out of school; parenthood may offer an escape route for these students. Though it is apparent that poor school performance and low ambition are predictive of school dropout for many adolescent mothers, to attribute school dropout solely to individual factors is misleading because it fails to take into account environmental factors associated with adolescent parenting. In addition, data from Furstenberg (1976c), Moore and Waite (1977), and Presser (1980) have indicated that many young mothers enjoy school and do moderately well. Many even manage to return to school despite their new roles and responsibilities. As educational programs for pregnant teens and young mothers have also demonstrated (Bennett & Bardon, 1977; Colletta, Gregg, Hadler, Lee, & Mekelburg, 1980; Osofsky, Osofsky, Kendall & Rajan, 1973), many young mothers will continue school if given the opportunity.

As previously discussed, teenage parenting involves a higher likelihood of experiencing stressful events (Bacon, 1974). This stress is partly determined by a social system unable to deal effectively with this nonnormative transition. The educational system's practices and policies have been implicated as partly responsible for the high dropout rate of pregnant adolescents and adolescent parents (Braen & Forbush, 1975). Schools have typically avoided providing information that could possibly prevent pregnancy and have discouraged or prevented pregnant girls and mothers from continuing their educations.

The importance of educational continuity has been discussed by Colletta *et al.* (1980), Furstenberg (1976c), Klerman (1975), and Plionis (1975). The general conclusion of these authors, based on an analysis of existing educational programs, revealed that most girls want to return to school after delivery. In addition, those girls who continue their educations during pregnancy are more likely to continue their educations after delivery. Furstenberg (1976c) suggested that school disruption may entail a status disruption for the individual. A higher probability of school termination was experienced by the girls in his Baltimore study because of school departure resulting from pregnancy. The departure usually entailed a loss of contact with peers and a stigma of failure from being behind in school on return.

Moore and Waite (1977), after reviewing data from a nationwide sample of 5000 teenagers, concluded that the negative association found between age and school attendance was probably due to complications with early childbearing. These complications included the difficulty and cost of arranging child care, the time involved in childrearing and home maintenance, the need to earn a living, and pressures from family and friends for mothers to devote themselves to child care. In addition, Furstenberg (1976b, 1976c) found that the inability to prevent further pregnancies was related to school attendance; as the number of children increased, the number of dropouts increased. Additional childbearing may further compound the factors discussed by Moore and Waite (1977), making degree attainment more difficult for the young parent.

The burdens faced by young parents may be lessened if alternate sources of income and child care can be arranged. Furstenberg (1976c), Furstenberg and Crawford (1978), and Presser (1980) have found that girls who receive child care help and financial assistance from their families are most likely to return to school and obtain their high school diploma, particularly if they remain unmarried and at home. Moore and Waite (1977) found that whites are more disadvantaged than blacks regarding degree attainment. Within the white population, marriage and child care by the mother are often expected. Because of a higher tolerance for illegitimacy among blacks, mechanisms to deal with teenage pregnancy, such as alternate child care arrangements, are better developed within the family. In addition to financial support from the family, public assistance may aid young mothers in achieving an education (Presser, 1980).

It appears that the existence of a nonpunitive, accepting school atmosphere that encourages educational continuity and the availability of financial and child care assistance are factors that facilitate school attendance. By assisting young parents to remain in school by relieving some of the pressures associated with early parenting, the future life circumstances for these individuals and their children are more favorable. In completing an education, the young parent is better able to compete for jobs in the labor force, making financial security and independence possible.

C. Income and Assets

Early childbearing has been associated with diminished income and assets, as well as poverty, in comparison to individuals who delay childbearing (Bacon, 1974; Furstenberg, 1976a, 1980; Furstenberg & Crawford, 1978; Honig, 1978; Klein, 1974; Presser, 1980; Russ-Eft, Sprenger, & Beever, 1979; Trussell, 1976). Adolescent parents are more likely to enter the labor force early, often with limited educations. Because they are often inexperienced and lack high school diplomas, they are unable to compete successfully with their peers for jobs within a limited job market. Even if they are able to find work, the work typically involves less income and prestige for the young parent.

The effect on economic circumstances are particularly severe for women (Card & Wyse, 1978; Furstenberg, 1976c) and most severe for women unmarried at conception or birth (Freedman & Coombs, 1966; Freedman & Thornton, 1979; Furstenberg, 1976c). In addition to entering a limited job market undereducated and inexperienced, young mothers are also discriminated against on the basis of gender.

The initial economic circumstances and disadvantages of adolescent parents, relative to deferred childbearers, often dictates long-term economic consequences. Freedman and Thornton (1979) assessed the economic status of white married women in Detroit who conceived before marriage. They found that the long-term economic consequences were negative for these families relative to families whose children were conceived after marriage. The adequacy of income for families with premaritally conceived births was lower because of lower incomes, fewer assets, and more people to support because of a higher fertility rate. Because of this inadequacy, vacations were shorter and less expensive, and fewer children in the family were likely to attend college because of limited savings, despite the fact that these parents' educational aspirations were similar to the controls. Though long-term consequences are apparent, the initial disadvantages diminish over time.

Card and Wise (1978) found that early childbearers, when measured at age 29, are overrepresented in blue-collar jobs and underrepresented in the professions. The men who become fathers as teenagers have higher incomes than men who deferred childbearing until their 20s. However, these young fathers were likely to enter initially higher paying union jobs, whereas the controls were more likely to pursue advanced education; their investment in education may just be beginning to pay off. Women who become mothers as teenagers are likely to marry men with lower educational and occupational attainment and are more likely to report lower incomes and higher job dissatisfaction at age 29 than their peers who deferred childbearing. Similar results are reported by Russ-Eft et al. (1979).

The family's response to adolescent pregnancy is often critical for the future economic circumstances of young mothers (Furstenberg, 1976b, 1976c, 1980; Presser, 1980). By providing child care, housing, and financial assistance to enable the young mother to finish high school, her employment prospects are enhanced. As Furstenberg and Crawford (1978) have shown, with an education completed and a child old enough to attend school, women are more prepared to separate from their families and become financially independent. Without such support, the young mothers were less likely to control further childbearing, less likely to advance educationally, and more likely to be economically disadvantaged.

The inability to find gainful employment may predispose the young parent to become a welfare recipient. The economic disadvantages that are associated with a higher likelihood of being a welfare recipient are felt by white and nonwhite adolescent parents (Moore, 1978; Trussell, 1976). A major source of welfare assistance, Aid to Families with Dependent Children (AFDC), was investigated by Moore (1978). The author found that AFDC mothers were more likely to have had a child as a teenager than non-AFDC mothers (61% versus 35%, respectively). Also, the older the mother at her first child's birth, the less likely she was to receive AFDC assistance.

Additional factors associated with welfare assistance are marriage and parity. Unmarried women and women with additional children were found by Furstenberg (1976c) more likely to be on welfare. However, the "brood sow" myth (Placek & Hendershot, 1974), which maintains that public assistance not only encourages childbearing out of wedlock, because it allows unmarried mothers to support children, but also encourages additional childbearing because of increased benefits, was discredited by Furstenberg (1976b, 1976c) and Presser and Salsberg (1975). They found that the fertility rates of welfare mothers were not significantly higher than mothers not on welfare. In addition, almost all the subjects in Furstenberg's Baltimore sample regarded welfare as unacceptable; 79% said they would work immediately even at low wages. Nevertheless, two-thirds of the mothers were on welfare at some time during the 5-year period after the birth of their first child.

The major reason for not working, given by two-thirds of the women in Furstenberg's (1976b, 1976c) study, was child care. It was more advantageous economically to receive welfare than to work in a low-paying job while paying for child care, particularly if the mother had more than one child. If the family of origin provides child care, so that mothers may work as well as complete an education, not only are the mother's future life chances likely to improve but society may also benefit by having a contributing wage earner. Another major factor influencing whether a parent will work is the availability of jobs. As previously indicated, young parents enter a limited job market undereducated and underskilled. One-third of the women on welfare in Furstenberg's (1976b, 1976c) study reported the unavailability of job opportunities as the only reason for not working.

D. Fertility

The life circumstances of individuals who begin childbearing as teenagers are characterized not only by more children but also by a faster rate of childbearing, in comparison to individuals who begin childbearing at a later age (Drillien, 1969; Keeve, Schlesinger, Wight, & Adams, 1969; Klein, 1974; Millman & Hendershot, 1980; Oppel & Royston, 1971; Russ-Eft, et al., 1979; Sarrel, 1967), regardless of marital status (Trussell & Menken, 1978). Within the teenage population, 18- to 19-year-olds have a lower subsequent fertility rate than 15- to 17-year-olds. The mediating factor for this finding is most likely the higher educational levels completed by the older teenagers.

In both the 5-year follow-up in Furstenberg's (1976b, 1976c) study and the follow-up at age 29 of the subjects from project TALENT (Card & Wise, 1978), early childbearers had exceeded their expectations for family size. In both studies, the teenage parents' aspirations for family size were equivalent to controls. Though the dynamics remain unclear, it is evident that the early childbearers were less capable of regulating further childbearing. One possibility suggested by Furstenberg (1976c), is that the resources for controlling unwanted pregnancies are less available to the teenage parent.

The continuation of educational pursuits is a major factor related to controlling subsequent pregnancies. Women with strong commitments to school or career are more likely to remain single, to stay in school, and are less likely to want a second child (Furstenberg, 1976c; Jekel, Klerman, & Bancroft, 1973). These mothers have lower fertility rates than mothers who drop out of school. Women who pursue their educations are also more likely to use contraceptives. The family of origin's role in providing support for young mothers to continue their educations is also instrumental in regulating further childbearing (Furstenberg, 1976b, 1976, 1980).

Heightened fertility usually has a negative impact on the life circumstances of early childbearers: A woman's marriage prospects may be impaired (Furstenberg, 1976b, 1976c), family support may be cut off (Furstenberg, 1980), and her education is likely to stop (Furstenberg & Crawford, 1978; Russ-Eft et al., 1979). Her likelihood of being on welfare increases (Furstenberg, 1976c), and her income and assets are impaired because of lower paying jobs and additional family members to support (Card & Wise, 1978). Although early childbearers are disadvantaged by higher fertility rates, mothers who begin childbearing early will end their childbearing earlier than deferred childbearers (Millman & Hendershot, 1980). One implication is that childrearing responsibilities will end earlier. In the later life development of these women, an unexplored area, possibilities exist for pursuing educational, occupational, or other interests. These options may not be possible for deferred childbearers who may be tied down with childrearing responsibilities until a later age.

In addition, it may be naive to equate economic adequacy directly with life satisfaction. The subjects in project TALENT (Russ-Eft et al., 1979), though economically disadvantaged due to factors associated with early childbearing and higher fertility, rated their relationships with their children as of greater importance than did deferred childbearers with smaller families. Russell (1980) suggested that teenage parents, undereducated and in low-prestige jobs, may be particularly sensitive to the rewards of first-time parenting. This statement was based on a finding that education was negatively related to perceived gratification with a parenting role for both men and women. Additional research needs to be directed into the present and future life satisfaction of adolescent parents to determine the full impact that early childbearing and higher fertility has on their lives.

E. Summary

The common thread running through all of these studies is the critical importance of education to social and economic success. The stresses related to early role transition are significantly compounded by economic hardship caused by lack of adequate educational and vocational training. To prevent these negative outcomes, educational and social service agencies will need to alter their existing systems to accommodate teenage parents. This will not eradicate the problems of adolescent families, but it will most certainly alleviate one of the primary stress factors.

VI. The Adolescent as Parent

The majority of teenagers who currently give birth in the United States make the decision to raise the child alone, with the child's father, or with the help of their own families. The most prevalent social attitude concerning these young mothers is that they are inadequately prepared to provide a supportive, healthy climate in which to raise a child. They are children attempting to raise children. Although in a number of cases the stresses placed on the young parent result in a poor childrearing environment, and in some instances abuse and neglect, it is more often the case that the adolescent is able to parent successfully, particularly with familial and social supports. The factors that contribute to success or failure of adolescent parenting are reviewed here.

A. The Family of Origin

The unwanted pregnancy of an adolescent daughter can be a very disruptive occurrence in a family. The teenager expecting a child represents a crisis for the entire family. One of the main reasons for considering teenage parenting as a family crisis is that having a child at a young age is most often considered socially deviant. As a result, family members are frequently not prepared to cope with this nonnormative life crisis. Oftentimes, however, this crisis has a positive rather than negative resolution. Though obviously a stressful event for the entire family, it may provide an opportunity for family growth and development (Bryan-Logan & Dancy, 1974; Furstenburg, 1980; Polsby, 1974; Russell, 1980) that may leave the family better able to cope with future stressful events. As indicated by Von Der Ahe (1969) in a study of 150 predominantly white unwed mothers, family relationships were reported to have improved in two-thirds of the cases and remained unchanged for one-third when the families were told of the pregnancies. Furstenburg (1980), in discussing results from his Baltimore study of predominantly black teenage mothers, reported that 31% of his sample said their relationship with their parents improved, whereas 15% felt the relationship was more distant.

Of particular importance is the relationship between the adolescent and her mother. Some authors (e.g., Sugar, 1976) feel that the relationship that a girl has with her own mother determines much of her own mothering behavior. It is generally agreed that pregnancy either produces conflict in a close mother–daughter relationship or serves to heighten stress in an already conflicted relationship (Bryan-Logan & Dancy, 1974; Smith, 1975). Because the adolescent's mother is her primary maternal role model, and because the adolescent is still her mother's child, the transition to mother-hood and grandmotherhood may be difficult and stressful. With an absence of clear-cut roles to follow, particularly in the situation where the girl is unmarried and living at home, decisions as to how much independence the young mother should have and how much childrearing responsibility the grandmother should assume may be especially difficult to make.

The initial reactions by the girl's mother may serve to enhance dis-equilibrium in the mother–daughter relationship. Bryan-Logan and Dancy (1974) have suggested that a mother may view her daughter's pregnancy in a variety of ways: as a sign of her own inadequacy as a parent, as a reflection of her own past mistakes, as the daughter's failure to conform to the behavior expected of her, or as a threat to her daughter's achievements. Smith (1975) has suggested that the initial reactions may include shame, shock, guilt, anger, and sorrow. In a society oriented toward youth, becoming a grandmother may be difficult to accept because it carries with it negative connotations associated with aging. In addition, the grandmother's own role transition may be disrupted; she may be preparing to resume work or school in anticipation of her children leaving home, and her daughter's pregnancy may force her back into a childrearing role.

This initial period of disequilibrium and conflict in the mother–daughter relationship has been generally regarded as temporary. Once the initial reactions and adjustments are made, a closeness appears to develop in the relationship. Smith (1975) has reported that this closeness develops by the third trimester of pregnancy. The mother–daughter relationship changes to a mother–mother relationship, brought about by the common experience of pregnancy. In both Furstenberg's (1980) and Sugar's (1976) studies, it was suggested that the common occurrence of sharing mothering may partially account for the improvement of the mother–daughter relationship. When the grandmother assisted in childrearing, an atmosphere ensued in which the mother would reciprocate child care favors, creating a situation of high social exchange leading to positive emotional feelings between interacting family members.

That the mother–daughter relationship can be critical for the young mother's further development and future life circumstances has been demonstrated by a number of authors. Friedman (1966) maintained that a mother's participation in her daughter's out-of-wedlock pregnancy may make the daughter feel less isolated. Because she has her mother's support, she may be more accepting of her baby and her own role as a mother. Furstenberg's (1976c) results from his Baltimore study have suggested that the mother–daughter relationship is important to the daughter's further educational attainment. The mother–daughter relationship also has been shown to be related to repeat pregnancies (Barglow *et al.*, 1968). In their study of unwed, low-SES, black women, aged 11 to 16, Barglow *et al.* (1968) found that if the girl's relationship with her own mother became more positive after the first pregnancy, then the chance of getting pregnant again decreased. In addition, these young mothers reported that adaptation to pregnancy and motherhood was more favorable if their relationship with their mothers had become more positive.

Little information concerning the adolescent's relationship with her father is available. Most of the available literature has described this relationship as being either pathological or describes the pregnancy as related to father-absence (Abernathy, 1974; Babikian & Goldman, 1971; Hertz, 1977; McKenry *et al.*, 1979; Zongker, 1977). Particularly because of the clinical nature of the samples being reported, the lack of comparative controls, and a social bias against father-absent families, these results may not be representative of the father–daughter relationship. More positive results were found in Presser's (1980) sample: Though 25% of the young unwed mothers had no father or father-substitute, 49% reported the relationship with their own fathers as very close. Barglow *et al.* (1968) have also suggested that the presence of the father figure may be crucial in avoiding repeated pregnancies. If the father is absent, the young mothers had a 78% chance of getting pregnant again.

As demonstrated in Furstenberg's (1976c) Baltimore sample, family acceptance may be instrumental in the adolescent's adjustment to pregnancy and parenting. The pattern of family acceptance is at first characterized by stress or disequilibrium. These initial reactions eventually give way to an understanding and acceptance of the situation to eventual positive attitudes concerning the young mother. Providing child care assistance is a major way in which families assist the young mother. Without such assistance, it may be very difficult for a young woman either to stay in school or to work. As Furstenberg (1976c) and Furstenberg and Crawford (1978) have indicated, child care help is more likely to be received if the young mother is living with her family and is unmarried. The importance and extensiveness of such help, particularly for mothers in school or working, is evident in Presser's (1980) sample. Seventy-seven percent of the sample received child care assistance at the first interview (children aged 7 months to 2.5 years); 45 months later 56% of the sample still reported receiving such assistance, which was provided by the grandmother in 70% of the cases.

In addition to child care, families provide financial support in the forms of direct monetary contributions, housing, food, and clothing (deLissovoy, 1975a, 1975b). Such financial assistance may be more available if the girl remains unmarried (Furstenberg 1976c; Furstenberg & Crawford, 1978) and if she lives at home (Furstenberg, 1980; Furstenberg & Crawford, 1978; Presser, 1980). As Furstenberg (1976c) has suggested, the adolescent's mother may fear that an early marriage may harm her daughter's life chances. Providing aid and childrearing assistance may be one way of keeping the daughter at home and unmarried. In Presser's (1980) study, 65% of the sample had reported receiving financial aid by the time their child was between 4 and 7 years of age: 85% of those living with parents compared with 36% not living with parents. Also, a family's ability to provide support is important. Furstenberg (1980) reported that couple-headed households were better able to assist their daughters financially, particularly with child care, then female-headed families.

Although an adolescent's pregnancy and parenting may be advantageous to both the young mother and her family, and may even stabilize an unfavorable family situation (Furstenberg, 1980), a number of potential dangers may result from this situation. Even though a young mother's status in the family may improve, her siblings may lose out. The youngest sibling may lose a favored position with a baby in the house or conflicts may arise with female siblings of approximate age. Also, whether dependency on the family hinders the adolescent's personal growth and the formation of an independent family unit remains to be explored by longitudinal research (Furstenberg, 1980). As demonstrated by Furstenberg (1980), maintaining such strong ties with one's family of origin may hinder marriages and marriage security, as well as father participation in childrearing. Wise and Grossman (1980) studied 30 black unwed mothers aged 14 to 19 and reported that girls who were more independent of their families exhibited greater child care responsibility, felt less depressed, and felt more positive about their pregnancies and their babies.

Little information exists on social support systems outside of the family. For many adolescents, having a child may separate them from their peer-group structure. Nakashima (1977), in an analysis of a nationwide sample, reported that social isolation was a problem for young unmarried mothers. The common activities of school and dating are often abandoned, and as a result these young mothers experience a loss of friends. Similar results were reported by Shaffer, Pettigrew, Wolkind, and Zajicek (1978), for girls who terminated school in response to teen pregnancy and parenting. In deLissovoy's (1975a, 1975b) study of semirural adolescent couples, mothers experienced feelings of loneliness, a lack of social life, and a loss of former friends. The fathers in this sample, however, kept their old friendships and participated in social activities with these friends.

Though isolation from friends affects some adolescents, others appear to benefit from the support their friends provide. In Presser's (1980) sample of urban black women, child care services were often provided by friends. Also, 69% of the women who remained unmarried by the time their children reached the ages of from 4 to 7 years reported that at least one of their two closest friends who lived near them assisted in child care. Stack (1974) also reported such assistance within an urban black community, and Furstenberg (1976c) suggested the peers can be influential in a girl's decision either to stay in or to drop-out of school.

B. The Mother–Child Relationship

Because teenage births have a high likelihood of being unplanned, particularly for unwed mothers, the mother–child relationship is assumed to be at risk. Presser (1974) found that only 19% of a sample of urban black and white women aged 15–19 reported that their child was planned, compared with 44% for 20- to 23-year-old women and 70% for 24- to 29-year-old women. In addition, teenagers were more likely to report that their babies came at the wrong time. Zelnik and Kantner (1978), using data from a national sample, reported that 82% of live births to unwed mothers aged 15–19 were unplanned compared with 42% of births to married women of the same age. They concluded that since the pregnancies were initially unplanned, young mothers may be less prepared to accept the responsibility of a child. In addition, because half of teen pregnancies occur within the first 6 months of becoming sexually active and one-fifth occur in the first month (Zabin, Kantner, & Zelnik, 1979), girls may possess not only limited knowledge of sexuality and contraception but also of child rearing. In deLissovoy's (1973) study of 48 white couples living in a semirurual area, it was found that adolescent mothers possessed little information on child development, had unrealistic expectations for their children's behavior, and were impatient, irritable, and insensitive to their children's needs. Only five of these mothers reported that they enjoyed playing with their children. According to these characteristics, deLissovoy (1973) maintained that these mothers may be more prone to use physical punishment. Based on questionnaire data from 80 expectant unmarried black women aged 15–19,

Gutelius (1970) found a preference for physical punishment as a disciplinary technique. These researchers also reported that these mothers had few ideas about ways to prepare children early in life for later school success, and they also exhibited inconsistency in attitudes about discipline. Both deLissovoy's (1973) and Gutelius's (1970) studies had no control or normative comparison group, however, which makes these results difficult to interpret.

The early mother–infant attachment process may also be disrupted because of the relatively high frequency of extended hospitalization of the infant at birth due to prematurity or illness. As has been suggested by Klaus and Kennell (1976) and Sugar (1976), this early mother–infant separation may adversely affect the development of a secure attachment relationship. The combination of personal, social, and economic stresses common to teenage parents can also have a negative impact on the attachment bond. These disruptions in the mother–infant relationship have been shown to be directly correlated with child abuse and maltreatment (Helfer & Kemp, 1968; Klein & Stern, 1971). The mother's unresolved needs, combined with low self-esteem, which may partially be the result of social isolation, may make the mother dependent on the child for the fullfillment of her needs. Because of inadequate knowledge of child care and development, unrealistic expectations for the child's behavior may develop, with maltreatment resulting.

Two studies by Bolton, Laner, and Kane (1980), and Kinard and Klerman (1980) have similarly suggested that though a higher incidence of maltreatment is found among the adolescent population, these results must be interpreted with caution. Bolton *et al.* suggested that official records may be misleading because of minority group overrepresentation. Not only are higher SES groups less likely to have child maltreatment reported, low-SES minority group parents are at a higher risk for financial stress and marital disruption that are related to maltreatment. Their overrepresentation may therefore skew the distribution toward an unfavorable description of adolescent parents as maltreaters. In addition, the dynamic variables associated with maltreatment by the adolescent and older mothers were found to be very similar. A tendency has emerged for environmental factors (parental history of child abuse, continuous child care responsibility, insufficient economics) to be associated with adolescent maltreaters and psychodynamic factors (alcohol dependence, loss of control, mental health problems) to be associated with older maltreaters. Kinard and Klerman (1980) have stated that no research is yet available to confirm or deny the relationship between adolescent parenting and maltreatment. They conclude that impoverished backgrounds and disturbed family life, and their relationship to social class, confounds such a relationship.

Furstenberg (1976c), has responded to much of the literature just cited by commenting that there is much negative opinion about adolescents as parents but little empirical evidence to support this view. He pointed out that many studies that have reported unfavorable psychological characteristics of teenage mothers have concentrated on the stressful period immediately following delivery and have not looked at how motherhood is managed across time. In reviews of the literature, Wise and Grossman (1980) and Phipps-Yonas (1980) have also commented on the negative assumptions concerning teenage parents without available empirical evidence. According to Phipps-Yonas, studies reporting teenage parents as deviant and inadequate often lack appropriate controls and data is often interpreted subjectively or post hoc.

A more favorable outlook is evidenced in Gutelius's (1970) study of 80 young unmarried black mothers. A sensitivity for infant needs and a fondness for children was apparent in their questionnaire responses. Also, the assumption that adolescent mothers may be inadequate in child care is somewhat tempered by the results reported by Furstenberg (1976c, 1980) and La Barre (1968). Prior child care experience with nieces, nephews, or siblings was reported by the majority of the mothers in these studies.

Data reported by Williams (1974) indicated that younger mothers may exhibit much energy and enjoy playing with children. Magid, Gross, and Shuman (1979), in a parenting program for pregnant teens, demonstrated that positive interactions can be enhanced between these women and children, and that participants in the program expressed increased interest in acquiring additional knowledge of child development. Osofsky et al. (1973) reported that if medical and school programs are made available, individuals will take advantage of them. These few studies suggest that adolescent mothers may possess the energy and desire to engage in educational interactions, and that given the appropriate resources, positive interactions may be enhanced.

Wise and Grossman (1980) suggested that age, race, SES, and education may not be the most important variables in a mother's psychological adjustment. Rather, they found planning and emotional involvement, which was related to independence from their families, to be positively correlated with positive feelings about the baby and a realistic view of infant behavior during pregnancy. Planning and emotional involvement were also correlated with attachment to infant at 6 weeks of age. Furstenberg (1976c), using data from his Baltimore study, found that the younger teenage mothers (those under 17) perceived themselves as less prepared during pregnancy. However, younger mothers were found to be just as committed to a maternal role in terms of enthusiasm, literature read, familiarity with their children's friends, and visits to their children's schools. This result may be partially due to the fact that younger mothers relied more on assistance from their families, which mediated potential problems that could negatively affect the mother–child relationship.

Observational studies of mother–infant interaction have shed much-needed light on the qualitative relationship of the adolescent and her infant. Osofsky and Osofsky (1970) studied a predominantly black population attending a medical educational program. They were the first to report adolescent maternal behaviors as being high in warmth and physical interaction and low in verbal interaction. These maternal behaviors seemed to be complimented by the infant characteristics of high activity and low affectivity and responsiveness on the Brazelton Neonatal Behavioral Assessment Scale. These same results were reported again by Osofsky et al. (1973), giving further support to the notion that the behaviors of young mothers and their infants may be mutually reinforcing and result in secure mother–infant attachment.

Osofsky and Osofsky (1970) and Osofsky et al.'s (1973) results are supported by a questionnaire study conducted by Epstein (Note 2) on pregnant teenagers' knowledge of child development. The author found that the adolescents' knowledge of perceptual and motor development was accurate. However, these adolescents underestimated cognitive, language, and social development, particularly with infants under 8 months of age. This is the direct opposite of notions presented by some authors that indicate that adolescent mothers may have unrealistic expectations for their children's early behavior.

Much additional research is needed to delineate clearly the relationship between the young mother and her child. Whereas some data suggest that the relationship may not always be optimal for mother or child, other data indicate that the teenager is sensitive to her infant's needs and capable of fulfilling parental responsibilities.

C. The Adolescent Father

The contribution that fathers make to their infants' and young children's development has been seriously neglected by social scientists as well as by our social institutions, including health, educational, and legal systems. Only recently have fathers begun to be accepted as important in their children's development. As a subset of fathers in general, adolescent fathers have been at a particular disadvantage in gaining acceptance as contributors to their children's development.

Social prejudice exists against adolescent fathers because of their youth, which implies incompetence, and their marital status, which is often single (Parke, Power, & Fisher, 1980). Society has regarded the father as one either to be punished or ignored because of his misdeeds (Juhasz, 1974). The concern of the legal system has been to make the "alleged" father into the "legal" father. In the process he should be forced to admit his mistakes and pay child support (Pannor, Evans, & Massarik, 1968; Platts, 1968) with little regard for him as a person. Also, assumptions are made about adolescent fathers (i.e., they are insensitive, they take advantage of girls, and they do not care about either the mother or the baby). These assumptions only influence social scientists to ignore the actual circumstances of adolescent fatherhood (Pannor, 1971; Parke et al., 1980).

Earls and Siegel (1980) and Parke et al. (1980) have found little research on adolescent fathers and their interactions with their children. Earls and Siegel have also pointed out that research describing the father has failed to interview him directly, and the reports of others may therefore be biased against him. This disregard of the young father is paradoxical, particularly since teenage pregnancy is recognized as one of our most important national health problems.

Delissovoy's (1973) study of 48 semirural married white adolescent couples maintained that the fathers were less familiar with developmental norms than were mothers. More specifically, estimates on the frequency of crying, the age at which to begin obedience training, and the age at which children can recognize wrongdoing were all unrealistic. Generalizability of these findings are questionable however because of the restrictiveness of the sample and the lack of a nonadolescent control group (Parke et al., 1980).

Psychological profiles of teenage fathers that show maladjustment have usually been taken shortly after the pregnancy (Pauker, 1968), a time characterized by anxiety, fear, and uncertainty. Realizing this, Pauker investigated the Minnesota Multiphasic Personality Inventories (MMPIs) of 11, 349 ninth graders in Minnesota and located 94 males reported to have fathered an out-of-wedlock child at a later date. Compared with controls matched for age, SES, and high school attended, he found similar IQ scores and MMPI profiles, with the out-of-wedlock fathers somewhat more active and less controlled. Results from an outreach program for adolescent fathers (Pannor, 1971; Pannor et al., 1968) have also indicated the psychological normalcy of young fathers when compared with controls.

Fathers are not insensitive and are affected by conceiving and having a child, according to reactions they express during pregnancy and delivery. The fathers in Pannor et al.'s (1968) study were interested in the girls' welfare and were often willing to enter marriage and help financially.

Platts (1968) has also found adolescent fathers to be available, concerned, troubled, anxious to help, and willing to assume responsibility. In Presser's (1980) study, few fathers (11%) wanted the girls to have an abortion. Other reactions (Pannor, 1971) include depression, fear, guilt, and disbelief. Of the 30 out of the 162 predominantly black fathers in Lorenzi et al.'s (1977) study that were present during delivery, 20% reported being highly excited, 60% happy, and 20% pleased. Seeing the baby (Pannor, 1971) made fathers more aware of the problem and left them with a sense of pride. These results imply that adolescent fathers' reactions to pregnancy and birth may be similar to the reactions of older fathers, providing that social and economic circumstances are not overwhelming.

After the birth of the child, adolescent fathers maintain varying levels of involvement with their children. In Furstenberg's (1976c) study, 63% of the natural fathers maintained contact with their children 5 years after their birth—21% living with the child, 21% as "supportive biological fathers" visiting their child at least once a week, and 21% visiting their child occasionally. A nonresidential father was more apt to visit his child if he was formerly married to the mother; marrying apparently establishes a claim to visiting rights. Nevertheless, 30% of the unmarried fathers visited regularly, often behaving like a residential father. In addition, a father's authority and decision making was related to whether or not he contributed financially to child support. If he did, he was more likely to maintain his authority. A factor that inhibits paternal involvement is the mother's marriage to a stepfather. When this occurred, the natural father's contact with his child almost always diminished.

In Lorenzi et al.'s (1977) study, even though many fathers were nonresidential, 75% of the fathers were reported to visit their child. Stack (1974) has implied that living apart does not mean disinterest for black urban fathers. Though they live apart, they visit regularly, live-in for variable intervals, give gifts, and are proud of their children, boasting of them to their relatives.

Encouraging the father's participation in the mother's pregnancy, birth, and child care decisions may be beneficial for all concerned. Through participation in the mother's pregnancy, the father's self-esteem and self-worth (Pannor et al., 1968) and his responsibility in a fathering role (Earls & Siegel, 1980) may be enhanced. He may enhance his child's welfare directly through financial contributions (Parke et al., 1980). His presence also affects his child's social, emotional, and cognitive development. Indirectly, his participation may increase the mother's self-assurance, confidence (Earls & Seigel, 1980), and sense of security (Parke et al., 1980). These strengths may help her deal more effectively with her own ambivalence concerning her situation (Pannor & Evans, 1975). By assisting the mother, the father enhances her interactions with their child. By strengthening the father's self-respect and sense of responsibility (Platts, 1968) and by directly and indirectly enhancing family and child development, the community or society at large may benefit.

Evidence indicates that the social and psychological correlates of adolescent fatherhood are similar to those of the adolescent mother (Earls & Siegel, 1980). Nevertheless, information is seriously lacking. Areas in which research is needed include behavioral investigations of adolescents' father–child interactional patterns; the social and psychological factors related to pregnancy and fatherhood; and how outcomes such as abortion and involving the father in decisions throughout pregnancy, birth, and early child care affect his behavior. It remains to be seen whether information that has demonstrated the importance of older fathers to their children's development (Lamb, 1976; Parke, 1978) can also be applied to the adolescent father.

D. The Mother–Father Relationship

Of particular importance in an adolescent's adjustment to parenting are the direct and indirect effects that mothers and fathers exert on each other's behavior. However, little information exists outside of descriptive studies of marital instability and contact between mothers and fathers.

One way to view the transition to adolescent parenting is as an accelerated role transition (Russell, 1980). The impact that pregnancy and birth has on an adolescent's life depends on its timing with a socially prescribed course for individual and family development. The degree to which an individual or a family deviates from a prescribed course is related to the degree of stress experienced. As Furstenberg (1976b), Kruger (1973), and Russell (1980) have indicated, school-age parenting may produce heightened stress when it is out of synchrony with a normative life course. Adolescents may be entering parenting at an age when they are not financially, educationally, and emotionally ready to deal with it effectively. Also, Rossi (1968) suggests that additional uncertainty and stress may result because adolescent parenting may be an unplanned or unwanted status.

One direct effect of marriage and childbearing at an early age may be marital instability. As the previous review of marriage has indicated, the separation and divorce rate of marriages for individuals under the age of 20 is two to three times higher than for those 20 and over (Alan Guttmacher Institute, 1976; Bacon, 1974; Baldwin & Cain, 1980; Bartz & Nye, 1970; Furstenberg, 1976c). Although these figures do tell us that teen marriages are more likely to break up, they do not tell us about the relationship between the mother and father.

Whether or not marriage occurs, research dealing with the mother–father relationship prior to conception has indicated that a closeness exists for many young couples. The myths of male exploitation and female promiscuity were not supported by results from a longitudinal study of black and white females conducted by Bowerman, Irish, and Pope (1966). They found that the relationship between the unwed mother and father was similar in many respects to courtship: that the father usually knew the expectant mother's family and friends; that the couples were similar in age, education, and SES; and that the pregnancy usually resulted from an exclusive relationship between the couple that lasted at least 6 months. Pope (1967) extended these findings and indicated that mothers reported the relationship as exclusive, and that they loved and were committed to the fathers. In Von Der Ahe's (1968) interviews with 150 predominantly white unwed mothers, it was found that the pregnancy was reported to be the result of a deep emotional involvement with the father, characterized as love by 80% of these women. Pannor (1971) also pointed out that adolescents who eventually have a baby are usually in long-standing involvements. Wise and Grossman (1980) found that 67% of the sample had a relationship with the father over 1 year and that 87% had continued this relationship during pregnancy.

A relationship between prior contact and marriage success was demonstrated by Furstenberg (1976a, 1976c). He found that the separation rate was only half as high for couples who had prior frequent and intensive contact. The best chance for marriage survival occurred if the mother married the partner of a long-standing exclusive relationship soon after conception. It was suggested that in such a relationship the child may reinforce the bond between parents. If the relationship was not close initially, then the child served as a "splitting wedge." Russell (1974) has also found, that good communication between parents was related to more effective family planning and higher marital adjustment. It was suggested that good communication could even be effective in overcoming the negative effects of unplanned pregnancies and marriages following conception. Wise and Grossman (1980) report similar results in their sample of unwed teenage mothers. The relationship between parents during pregnancy was found to be related to better planning and greater amounts of emotional involvement with the pregnancy.

Contact with the father after the birth of the child has also been investigated. Presser (1980) reported that for the 51 never-married women in her sample, 29% were seeing the father one or more times per week, 26% one to three times per week, 16% one time per month, with 29% reporting no contact when their children were between the ages of 18 months and 3 years. Over time, 44% reported increased contact, 23% decreased contact, and 33% no change. By the time the children were between the ages of 3 and 5, 67% had reported contact with the father from birth. Lorenzi *et al.* (1977) investigated the permanency of the relationship in a predominantly black sample interviewed at 3-, 15-, and 26-month intervals. They found that marriage to fathers increased over time, from 7% at 3 months to 17% at 15 months to 23% at 26 months. Those reporting steady contact (married and unmarried) decreased from 63% to 57% to 46%, respectively, whereas mothers reporting occasional contact remained stable at 18% across the three intervals.

An important factor that may determine the course of the mother–father relationship is the financial capability of the father. Whether marriage occurs may depend on whether the husband can support the family (Furstesnberg, 1976b). As age and employment prospects increase, more marriages occur. This may explain why a large number of marriages from Furstenberg's Baltimore sample occurred in the 2 years following delivery, and may also explain the increases reported in Lorenzi *et al.*'s (1977) sample. If marriages had not occurred after 2 years, the mother–father relationship usually deteriorated (Furstenberg, 1976b). Lorenzi *et al.* concluded that the duration of financial support may imply a meaningful relationship for unmarried couples. Similarly, Presser (1980) found that the mothers who received support when their children were aged 3 to 5 (33% of the sample) were also more likely to see the father at least once a month.

Marriage as a resolution of teenage pregnancy may be an appropriate solution for some adolescents, particularly those who have had a prior and long-standing exclusive relationship. Marriage may even serve to alleviate the immediate stress experienced by young expectant parents. In fact, mothers in Furstenberg's (1976c) study were three times more likely to report having unambivalent, positive feelings if they married during their pregnancy. However, as the separation and divorce statistics imply, the stresses encountered by young couples (i.e., financial insecurity, social isolation, and lack of familial and social support) are often too great for even many close marriages to survive.

It is important to recognize that positive relationships may continue outside the institution of marriage. Because it is often beneficial to remain unmarried, in terms of continued support from the family and social services, young mothers and fathers may develop alternate avenues of interacting with one another and their children. Stack (1974) has suggested that the birth of the first child (at least for some couples) may be a preparation for marriage and co-residence that may take place with the birth of a second child.

As this review of the mother–father relationship suggests, the potential for satisfying relationships exists for many adolescent parents. However, in a society largely unwilling and unprepared to deal effectively with their situation, the likelihood of relationships surviving is undermined.

E. The Child of Adolescent Parents

The importance of a child's early experience with his or her parent(s) is exemplified by the following quote by Honig (1978), based on the early stage of trust versus mistrust in Eriksonian theory (Erikson, 1950). "The need of a baby for satisfying mutual interactions with a caring special person is essential for good development. Mutual give-and-take, physical loving, talking and cooing to each other, caresses, snuggles, positive communication—lay foundations of infant trust in their world as basically a good place to grow up in [Honig, 1978, p. 118]." That a child is negatively affected by being raised by an adolescent parent or parents has been suggested by a number of authors. Delissovoy (1973; 1975a, 1975b) has maintained that adolescent parents lack knowledge and experience and have unrealistic expectations for child development. Because of this, young parents may attribute intentions far beyond a child's capabilities that may lead to undue harshness in childrearing (Honig, 1978). However, because of the methodological problems with studies reporting that teenagers are psychologically and/or emotionally at a disadvantage in a parenting role, firm conclusions cannot be drawn. As Honig (1978) points out, it may be that the lack of social supports influences adolescent parent–child interactions rather than age per se. "Someone who feels overwhelmed, rejected, bewildered, and frustrated in her move toward her own life goals for herself by an unwanted pregnancy will find it hard to summon up the sustained life energy and tender caring feelings that high quality infant caregiving and parenting require [p. 118]."

The higher likelihood of prematurity, low birth weight, and neurological defects of infants born to teenagers (Alan Guttmacher Institute, 1976) has been suggested as a link to child abuse. However, because good prenatal care is related to a positive obstetric outcome, and since teenagers are less likely to have appropriate prenatal care and nutrition, the relationship between age and abuse is confounded. Additional factors associated with the life circumstances of adolescent parents, most particularly marriage instability and financial insecurity, further confounds the relationship between adolescent parenting and maltreatment. It is highly likely that enhancing positive obstetric outcome through good prenatal care, education, and nutrition, and reducing potential life stressors through educational incentives and job training, can help reduce negative parent–child interactions.

The long-term cognitive, physical, emotional, and social effects on children born to adolescent parents have been investigated. Oppel and Royston (1971) found differences in the nurturing behaviors of 86 mothers under 18 years of age compared with 86 mothers 18 and older, matched for SES, race, infant's birth weight, and number of previous live births. They found that the younger mothers were more likely to think that their 6- to 8-year-old children should act independently. Also, there was emotional and behavioral involvement with their children along with less reported desire to control the children and keep them closely attached. The younger mothers were also less likely to have intellectual aspirations for their children. In looking at physical, psychological, and intellectual characteristics of the children at ages 8–10, they found that children born to the younger mothers were shorter and lighter, and were behind an average of .38 years in reading. However, IQ scores indicated no significant differences. The psychological ratings of the children revealed that children of younger mothers were more likely to have infantile and acting-out difficulties, have more behavior problems, be more outgoing, dependent, and distractible.

The authors also found that 67 of the 86 mothers under 18, and 24 of the 86 fathers, were still living with their children 8 to 10 years after birth. This compared with 82 of 86 mothers 18 and over and 48 of 86 of the fathers. The fertility rate, measured when the first-born children were aged 8–10 was 3.45 versus 2.93 children for younger and older mothers, respectively. Based on these results, Oppel and Royston (1971) concluded that young mothers are less likely to raise their children in a "healthy" family environment and their less adequate nurturing of children may lead to physical, social, and psychological deficits later. However, because the group was not matched initially for illegitimacy, and because children born to adolescent mothers had a higher likelihood of being raised by others, these results should be interpreted with caution.

Furstenberg (1976c) measured the cognitive development and social maturity of the children in his Baltimore study when they were 42 months old. A comparison of girls 17 and older with those under 17 at the time of birth found that younger mothers were no more likely to have children with behavior problems. Also, children of mothers under 16 performed as well as children of older mothers on the cognitive and social maturity indexes administered. Younger mothers, though less likely to marry, complete school, or achieve economic self-sufficiency, were more likely to receive child care and financial assistance from their families, which may have accounted for the lack of age differences. In addition, the father's relationship with his child seemed to be a critical factor in his child's cognitive development. Parents who married early and had remained married had children with the highest scores. If the mothers married someone other than the father, they were more likely to report difficulty in managing motherhood and to express doubts about their parenting ability. They were also more critical of their children and had children with lower cognitive scores and a higher likelihood of having behavior problems.

A negative relationship was found between the extent of maternal participation and the child's cognitive score. It appears that if the child is exposed to an additional caretaker (usually the grandmother), who has an active interest in the child's development, along with a mother who has high educational goals for the child, then the child benefits cognitively.

In an analysis of 49,913 births in Birmingham, England, between 1950 and 1954 (Record, McKeown, & Edwards, 1969) a relationship was found between maternal age, birth order, and verbal reasoning at age 11. Verbal-reasoning scores of children rose with increasing maternal age at birth and fell with increasing birth order. The children of women under 20 at the time of birth achieved the lowest scores, except for children in families with three or more older siblings. However, because low SES was also associated with low scores, obvious validity problems arise.

Bennett and Bardon (1977) found a positive relationship between a mother's education and her child's later development. Based on results from a program for 86 mothers that provided prenatal care, continuing education, and information concerning parenting and socioemotional adjustment, the authors concluded that continuing school was related to a greater ability to find satisfactory employment, which led to a reduced likelihood that their children would repeat a cycle of poverty and early childbearing. The mothers higher education was associated with the early social competence and later cognitive and academic achievement of their children, relative to a sample of 30 control mothers and their children.

Long-term effects were also evidenced by Baldwin and Cain (1980) in a review of final reports to the National Institute of Child Health Development. A Danish study investigating the health status of 1-year-old infants found no difference between infants of adolescent mothers versus those of mothers 20 years and over. However, if neither the father nor the maternal grandmother was present to assist the mother, health-status scores were lower for the infants of young mothers. The authors' review of socioemotional development indicated that maternal age had little effect at age 4, but at age 7 differences emerged. Children of adolescent parents were more likely to be characterized by overactivity, resistiveness, hostility, and a lack of impulse control.

Regarding a child's early mental and motor development, the authors reported differences in younger and older mothers' interactions at 1, 3, 6, and 12 months of age. These differences were related to higher scores on mental and motor indexes at 9 months of age for infants of older mothers. Their review of cognitive development across the first 7 years of life indicated deficits for children of adolescent parents, particularly for boys. Similar deficits were found for the academic achievement of 10- and 11-year-old children born to adolescent parents. In addition, children born to girls under age 17 were found to have a harder time adjusting to school at age 6. Again, this negative effect was most severe for male children, and the effects were lessened if a father or a grandmother was present in the home.

F. Summary

It appears that the future development of children born to teenage parents may be negatively affected by factors associated with adolescent parenting, such as a more negative obstetric outcome, reduced parental education, financial insecurity, and marital instability. There is some indication, however, that despite these negative consequences of adolescent parenting, the relationship that a parent and child have with each other may be very rewarding. A factor that may be essential to a child's development is the role of the father, particularly for male children. For the child of an adolescent parent, the negative effect on their socioemotional and cognitive development appears to be mediated by the ongoing relationship with fathers, or by having either the father or other concerned person (grandmother) available to assist the mother.

VII. Conclusion

The content of this chapter is both troubling and encouraging. The accelerated, out-of-sequence role transition caused by adolescent pregnancy has a profound impact on the young woman's development, as well as on the lives of the father, child, and significant others. The nonnormative event, however, is an example of both the positive and negative meanings of the term crisis. For many of the individuals involved, the pregnancy is viewed as a tragic occurrence, with a subsequent downward spiraling of the life course, but for many others the pregnancy is an opportunity for growth and positive development. Our stereotype of the teenage mother is usually one that involves the images of promiscuity, little ambition for education or job attainment, reliance on welfare, and neglectful parenting. This profile, however, is representative of only a small minority of these women. When provided with educational opportunities, emotional and financial support from family members and the baby's father, the adolescent mother and family form a viable familial system.

It is imperative that our social, educational, and medical systems respond to the needs of the 1 million young women who become pregnant every year in the United States. Safe, available methods for preventing adolescent pregnancy are needed. In the advent that prevention fails, termination of adolescent pregnancy as a safe, available, alternative solution should also be recognized. The most important point to work toward is the establishment of strong support networks for all adolescents who conceive a child in order to provide for the optimal growth and continued development of all concerned.

Reference Notes

1. Gilligan, C., & Notman, M. *The recurrent themes in women's lives: The integration of autonomy and care.* Paper presented at the Eastern Sociological Meeting, Philadelphia, March 1978.
2. Epstein, A. *Pregnant teenager's knowledge of infant development.* Paper presented at the biennial meeting of the Society for Research in Child Development, San Francisco, March 1979.
3. Pannor, R., Evans, B., & Massarik, F. The unmarried father—findings and implications for practice. Effective services for unmarried parents and their children: Innovative community approaches. New York: National Council on Illegitimacy, 1968.

References

Abernathy, V. Illegitimate conception among teenagers. *American Journal of Public Health*, 1974, *64*, 662–665.

Aiman, J. X-ray pelvimetry of the pregnant adolescent: Pelvic size and the frequency of contraction. *Obstetrics and Gynecology*, 1976, *48*, 281–286.

Alan Guttmacher Institute. *11 million teenagers: What can be done about the epidemic of adolescent pregnancies in the U.S.* New York: Planned Parenthood Federation of America, 1976.

Annis, L. F. *The child before birth.* Ithaca, N.Y.: Cornell University Press, 1978.

Babikian, H., & Goldman, A. A study in teenage pregnancy. *American Journal of Psychiatry*, 1971, *128*, 755–760.

Bacon, L. Early motherhood, accelerated role transition, and social pathologies. *Social Forces*, 1974, *52*, 333–341.

Baizerman, M., Sheehan, C., Ellison, D. L., & Schlesinger, E. A critique of the research literature concerning pregnant adolescents, 1960–1970. *Journal of Youth and Adolescence*, 1974, *3*, 61–75.

Baldwin, W., & Cain, V. The children of teenage parents. *Family Planning Perspectives*, 1980, *12*, 34–43.

Barglow, P., Bornstein, M., Exum, D., Wright, M., & Visotsky, H. Some psychiatric aspects of illegitimate pregnancy in early adolescence. *American Journal of Orthopsychiatry*, 1968, *38*, 672–687.

Bartz, K., & Nye, F. Early marriage: A propositional formulation. *Journal of Marriage and the Family*, 1970, *32*, 258–268.

Bennett, V., & Bardon, J. The effects of a school program on teenage mothers and their children. *American Journal of Orthopsychiatry*, 1977, *47*, 671–678.

Bibring, G. L., & Valerstein, A. F. Psychological aspects of pregnancy. *Clinical Obstetrics and Gynecology*, 1976, *19*, 357–371.

Bolton, F., Laner, R., & Kane, S. Child maltreatment risk among adolescent mothers: A study of reported cases. *American Journal of Orthopsychiatry*, 1980, *50*, 489–504.

Bowerman, C., Irish, D., & Pope, H. *Unwed motherhood: Personal and social consequences*. Chapel Hill: University of North Carolina Press, 1966.

Boyce, J., & Benoit, C. Adolescent pregnancy. *New York State Journal of Medicine*, 1975, *75*, 872–874.

Braen, B., & Forbush, J. School-age parenthood: A national overview. *The Journal of School Health*, 1975, *45*, 256–262.

Bryan-Logan, B., & Dancy, B. Unwed pregnant adolescents. *Nursing Clinics of North America*, 1974, *9*, 57–68.

Card, J., & Wise, L. Teenage mothers and teenage fathers: The impact of early childbearing on the parent's personal and professional lives. *Family Planning Perspectives*, 1978, *10*, 199–205.

Chilman, C. *Growing Up Poor*. Washington, D.C.: U.S. Government Printing Office, 1966.

Christensen, H. Cultural relativism and premarital sex norms. *American Sociological Review*, 1960, *25*, 31–39.

Cobliner, W. Pregnancy in the single adolescent girl: The role of cognitive functions. *Journal of Youth and Adolescence*, 1974, *3*, 17–29.

Cobliner, W., Schulman, H., & Romney, S. The termination of adolescent out-of-wedlock pregnancy and the prospects for their primary prevention. *American Journal of Obstetrics and Gynecology*, 1973, *115*, 432–444.

Colletta, N., Gregg, C., Hadler, S., Lee, D., & Mekelburg, D. When adolescent mothers return to school. *The Journal of School Health*, 1980, *50*, 534–538.

Coombs, L., & Freedman, R. Premarital pregnancy, childspacing, and later economic achievement. *Population Studies*, 1970, *24*, 389–412.

Cvejic, H. *et al.* Follow-up of 50 adolescent girls 2 years after abortion. *Canadian Medical Association Journal*, 1977, *116*, 44–46.

deLissovoy, V. Child care by adolescent parents. *Children Today*, 1973, *2*, 22–25.

deLissovoy, V. Concerns of rural adolescent parents. *Child Welfare*, 1975, *54*, 167–174. (a)

deLissovoy, V. High school marriages: A longitudinal study. *Journal of Marriage and the Family*, 1975, *37*, 245–255.

Drillien, C. School disposal and performance for children of different birthweight born 1953–1960. *Archives of Diseases of Childhood*, 1969, *44*, 562.

Duenhoelter, J. H., Jimenez, J. M., & Baumann, G. Pregnancy performance of patients under fifteen years of age. *Obstetrics and Gynecology*, 1975, *46*, 49–52.

Dwyer, J. F. Teenage pregnancy. *American Journal of Obstetrics and Gynecology*, 1974, *118*, 373–376.

Earls, F., & Siegel, B. Precocious fathers. *American Journal of Orthopsychiatry*, 1980, *50*, 469–480.

Elkind, D. Egocentrism in adolescence. *Child Development*, 1967, *38*, 1025–1034.

Erikson, E. *Childhood and Society*. New York: Norton, 1950.

Erikson, E. *Identity: Youth and Crisis*. New York: Norton, 1968.

Evans, J., Selstad, G., & Welcher, W. Teenagers, fertility control behavior and attitude before and after abortion, childbearing or negative pregnancy test. *Family Planning Perspectives*, 1976, *8*, 192–200.

Fielding, J. Adolescent pregnancy revisited. *New England Journal of Medicine*, 1978, *299*, 893–896.

Fischman, S. The pregnancy resolution decisions of unwed adolescents. *Nursing Clinics of North America*, 1975, *10*, 217–227.

Fischman, S. H. Delivery or abortion in inner city adolescents. *American Journal of Orthopsychiatry*, 1977, *47*, 127–133.

Flavell, J. H. *The Developmental Psychology of Jean Piaget*. New York: D. Van Nostrand Co., 1963.

Flavell, J. H. Metacognition and cognitive monitoring: A new area of cognitive-developmental inquiry. *American Psychologist*, 1979, *34*, 906–911.

Freedman, D., & Thornton, A. The long-term impact of pregnancy-at-marriage on the family's economic circumstances. *Family Planning Perspectives*, 1979, *11*, 6–20.

Freedman, R., & Coombs, L. Childspacing and family economic position. *American Sociological Review*, 1966, *31*, 631–648.

Freud, A. Adolescence. *Psychoanalytic Study of the Child*, 1958, *13*, 255–278.

Freud, S. *A General Introduction to Psychoanalysis*. New York: Permabooks, 1953.

Friedman, H. The mother–daughter relationship: Its potential in treatment of young unwed mothers. *Social Casework*, 1966, *47*, 502–506.

Furstenberg, F. Premarital pregnancy and marital instability. *Journal of Social Issues*, 1976, *32*, 67–86. (a)

Furstenberg, F. The social consequences of teenage parenthood. *Family Planning Perspectives*, 1976, *8*, 148–164. (b)

Furstenberg, F. *Unplanned parenthood: The social consequences of teenage childbearing*. New York: The Free Press, 1976. (c)

Furstenberg, F. Burdens and benefits: The impact of early childbearing on the family. *Journal of Social Issues*, 1980, *36*, 64–87.

Furstenberg, F., & Crawford, A. Family support: Helping teenage mothers to cope. *Family Planning Perspectives*, 1978, *10*, 322–333.

Gallatin, J. Theories of adolescence. In J. F. Adams (Ed.), *Understanding Adolescence*. Boston: Allyn & Bacon, 1980.

Gottschalk, L., Titchener, J. L., Piker, H. N., & Stewart, S. S. Psychological factors associated with pregnancy in adolescent girls: A preliminary report. *Journal of Nervous and Mental Disorders*, 1964, *138*, 524–534.

Gutelius, M. Child-rearing attitudes of teenage negro girls. *American Journal of Public Health*, 1970, *60*, 93–104.

Hale, M. Meeting the health needs of the sexually active adolescents. *Contemporary Obstetrics/Gynecology*, 1978, *12*, 80–97.

Hamachek, D. E. Psychology and development of the adolescent self. In J. F. Adams (Ed.), *Understanding adolescence*. Boston: Allyn & Bacon, 1980.

Helfer, R., & Kempe, C. *The battered child*. Chicago: University of Chicago Press, 1968.

Hertz, D. Psychological implicaitons of adolescent pregnancy: Patterns of family interaction in adolescent mothers-to-be. *Psychosomatics*, 1977, *18*, 13–16.

Hogan, D. The variable order of events in the life cycle. *American Sociological Review*, 1978, *43*, 573–586.

Honig, A. What we need to know to help the teenage parent. *The Family Coordinator*, 1978, *27*, 113–119.

Jekel, J., Klerman, L., & Bancroft, D. Factors associated with rapid subsequent pregnancies among school-age mothers. *American Journal of Public Health*, 1973, *63*, 769–773.

Juhasz, A. The unmarried adolescent parent. *Adolescence*, 1974, *9*, 263–272.

Keeve, J., Schlesinger, E., Wight, B., & Adams, R. Fertility experience of juvenile girls: A community-wide ten-year study. *American Journal of Public Health*, 1969, *59*, 2185–2198.

Kerckhoff, A., & Parrow, A. The effect of early marriage on the educational attainment of young men. *Journal of Marriage and the Family*, 1979, *41*, 97–107.

Kinard, E., & Klerman, L. Teenage parenting and child abuse: Are they related? *American Journal of Orthopsychiatry*, 1980, *50*, 481–488.

Klaus, M., & Kennell, J. *Maternal–infant bonding*. St. Louis: Mosby, 1976.

Klein, L. Early teenage pregnancy, contraception, and repeat pregnancy. *American Journal of Obstetrics and Gynecology*, 1974, *120*, 249–255.

Klein, M., & Stern, L. Low birth weight and the battered child syndrome. *American Journal of the Disabled Child*, 1971, *122*, 15–18.

Klerman, L. Adolescent pregnancy: The need for new policies and new programs. *The Journal of School Health*, 1975, *45*, 263–267.

Konopka, G. Life-situational and psychodynamic factors in the pregnancy experiences of married adolescents. *American Journal of Orthopsychiatry*, 1967, *37*, 265.

Kruger, W. Education for parenthood and the schools. *Nurse Practitioner*, 1973, *2*, 4–7.

La Barre, M. Pregnancy experience among married adolescents. *American Journal of Orthopsychiatry*, 1968, *38*, 47–55.

Lamb, M. *The role of the father in child development*. New York: Wiley, 1976.

Lorenzi, M., Klerman, L., & Jekel, J. School age parents: How permanent a relationship? *Adolescence*, 1977, *12*, 13–22.

Magid, T., Gross, B., & Shuman, B. Preparing pregnant teenagers for parenthood. *Family Coordinator*, 1979, *28*, 359–362.

Marinoff, S. C., & Schonholtz, D. H. Adolescent pregnancy. In A. Altchek (Ed.), *The Pediatric Clinics of North America*, 1972, *19*, 795–802.

Martin, C. Psychological problems of abortion for the unwed teenage girl. *Genetic Psychology Monographs*, 1973, *88*, 23–110.

McCarthy, J., & Menken, J. Marriage, remarriage, marital disruption, and age at first birth. *Family Planning Perspectives*, 1979, *11*, 22–30.

McKenry, P., Walters, L., & Johnson, C. Adolescent pregnancy: A review of the literature. *The Family Coordinator*, 1979, *28*, 17–28.

Millman, S., & Hendershot, G. Early fertility and lifetime fertility. *Family Planning Perspectives*, 1980, *12*, 139–149.

Moore, K. Teenage childbirth and welfare dependency. *Family Planning Perspectives*, 1978, *10*, 233–235.

Moore, K., & Waite, L. Early childbearing and educational attainment. *Family Planning Perspectives*, 1977, *9*, 220–225.

Neugarten, B., Moore, J., & Lowe, J. Age norms, age constraints, and adult socialization. In B. Neugarten (Ed.), *Middle age and aging*. Chicago: The University of Chicago Press, 1968.

Nakashima, I. Teenage pregnancy: Its causes, costs, and consequences. *Nurse Practitioner*, 1977, *2*, 10–13.

Olson, L. Social and psychological correlates of pregnancy resolution among adolescent women: A review. *American Journal of Orthopsychiatry*, 1980, *50*, 432–445.

Oppel, W., & Royston, B. Teenage births: Some social, psychological, and physical sequelae. *American Journal of Public Health*, 1971, *61*, 751–756.

Osofsky, H., & Osofsky, J. Adolescents as mothers: Results of a program for low-income pregnant teenagers with some emphasis upon infants' development. *American Journal of Orthopsychiatry*, 1970, *40*, 825–834.

Osofsky, H., Osofsky, J., Kendall, N., & Rajan, R. Adolescents as mothers: An interdisciplinary approach to a complex problem. *Journal of Youth and Adolescence*, 1973, *2*, 233–249.

Pannor, R. The teenage unwed father. *Clinical Obstetrics and Gynecology*, 1971, *14*, 466–472.

Pannor, R., & Evans, B. The unmarried father revisited. *The Journal of School Health*, 1975, *45*, 286–291.

Parke, R. Parent–infant interaction: Progress, paradigms, and problems. In G. D. Sackett (Ed.), *Observing behavior: Theory and applications in mental retardation* (Vol. 1). Baltimore: University Park Press, 1978.

Parke, R., Power, T., & Fisher, T. The adolescent father's impact on the mother and child. *Journal of Social Issues*, 1980, *36*, 88–106.

Pauker, J. Fathers of children conceived out of wedlock: Pregnancy, high school, psychological test results. *Developmental Psychology*, 1968, *4*, 215–218.

Perez-Reyez, M. & Falk, R. Follow-up after therapeutic abortion in early adolescence. *Archives of General Psychiatry*, 1973, *28*, 120–126.

Phipps-Yonas, S. Teenage pregnancy and motherhood: A review of the literature. *American Journal of Orthopsychiatry*, 1980, *50*, 403–431.

Piaget, J. Intellectual evolution from adolescence to adulthood. *Human Development*, 1972, *15*, 1–12.

Placek, P., & Hendershot, G. Public welfare and family planning: An empirical study of the "brood sow" myth. *Social Problems*, 1974, *21*, 658–673.

Platts, H. A public adoption agency's approach to natural fathers. *Child Welfare*, 1968, *47*, 530–537.

Plionis, B. Adolescent pregnancy: Review of the literature. *Social Work*, 1975, *20*, 302–307.

Polsby, G. Unmarried parenthood: Potential for growth. *Adolescence*, 1974, *9*, 263–272.

Pope, H. Unwed mothers and their sex partners. *Journal of Marriage and the Family*, 1967, *29*, 756–764.

Presser, H. Social consequences of teenage childbearing. In W. Petersen & L. Day (Eds.), 8–14.

Presser, H. Social consequences of teenage childbearing. In W. Peterson & L. Day (Eds.), *Social demography: The state of the art*. Cambridge, Mass.: Harvard University Press, 1977.

Presser, H. Sally's Corner: Coping with unmarried motherhood. *Journal of Social Issues*, 1980, *36*, 107–129.

Presser, H., & Salsberg, L. Public assistance and early family formation: Is there a pronatalist effort? *Social Problems*, 1975, *23*, 226–241.

Record, R., McKeown, T., & Edwards, J. The relation of measured intelligence to birth order and maternal age. *Annals of Human Genetics*, 1969, *33*, 61–69.

Rossi, A. Transition to parenthood. *Journal of Marriage and the Family*, 1968, *20*, 26–39.

Russ-Eft, D., Sprenger, M., & Beever, A. Antecedents and consequences of adolescent parenthood and consequences at age 30. *The Family Coordinator*, 1979, *28*, 173–179.

Russell, C. Unscheduled parenthood: Transition to "parent" for the teenager. *Journal of Social Issues*, 1980, *36*, 45–63.

Sarrel, P. The university hospital and the teenage unwed mother. *American Journal of Public Health*, 1967, *57*, 308–313.

Schaffer, C., & Pine, E. Pregnancy, abortion, and the developmental tasks of adolescence. *American Academy of Child Psychiatry* , 1972, *11*, 511–536.

Shaffer, D., Pettigrew, A., Wolkind, S., & Zajicek, E. Psychiatric aspects of pregnancy in school girls: A review. *Psychological Medicine*, 1978, *8*, 119–130.

Sklar, J., & Berkov, B. Teenage family formation in postwar America. *Family Planning Perspectives*, 1974, *6*, 80–90.

Smith, E. The role of the grandmother in adolescent pregnancy and parenting. *Journal of School Health*, 1975, *45*, 278–283.

Stack, C. *All our kin: Strategies for survival in a black community*. New York: Harper & Row, 1974.

Sugar, M. At-risk factors for the adolescent mother and her infant. *Journal of Youth and Adolescence*, 1976, *5*, 251–270.

Trussell, J., & Menken, J. Early childbearing and subsequent fertility. *Family Planning Perspectives*, 1978, *10*, 209–218.

Trussell, T. J. Economic consequences of teenage childbearing. *Family Planning Perspectives*, 1976, *8*, 184–190.

Von Der Ahe, C. The unwed teenage mother. *American Journal of Obstetrics and Gynecology*, 1969, *104*, 279–285.

Williams, T. Childrearing practices of young mothers: What we know, how it matters, why it's so little. *American Journal of Orthopsychiatry*, 1974, *44*, 70–75.

Wise, S., & Grossman, F. Adolescent mothers and their infants: Psychological factors in early attachment and interaction. *American Journal of Orthopsychiatry*, 1980, *50*, 454–468.

Youngs, D., & Neibyl, J. Adolescent pregnancy and abortion. *Medical Clinics of North America*, 1975, *59*, 1419–1427.

Zabin, L., Kantner, J., & Zelnik, M. The risk of adolescent pregnancy in the first months of intercourse. *Family Planning Perspectives*, 1979, *11*, 215–222.

Zelnik, M., & Kantner, J. The resolution of teenage first pregnancies. *Family Planning Perspectives*, 1974, *6*, 74–80.

Zelnik, M., & Kantner, J. First pregnancies to women aged 15–19: 1976 and 1971. *Family Planning Perspectives*, 1978, *10*, 11–20.

Zongker, C. The self concept of pregnant adolescent girls. *Adolescence*, 1977, *12*, 477–488.

CHAPTER 5

The Birth Defective Child and the Crisis of Parenthood: Redefining the Situation[1]

ROSALYN BENJAMIN DARLING

CITY–COUNTY CLINIC
JOHNSTON, PENNSYLVANIA

I. Introduction: Defining the Situation

W. I. Thomas stated that situations defined as real are real in their consequences. Human behavior is a direct result of one's definition of the situation, and each individual functions within a uniquely conceived reality. The present is constantly being defined in terms of the past, and the past is constantly being redefined in terms of the present. All human beings rely on their past experiences to "make sense" of the world around them and to select behaviors appropriate to their interpretations of the day-to-day events of their lives. The process of defining the situation is typically subconscious because life events normally proceed in a predictable manner. In recent years, ethnomethodologists and other investigators have become interested in the *un*predictable event and the problem of how the defining process

---

[1] The excerpts from *Families Against Society* by Rosalyn Benjamin Darling (SAGE LIBRARY OF SOCIAL RESEARCH Volume 88) copyright 1979, are reprinted by permission of the Publisher, Sage Publications, Inc. (Beverly Hills/London).

LIFE-SPAN DEVELOPMENTAL PSYCHOLOGY
Nonnormative Life Events

proceeds when the present *cannot* be explained in terms of the past. The unanticipated birth of a child with a permanent defect is an event of this type.

The definition of the situation includes several components: (*a*) definition of self; *b*) definition of others involved in the situation; (*c*) definition of time and place; (*d*) definition of context or purpose; and (*e*) definition of process or "what is happening" in the situation. In addition, actors generally feel that they have some degree of power in a situation so that they are more or less "in control" of what is happening. When an actor's definition is congruent with those of others in the situation, events are likely to proceed in an orderly fashion. When entering a new situation, one constructs a preliminary definition based on past experience. As interaction proceeds, this preliminary definition is modified and supplemented by a continual process of interpretation and reinterpretation. Thus, the process of defining the situation of becoming and being a parent begins with preexisting conceptions of pregnancy, birth, and parenthood. As expectations concerning time, place, context, process, or the attributes or definitions of others are not fulfilled, definitions of "what it is like" to become and be a parent will continue to be altered.

McHugh (1968) suggests that social order is contingent on the successful process of definition of the situation. Conversely, a definitional breakdown will generally result in *anomie*. Order, McHugh argues, is characterized by "emergence" and "relativity." These characteristics, in turn, include components such as "theme," "fit," and "revelation." Situations are like puzzles that are put together uneventfully as long as the pieces readily fit into place. Sometimes, a piece does not seem to fit into the puzzle at all, but then revelation occurs, the piece fits, and the process continues. On occasion, pieces are *made* to fit by forcing them together: Human beings tend to rationalize events that seem inappropriate, incorrect, or unlikely. The tendency is always toward creating order, even when the logic of events is not readily apparent.

When attempts at rationalization fail to restore order, anomie ensues. In the anomic situation, the theme disappears, and no new theme can be found to replace it. When no intelligible purpose or context can be constructed, events become *meaningless*. In a second type of definitional crisis, meaning is present but control is lost. The actor is able to rationalize events but is unable to make this rationalization clear to the other actors in the situation. Like meaninglessness, *powerlessness* results in a communication breakdown, because interaction can proceed only when all actors share a similar definition of the situation.

This chapter will focus on the occurrence of meaninglessness and powerlessness in the situation of becoming and being a parent. The relative proportion of order and anomie in the situation of becoming and being the parent of a birth defective child will be assessed and compared with an analysis of the situation of becoming and being the parent of a normal child. One might expect that the former situation would be considerably more anomic than the latter. However, as the following discussion will show, at least during birth and the postpartum period, anomie may be a pervasive component of *most* situations, whether the child is normal *or* defective.

II. The Birth and Parenting of a Normal Child: The Prevailing Crisis Model

The process of defining the situation of birth and parenting will be discussed in terms of the "career" model suggested by Becker (1963) and others. In this model, events are conceptualized as following in a connected sequence from one time period to another. For the purposes of this discussion, the parenting career will be defined as beginning with the acquisition of the pregnant identity and proceeding through the prenatal months, birth, the immediate postpartum period, the remainder of the first postpartum year, and the subsequent years of childhood.

A. The Prenatal Period

Miller (1977) has suggested that pregnancy *as a social role* does not begin until a parent's suspicions of pregnancy are confirmed by a medical authority. Thus, the physician establishes the theme, "going to have a baby." The meaning of that theme to various prospective parents will depend on whether the pregnancy is planned or unplanned, whether this pregnancy is the first, and on the prevailing definitions of pregnancy present within the expectant couple's social world.

Certainly, the confirmation of a planned pregnancy is likely to evoke a favorable reaction in the expectant parents, especially if they have been trying to achieve conception for a long time. Even an unplanned pregnancy can come to be defined in positive terms, as parents rationalize the turn of events by redefining goals and restructuring values. Thus, the "change of life" baby becomes defined as "a special blessing," and the pregnant adolescent decides that educational or career plans can be postponed.

The couple who have had children are likely to rely on past pregnancy experience to define the situation—noting differences in how they feel, how much the baby's movements are felt, or how the obstetrician reacts. Sometimes these differences are interpreted as indicating the sex, size, or temperament of the unborn child.

Among primiparae, past experience is not as ready a guide, although many expectant parents have had close relationships with others—relatives, neighbors, and friends—who have been pregnant and given birth. Typically, new parents engage in much mutual socialization, so that first-timers can interpret their experiences on the basis of the experiences of others. In addition, many read books and articles in the popular press or take special courses in preparation for parenthood given in schools and hospitals by the American Red Cross and other organizations.

La Rossa (1977) has argued that a couple's first pregnancy creates a crisis that is a potential strain for the marital relationship. Similarly, Doering, Entwisle, and Quinlan (1980) claim that a first pregnancy is seen as a progressively developing crisis, marked by threat of damage to the self-concept. The uncomplicated first pregnancy, however, does not often destroy an otherwise stable marriage.

Occasionally, a pregnancy may cause concern to a childless couple who have experienced one or more miscarriages or stillbirths. The following quote from a first-time mother is suggestive: "I had two miscarriages before I became pregnant with Ricky. I thought maybe I had bad genes or something . . . It was in the back of my mind through the whole pregnancy [Darling, 1979, p. 127]."

Both first-time and experienced parents also express concern over the health of the unborn child. These comments from fathers are illustrative:

> My sister had a child who died of cystic fibrosis, and it was a very sad experience for the whole family . . . The chances were very slight, but there was some concern that it could happen to us . . . I've always been worried about having a child who was handicapped . . . one of our friends has a terribly retarded child—terribly retarded. We were concerned. We just wanted a healthy child.

> We had a very healthy child the first time and here we were "going to bat" again, so to speak. I was aware of the chance that this time we might "strike out" [Darling, 1979, p. 127].

Views of pregnancy are also colored by definitions received from friends, relatives, and neighbors. Rosengren (1962) has noted that reactions to pregnancy vary by social class. Lower class people are more likely to define pregnancy in terms of the sick role, whereas the upper classes view the gestation period as a time of normalcy. Whether or not the prenatal period is defined in terms of illness, once labor begins, medical definitions and medically based authority almost always prevail.

B. The Birth Situation

At the onset of labor, then, most expectant parents have had some anticipatory socialization in childbirth. Those who have already had a baby or have taken courses in prepared childbirth have a definite set of expectations about the events and procedures that will occur. Others have heard stories about or have witnessed or read about birth in the media. To the extent that actual events deviate from what is expected, the definition of the situation will be threatened.

A number of studies (see, for example, Doering et al., 1980; Norr, Block, Charles, Meyering, & Meyers, 1977) have suggested that the defining process is smoother and consequently more enjoyable for those who have taken classes in prepared childbirth. Norr et al. (1977) have noted that those who prepare for childbirth in this way are more likely to be of high status, to have a close marriage, and to have less traditional sex-role attitudes. Typically, in prepared childbirth, the husband is present in the labor and delivery rooms to provide support, which also diminishes his wife's pain and adds to enjoyment. As long as a prepared birth proceeds normally, anomie is likely to be avoided—events will be meaningful, and the birthing couple will feel that they are in control of the situation.

Rothman (1978) has argued, however, that although prepared childbirth might seem meaningful to the parents, it actually places them in a situation as powerless as that experienced by parents in the traditional, medically controlled birth situation. She suggests that any birth that takes place in the hospital is defined as a medical event; the baby is a product of the hospital rather than a product of the mother, and the birth and care of the child are scheduled to fit the institutional rhythm. Even admission to the hospital is controlled by medical personnel who must verify whether the labor in question is "real." The feeling of powerlessness is then magnified by various admission procedures: stripping the woman of her clothing and jewelry, shaving the pubic area, administering an enema. Danziger (1979) notes, too, that medical control is expressed directly through stimulation of labor and intervention in delivery. The couple is also dependent on staff assessments in defining labor stages and for defining appropriate behavior in each stage. Typically, the hospital staff uses the same interpretations regardless of the needs of the individual couple. Rothman (1978) argues that childbirth education classes only prepare a couple for the hospital and acceptance of the medical model. The birthing woman has power only as long as she follows the institutional rules (Danziger suggests that these include passivity or quiet acceptance), and as long as the husband acts as "coach" to keep the woman "in her place."

Similarly, in a study of mothers who had attended prenatal classes, Larsen (1966) found a number of complaints about the situations of labor and delivery: lack of interest and support from nurses, conflicting advice from professionals, and unmet needs for support from the husband and physician. Thus, even though events might be somewhat more meaningful for the prepared mother, anomie in the form of powerlessness may still be present, even in uncomplicated births.

C. The Postpartum Period

Feelings of powerlessness may linger into the postpartum period when the new baby is kept in a nursery apart from the mother, although "rooming-in" may serve to alleviate some of the anomie felt at this time. Larsen (1966) notes that the mothers she studied had the fewest complaints about the hospital stay compared to other periods in the childbearing year. Among the complaints she did note were a desire to see more of the baby and irritation over certain routines and environmental conditions in the hospital.

Powerlessness is likely to be increased when, for medical reasons, a baby must be kept in the nursery for an extended period of time. In a study of an intensive care nursery, for example, Wiener, Strauss, Fagerhaugh, and Suczek (1979) found that parents attempted to define events in terms of their "biography," or life history, and to relate their baby's condition to life outside the hospital, while staff focused on the baby's condition during the hospital stay. Meaning also had to be reassessed as parental expectations— financial, emotional, and social—were realigned.

Once the baby comes home, feelings of powerlessness may end, at least momentarily. However, especially in the case of primiparae, the demands of a new baby may seem overwhelming at first. Many writers have suggested that a baby's homecoming is likely to precipitate a major crisis in the family. Shainess (1963) writes, "Motherhood is a shock, a blow on the head, from which many women never recover. Little in our culture prepares women for its ultimate realities [p. 146]." She suggests that the period from birth to 8 months is a "parasitic" phase during which the mother must subordinate her own needs to those of her child.

A series of studies of "parenthood as crisis" (Dyer, 1963; Hobbs, 1965; Le Masters, 1957) found that among urban, middle-class couples, from 53 to

83% reported extreme or severe crises in adjusting to their first child, even though the pregnancies were planned, the parents showed no other evidence of psychiatric disability, and regardless of whether their marriages were good or poor. Among the problems of adjustment noted were loss of sleep, chronic exhaustion, extensive confinement to the home and resulting curtailment of social contacts, giving up the satisfactions of outside employment, additional laundry, feelings of guilt and inadequacy in the parental role, long hours of infant care, decline in housekeeping standards, concern with appearance, and decline in the wife's sexual response. In addition, Larsen (1966) mentions physical discomforts and complications, complications of the baby such as colic, difficulty in adjusting to the needs of other children, too much company, and interference by relatives and neighbors. She also notes that the first 3 months at home produced more stresses than any other period in the childbearing year. In addition to the stresses producing feelings of powerlessness, feelings of meaninglessness are also present, especially among first-time parents, with respect to interpreting the infant's cues (Shereshefsky, Liebenberg, & Lockman, 1973). The infant who continues to cry after parents have tried feeding, diaper changing, rocking, and other measures is also likely to arouse feelings of powerlessness in the parents.

Le Masters (1957) notes that most parents in his study had little effective preparation for the parental roles and, as a result, had romanticized parenthood. Shereshefsky et al. (1973) quote a new mother: "I don't think I was prepared at all because you read in books and you talk with people and you think that all of a sudden there is going to be this motherly surge of love, which is not true . . . I had this colicky baby that spit up and we had to stay home. It took me a long time [p. 175]." Dyer (1963) notes that 80% of both the husbands and wives he studied "admitted that things were not as they expected them to be after the child was born [p. 200]."

Le Masters (1957) suggests that the transition to parenthood is particularly painful for primiparae because "the arrival of the first child destroys the two-person or pair pattern of group interaction and forces a rapid reorganization of their life into a three-person or triangle group system [p. 354]." Both husband and wife must accept the child's priority, and this acceptance is often accompanied by resentment and anxiety (Shereshefsky et al., 1973).

Dyer (1963) notes the crisis is less severe in the case of first-time parents when certain conditions prevail: (a) the marital relationship is strong prior to the birth of the child; (b) parents have taken preparation for marriage courses; (c) parents have been married a long time, (d) the husband has a high educational level, and (e) parenthood is planned.

A few more recent studies (Cole & Hobbs, and Maynard & Hobbs, reported in Bigner, 1979) have questioned whether the transition to parenthood is as severe a crisis as earlier writers had suggested. However, Rollins and Feldman (1970) have shown that marital happiness tends to be lowest after birth of the first child. Bigner (1979) suggests that whether a birth is a "crisis" or merely a "transitional event" for parents is only a semantic difference in what is in either case a true turning point in family structure and relationships.

In all studies, the crisis is found to diminish during the second half of the child's first year of life, and all but a few couples eventually make a successful adjustment to parenthood. Some writers even suggest that the reintegration that takes place results in a better relationship than that which existed prior to the child's birth. Le Masters (1957) postulates that "parenthood (not marriage) marks the final transition to maturity and adult responsibility in our culture [p. 355]." Similarly, Meyerowitz and Feldman (1966) write, "The 'crisis' of the first child is suggested to be a significant transitional point in the maturation of the marital relationship—transition from the dyadic state to a more mature and rewarding triadic system [p. 84]."

As Le Masters (1957) notes, then, "the fact that parenthood is 'normal' does not eliminate crisis [p. 355]." However, for most couples, the crisis of giving birth to a normal child appears to be short-lived. Feelings of meaninglessness and powerlessness give way to successful definition of the situation, as the baby responds to parental handling and significant others offer social support. Even if such support were not forthcoming, the normal baby would eventually become less dependent as a result of growth and development, and parental problems, such as chronic exhaustion, would simply fade away.

D. Childhood: The Postinfancy Experience

In contrast to the infancy period, later childhood typically involves smaller crises rather than a major transitional experience. The parent role has been established and, barring a catastrophic event such as the death of a child, will remain unchallenged until the onset of the "empty nest" crisis some years later.

The smaller crises of early childhood may involve either meaninglessness or powerlessness, or both, although anomie, involving a complete definitional breakdown, is unlikely in most cases. As in the infancy period, meaninglessness is more likely to occur among primiparae, especially those who are poorly prepared for the behaviors common in early childhood. Prepared parents are more likely to define the "terrible twos," for example, as a normal and transitory phase of child development, whereas unprepared parents might see their 2-year-old's tantrums as pathological and meaningless. Even unprepared parents, however, typically learn quickly, and the slow learners still have time on their side, as childhood stages are rarely permanent.

Crises of powerlessness are also more likely to occur among those who are not well prepared for parenthood. Erikson (1950) has suggested that the child's primary tasks during the preschool years involve establishing autonomy and learning to take initiative in behavior. Correspondingly, the parent's primary task involves imposing the parental philosophy on the child (see Shainess, 1963) while breaking some of the close ties of early infancy. A rebellious preschooler can make an unprepared parent feel out of control at times. The self-esteem of powerless parents may decrease as they question their ability to rear their own child. As a result of effective limit setting by parents and simple growth and maturity in the child, however, control is likely to be reestablished within a reasonably brief period. At the same time, parents typically learn rationalizations from friends and neighbors who reassure them that "it's only a passing stage."

Later childhood is also likely to involve definitional ups and downs for parents, marked by minor turning points such as school entrance. Children become increasingly independent during this period, which creates more freedom for parents but, at the same time, may lead parents to question their life goals. Many parents become more deeply involved in careers or activities outside the home at this point.

When children become adolescents, their parents' definitional problems may begin once more. The peer group gains in importance at this time, which may generate feelings of powerlessness in parents who previously felt they were in control of their children's lives. The child is also likely to become more assertive in rejecting parental control over everyday activities and decisions about the future.

The specter of meaninglessness may also arise again at this time as parents no longer feel needed by their children and must find a new purpose in their lives. As children grow from total dependence to total independence, parents are likely to move from powerlessness, to control and order, to meaninglessness. Finally, order and meaning are restored by the acquisition of new goals and rationalizations, such as an appreciation for newfound freedom and the chance to explore new careers, hobbies, and interests.

In summary, for parents of normal children, anomie is likely to be highest shortly after the birth of the first child and again when the last child becomes an adolescent and leaves home. Further, during both of these periods, anomie is more likely to occur among parents who have not been well socialized for parenting. In either case, though, anomie is typically a transient phrase that is quickly replaced by new definitions and appropriate rationalizations.

III. The Birth of a Defective Child: Permanent Crisis?

A. *The Prenatal Period*

For most parents, the birth of a defective child is an unanticipated event. Consequently, the prenatal period is not significantly different from that of parents whose children are normal. Some parents are concerned, however, just as the parents of normal children are, with the possibility that their child might not be normal. Such concerns are more likely to arise when the events of a pregnancy do not fit preconceived notions or expectations based on past experience. The following mothers' observations are illustrative:

I always said if it wasn't a girl [respondent already had two normal boys], there was something wrong. It just felt different from my other pregnancies.

I felt very strongly that she was deformed . . . She didn't kick as much as I thought she should.

I thought something might be wrong because I was sick all the time and I wasn't sick at all during my first pregnancy [Darling, 1979, pp. 125–126]

In all of these cases, however, the mothers' concerns were discounted by family, friends, and physicians, and therefore most of these mothers did not really anticipate anything other than a normal baby.

With advances in technology, prenatal diagnosis has become somewhat more common in recent years. As a result of ultrasound screening and other techniques, a small minority of parents do know, prior to birth, that their baby has a problem. In one such case, the parents reported feeling "shocked, sad, and depressed" after being told that their baby's head was enlarged and that brain damage might have occurred (Darling & Darling, 1982, p. 98). However, they were also able to hope that physicians had "made a mistake." After the baby was born these parents no longer doubted the diagnosis and entered a process of adjustment similar to that experienced by parents who have no prior knowledge of their baby's defect.

The majority of parents have little knowledge of birth defects before their child is born. Childbirth preparation classes present only the situation of having a normal baby, and past socialization in this area is usually limited. These comments from parents of congenitally handicapped children are typical:

> I never heard of Down's . . . Mental retardation wasn't something you talked about in the house . . . There wasn't much exposure.

> I've heard Mongoloid—something I had read in passing in a book or something. Just a freak of nature.

> I remember thinking, before I got married, it would be the worst thing that could ever happen to me [Darling, 1979, p. 124].

Thus, most parents enter the birth situation with the expectation that events will proceed normally. Some may have fleeting concerns about the child's normality, but virtually none dwells on these concerns or thinks in terms of specific defects.

B. The Birth Situation: A Turning Point

At the outset, the birth situation in most cases is the same for parents of defective and normal children. The same degree of powerlessness is likely to be felt by all prior to the delivery of the child. Once the baby is born, however, events may differ dramatically from those of the normal birth situation.

Almost always in the case of permanently disabling defects, the true nature of the defective infant's condition is not revealed to parents immediately. Even in the case of a defect apparent at birth such as spina bifida or Down's syndrome, delivery room staff will typically deny that anything is wrong on the assumption (or pretext) that parents are "not ready" to hear the truth at this point. Parents, however, can usually pick up cues from staff behavior that do not fit the theme of "birth of a normal baby." D'Arcy (1968) and Walker (1971) note cues such as "the look on the nurse's face," consultations between nurses in hushed voices, and nurses who "looked at each other and pointed at something." The mother of a Down's Syndrome child recalled,

> I remember very vividly. The doctor did not say anything at all when the baby was born. Then he said, "It's a boy," and the way he hesitated, I immediately asked, "Is he all right?" And he said, "He has ten fingers and ten toes," so in the back of my mind I knew there was something wrong. [Darling, 1979, p. 129]

Feelings of meaninglessness and powerlessness may even be magnified by staff overreaction, as seen in this Kafkaesque experience reported by the mother of a spina bifida child:

> When the baby was born, they said, "Oh my God, put her out." That's the first thing they said, "Oh my God, put her out." . . . and the next thing I remember was waking up in the recovery room . . . I had my priest on my left hand and my pediatrician on my right hand . . . and they were trying to get me to sign a piece of paper . . . I just couldn't believe that this was happening to me and I said to my priest, "Father, what's the matter?," and he said, "You have to sign this release. Your daughter is very sick." And I said to the pediatrician, "What's the matter with her?," and he said, "Don't worry honey, she'll be dead before morning." . . . He said she had something that was too much to talk about, that I shouldn't worry myself . . . Nobody was telling me what this was . . . I was very depressed. [Darling, 1979, p. 130]

Such denial and avoidance by medical staff are likely to provoke strong feelings of anomie in parents. To make sense of events, parents sometimes try to rationalize dissonant cues. They may, for example, try to explain a baby's unusual features by attributing them to normal variation: "She had a high forehead, but my husband has a high forehead too." Other parents convince themselves that the anomalies they have observed are meaningless after all: "I really thought her ears looked funny and I had this funny feeling, so I asked the doctor, 'Is there anything wrong?' and he looked right at me and said, 'No.' So I assumed she was O.K. [Darling, 1979, p. 131]." (This mother was told the following morning that her baby was retarded). The physician's "professional dominance" typically prevails in such cases, and parents defer to the professional's expertise.

C. The Postpartum Period

Sometimes, the truth is withheld from parents for a protracted period of time. In these cases, the definition of the situation as normal becomes more and more difficult to maintain as dissonant cues accumulate:

> He was born on Tuesday, and by Thursday, I was suspicious. Nurses would come in and ask to see pictures of my first child; then they would leave quickly . . . The baby wasn't eating well, and once when a nurse came in after a feeding, I told her I was worried. She said, 'It's all due to his condition.' I asked, 'What condition?' but she just walked out . . . Then, the doctor asked me when I was going home. When I said, 'Tomorrow,' he said, 'Good. That will give us more time to observe the baby.' . . . The obstetricians kept asking if I noticed any difference between Joey and my first baby [reported in Darling, 1979, p. 129].

A high degree of meaninglessness is likely to prevail in such a situation. In a study of mothers of children with Down's syndrome, Carr (1970) found that half of those told within the first week would have like to have been told even sooner. The earlier they were told, the more satisfied they were.

In some cases, physicians continue to procrastinate in informing parents for several months after a defective child is born. These cases usually involve developmental problems such as cerebral palsy or nonspecific mental retardation, in which the prognosis is somewhat uncertain. In most of these cases, however, parents are aware of their children's "differentness" and feel meaninglessness when physicians continue to deny that any problem exists. Hewett (1970) noted, for example, that 90% of the mothers of cerebral palsy children she studied felt that something was wrong before a diagnosis was made.

In one such case reported by the parents of a retarded child (Darling, 1979), the mother, who was a nurse and had an older child, felt from the time of birth that something was wrong with the baby. Her daughter would not nurse, her eyes were crossing, "and she always seemed to be looking at her right side [p. 140]." The mother asked her pediatrician about the baby's vision and hearing but was told that nothing was wrong. When the baby was 3-months-old she kept falling asleep. The mother again questioned her pediatrician and was told that nothing was wrong. At 5 months, the baby began to have seizurelike periods, and the mother became increasingly concerned. Both her husband and her pediatrician continued to deny the problem. Her husband said, "I thought she was a little paranoid about it . . . When you're not home all day you don't see the (baby's) lack of activity or anything like that [p. 141]." As a result, the mother tried harder to rationalize and began blaming herself, feeling that perhaps she had been neglecting the baby in favor of her older child. Finally, when the baby was 6-months-old, the mother "broke down and started crying" in the pediatrician's office, and the physician reluctantly initiated diagnostic tests.

Occasionally, meaninglessness is resolved in stages by physicians who hint that something might be wrong and then progressively reveal more and more details about the baby's condition and prognosis (presumably in the interest of protecting the parent). This procedure typically does little to relieve parents' definitional crises, as explained by the mother of a retarded child with cerebral palsy:

> (The neurologist said), "I think I know what's wrong with your son but I'm not going to tell you because I don't want to frighten you" . . . Every time we went, they told us something else. It's my feeling that you can't really cope unless you know the whole truth . . . You can't cope in stages . . . Everyone was pablum-feeding us, and we wanted the truth [Darling, 1979, pp. 137–138, 147].[2]

Two of the most critical early turning points for parents who have not yet rationalized their situation are: (a) telling friends and relatives about the baby's defect; and (b) taking the baby out in public for the first time. When their situation does not yet have meaning for the parents themselves, they naturally have difficulty in explaining the situation to others.

Some parents postpone telling friends and relatives about a baby's defect because they "just don't want to explain." They soon realize, however, that avoiding the truth increases their feelings of isolation and anomie. As a result, most do attempt to explain their child's condition to significant others within a short time after a diagnosis has been made. As one couple said, "After a week we told people. We realized that we were going to have to live with it [Darling, 1979, p. 146]."

Although close friends and relatives are informed fairly soon, strangers are typically denied the truth at first. Most parents of handicapped infants realize, after their first uneasy attempts to take their child out in public, that even severely retarded young infants usually pass as normal. During their initial public excursions, parents often engage in various forms of "impression management" (see Darling, 1979; Voysey, 1972), such as hiding a baby's small ears with a hat or hiding deformed hands under long sleeves. Often, as the baby gets older but still looks like an infant, parents will lie about their child's age to avoid explanations. As one mother said, "I never knew whether to give his right age, because other people got embarrassed. If it was just someone in a store, I just told them how old he *looked* [Darling, 1979, p. 157]." As a result of such tactics, most strangers make only positive comments. This mother's report is typical: "In stores, people say, 'Oh, what a beautiful baby!' I want to say, 'She's a Down's baby,' but I don't [Darling, 1979, p. 155]."

As these infants get older and their defects become more obvious, parents are no longer able to pass. By then, however, most have solved their problems of meaninglessness and are more comfortable about explaining their situation to others. The majority of parents are prepared to offer a standard explanation such as "He's handicapped" or "She's brain-damaged," or, in the case of a rare defect, "Yes, it's kind of like cerebral palsy."

---

[2]The physicians in all of these cases were not deliberately attempting to increase parental anxiety. In fact, most withheld information on the assumption that the *truth* would provoke anxiety. By stalling or hinting, they felt that they were breaking the bad news of a child's defect more gently. Of course, such tactics also served to delay any direct (and uncomfortable) confrontation between parent and physician, enabling the physician to maintain control over the situation for a long period of time. See Darling, 1979, Chapter 6, for a further discussion of the physician's perspective.

Once meaning is established, most parents continue to feel powerlessness because they are given little information about treatment. With physical defects that can be medically or surgically corrected shortly after birth, physicians are likely to adopt an action orientation. They have been trained to react promptly to a problem that can be solved. When complete cure is not possible, however, physicians sometimes regard any treatment as futile. As a result, parents of permanently handicapped children often are not informed about infant stimulation or other training or therapy programs that might maximize their child's potential.

Unlike their physicians, parents of children with incurable defects do have an action orientation. They feel the need to *do something* for the child in order to alleviate the powerlessness they feel and to restore their self-esteem as parents. Consequently, they become researchers: They go to the library, they write letters to national organizations, they seek second opinions, they call everyone they know with a background in health or education. As one parent commented, "I was looking for a door at that point—somebody who could give us any help at all [Darling, 1979, p. 149]."

D. Later Infancy and Early Childhood: Emerging Adjustment Strategies

Eventually, most parents find their way to sympathetic physicians, parents' associations, appropriate literature, and helpful programs in special education, behavior modification, physical therapy, self-help training, or other areas of need. Once they find help, these parents no longer feel powerless. This mother's experience is typical:

> I met other parents of the retarded after we moved here. I felt that made the biggest difference in my life . . . Down there (where we lived before) with my husband working so much and no other families with retarded children I felt I was just singled out for something, that I was wierd. I felt a lot of isolation and bitterness . . . Meeting other parents you get practical hints—like how someone got their child to chew—that normal parents take for granted [Darling, 1979, pp. 162–163].

In a few cases, especially when children are hospitalized for long periods of time, parents continue to feel powerless as a result of professional control over their and their child's lives. As one mother of a child with spina bifida said, "We had to go to doctors, doctors, doctors . . . We never could get to know our own child . . . We got to the point where we hated doctors, we hated _____ Children's Hospital [Darling, 1979, p. 154.]" These feelings are magnified when medical procedures do not work or prove to be unnecessary. Many parents eventually become assertive and refuse to accept without question the insults of hospital bureaucracy and professional dominance.

Although almost all parents of congenitally handicapped children experience some degree of anomie during the early postpartum period, most ultimately manage to redefine the situation successfully. Much has been made in the literature of families that are unable to cope with the problems created by handicapped children. Some more recent literature (see, for example, Darling, 1979; Darling and Darling, 1982; Hewett, 1976; Voysey, 1975), however, has indicated that although such families exist, most parents learn to adjust to their nonnormative situation.

Although earlier studies suggested that the birth of a handicapped child was likely to precipitate family breakdown, more recent literature overwhelmingly suggests that marital deterioration in such cases is largely attributable to problems that existed prior to the birth of the disabled child (see, for example, Dorner, 1975; Hewett, 1976; Korn, Chess & Fernandez, 1978; Martin, 1975). In fact, some marriages seem to improve as a result of the cohesiveness necessitated by social stigma. As one mother said, "It's deepened the relationship between (my husband) and myself. Coming across a problem that can't be solved is a maturing thing [Darling, 1979, p. 172]."

Siblings also seem to be able to adjust to their atypical situation. Some studies, however, have shown adjustment difficulties among siblings, especially among older sisters who are recruited to help with child care (see, for example, Fowle, 1968; Gath, 1973; Kew, 1975). However, well-controlled studies (see, for example, Gath, 1972; Hewett, 1970) report no major differences between siblings of normal and handicapped children. Parents interviewed by the author also reported that their normal children had few interactional difficulties as a result of their handicapped brothers and sisters. In fact, many felt that normal siblings *benefited* from their situation. As one mother said, "I think my children will be better human beings . . . They will be more understanding . . . more prepared for difficulties in life . . . more loving [Darling, 1979, p. 165]."

Family adjustment is made possible through rationalization and support for these rationalizations from other parents, friends, and professionals. Voysey (1975) argues that parents are able to use a normality framework in interpreting their experiences because they are *expected* to be normal by other agencies in society. Parents' associations, magazine articles, clergy, and various helping professionals teach parents that they are not responsible for their child's defect, that having a defective child is a maturing experience, that a defective child is "special" or a "a gift from God," and that parents must work to overcome societal ignorance and stigma.

Voysey (1975) suggests that the ideology of normalization adopted by these parents contains the following elements: (*a*) acceptance of the inevitable ("It could happen to anyone"); (*b*) partial loss of the taken-for-granted ("Taking it day-to-day"—but—"Anything can happen"); (*c*) the redefinition of good and evil ("There's always someone worse off"); (*d*) the discovery of true values ("You appreciate your child's progress more when you don't just take it for granted"); (*e*) the positive value of suffering ("It brings you closer together"); and (*f*) the positive value of differentness ("It's for his own good").

Parents' definitions are shaped both by interaction with outside agencies and by interaction within the family. Outside agencies supply the rationalizations, and these are supported emotionally by the growing relationship between parents and child. Even a severely retarded child responds in some manner to parental attention, and that response becomes rewarding to parents. Just as parents of normal children, these parents come to feel needed and their self-esteem as parents grows. Thus, by the end of the first year, most parents have overcome their anomie.

Some problems do remain. Even after parents have successfully defined their situation, they must deal with others in society who continue to stigmatize their children in various ways. School systems may not admit their children to appropriate classes, physicians may refuse to treat their children, and grandparents may continue to insist that their children should have died at birth. Parents may also have to fight for services such as respite care or financial aid. Unlike normal children who become increasingly independent, the severely disabled are a continuing burden to their parents. As one mother said, "It's really like having a little baby, only he doesn't outgrow it [Darling, 1979, p. 171]." This permanent dependency could conceivably produce a continuation of the feelings of powerlessness that parents have during the first few months of their children's lives—and some parents do experience a continuing crisis of this sort.

Most parents learn, however, to place to blame for their problems on outside agencies. They come to realize that if good day care facilities were available, for example, they would have some relief from their children's permanent dependency. As a result, more and more parents are fighting for such community-based alternatives to institutionalization that would relieve them of some of their burden without affecting their self-esteem as parents. An activist orientation has, thus, become quite popular—parents' associations have evolved into lobbying organizations and assertiveness-training courses are being offered for parents of handicapped children (see, for example, Markel & Greenbaum, 1979), as parents seek to *impose* their definition of the situation on others. By becoming involved in such efforts, parents are able to overcome their feelings of powerlessness and maintain a sense of order in their lives.

E. Later Childhood and Adolescence: Long-Term Styles of Adjustment

As their children grow, parents' adjustment strategies may change. In general, the most important determinants of strategy through the life cycle are parents' perceptions or the availability of means for establishing meaning and achieving control. When means are seen as readily available, parents are likely to adopt a strategy of *normalization*. On the other hand, when the opportunity structure is perceived as limited, *crusadership* is likely to result.

Birenbaum (1970, 1971) argues that parents of retarded children seek to establish a "normal-appearing round of life," and indeed, normalization is the most common adaptation found in such families. As one father remarked, "Retardation is not number one around here. It's just something that Karen has [Darling, 1979, p. 190]." Normalization is possible after parents have passed through the "seekership" phase of the first year and have found appropriate services for their children, including responsive medical care, a satisfactory educational placement, and family acceptance.

Families who achieve normalization typically decrease their involvement in parents' associations and other support groups, although an altruistic adaptation, in which parents remain active for the sake of children other than their own, is also possible. The normalized family typically draws its support from "normal" society—accepting neighbors, an adaptable school system, and relatives who help with child care or finances. Such families are able to remain in control of their lives and to have a life style that is similar to that of others of their social status.

The normalization equilibrium is always precarious, however. At any time, society could become less accepting and threaten a family's control. A new school administrator, for example, might feel that all Down's syndrome children should be in trainable classes regardless of their abilities. Parents who believe that their Down's child is educable might at that point be faced with a confrontation with the school system if they want their child moved out of the trainable class (cf. Darling, 1979, p. 175). In such cases, anomie is typically alleviated through parental activism. Assertiveness, thus, serves to restore normalization.

Even when normalization is maintained through childhood, a child's adolescence and approaching adulthood often produce a new threat. As one father said, "We'll never reach the stage that other people reach when their children leave home, and that's depressing . . . I also wonder what will happen to Brian when he no longer looks like a child. [Darling, 1979, p. 184]." Many parents become concerned that their children will outlive them and will be institutionalized. Their old rationalization of "taking one day at a time" begins to wear thin as the future becomes the present. Most parents meet this threat by becoming active seekers once again in an attempt to find programs such as sheltered workshops or community living arrangements that will meet their child's needs on a long-term basis.

Although most parents achieve normalization during the greater part of the childhood years, some cannot easily establish normalized routines. In particular, parents whose children are multiply handicapped or are very low functioning are likely to have difficulty finding the social supports necessary for normalization. To prevent or alleviate anomie, these parents typically become involved in crusades to change society.

Crusadership takes many forms. Some parents write books in an effort to change public attitudes, some take legal action against school systems, and some march in picket lines demanding the elimination of architectural barriers. In general, these parents become *more* involved in parents' associations as their children grow older, and many are leaders of national organizations. Some writers have argued that such parental entrepreneurship results from guilt. More likely, it results from a simple lack of supportive resources preventing normalization.

Although uncommon, a final type of adaptation among parents of children with unmet needs is *resignation*. Such parents succumb to the forces of anomie and become fatalistic. Rather than trying to change society, they resign themselves to its unwelcome control over their lives. Many develop neurotic symptoms, and some even break down completely under the stress.

Parents who adopt the resignation mode are typically those who are doubly isolated: They are not supported by "normal society," and, for one reason or another, they never become integrated into alternative support groups such as parents' associations. Highly represented among such parents are those who are foreign-born, those with family problems apart from the handicapped child, those in poor health, and those living in isolated areas. In all, they constitute only a small minority of parents with disabled children.

IV. Discussion: Parents' Definitional Careers

A. Becoming a Parent: Preparation and Anomie

The situation of giving birth to a permanently disabled child is both similar to and different from the situation of giving birth to a normal child. In both cases, birth and the first postpartum months may provoke a definitional crisis. In many ways, parents of a first defective child are like all primiparae even if they have had children, because caring for a disabled child is a new experience for them. With time, parents of both normal and handicapped children are generally able to reestablish meaning and control, although the process may be simpler for the former than the latter.

In general, the literature indicates that definitional problems are likely to be more severe when parents are not adequately prepared for childbirth and/or parenting. Table 5.1 indicates the differences in anomie present in prepared and unprepared childbirth. In prepared childbirth, meaning is preserved in the case of a normal child, because events in labor and delivery proceed as expected. As some of the literature has suggested, however, powerlessness may still prevail as a result of medical control of the situation. The unprepared mother, on the other hand, is likely to experience meaninglessness, even if her child is normal, because she will be unable to interpret her contractions or the responses of the medical personnel around her within a context of progress toward delivery.

Parents of defective children are likely to experience both meaninglessness and powerlessness in the childbirth situation *regardless* of their level of preparation. Childbirth preparation classes or the experience of having had a normal child do not prepare a parent for the atypical events likely to take place after the delivery of a defective baby. Unusual remarks by or strange silences on the part of delivery room personnel do not fit the context of normal childbirth and are likely to arouse suspicion, even in parents who are well prepared.

Just as anomie in the childbirth situation will depend to some extent on the quantity and quality of parents' preparation, the degree of definitional crisis in the early postpartum months will also depend on whether parents' prior expectations are fulfilled. Table 5.2 shows the effect of preparation on the amount of anomie felt during the period following the baby's birth. In the ideal–typical case, preparation minimizes anomie for parents of normal children but has little effect when a child is defective. As Table 5.3 indicates,

TABLE 5.1
Types of Anomie Found in Different Childbirth Situations

Type of child	Prepared childbirth	Unprepared childbirth
"Normal" child	Powerlessness only	Powerlessness and meaninglessness
Defective child	Powerlessness and meaninglessness	Powerlessness and meaninglessness

TABLE 5.2

The Effect of Preparation for Parenthood on Anomie during Successive Postpartum Periods

Type of child	Time Period							
	Hospital stay		First 6 months at home		6 months–1 year		After 1 year	
	Prepared parenthood	Unprepared parenthood	Prepared parenthood	Unprepared parenthood	Prepared parenthood	Unprepared parenthood	Prepared parenthood	Unprepared parenthood
"Normal" child	In control or anomie (powerlessness only)	In control or anomie (meaninglessness and/or powerlessness)	In control	Anomie (meaninglessness and powerlessness)	In control	In control	In control	In control
Defective child	Anomie (meaninglessness and powerlessness)	Anomie (meaninglessness and powerlessness)	Anomie (meaninglessness and powerlessness)	Anomie (meaninglessness and powerlessness)	Anomie (powerlessness only)	Anomie (powerlessness only)	In control	In control

TABLE 5.3

Emergent Patterns by Type of Parenthood Preparation and Type of Child

	Time Period			
	Hospital	First 6 months	6 months–1 year	After 1 year
I. Normal child, prepared parenthood	In control→	In control→	In control→	In control
II. Normal child, unprepared parenthood	In control→	Anomie[a]→	In control→	In control
III. Defective child (prepared or unprepared parenthood)	Anomie[a]→	Anomie[a]→	Anomie[b]→	In control

[a] Meaninglessness and powerlessness
[b] Powerlessness only

three ideal–typical patterns emerge. In Type I (normal child, prepared parenthood), the parent is generally in control throughout the postpartum year. At the opposite pole, in Type III (defective child, either prepared or unprepared parenthood), anomie tends to prevail, although meaninglessness is likely to disappear before powerlessness. Finally, Type II (normal child, unprepared parenthood) lies between Types I and III: Anomie dominates the first postpartum months only. In all three types, control is likely to be restored by the end of the first postpartum year. The definitional processes marking each of these time periods will be discussed separately.

B. The Hospital Stay

As indicated earlier, the hospital stay is often the least traumatic time in the childbearing year for new parents of normal children. In contrast, the hospital stay is often the *most* traumatic time for parents whose children are not normal. The hospital stay is a plateau phase for parents of normal children; prenatal anxiety and the trauma of birth are over, yet parents do not yet have full responsibility for the care of the infant. The hospital staff is present to interpret the baby's cues, and meaninglessness is deferred as a result. Powerlessness may still be felt, however, as the needs of the individual parent are subordinated to hospital routines.

Parents of defective newborns typically experience much anomie during the hospital stay. They are surrounded by parents whose babies are normal, and they often feel slighted by the preferential attention that the hospital staff gives the other mothers. Many stay only a day or two, demanding an early discharge from their physicians. In general, the hospital stay is a time of acute self-pity, marked by feelings of anger, resentment, guilt, sorrow, mourning for the normal child that never was, and rejection of the defective child that was born instead. Parents have not yet rationalized their situation and cannot find meaning in what has happened to them.

When a diagnosis is withheld by physicians during the hospital stay, the definitional crisis is somewhat different. The parent typically suspects that something is wrong, and when these suspicions are not confirmed by the hospital staff, parents are likely to waver between anomie and rationalization. They try to assure themselves that everything is all right, but the baby's appearance or behavior and the reactions of the hospital staff tell them that everything is not all right. Both meaninglessness and powerlessness are likely to be strong in such a situation.

C. The First Months at Home

When the normal baby comes home, parents' feelings of powerlessness resulting from the hospital's domination in the care of the infant will be replaced by feelings of being in control if the parents are well prepared. Parents who have other children or who have had experience in caring for children may learn to interpret their infant's cues without undue difficulty. They will also be prepared to expect the burdens of caring for a young and highly dependent infant and the chronic fatigue that typically accompanies the first months. Certainly, some readjustment may be necessary, especially if a second child is colicky after a first child was unusually placid. However, well-prepared parents are able to rationalize the situation as one that will improve as the child grows older. Feelings of anomie are, thus, minimal.

For the unprepared parent, the first few months at home may seem quite frenzied compared to the relative calm of the hospital stay. When the continuous demands of a new baby have not been anticipated, the parents are likely to feel powerless and trapped by their new situation.

Such parents regain control over their lives in a variety of ways. Those whose self-esteem was high prior to the birth are generally able to achieve reintegration of the self most quickly. Social support is also important: Those whose marriages were strong prior to the birth are also likely to overcome the crisis fairly soon. In the case of a normal baby, social support is also likely to be forthcoming from friends, relatives, and neighbors. All of these people, in addition to medical professionals and readily available child care literature, are likely to offer advice and guidance to help parents reestablish meaning.

Finally, and perhaps most important, parents' trial and error in child care is likely to be successful. As the baby responds to parental handling, bonding develops and parents are reassured about their ability to parent.

Even when parents' efforts are not always successful, *time* is on their side. As a result of simple growth and maturity, the baby will eventually sleep through the night, alleviating parents' chronic fatigue, and even the children of the most inept parents usually start smiling by the time they are 3 months old, rewarding parents for their efforts. As the baby becomes increasingly independent, parents' freedom and control over their lives slowly returns.

Parents of defective children cannot rely on these supports that normal parents take for granted. Instead of social acceptance, they may encounter stigma from friends, relatives, and neighbors. Sometimes, strangers may be accepting, but the *fear* of stigma causes parents to withdraw from participation in social life. Readily available child care guides may also offer little help to parents whose children may not even have the basic reflexes of a normal newborn, such as sucking ability. Further, the "wait and see" attitude often taken by pediatricians does not offer concrete help for the day-to-day problems of child care that parents face and does not fulfill the parents' need to feel as though they are "doing something" for their baby. Finally, the severely impaired baby is often not as rewarding to parents because of an inability to respond to parental efforts.

Parents must, therefore, cultivate other resources to help them find meaning in their situation. The nuclear-family group may become more cohesive, or parents may look to external sources of support such as parents' groups, library research, or radical treatment programs. These sources help them to redefine their goals in terms of an ideology of acceptance. The impaired child thus becomes redefined as a "special child," and social stigma is interpreted as a psychological problem that normal people have or a form of ignorance.

Time is an unreliable ally for parents of disabled children, because some problems are never outgrown. Because parenting success cannot always be measured in terms of a child's accomplishments, these parents must substitute other criteria. As long as these parents *try* to do something for their children, their self-esteem can be maintained. Although they are aware that cure is not possible, they are likely to become involved in all kinds of treatment programs for their children and counseling programs for themselves during the early months.

D. The Later Postpartum Period

By the second half of their children's first year of life, parents of normal children have generally resolved any crisis that may have existed in the early postpartum period, *regardless* of whether they had been well prepared for parenting previously. Certainly, life is never quite the same as it was before the baby was born, but most parents eventually adjust to their new status and come to define it as a more rewarding and maturing stage of life.

By the second half of the postpartum year, most parents of handicapped children have also done some readjusting. The crisis of meaninglessness has generally been resolved (often as a result of parental pressure) by the issuance of an accurate and realistic diagnosis by a physician and by the rationalization of that diagnosis by means of a socially supported ideology of acceptance.

Anomie, in the form of powerlessness, may still remain, however, in the face of social stigma and professional dominance. As the child moves out of the family circle and continues to become involved in new interactional areas, parents' control will continue to be threatened. Confrontations may continue to occur with physicians, educators, and eventually even employers, who challenge the parents' knowledge of "what is best" for the child. Repeated confrontations of this type are likely to provoke assertive responses by parents. Even parents who are relatively shy in other interactional areas are likely to come to their own defense in order to maintain their self-esteem as parents and replace the anomie in their lives with a sense of order and control.

E. The Later Childhood and Adolescence Years

During the later childhood and adolescent periods, the major crisis facing parents of normal children is likely to result from the child's growing *independence*. Paradoxically, in the case of parents of permanently disabled children, the crisis arising at this time is likely to center around the child's continuing *dependence*. In either case, powerlessness will prevail until rationalizations and solutions are found.

For parents of normal children, rationalizations and solutions can readily be found in the media and the advice of friends and relatives. Special courses in "parent effectiveness training" are also available. Thus, parents learn to cope with their children's increasing independence by setting effective limits, finding interests outside the home for themselves, and finally by simply "letting go" and recognizing their child's independence striving as a normal, healthy process.

For parents of impaired children, four general modes of adjustment prevail during most of the childhood years. These are shown in Table 5.4.

The "altruistic" parent receives positive definitions from normal society in the form of support for and acceptance of the handicapped child. Although their own child is accepted by normal society, these parents continue to be active in parents' associations or other forms of alternative groups that promote social change for the handicapped.

The vast majority of parents adopt the "normalization" adaptation during later childhood and adolescence. These families have found enough support to overcome the effects of stigma and lead relatively normal lives. Parents' associations decline in importance for this group. Normalcy-promoting rationalizations are also common among these parents: The still-dependent adult child is defined as a "pal" rather than a burden, and the "old maid" retarded daughter becomes "a doting aunt."

The "crusadership" mode is the second most common adaptation. These parents reject normalization because it is unavailable to them. Instead, they become increasingly immersed in alternative groups of various kinds that support their efforts to bring about social change in the form of community living arrangements or other supports for the permanently dependent.

Finally, a few parents whose children are denied social acceptance do not adopt the crusadership mode because it is unavailable to them. They become resigned to their situation and may exhibit various symptoms of disturbance as a result.[3]

None of these modes of adaptation is necessarily permanent. In fact, most parents tend to fluctuate between types. Even the most active crusaders may become temporarily resigned to their situation after losing a major battle with the school system or some other agency. Fleeting periods of powerlessness are common for all parents, and feelings of resignation are likely to increase as children who remain highly dependent reach adulthood. In general, new adaptations must be made in all cases when handicapped adolescents become adults. However, most parents are eventually able to recover and resume a more controlled mode such as normalization or crusadership. Normalization becomes more attainable as society changes and creates new opportunities for handicapped children and adults through legal mandates for education, community living arrangements, and other regulations and services.

As their children grow, then, parents also grow and change. Most of all, they learn to cope by continually redefining the situation to reflect the social opportunity structure. As social opportunities increase, normalization is likely. On the other hand, when opportunities become limited, parents are likely to seek out alternative definitions that enable them to maintain their

---

[3]This typology closely parallels the "opportunity structure theory" developed by Cloward and Ohlin (1960) to account for various forms of juvenile delinquency, perhaps suggesting the universal applicability of their theory as a partial explanation of human choice behavior.

TABLE 5.4

*Modes of Adaptation among Parents of Handicapped Children
according to Type of Definition–Acceptance*[a]

Mode of Adaptation	Definition–acceptance	
	"Normal" society	Alternative subculture
I. Altruism	+	+
II. Normalization	+	−
III. Crusadership	−	+
IV. Resignation	−	−

[a] + = acceptance; − = rejection.

sense of control, and, in turn, their self-esteem. Parents of both normal and handicapped children respond to the opportunity structure in this manner; the major difference between the two is in the content of the opportunity structure and the degree of support it offers.

V. Conclusion: The Normality of the Nonnormative

Eventually, then, *all* parents, whether their children are normal or disabled, will strive to achieve meaning in and control over their situation. Parents of normal children generally achieve those goals within the first few months of their children's lives. For parents of disabled children, the process may take a little longer. In the end, however, a human tendency toward rationality seems to prevail.

The potential for human adjustment seems almost infinite. When people are prepared in advance for the situations they will face in life, adjustment usually proceeds smoothly. Even when they are not prepared at all, however, they learn to accept the unacceptable in time. Resocialization seems possible at almost any point in the life cycle, and the parent who says, "I remember thinking, before I got married, it would be the worst thing that could ever happen to me," may be the very one who achieves the greatest degree of acceptance after she gives birth to a retarded child.

Much of the early, clinical, literature on parents of handicapped children focused on parents who did *not* adjust. (See Darling, 1979 and Darling and Darling, 1982 for a further discussion of these studies.) As a result, the pathological attitudes of a small minority came to be seen as normative for all parents of the disabled. More recent studies have increasingly demonstrated that, even in a nonaccepting society, parents learn to accept. They have no choice but to accept; if they adopted society's negative attitudes, they would be forced to see themselves as failures. Looking at the adjustment process as one of learning to overcome societally imposed anomie is suggested as a more conceptually profitable alternative to the more traditional view of adjustment as a problem of coping with an individualistic neurotic reaction. As Le Masters (1957) has written, the fact that parenthood is 'normal' does not eliminate crisis. The obverse is also true: The fact that giving birth to a permanently impaired child is nonnormative does not necessitate permanent crisis.

References

Becker, H. S. *Outsiders: Studies in the sociology of deviance*. New York: Free Press, 1963.

Bigner, J. J. *Parent–child relations: An introduction to parenting*. New York: Macmillan, 1979.

Birenbaum, A. On managing a courtesy stigma. *Journal of Health and Social Behavior*, 1970, *11*, 196–206.

Birenbaum, A. The mentally retarded child in the home and the family cycle. *Journal of Health and Social Behavior*, 1971, *12*, 55–65.

Carr, J. Mongolism—telling the parents. *Developmental Medicine and Child Neurology*, 1970, *12*, 213.

Cloward, R. A., & Ohlin, L. E. *Delinquency and opportunity*. New York: Free Press, 1960.

Danziger, S. K. Treatment of women in childbirth: Implications for family beginnings. *American Journal of Public Health*, 1979, *69*, 895–901.

D'Arcy, E. Congenital defects: Mothers' reactions to first information. *British Medical Journal*, 1968, *3*, 796–798.

Darling, R. B. *Families against society: A study of reactions to children with birth defects*. Beverly Hills, Calif.: Sage, 1979.

Darling, R. B. and Darling, J. *Children who are different: Meeting the challenges of birth defects in society*. St. Louis: C. V. Mosby, 1982.

Doering, S. G., Entwisle, D. R., & Quinlan, D. Modeling the quality of women's birth experience. *Journal of Health and Social Behavior*, 1980, *21*, 12–21.

Dorner, S. The relationship of physical handicap to stress in families with an adolescent with spina bifida. *Developmental Medicine and Child Neurology*, 1975, *17*, 765–776.

Dyer, E. D. Parenthood as crisis: A re-study. *Marriage and Family Living*, 1963, *25*, 196–201.

Erikson, E. *Childhood and society*. New York: Norton, 1950.

Fowle, C. M. The effect of the severely mentally retarded child on the family. *American Journal of Mental Deficiency*, 1968, *73*, 468–473.

Gath, A. The mental health of siblings of congenitally abnormal children. *Journal of Child Psychology and Psychiatry*, 1972, *13*, 211–218.

Gath, A. The school age siblings of mongol children. *British Journal of Psychiatry*, 1973, *123*, 161–167.

Hewett, S. *The family and the handicapped child: A study of cerebral palsied children in their homes*. Chicago: Aldine, 1970.

Hewett, S. Research on families with handicapped children—an aid or an impediment to understanding? *Birth Defects: Original Article Series*. New York: The National Foundation, 1976, *12*(4), 35–46.

Hobbs, D. F. Parenthood as crisis: A third study. *Marriage and Family Living*, 1965, *27*, 367–372.

Kew, S. *Handicap and family crisis: A study of the siblings of handicapped children*. London: Pitman, 1975.

Korn, S. J., Chess, S., & Fernandez, P. The impact of children's physical handicaps on marital quality and family interaction. In R. M. Lerner and G. B. Spanier (Eds.), *Child influences on marital and family interaction*. New York: Academic Press, 1978.

La Rossa, R. *Conflict and power in marriage: Expecting the first child*. Beverly Hills, Calif.: Sage, 1977.

Larsen, V. L. Stresses of the childbearing year. *American Journal of Public Health*, 1966, *56*, 32–36.

Le Masters, E. E. Parenthood as crisis. *Marriage and Family Living*, 1957, *19*, 352–355.

Markel, G. P., & Greenbaum, J. *Parents are to be seen and heard: Assertiveness and educational planning for handicapped children*. San Luis Obispo, Calif.: Impact, 1979.

Martin, P. Marital breakdown in families of patients with spina bifida cystica. *Developmental Medicine and Child Neurology*, 1975, *17*, 757–764.

McHugh, P. *Defining the situation*. Indianapolis: Bobbs-Merrill, 1968.

Meyerowitz, J. H., & Feldman, H. Transition to parenthood. *Psychiatric Research Reports*, 1966, *20*, 78–84.

Miller, R. S. The social construction and reconstruction of physiological events: Acquiring the pregnant identity. In Norman Denzin (Ed.), *Studies in symbolic interaction*. Greenwich, Conn.: JAI Press, 1977.

Norr, K. L., Block, C. R., Charles, A., Meyering, S., & Meyers, E. Explaining pain and enjoyment in childbirth. *Journal of Health and Social Behavior*, 1977, *18*, 260–275.

Rollins, B., & Feldman, H. Marital satisfaction over the family life cycle. *Journal of Marriage and the Family*, 1970, *32*, 20–28.

Rosengren, W. R. The sick role during pregnancy: A note on research in progress. *Journal of Health and Human Behavior*, 1962, *3*, 213–218.

Rothman, B. K. Childbirth as negotiated reality. *Symbolic Interaction*, 1978, *1*, 124–137.

Shainess, N. The structure of the mothering encounter. *Journal of Nervous and Mental Disease*, 1963, *136*, 146–161.

Shereshefsky, P. M., Liebenberg, B., & Lockman, R. F. Maternal adaptation. In P. M. Shereshefsky and L. J. Yarrow (Eds.), *Psychological aspects of a first pregnancy and early postnatal adaptation*. New York: Raven, 1973.

Voysey, M. Impression management by parents with disabled children. *Journal of Health and Social Behavior*, 1972, *13*, 80–89.

Voysey, M. *A constant burden: The reconstitution of family life*. London: Routledge and Kegan Paul, 1975.

Walker, J. H. Spina bifida—and the parents. *Developmental Medicine and Child Neurology*, 1971, *13*, 462–476.

Wiener, C., Strauss, A., Fagerhaugh, S., & Suczek, B. Trajectories, biographies and the evolving medical technology scene: Labor and delivery and the intensive care nursery. *Sociology of Health and Illness*, 1979, *1*, 261–283.

CHAPTER 6

Fetal Loss and Sudden Infant Death: Grieving and Adjustment for Families

EDWARD J. CALLAHAN
WILLIAM S. BRASTED
JUAN L. GRANADOS
WEST VIRGINIA UNIVERSITY
MORGANTOWN, WEST VIRGINIA

The death of a child is typically a disruptive and emotionally intense event for the family. Children are simply not supposed to die, yet many do. How such deaths affect the family and, more specifically, the parents is the focus of this chapter. We hope to demonstrate that the specific effects of a child's death on a family depend on such factors as preparation, prior exposure to death, and how the death is handled by hospital personnel, the extended family, and friends.

The particular kinds of death that are of interest here are prenatal, neonatal, perinatal, and sudden infant death. *Prenatal deaths* involve all forms of death before birth and include: (*a*) abortion, which refers to the loss of any pregnancy under 20 weeks gestation or any fetus weighing less than 500 grams (this includes both spontaneous and induced abortions, though we will restrict our discussion to the former); and (*b*) fetal death, which is the death in utero of any fetus between 20 weeks gestation and term (40 weeks), or the death of any fetus weighing more than 500 grams. *Neonatal deaths* include the deaths of any infant born alive who dies before 1 month of age. A further distinction in terms that should be noted involves *perinatal deaths*, which include both fetal and neonatal deaths. Finally, *sudden infant deaths*

LIFE-SPAN DEVELOPMENTAL PSYCHOLOGY
Nonnormative Life Events

are quickly occurring infant deaths attributed to Sudden Infant Death Syndrome (SIDS), which describes the sudden, unexplained loss of any infant not attributable to trauma or recognizable illness. SIDS usually occurs between 2 and 3 months of life.

Each of these types of deaths occur very early in the lifespan during the period when parents are typically bonding to their offspring as he or she progresses through the most rapid stage of growth. Suddenly, and often unexpectedly, parents must shift from bonding to their child to a process of grieving not only for the literal reality of their infant but also for their perceptions of the person who their child would have become.

The family must often deal with this tragedy alone, since few others have lost a child. Thus, in view of the uniqueness of the event, such deaths might be considered nonnormative. However, determining what is a nonnormative life event is a difficult and controversial task. An event may be nonnormative because it is statistically infrequent, because it is culturally proscribed, or because it has a disruptive impact on the family (see Burgess et al., Chapter 4, this volume). On each of these criteria, the death of a fetus or infant is a nonnormative life event. In this chapter we will examine these forms of early death and how they affect both families and professionals. We will discuss these issues from both a theoretical and a practical standpoint evolved from working with parents who have experienced such losses and the medical personnel involved as well. We will attempt to integrate these experiences with the theoretical and scant empirical work of others and to lay out a practical and useful analysis of prenatal death, neonatal loss, and Sudden Infant Death syndrome as nonnormative life events. Let us look first at commonalities and differences in early loss.

There are several commonalities as well as several differences in these early life tragedies. First, the incidence of each is much greater than is ordinarily assumed. Some contend that one-third of all conceptions fail to result in a viable child (Peppers & Knapp, 1980). Perinatal deaths occur in about 8 per 1000 births, whereas the incidence of Sudden Infant Death syndrome is 1 in every 450 infants (Limerick, 1979). Though the data indicate that these deaths are relatively frequent occurrences, in most cases family and friends are reluctant to talk about the problem openly. This results in an underestimation of the incidence by family members who feel quite alone ("I don't know anyone who has lost a child to SIDS").

A second similarity among these forms of early loss is that the cause of death is often unknown. No clear cause is usually apparent in first trimester abortions (those less than 14 weeks gestation). Fetal death can be caused by a placental abruption (a significant mass of placenta separating from the uterine wall), but the cause of such abruptions is usually unknown. Death of an infant due to SIDS is now an acceptable legal cause of death, but it does not say why the child has stopped breathing. Indeed, the mystery of cause is a hallmark of the syndrome.

Since scientific causes are not discovered, these problems are similar in a third sense: old wives' tales have sprung up to fill in the etiological void. Women who have miscarried are told they have done so because they did not want the child enough; the mother of an infant delivered dead with its cord around its neck is told she caused it by stretching for items on high shelves; the family cat is said to have sucked away the breath of the SIDS infant. In these instances, the need to understand *why* unexpected death has occurred often overshadows the response of helping the parents. The price for "understanding" a death that cannot be explained is often great: Irrational blame is often laid because of the need to understand. Thus it can lead one parent to accuse the other of neglect or abuse, or it can elicit similar accusations at both parents by family and friends. Unfortunately, such accusations erode the support network parents need so desperately at that time.

This erosion of the support is further enhanced by a fourth factor common to these losses: Professionals, family members, and friends often lack the skills to talk about the death. In these cases, the uncommonness of the death means that people have few opportunities to learn how to talk about the loss. Because of the sensitivity of the issue, much of the talk is done privately, depriving young medical students and residents of the chance to observe skilled models discuss death. Professionals often are sorely pressed for time; painful discussions are easily avoided by becoming immersed in a busy schedule. Finally, professionals, families, and friends cannot be sure whether it is better to avoid the topic or to bring the grieving parent into contact with the loss again. In fact, appealing to the painfulness of the discussions for the other person is an avenue especially valued by anyone feeling a lack of skills in the area.

Thus, there are many similarities among these types of early losses. There are also significant differences that deserve attention. First, prenatal and neonatal deaths are much more common than SIDS. More support will be available from others who have undergone a similar loss. That support may well ease the grieving process and the disruption of one's life. Second, the child lost in a SIDS death is older, better known to the parents and to family and friends. This greater realism of the child means that fewer people will claim that a SIDS infant was not really a person, whereas such a claim is often made in cases of abortion or perinatal death. Third, there is greater variability in the developmental age of the fetus in prenatal loss, whereas the loss of a SIDS infant usually occurs in the second to third month of life. This also distinguishes prenatal from neonatal and SIDS death because there is a greater distinction between a loss at 6 weeks gestation and 38 weeks gestation than between a 6-week-old infant and a 38-week-old infant. A fetus more than 20 weeks gestational age (fetal death) is likely to be buried with some ceremony, whereas a loss before 20 weeks (abortion) is rarely accorded such status. With the loss of such status, the early loss is less likely to be adequately grieved. A fourth distinction is related to the parents' support group. As the gestational age of the pregnancy increases, the size of the support group aware of the pregnancy increases.

Let us turn now to consideration of grief and how it might be different in a nonnormative loss (fetus or infant) versus a normative loss (e.g., that of an elderly parent, grandparent). This discussion is essentially theoretical, and as such may appear of little practical importance. However, it is only with such a theoretical background that the salience of the practical issues can be recognized for those dealing with the death of a child.

I. Grief Defined

The occurrence of a death is rarely an isolated event. More typically, death involves numerous participants including the individual who dies and the survivors who are left to encounter the experience of grief (Toynbee, 1976). *Grief* refers to the set of cognitive, physiological, and behavioral responses elicited by a significant loss that when viewed in total represent a process through which the bereaved learns to accept and adapt to the death of a loved one (Averill, 1968). Grief is generally characterized as consisting of (*a*) an initial period of somatic distress and a perceived state of unreality; (*b*) a period of behavioral and physiological arousal involving agitated, nongoal-directed behavior; (*c*) a period of generalized sleep and appetite disturbances; and (*d*) a period of reintegration during which the individual reestablishes social contacts, career goals, etc. (e.g., Averill & Wisocki, 1981; Bowlby, 1980; Gorer, 1965; Lindeman, 1944).

Why the death of a significant other elicits the pattern of behavior referred to as grief is still an empirical question. Stage theorists (e.g., Bowlby & Parkes, 1970; Engel, 1961) have provided descriptions of the grief process but have failed to suggest why the process occurs. Behavioral psychologists have only recently begun to hypothesize reasons for the surprising uniformity of grief responses. Averill and Wisocki (1981) suggest that the concepts of reinforcement, punishment, and extinction may play a fundamental role in determining the topography of grief. *Reinforcement* refers to the process by which the occurrence of a particular behavior increases after being followed by a positive event. For example, verbal statements of emotional pain during grieving may increase because they receive the consequence of attention and sympathetic verbal responses of a particular audience. *Punishment* refers to the process by which the occurrence of a particular behavior decreases after it is followed by an aversive event. For example, a grieving person may bring up their loss with a stranger and consequently be shunned by that person. If being shunned is punishing, then the probability of the griever opening up to strangers will be decreased. *Extinction* refers to the process by which a behavior emitted by an organism that is typically reinforced (i.e., followed with a positive event) is no longer reinforced. The result of the extinction process is that the behavior will eventually no longer be emitted. For example, over time checking the baby's crib will stop because it never results in finding the baby. In the case of extinction during grief, Averill & Wisocki state:

> Following bereavement, reinforcement may be reduced for any of four different reasons: (1) customary reinforcers, e.g., those directly dependent on the presence of the deceased, may no longer be available; (2) customary reinforcers, although available, may no longer be effective, as when previously pleasurable activity becomes affectively neutral; (3) the person may no longer have the desire or ability to make the responses required to achieve reinforcement, e.g., due to apathy; or (4) the person may refrain from responding because of negative consequences, e.g., the response might serve as a painful reminder of the deceased or be the source of guilt or social criticism [p. 222].

Thus reinforcement, extinction, and punishment may explain much of the topography of grief. In fact, other writers have suggested that these concepts may be extended to account for the effect of the support network in determining grief response. Gauthier and Marshall (1977) suggest that normal grief occurs following the death of a significant other because the people in the bereaved individual's environment reinforce grieving and mourning behaviors by providing contingent sympathy and support. Eventually, these individuals reduce the support (or reinforcement) for grieving and conversely provide reinforcement for alternate, more adaptive behaviors such as renewing social contacts and activities. This results in the extinction of behaviors typically associated with the grieving period and the eventual reintegration into normal activity.

Various other factors have been implicated in further mediating the form of grief. For example, Marriss (1958) and Averill (1968) have suggested that the degree to which the survivor's role was dependent on the deceased is a crucial determinant of the topography of the grief response. Averill (1968) thus discriminates between role-loss and object-loss, with the former providing a greater disruption of behavior. Therefore, if a significant portion of one's daily activity involved interacting with and caring for the needs of the deceased, then the occurrence of the death will represent a greater disruption of one's activity than, for example, the loss of a relative who one rarely saw.

Hence, in the case of an infant's death, there is typically a more profound effect on the mother than the father (e.g., Benfield, Leib, & Vollman, 1978), which may be related to the fact that mothers are usually more involved with the daily routines of raising an infant. Similarly, there is often a more difficult adjustment for the woman who loses her fetus after leaving work than for the woman who has not yet left her job.

Another factor involved in the topography of grief is one's prior exposure to death. In the human life span one typically has little exposure to death while young, but as we age death becomes a more frequent event. First, we experience the death of grandparents, later parents and friends, and eventually we may experience the death of a spouse. Thus, most persons are gradually exposed to more significant deaths. Perhaps this gradual exposure allows for the occurrence of an adaptation process, which is reflected in the fact that elderly people exhibit flatter or less dramatic responses to the loss of a spouse than do younger people (e.g., Parkes, 1964; Skelskie, 1975). It is interesting that animal studies have demonstrated that gradual exposure to aversive stimuli results in a decrease in the effectiveness of the aversive event (i.e., adaptation); that is, if an organism has repeated, gradually intensifying exposure to an aversive event, that aversive event will prove less disruptive to behavior (e.g., Karsh, 1963; Miller, 1960). Thus, parents of infants are usually at an age when death has not yet become a frequently encountered event. They are essentially robbed of the graduated experience and are immediately faced with perhaps the most significant death they will ever experience. In fact, this experience might even result in increasing the disruptiveness of later deaths of older relatives or friends, which is referred to as a sensitization process.

In experimental psychology literature, *sensitization* describes the process of an aversive event becoming more disruptive, suppressing more ongoing behavior, after an animal has experience with an extremely intense form of the event. For example, before sensitization a .1-ma shock might not disrupt the barpressing of a rat for food. After the rat experiences a .9-ma shock, however, later presentations of .1-ma shocks disrupt barpressing much more than shock presentation with preexposure (cf. Catania, 1973). In the human analogue, early infant loss might cause parents to become quite disrupted by deaths of family members or friends occurring after the loss of their fetus or infant, because of the intense nature of their first experience with death. This might be displayed by avoiding funerals and cemeteries; in one extremely severe instance, one of our clients became obsessed that she herself was going to die. This occurred 3 months after the loss of an 18-week-old fetus—a loss she refused to consider "real" or to tell her 3-year-old daughter about.

The distinction between adaptation and sensitization may reflect an important difference in the effects of nonnormative versus normative deaths. Normative deaths typically occur later in the life span and are thus likely to produce an adaptation effect. However, nonnormative deaths occur early in the life span and are more likely to produce a sensitization effect because they are significant and because they can occur before any natural adaptation process prepares parents for such deaths.

Thus far, we have discussed some theoretical issues based on experimental animal literature that appear to be important in the explanation of grief expressed by the individual. Before discussing the actual research findings concerning the effects of infant deaths, we will briefly consider theoretical issues derived from sociobiological literature that will hopefully illuminate some functions of grief within a social arena.

Averill (1968) and others (e.g., Bowlby, 1961; Rosenblatt, Walsh, & Jackson, 1976) suggest that grief may play an adaptive role in all social-living species whose survival depends on the existence of social networks such as families and prolonged mother–infant relationships. For example, if grief is a painful biological state that is elicited by the loss of significant others, then it would be likely that group members would work to avoid the loss of members. This would make it less likely that a member of a particular social network would permanently leave the network. Further, the potential effects of grief on the mother–infant relationship is important for species survival. When separation occurs, the aversive consequences of loss function to motivate the mother to search for the lost child. Therefore, the probability of prolonged care for the infant is enhanced. In both cases the consequences of grief function to elicit searching for the lost object. However, when a significant person dies, such as a spouse or child, behaviors such as searching cannot function to avoid grief forever, and thus grief must play out its natural course.

In support of this concept, Averill (1968) refers to numerous articles that demonstrate that various species of higher primates evidence grief reactions similar to that seen in humans. He summarizes these by stating: "At first there is typically an unwillingness to relinquish the lost object: This may be followed by restlessness and/or apathy, withdrawal, aggression directed towards self and others, a loss of appetite and sexual interest, an inability to establish new relationships, and so forth [p. 731]." Averill indicates that numerous authors have reported the presence of some or all of these components in various species such as chimpanzees (Yerkes & Yerkes, 1929), orangutans (Zedwitz, 1930), baboons (Zuckerman, 1932), rhesus monkeys (Tinkelpaugh, 1928), dogs (Bowlby, 1961), and geese (Lorenz, 1966). Furthermore, in each of these species, social organization and the mother–infant relationship appear to play a primary role in species survival.

In fact, some early behavior following an infant's death resembles looking for a lost child. This sort of seeking is found in the early stages of grieving (Lindemann, 1944). The strength of this searching for the dead infant can be seen as bizarre or maladaptive; more simply, though, the behavior may be akin to an extinction burst in the laboratory. In an extinction burst, an animal works much harder than usual for a reward soon after the reward is discontinued. Similarly, bereaved parents tell us of their repeated checks on the empty crib vacated by a SIDS loss. Mothers carrying dead fetuses in utero report continuing to feel kicks and hope to deliver a live baby. For some of our clients, these kicks were even experienced for a time after the delivery. All of these are behaviors oriented to keeping the infant or fetus alive—or toward denying his or her death.

Now that some basis (albeit tentative) has been established for considering grief as a family experience, let us now look at research in the area of grieving.

II. Research Findings

There is a dearth of actual research findings evaluating the specific effects of the loss of a fetus or infant on parents and other family members. Perhaps the major reasons for this are the numerous difficulties inherent in working with such a population. To begin, serious ethical issues confront researchers wishing to examine the phenomenon of grief. There is a fear that assessments of the impact of a child's death may have deleterious effects on the family's psychological well-being. Perhaps this is only a professional version of the awkwardness most people experience in discussing a loss with the bereaved. Just as family and friends may rationalize their avoidance of a bereaved individual, so psychologists may rationalize not studying grief because it may violate privacy. In fact, however, Parkes (1964) suggests that the subjects in his studies evaluating the effects of loss of spouse on widows indicated that discussing their losses was reported to be beneficial. SIDS parents have pointed out that talking to other parents who have lost a child to SIDS helped them accept their own loss better. Interestingly, though, SIDS parents who filled out questionnaires for us universally offered to help others; none asked for someone to talk to them. Perhaps helping others is a socially acceptable way of trying to deal with one's own distress.

Another problem facing researchers is the apparent discomfort in dealing with death found in Western culture in general. Today, death typically occurs in hospitals in out-of-the-way rooms surrounded by hushed voices. Even within the hospital, death is most often discussed as a failure of medical technology, not as a pressing human experience. This removal of death from everyday existence appears to have created an aura of privacy and secrecy. The result of this for research is that medical personnel are often reluctant to reveal the identity of the individuals who have experienced an abortion, perinatal loss, or SIDS death. Realistically, such reluctance also reflects the need for sensitivity in dealing with families during such a crisis. Thus, it is often difficult for researchers to find an adequate population with which to work.

The sublimation of death also has effects for potential clinical researchers themselves. Death is a difficult topic to confront, and as such it is not a pleasant task to interview individuals who are experiencing this trauma. It was an interesting realization to us that we often read charts more thoroughly and consulted others at greater length before talking to grieving parents. This might be justified by pointing out that accurate information is needed before talking to grieving parents. Such an explanation does not cover the sudden strong need for a cup of coffee at this point, however. Avoidance is a far simpler explanation.

Thus clinicians and researchers must deal with their own feelings concerning death to confront others' experiences openly. Additionally, there is little data to suggest how one should go about the business of evaluating grief; researchers have few models to mold their efforts.

Fortunately, in the past 10 years scientists have begun to transcend these difficulties and there is now an expanding literature concerning the phenomenon of grief. The majority of this work has been done using interview formats in which subjects are asked to recollect their experiences following their child's death. Though this type of retrospective evaluation is known to be subject to bias and distortion (e.g., Sherman, Trief, & Sprafkin, 1975), it is perhaps the most ethically justifiable method for data collection considering the sensitivity of the issue.

The previous discussion of the problems in doing valid research in grief is not meant to discredit what findings are available. Rather, it is meant to suggest that the reader should be wary of the findings and should remember that individual variation will occur. What is presented here is a *somewhat* typical set of responses to these deaths. Taking any description of the grief process as absolute is a serious error—it denies the validity and normality of idiosyncratic responses to loss. Bearing that in mind, let us look at the "usual" process of grief in abortion, neonatal death, and SIDS loss.

III. The Grieving Process

The immediate effects of determining that a fetal demise or SIDS death has occurred is similar to that seen in normal grief. There is an immediate reaction of shock, disbelief, and typically anger (e.g., Helmrath & Sternitz, 1978; Kowalski, 1980; Smialek, 1978). The disbelief can be evidenced by repeated attempts to have the physician check again, as in the case of abortion and fetal demise, or repeated attempts to revive the baby in the case of SIDS. The anger can be directed in numerous directions such as toward the health care professional, one's spouse or oneself for allowing the death to occur, toward God for taking the child (if parents are religious), and even toward the infant for dying.

After a short period of time, which can vary from hours to weeks, the death becomes a reality to the parents and the denial phase ends. At this time (or earlier) a new set of problems arises. Typically, parents begin to express extreme guilt over the death (e.g., DeFrain & Ernest, 1978; Kennell, Slyter, & Klaus, 1970; Smialek, 1978). The guilt is usually based on perceptions of past faults that may have caused the death. For example, parents of stillborns will search through the period of the pregnancy and determine things they did that may have been harmful. If there were any such events, they may focus on these as the cause of the baby's death (e.g., "I didn't want the baby enough and that's why he died," or "I knew I shouldn't have made love that night—it ended the pregnancy.") Parents of SIDS infants will typically express guilt over more immediate problems such as leaving the baby alone in his or her room, or leaving the baby with a babysitter. In one case, a mother recounted to us that she had stayed up most of the night with her cranky infant and then had lain down. Her intent was to check the baby once again before going to sleep. Instead she awoke to find her daughter dead, and consequently she ruminated "If only I had checked once more . . . "

Concurrent with dealing with their own guilt, parents must also face external problems: Interacting with other family and friends. Dealing with others has been reported to be one of the most difficult aspects of the grieving period (e.g., DeFrain & Ernst, 1978; Helmrath & Sternitz, 1978). Because the death of an infant is even more atypical for laymen than professionals in a medical setting, people simply do not know how to respond to parents experiencing their child's demise. Thus, they either will avoid the parents altogether or they will avoid the issue when attempting to interact with the parents. Helmrath & Sternitz (1978) have referred to this aspect as the "conspiracy of silence." Yet another common response of families and friends to parents, especially in the case of stillbirth, is to gloss over the problem. Such statements as, "It's OK, you can always have another," are common. Two parents reported being told "It's OK, you have another at home" when in fact they had no other children. This minimization of the problem serves only to isolate the parents further. In the case of SIDS, outsiders often intimate that the parents are to blame (e.g., DeFrain & Ernest, 1978). Among the SIDS parents we dealt with, such stories were common. In one case, a local newspaper published a report that the mother left her child unattended in a hot, closed car before its death. Only 2 years of litigation and several eyewitnesses convinced the newspaper to brand the story an error and print a short retraction buried in the entrails of the paper. The original story, however, had made the front page and still follows the parents. Such accusations serve only to increase the irrational guilt that is already present.

Problems can also arise within the relationship. Individuals respond differently to grief, and thus one parent may wonder why the other is not experiencing the death in the "right" way: "You should be feeling what I am feeling now." Without good communication skills, such misunderstanding can end the marriage. Also, in our society there is a tendency for males to assume the role of protector, to be the "strong one." In our experience, men are not alone in this trap. Either partner may decide to protect the other, and thus not take time to feel the grief. This also appears to exacerbate the differences between spouses' reactions and may enhance communication problems. In fact, in a rare study of fathers' reactions to their infants' death Mandell, McAnulty, and Reese (1980) found that most fathers reported a need to be strong for their wives. They additionally reported increasing their involvement in activities outside the home while also feeling diminished self-worth; their adjustment was further marked by a tendency to intellectualize their grief. These factors led to problems in the relationship that eventually led to 6 of the 28 subjects reporting severe marital dysfunctions.

Other sources have reported subsequent marital dysfunctions (e.g., Davis, 1975; Kubler-Ross, Note 1). However, it should not be assumed that the death of an infant will result in marital problems. For example, all seven couples interviewed by Helmrath and Sternitz (1978) reported that they perceived their relationship as having improved. Thus, it may be that couples who have communication difficulties already may see these problems increase as a result of the crisis. Those who have good communication skills at the point of the loss may find that the crisis enhances the use of these skills and results in an overall improvement of their marital bonding.

One must also ask how long grief will last. Once again longitudinal responses to loss of an infant appear to mirror the effects in other forms of grief. Though the death is never forgotten, the acute stages of grief appear to subside after a period of months, and by the end of a year most parents have been reintegrated into normal behavior patterns. This was validated in a cross-sectional study by DeFrain and Ernst (1978) in which they interviewed 50 parents at various times following their infant's death. However, it should be noted that some effects never subside. For example, Davis (1975) reports that many couples determine never to have more children. Other couples find themselves unable to conceive another child within the first year after the loss. Perhaps this reflects the sensitization to death that we described earlier. In this case, the new fear of death is so great that parents are afraid to have other children.

This section has attempted to present a "clinical picture" of the grieving parent. It cannot be assumed that a particular response pattern will occur in every individual experiencing a child's death. In fact, that individual variation is probably more the rule than the exception is an essential point for clinicians dealing with families. The understanding of parental grief would be incomplete without considering the amount of bonding (Klaus and Kennel, 1976) that parents have engaged in with their child and what effects the loss has on siblings.

IV. Bonding and Grieving

Bonding is the process of establishing positive emotional ties with a child. In an important early study, Klaus, Kennel, Plumb, and Zuehlke (1970), reported that early mother–child skin-to-skin contact appeared to facilitate bonding. The absence of good evidence of bonding (parent–child eye contact, talking, cuddling) may indicate an increased probability of child abuse (Lynch & Roberts, 1977). Premature children may be more difficult to bond with: There is often little opportunity to hold and touch the child while important life-monitoring procedures continue. Infant responsiveness is also depressed. The experience of dealing with a prolonged stay in neonatal intensive care is difficult for most parents. One mother in our sample had experienced both neonatal death of her first child and intensive care for her second child; she reported that the death was easier to deal with.

What is bonding? The Klaus and Kennel (1976) definition resembles that of imprinting. That is, it is described as a possible biochemical process that ties the parent, usually the mother, closely to the child in the early hours after birth. Other research suggests that bonding can occur strongly and well at any of several points after birth (Campbell and Taylor, 1979; Svejda, Campos and Emde, 1980; Svejda, Pannabacker and Emde, 1982). However, these definitions do not explain bonding before birth.

Perhaps a parsimonious, nonbiochemical explanation of bonding is possible. Bonding appears to be an increase in verbal and physical demonstrations of concern for another that increase in probability with repeated occurrence of exchange of reinforcers. The presence of the fetus can and usually does result in an increased availability of social reinforcers for the parent. Let us look first at fetal loss through pregnancy and birth to consider the development of a parent–child bond and how such bonding may contribute to the strength of the grief reaction. After considering this issue with abortion and prenatal loss, let us look at the same process with SIDS loss. In this way we can integrate the age of the child (from conception through approximately 4 months) and the effects on bonding and grieving.

Although up to one-third of all conceptions do not result in a live birth (Peppers & Knapp, 1980), these losses are not distributed evenly across the 40-week gestation period. The most common losses occur before 10 weeks of gestation; some of these occur so early (i.e., 4 to 6 weeks after the last menstrual period) that there is often no assurance that pregnancy has indeed occurred. Without such assurance, little bonding can occur because little outside reinforcement is yet available. Such early losses do not appear to result in as much grieving as later losses. Indeed, women grieving such losses would be unlikely to gain much social support. The loss is also likely to be kept private, since the pregnancy is unlikely to have been announced. The likelihood of social support increases throughout the pregnancy and infancy. Concurrent with increases in social support are progressive steps in parent–child bonding.

Several factors appear important in the process of parents bonding with their unborn child. First, confirmation of the pregnancy, usually by a physician, makes the event real. Second, announcing the pregnancy to friends and relatives establishes a basis for a support network through the pregnancy. Third, feeling movement for the first time further reifies a child whose existence may not yet be confirmed by a clothing change. The father's feeling of the child's movement makes the pregnancy more real for him as well. The child can reward the father's placement of his hand on the mother's stomach by kicking hard enough for him to feel. This in turn can increase the amount of close physical contact and talking between the couple. Each of these steps involves the infant becoming more real to the parents and facilitating bonding with the child. The fetus is now the occasion for reinforcement for the parents. "Congratulations" are heard, pregnancy stories told, and overall attention for both parents, especially for the mother, increases. Some of this attention may have its roots in protecting the mother from increased risk of fetal loss through straining, heavy exercise, or even tasks only superstitiously related to fetal losses.

Next, the mother may begin to wear maternity clothes. This changes her image considerably and announces her pregnancy to all who see her. Later, the couple begins acquiring furniture and clothing for the baby, considering names and making plans for the birth. Finally, the mother may leave her job in preparation for the birth of the child. As the couple experiences the child more and changes their behavior in expectation of its birth, social rewards increase. As the reinforcement generated by the pregnancy increases, bonding to the child increases. Further, grieving appears to become more intense as loss of reinforcers increases.

In addition, as the gestational age of the child advances, the likelihood of the support system accepting the child as a real person increases. The medical profession, for example, describes maternal history in terms of "gravidity" and "parity." "Gravida one," for example, indicates a first pregnancy. "Para one," however, indicates that the woman has carried one pregnancy to at least 20 weeks gestation. A pregnancy not reaching 20 weeks (an abortion) is not counted in such a description. Thus, the medical profession views the pregnancy differently after the twentieth week of gestation; the mother is then seen to have carried a child whether the child lives or not.

This change in attitude is paralleled by a change in how the body of the infant is dealt with. It is rare that a fetus lost before 20 weeks is named or buried, though these social rituals appear to be important in sanctioning and releasing grief of the parents. The absence of these procedures increases the likelihood of inadequate grieving. Thus, while less bonding occurs with earlier losses, less effective grieving releasers (e.g., funerals) are made available as well. Yet, it should also be noted that the absence of more effective grief-releasing techniques may only mean that such techniques are not needed. Each case is individual, however, and it may be important for some parents to bury an aborted fetus, whereas other parents may allow the hospital to dispose of an older fetus.

The likelihood of rewards and punishments from the support system or "extended family" varies here with the gestational age also. The mourning grandmother's experience of denial can translate to "that wasn't really a child you were carrying; it was only 16 weeks so you weren't really even pregnant." Such responses became less likely in our sample as gestational age approached 28 weeks—the age at which more premature infants survive than die.

Thus, before birth the amount of bonding that occurs seems to depend more on social system reinforcement than on the behavior of the fetus itself. However, the fetus's behavior can also affect bonding of the parents. The fetus's kicks and heartbeats, which can be first heard by stethoscope and later on by ear, contribute to the bond reinforcement.

Using this conceptualization, bonding is more likely when the social system and the fetus provide rewards to the mother during the pregnancy. It is also possible that the social system and the fetus can provide punishment for the mother. For example, a child conceived out of wedlock has traditionally resulted in upset for the mother—perhaps even her hiding away for the duration of the pregnancy. In a parallel way, some pregnancies result in excessive vomiting (hyperemesis gravidarum) or other physical discomfort for the mother. If these aversive events outweigh the positive support and physical reinforcers gained during the pregnancy, bonding may well be tenuous or nonexistent. Such occurrences may indicate an increased likelihood of poor prenatal self-care, placing a child for adoption, or later child abuse.

If the bonding that occurs is lessened, does this indicate less need for grieving? Unfortunately, the answer to this is not simple. In some of the cases we have seen, the lessened bonding predicts lessened disruption due to the fetus's demise; lessened grieving, but essentially no untoward long-term sequelae. However, other cases have shown a clear complication: Maternal guilt over not having loved the unborn child enough can complicate the grieving process. In fact, the mother may feel that, if she were a good mother, she would feel the loss more intensely. Or, as stated earlier, she may feel that her inadequate love for the child caused it to die. Overall, a strong prenatal bond appears to predict both more intense grief and a better long-term adjustment. Perhaps, if grief is a biological process as Averill (1968) suggests, it is a more complete and healthy process under conditions facilitating its full expression. Good bonding, appropriate to the point of development of the pregnancy, may well predict the optimal intensity and duration of grieving.

A new level of bonding occurs at birth. Although bonding increases with the birth of the child, the increase is also consonant with the increase in reinforcement available to the parents. At birth, reinforcement increases substantially. There is now a visual stimulus more recognizable than an enlarged stomach and kicks. For many, the birth process is experienced as an exhilarating experience. After birth, the child can be touched; touching appears to be a critical component in relating (Montagu, 1971) and an important conditioned reinforcer (touching is involved in early feeding, early comforting, and many later positive interpersonal contacts). The child can now make eye contact, track voices, make noise, and quiet down with comforting. Through birth the child has increased his or her capacity to reinforce his or her parents.

The birth is a signal for other increases in reinforcement: flowers, visits to the hospital, congratulatory cards, and gifts. The social system intensifies contact with the new parents. Parents of premature or handicapped infants experience concurrent aversive events as well, however. They must deal with an unusual looking child who does not meet their expectations or those of significant others. They must pay increased bills to maintain the life or increase the health of their infant. They do not receive the usual adulation from others for their child. As Darling (Chapter 5, this volume) points out, the birth of a handicapped child is usually attended by awkward silence in the delivery room, looks of upset, and little or no verbal explanation. Thus, bonding can be hindered. This may be important in those SIDS cases in which the child was born prematurely.

While the frequency of SIDS is higher in premature infants than in full-term births, the majority of SIDS infants are still full-term. The most common time of SIDS death is 2 to 3 months of age.

During the first 2 to 3 months of life, most infants make substantial progress. It is likely that they will learn to smile and coo at the parents. They will establish particular behavior patterns with their parents in terms of eating and sleeping. Parents, in turn, begin to understand how to predict and control the behavior of the infant, which also increases bonding. The control of infant behavior is far from complete, however, as all parents experience some exasperation with their infant. Such exasperation makes sense: The total amount of reinforcement an infant can provide is far outweighed by intense and virtually continuous demands. Most parents decrease their social contact during this period in order to provide for their infant's needs, and thus they experience some decrease in available reinforcement. The toll of parenthood often leads to some feelings of disenchantment with the role. When the death of a SIDS child is immediately preceeded by strong resentment from the parents, guilt is a likely end product.

Again, in all problems of unknown etiology, people are likely to establish and accept particular hypotheses about why the problem occurred. Thus far, we have discussed grief as it relates to parents. In the next section we will turn to a consideration of the effects of grief on other family members, such as siblings, and on professionals.

V. Sibling Reactions

Sibling reactions to death can be more complex than adult reactions. This may be caused by the adult reactions. There is often a tendency to keep the siblings away from the grieving in order to protect them from the pain of the death. Parents may pay less attention to siblings at the time of loss because of their preoccupation with their own pain. In either case, siblings often respond to isolation from parents who are grieving as a sign that they (the children) have done something wrong. Siblings, too, are less apt to have the verbal skill to make their own needs known. Their reaction to death is often expressed through somatic distress or acting out. Any jealousy of a real or promised baby can also result in guilt for most siblings just as it does for parents: "The baby died because I didn't love it." Thus, the parents' communication skills may play a large part in how a child will handle the death. Just as spouses must be able to understand and express their needs to one another they must also elicit expression from their children of both the child's needs for understanding the situation and the child's concerns about his or her role in the issues. Further, parents should be capable of expressing their own feelings and needs in language understandable to the child.

VI. Professional Response

In dealing with the loss experienced by patients and clients, it is important for professionals to be aware of their own response to the grieving process. Elements of denial, anger, and resolution must surely touch the professional, as well as the families with whom they are working. Not being aware of these responses can cloud scientific and clinical skills and make the practitioner much less effective with those with whom she or he deals. It is also critical to recognize that each death and the grieving it triggers is unique.

In attempting to formulate some ideas on how professionals can help parents through a death in their family, it is important to point out again that each death is a unique event and the reactions of the grievers will be unique. Thus, professional response must be flexible. Further, the responses suggested here are only minimal guides.

Fortunately, the behavior of the professional does not appear to have to conform to some strict standards at the time of an infant's death. Those families responding to our questionnaire reported that they did not remember much of what their physician said around the time of the death; what they did recall was whether or not he made an effort to be with them. Also, they remembered whether the health care providers listened; those whose eyes filled with tears were remembered especially fondly, as were those who conveyed caring by the touch of the hand.

Since denial is a strong response to the immediate occurrence of the death, it may take several repetitions of the news that the fetus or the infant is dead for the family to be able to accept the death. There is no reason to worry that the parents are going crazy if they cannot seem to grasp the problem at this point. Repeated gentle confrontation with the fact of death is an adequate process; failure to achieve the goal of acceptance by the parents in first talking about the death is acceptable as well. Often, too, the information is not clear to the physician at first. When evidence of likely fetal demise is strong, it can be shared with the parents. It can be shared first as a strong possibility, and then acceptance can occur gradually as more evidence of the fetal demise occurs.

It is hard to confront families with the likely loss of a fetus or infant without first accepting the inevitability of that loss. Life-saving techniques must always be employed when there is reasonable possibility of their success. However, it is not uncommon that these techniques are employed even when there is no chance of their success. This is a version of the professional's denial stage. It is possible that the professional would feel extreme guilt if such techniques were not applied. Thus, it is critical that professionals learn to recognize their own way of dealing with the urge to deny the possibility of a death.

In a recent case, an infant was thought to have little or no chance of living and was brought immediately after birth to the neonatal intensive care unit. One of the authors of this chapter was consulted when the mother did not seem to realize that her infant was going to die. On talking with the mother, it became apparent that she indeed did not seem to know her infant was about to die. When nurses came to help her move to a private room from a four-bed ward, she looked surprised and asked why she was being moved. The question was not asked with any force, however, and she quickly accepted the explanation that it had been discovered that her insurance policy allowed such a luxury. (In fact, she had no insurance; the cost of the move would have to be accepted as a loss by the hospital.) It soon became apparent that the reason she was so successful in denying the probability of her son's death was because of a silent conspiracy between the medical staff and her family not to mention the likelihood of death to her. Instead everyone talked about how some infants like hers (who had not shown voluntary movement since birth and was being passively supplied oxygen) made miraculous recoveries. When told her baby was likely to die, she burst into tears and asked that her husband be sent for. She too strongly suspected her son was going to die, but her denial and the denial of the medical staff around her contrived a poorly acted "he's going to live" theme.

The resident in charge of her care pointed out that he only held back the information because he feared she was not strong enough to handle the news; her husband and parents agreed. In talking about the case in this way, however, the participants were behaving in a manner that denied the impending death of the infant; the mother, however, was seen as the reason, and not their own denial.

It is a delicate question as to when appropriate efforts to save a life end and denial begins. Thus, each physician must deal with the issue of recognizing denial as a part of their professional response.

In addition, the anger response in grieving can also be found in professionals. The objects of the anger can be varied: the referring physician or hospital when a transferred case is dying, the nursing staff or other physicians on the case, the parents, or the physician him or herself. Anger can be engendered by blatantly poor practice on the part of the self or others, but more often, the anger is directed toward errors of omission, errors of not referring early enough, or errors in communication with the parents. (In fact, a study on malpractice suits reports that the most common reason for a person filing a malpractice suit is that they were unsatisfied with the communication process.)

Obviously, in some cases the anger is justified; someone has made a serious error and a life has been lost unnecessarily. However, in the vast majority of instances such an error did not occur. Instead, members of the health care team blame one another for not thinking of doing different tests or for failing to deal better with the parents.

Interestingly, we are not aware of any empirical work with physicians documenting their grieving process in the loss of someone with whom they are working. The most obvious way such investigative work could be carried out would be through self-reports from physicians. But it is likely that such self-reports might not be valid, since the issue is an emotional one in a profession reared on science. Our questionnaire data from families who have experienced a loss suggest that most health professionals do an excellent job of supporting the family. There were notable exceptions, however. In those exceptions, the physician avoided the family or made statements that denied the severity of the losses. In sum, then, health professionals ought to be aware of their own pattern of reacting to death. Such awareness can make it easier to meet the needs of families in the process of grieving.

Other more specific things can be done to help families who are grieving. In capsule form, professionals can assure families that:

1. People often find ways to feel as though they are responsible for the death. It is natural to have such feelings, but it is also important to recognize these feeling are merely a way of trying to control something that is beyond control.
2. It is natural to feel anger at a time like this; feeling anger does not make you a "bad" person. It is also important to be tolerant of anger expressed by others in the family and to talk about the anger.
3. All people who go through a grieving process experience their sorrow

and other emotion at different times; no one is feeling the wrong emotion or feeling it at a wrong time. Thus, it is important to accept another's responses and needs as appropriate for them.

4. It is a good idea to practice a simple response for others who ask what has happened. It is all right to choose not to share anything further than the simple response. It is also all right to choose to expand beyond that response whenever that need is felt and the person to whom you are talking seems responsive.

5. You need a simple response for those who seem awkward and do not know what to say. A simple statement of "it is hard for most people to know what to say about the death" can help many awkward friends and relatives to deal with the death.

6. If anything is known about the chances of a similar problem in future pregnancies or births, the parents will want to know that as well.

7. The death is a difficult thing to accept. The one positive thing about the death is that it gives people the opportunity to grow closer: The tragedy they have shared can bring them closer together if they make an effort to learn to communicate with one another. They can also learn a greater sensitivity to children and to the loss of other loved ones through this trauma; the sensitization to death can make them relate more closely and empathetically with others rather than leading them to avoid the issue of death altogether.

VII. Conclusion

Loss of a pregnancy or an infant is indeed a nonnormative event in our society. The effects of that death can be disruptive to the unit that shares it; that disruption can lead to a better integration of the family or to a disintegration. Which event occurs appears to depend on the communication skills that people have before the event and the effort that they make to learn to communicate after the death. Siblings, by virtue of their usually incomplete communication skills, can be particularly vulnerable to problems in dealing with the loss of a pregnancy or infant.

In this chapter we have reviewed theoretical issues of the grief process in families that experience a prenatal loss and those who experience the death of an infant due to Sudden Infant Death syndrome. The discussion is most appropriate to those populations but may also bear on other forms of death that strike early in the life span. The practical aspects of professional response to death best fit these populations but may be of use to professionals dealing with other populations as well.

Death apparently is a crisis like the others explored in this book: It offers both a problem and an opportunity. The problems of dealing with the death when it occurs often appear overwhelming; the opportunity for growth often appears absent. As some of our families have reported, however, growth is possible.

Reference Note

1. Kubler-Ross, E. *Until I die.* Videotape available from Center for Continuing Education, University of Chicago. Chicago, Illinois, 1970.

References

Averill, J. R. Grief: It's nature and significance. *Psychological Bulletin*, 1968, *70*, 721–748.

Averill, J. R., & Wisocki, P. A. Some observations on behavioral approaches to the treatment of grief among the elderly. In H. Sobel (Ed.), *Behavior therapy in terminal care: A humanistic approach.* New York: Ballinger, 1981.

Benfield, D. G., Leib, S. A., & Vollman, S. H. Grief response of parents to neonatal death and parent participation in deciding care. *Pediatrics*, 1978, *62*, 171–177.

Bowlby, J. Process of mourning. *International Journal of Psychoanalysis*, 1961, *42*, 317–340.

Bowlby, J. *Attachment and loss* (Vol. 3): *Loss: Sadness and depression.* New York: Basic Books, 1980.

Bowlby, J., & Parkes, C. M. Separation and loss. In E. J. Anthony & C. Koupernik (Eds.), *The Child and his family* (Vol. 1). International Yearbook of Child Psychiatry and Allied Professions. New York: Wiley, 1970.

Campbell, S. B. G. & Taylor, P. M. Bonding and attachment: Theoretical issues. *Seminars in Perinatology*, 1979, *3*, 3–13.

Catania, C. The nature of learning. In J. A. Nevin & G. S. Reynolds (Eds.), *The study of behavior: Learning, motivation, emotion, and instinct.* Glenview, Ill.: Scott, Foresman and Co., 1973.

Davis, D. M. Sudden Infant Death Syndrome: An opportunity for primary prevention. *American Journal of Psychiatry*, 1975, *32*, 648.

DeFrain, J. D., & Ernst, L. The psychological effects of Sudden Infant Death Syndrome on survivary family members. *Journal of Family Practice*, 1978, *6*, 985–989.

Engel, G. L. Is grief a disease? *Psychosomatic Medicine*, 1961, *23*, 18–22.

Gauthier, J., & Marshall, W. L. Grief: A cognitive-behavioral analysis. *Cognitive Therapy and Research*, 1977, *1*, 39–44.

Gorer, G. *Death, grief and mourning.* London: Crescent Press, 1965.

Helmrath, T. A., & Sternitz, E. M. Death of an infant: Parental grieving and the failure of social support. *Journal of Family Practice*, 1978, *6*, 785–790.

Kennell, J. H., Slyter, H., & Klaus, M. H. The mourning response of parents to the death of a newborn infant. *New England Journal of Medicine*, 1970, *283*, 344–348.

Karsh, E. B. Changes in intensity of punishment: Effect on running behavior of rats. *Science*, 1963, *140*, 1084–1085.

Klaus, M. H., & Kennell, J. H. *Maternal–infant bonding.* Saint Louis: C. V. Mosby Co., 1976.

Klaus, M. H., Kennell, J. H., Plumb, N., & Zuehlke, S. Human maternal behavior at first contact with her young. *Pediatrics*, 1970, *46*, 187–192.

Kowalski, K. Managing perinatal loss. *Clinical Obstetrics and Gynecology*, 1980, *23*, 1113–1123.

Kubler-Ross, E. *Coping with death and dying: Lessons from a dying patient*. Audiotape, 1973.

Limerick, S. R. Counseling parents who have lost an infant. *Journal of the Royal College of Physicians of London*, 1979, *13*, 242–245.

Lindeman, E. Symptomatology and management of acute grief. *American Journal of Psychiatry*, 1944, *101*, 141–148.

Lorenz, K. *On aggression*. New York: Harcourt, 1966.

Lynch, M. A., & Roberts, J. Predicting child abuse: Signs of bonding failure in the maternity hospital. *British Medical Journal*, 1977, *1*, 624–627.

Mandell, F., McAnulty, E., & Reese, R. M. Observations of paternal response to sudden unanticipated infant death. *Pediatrics*, 1980, *65*, 221–225.

Marriss, P. *Widows and their families*. London: Routledge & Kegan Paul, 1958.

Miller, N. E. Learning resistance to pain and fear: Effects of overlearning, exposure, and rewarded exposure in context. *Journal of Experimental Psychology*, 1960, *60*, 137–145.

Montagu, A. *Touching: The human significance of the skin*. New York: Columbia University Press, 1971.

Parkes, C. M. The effects of bereavement on physical and mental health: A study of the case records of widows. *British Medical Journal*, 1964, *2*, 274–279.

Peppers, L. G. & Knapp, R. J. *Motherhood and mourning: Perinatal death*. New York: Praeger, 1980.

Rosenblatt, P. C., Walsh, R. P., & Jackson, D. A. *Grief and mourning in cross-cultural perspective*. New Haven, Conn.: Human Relations Area Files Press, 1976.

Sherman, M., Trief, P., & Sprafkin, R. Impression management in the psychiatric interview: Quality, style, and individual differences. *Journal Consulting Clinical Psychology*, 1975, *43*, 867–871.

Shelskie, B. E. An exploratory study of grief in old age. *Smith College Studies in Social Work*, 1975, *45*, 159–182.

Smialek, Z. Observations on immediate reactions of families to Sudden Infant Death. *Pediatrics*, 1978, *62*, 160–165.

Svejda, M. J., Campos, J. J., & Emde, R. N. Mother–infant "bonding": Failure to generalize. *Child Development*, 1980, *51*, (3), 775–779.

Svejda, M. G., Pannabecker, B. J., & Emde, R. N. Parent-to-infant attachment: A critique of the early bonding model. In R. N. Emde & R. J. Harmon (Eds.), *The development of attachment and affiliation*. New York: Plenum, 1982, 83–93.

Tinkelpaugh, O. L. The self-mutilation of a male macacus rhesus monkey. *Journal of Mammology*, 1928, *9*, 293–300.

Toynbee, A. The relation between life and death, living and dying. In E. S. Schneidman (Ed.), *Death: Current perspectives*. Palo Alto, Calif.: Mayfield Publishing Co., 1976.

Yerkes, R. M., & Yerkes, A. W. *The great apes*. New Haven, Conn.: Yale University Press, 1929.

Zedwitz, F. X. von. Beobachtongers in zoologischen Garten Berlin. *Der Zoologische Garten*, 1930, *2*, 278–286.

Zuckerman, S. *The social life of monkeys and apes*. London: Kegan Paul, 1932.

CHAPTER 7

Rape: A Precursor of Change [1]

LOIS J. VERONEN
DEAN G. KILPATRICK
MEDICAL UNIVERSITY OF SOUTH CAROLINA
CHARLESTON, SOUTH CAROLINA[2]

I. Introduction

A. Overview

As rape researchers and activists in the antirape movement, we were flattered, challenged, and somewhat perplexed when requested to prepare a chapter on rape for this volume on nonnormative life events. Although we have spoken to and written for a variety of professional and lay groups about various aspects of sexual assault, we had never considered rape as a nonnormative event from a developmental, life-span perspective. We were flattered to be asked to participate in such an august endeavor. We were

---

[1]This research was supported by Grant No. 5 RO1 MH 29602, "Treatment of Fear and Anxiety in Victims of Rape," awarded by the National Center for the Prevention and Control of Rape of the National Institute of Mental Health.

[2]The authors are also affiliated with People Against Rape, a volunteer rape crisis center in Charleston, S.C.

LIFE-SPAN DEVELOPMENTAL PSYCHOLOGY
Nonnormative Life Events

challenged because we knew we would be addressing an audience that knew little about rape, therefore necessitating our giving a crash course on the topic. We were excited about the challenge of meeting the objective of the volume: to identify both positive and negative changes that might occur following a nonnormative life event. We were perplexed because we were not exactly sure what a nonnormative life event was or how to define it. Fortunately we are not alone in our definitional problems.

On the general premise that it is better to be overly inclusive in dealing with a topic with which many are unfamiliar, this chapter will cover the following topics in the order listed here:

1. Issues surrounding the definition of rape, nonnormative life events, and rape as a nonnormative life event
2. The impact of a rape experience on its victim
3. The reaction of victims to a sexual assault experience, which includes a description of the Sexual Assault Research Project and our findings to date
4. A presentation of several models, illustrated with case histories, that may promote positive changes following a sexual assault experience
5. A final section dealing with some general conclusions

B. Definitions of Rape

There are numerous definitions of and perspectives on rape. Because rape involves both sex and violence, it impinges on and threatens the basic institutions of our culture.

From the legal perspective, rape is a criminal act. Although old laws define rape as an act of illicit sex, new legislation regards rape as a type of assault. In South Carolina, the site of our research investigation, the new law, Criminal Sexual Conduct Statute, 1977, defines three degrees of sexual assault, based on the amount of force used. The new code includes forced or coerced acts other than intercourse that involve genital contact or contact with a woman's breast. The previous legislation required a penis to have entered a vagina for the act to be prosecutable under the rape statute. Under the new legislation, men as well as women can be victims. These new rape laws, with their increased emphasis on force, threat of force, and coercion, come much closer to capturing the psychological essence of rape.

From the perspective of the media (i.e., television, movies, books, and magazines), rape, for the most part, is presented as an act of sexual passion. In most media representations of rape, the male is presented as overcome by sexual passion to the point of acting forcibly to overwhelm the woman; the woman is presented as an attractive and resistant female who does not know her own mind. The act of rape overcomes her resistance and she becomes a docile and loving female. The rape segment in *Gone with the Wind*, when Rhett overcomes Scarlett, is illustrative.

Societal attitudes regarding rape, in large part, support the blaming of the victim (Burt, 1980). The myth is "Proper young women do not get raped; only bad girls get raped." Therefore, if a woman is raped, she must have behaved improperly and, therefore, she was "asking for it."

To complicate the definitional aspects of rape further, we have a male perspective of sexual conduct. Men in our culture are socialized to initiate sexual activity. In dating and courting situations, it is the man who is expected to behave aggressively to convince the woman that sexual contact would be enjoyable. Young men are said to "score" if they are able to have intercourse with the woman they have dated. Young men are taught that "No" really means "Yes." Again, the young man is led to believe a woman does not know her own mind as to whether she wants intercourse. This perspective may be further reinforced by the young woman's behavior: She initially resists sexual advances and later gives in.

The victim's perception of rape is, first of all, that it is a threat to life. The situation is out of her control to the extent that she feels she may be killed or seriously injured. Additionally, there is the element of degradation. The victim feels that she has been degraded and violated by being forced to participate in an action that she did not want.

To summarize, there are many perspectives and definitions of rape. The rapist can be a stranger, a casual acquaintance, a friend, or a family member. The key factor distinguishing rape, in our opinion, is that it is nonconsensual sexual activity obtained through coercion, threat of force, or force. If a woman considers herself to have been forced to have nonconsensual sexual activity, then we would consider her to be a victim. This definition is based on the strong ethical–moral principle that no person has the right to coerce another into unwanted sexual conduct. Another factor to be considered is that the amount of coercion and/or force used varies, and we contend that those rapists who use the most force or coercion are the most culpable.

C. Definition of Nonnormative Life Events

Since we are clinical researchers and antirape activists, we shall leave the fine-grained, hair-splitting defining of nonnormative life events to our developmental life-span colleagues. However, the following considerations assisted us in forming a working definition of the term. *Nonnormative events* can be defined as including those events that do not happen to everyone as a part of the normal developmental process. From the sociological use of the term *norm*, nonnormative could be defined as an event that does not conform to the norm for a given society (i.e., not normal). This latter definition implies some sort of relative statistical infrequency. Using either of these definitions, an event could be defined as nonnormative if it did not routinely occur to the majority or all of the relevant population in question. An event occurring to all or most of the population could scarcely be defined as nonnormative. Another assumption in discussing such events is that they should have a major impact on the life of the individual to whom they occur.

D. Nonnormative Aspects of Rape

Given the previously discussed definitions of rape and nonnormative life events, can rape be classified as such an event? With respect to the issue of frequency of occurrence, the problem of underreporting makes it extremely difficult to obtain accurate data regarding incidence and prevalence of rape (Chappell, 1976). However, although a substantial minority of women can expect to be assaulted sometime during their life, the majority of women are not victimized. Therefore, rape would appear to be a nonnormative event because it does not happen to everyone as a part of their normal development and because it occurs relatively infrequently (i.e., not to a majority of women).

Considering next the issue of whether rape produces a significant impact on the lives of victims, it is important to differentiate between rape and consensual sexual activity. Some people might ask: What is the big deal about rape? Why do feminists focus so much energy on the issue? After all, these people might reason, is not rape just sex when a woman does not want it? For a sexually experienced woman, there should be little problem. She has probably had sex many times when she was not "in the mood."

In the first place, rape is much more than just sex. When a woman does not consent, intercourse is a crime of violence and degradation. Two aspects of rape make it much more than sex when a woman does not want it. These two elements are the implicit violence or threat of violence and the contrast between rape and consensual sex. Among the sample of women we studied, approximately 50% were directly threatened with a weapon, either a knife or gun. Additionally, most women perceive the rape to be a life-threatening situation (Veronen, Kilpatrick, & Resick, 1979). At some time during the rape experience, the power the assailants have over the victims is so complete that most women feel they could be killed. They fear dying.

Additionally, forcing a woman to have sex, an act that under normal conditions occurs with an intimate and loving partner, further exacerbates her reaction since she may then experience considerable confusion when confronted with sexual cues. Therefore, rape is also nonnormative in that it is considerably different from normal consensual sexual activity.

E. Impact of a Rape Experience

It is our contention that rape is a nonnormative event that has powerful effects on the victim's life. Not only is the rape experience per se stressful but the rape sets into motion a complex set of events that impact on nearly all aspects of a woman's life.

The victim experiences a variety of concerns which, for the sake of clarity, will be discussed in chronological sequence. We define immediate concerns as those that occur within the first 24 hours after the assault. Intermediate and long-term concerns are those that occur between 24 hours and 6 months postrape: However, some victims experience rape-related problems many years after the assault. Much has been written about victim concerns (e.g., Burgess & Holmstrom, 1974; Kilpatrick, Best, & Veronen, 1978; Kilpatrick, Veronen, & Resick, 1982), and a reader interested in a more comprehensive presentation of victim concerns should consult these references.

1. Immediate Concerns of Rape Victims

Among the most pressing immediate concerns of victims are (a) whether to report the rape to law enforcement offices; and (b) whom they should tell about the rape. A discussion of issues involved in deciding whether to report a rape is beyond the scope of this chapter. It is important to realize, however, that most of what we know about rape victims is based on data collected from women who reported it, although there is general agreement that more victims do not report than do report (e.g., Chappell, 1976). If a woman decides to report a rape, she must interact with a variety of agencies, primarily with the health care delivery and criminal justice systems. Women who do not report a rape generally require medical care but do not interact with the criminal justice system. All victims experience concerns in the areas of family relationships, other interpersonal relationships, and self-concept. An outline of these concerns is presented in Table 7.1.

Victims who obtain medical care have a variety of concerns. In addition to receiving a pelvic examination, victims frequently undergo an examination to gather evidence in which samples and specimens are collected for use in

TABLE 7.1
Immediate Concerns of Rape Victims

1. Medical
    Exam
    Pregnancy
    Venereal disease
    Internal damage
2. Family relationships
    Whom do I tell?
    Will they see me as responsible?
    What will they think of me?
3. Other interpersonal relationships
    Will my significant others still care for me?
    Whom must I tell?
    What will people think?
4. Criminal justice
    What kind of questioning?
    If I go to court, what will they ask me?
5. Self-concept
    Feel unclean, dirty
    Feel responsible; should have acted differently

potential prosecutions (Kreutner & Hollingsworth, 1978). Victims often experience considerable anxiety about this process. Other medical concerns of the victim are pregnancy, venereal disease, and internal damage. For victims who were not using contraception at the time of the assault, there is the fear of pregnancy. For nearly all victims, there is concern that venereal disease may have been transmitted. Finally, victims are often concerned that they have been damaged or harmed internally by the assault.

Family concerns for the victim include whom among the family members should be informed about the assault, will the family members blame her or see her as responsible for the assault, and what will her family think of her?

Concerns that occur for the victim in the interpersonal realm are very similar to the family concerns. For example, many victims worry that they will be rejected by their boyfriend or significant other when they tell about the assault. Other victims are concerned that the significant person in their life will not know how to react. Many victims fear their boyfriend's or spouse's anger. Others fear that significant others in their lives will make negative judgments concerning their character, conduct, etc.

From the standpoint of the criminal justice system, many victims fear that the police will blame them for the rape. Among some victims, there is the desire to avoid all police contact. These victims may have been assaulted by someone they or a family member knew, and they fear retaliation. Among such victims, there is a definite decision that they do not want the police called or involved in the procedure, and there exists the fear that they will be forced to deal with the police.

Concerns for self are those that deal with the victim herself. Immediately following a rape experience, most victims express a desire to bathe or shower in an effort to get clean. They claim they feel dirty and want to wash away the odor left by sex.

Another concern for self relates to the victim's integrity. For example, how much will she see her self-respect altered by this event? In what ways should she have behaved differently? Cultural attitudes, childhood training, and media tend to present the woman as responsible for sexual encounters. Some victims of sexual assault express concerns that they were responsible for the assault. These concerns of responsibility for the assault may be expressed in relatively realistic ways. For example, a victim who was raped while hitchhiking said, "I should never have hitchhiked," or another who was abducted while leaving a bar said, "I should never have left that bar alone." Other victims' feelings of responsibility may be totally unrealistic. For example, one victim blamed herself for the assault by saying, "This rape would never have happened if I hadn't separated from my husband." Another victim, who was a new resident of the city, said, "My parents didn't want me to move to Charleston: I should have stayed home and worked in Ravenel."

2. Intermediate and Long-Term Concerns of Rape Victims

The concerns and problems expressed by the rape victim within the days and months following the rape experience are safety, independence, family, trust, sex, and criminal justice. Each of these will be briefly discussed, and an outline of concerns in each area is presented in Table 7.2.

Following the assault experience, victims are increasingly concerned about their personal safety. They experience feelings of increased vulnerability. They are concerned that they could be attacked again. There is a preoccupation with door locks, chains and peepholes, and other protective devices. Many victims who were raped in their homes or neighborhoods move to new locations. Some victims obtain dogs that they hope will offer protection from potential attackers. Additionally, many report constant vigilance about noise: They strain to hear faint sounds and are wary over any unusual noises.

TABLE 7.2

Intermediate and Long-Term Concerns of Rape Victims

---

1. Safety
   Do not want to go to new places.
   No longer feel secure doing what I did.
   Can I ever feel safe again?
   Will assailant or his family harm me?
2. Independent functioning
   I cannot stay alone, be alone, or go places alone.
3. Family
   Have done so much already, but they are getting tired of helping.
4. Trust
   Whom can I trust?
   Can I rely on my own judgment about people?
   I need other people so much.
5. Sexual
   Not particularly interested in a sexual relationship.
6. Criminal justice
   A. Police
      Will the police find my assailant?
      Are the police working on my case?
   B. Court
      Will the jury believe me?
      Will the lawyers ask me about my past sexual activity?

Another fear of the rape victim is that the assailant will seek to attack her again. This fear is shared both by the victim whose assailant has been apprehended and the victim whose assailant has not been apprehended. In the case of the apprehended assailant, victims are frequently contacted by family members of the rapist urging them to drop charges. Later, the victim may fear that the assailant may be released and seek revenge.

When the assailant is not apprehended, there is fear that he will return to attack again. This fear is not entirely groundless. In our sample of 105 victims, the assailant returned to assault, physically or sexually, the same victim in at least two cases. In a greater number of cases, victims have experienced phone or personal harassment that they believed was perpetrated by their assailant.

The ability to be alone, stay alone, and go places alone is a chief concern of rape victims after the assault. In our treatment study, 9 of 10 victims defined the fear of being alone as a target fear and a problem that they wished to alleviate by treatment (Veronen, Kilpatrick, & Best, Note 1). Victims have considerable difficulty resuming independent functioning in their lives after an assault. Fear of being alone is understandable: The woman was alone when she was attacked. Later, all conditions where she finds herself alone are fear-inducing. This fear of being alone is highly disruptive to a woman's life. If she cannot function independently and she is constantly seeking someone to go, do, and be with her, her mobility and range of activities are reduced. She becomes a burden for others, similar to a child who cannot be left unattended. She clings to the company and companionship of others in order to feel safe.

In the weeks and months following a sexual assault, victims may exhaust their support system. Family members, who are initially very supportive of the victim, gradually become frustrated because the victim does not resume her previous level of independence within the family. She may no longer perform household duties and tasks if they require her to go places alone. Due to her increased fearfulness, she wants more attention, concern, and companionship from her spouse and other family members. This situation arises frequently with military families. The husband may be brought back on emergency leave to be with his wife. After a few days or weeks, his command may require him to resume his duty post, but his wife is too fearful to resume her previous role and tasks. This situation creates conflict within the relationship and places the husband in a difficult position. He may want to remain with his wife to protect and comfort her, yet his job requires him to be away from her. We have seen many cases in which a military man has requested a change in his duty because of his wife's increased fearfulness and inability to resume her previous roles.

Another concern that arises for victims following an assault is trust. Many victims stop dating and avoid any situations in which they will be alone with a man. Some complain that they are afraid of someone walking up behind them, afraid of being touched. For many victims, there is a confusion between affectionate and sexual contact.

For victims who were assaulted by someone they knew or were acquainted with, the issue of trust is slightly different. It is often expressed as doubt in their own judgments about men. For example, one victim who was raped by someone she had seen several consecutive weeks at a disco where she danced said, "He always smiled at me; he looked like a nice fellow; I never thought he'd do anything like that to me."

Sexually, the concern of victims is not a disruption in sexual functioning as much as it is a lack of desire. Victims of sexual assault tend to avoid situations in which sexual behavior might occur. For those who have a regular sexual partner and a good sexual relationship prior to the assault, postrape sexual adjustment tends to be good. For victims who do not have a sexual partner, there is a tendency to avoid becoming involved with one.

Victims have many police and court concerns. During the weeks following the assault, concern regarding the police is greatest if the victim's assailant has not been apprehended. Victims often express concern by calling the police and asking for information about the case. They are eager to determine if their assailant has been apprehended. If the assailant has been apprehended, they want to find out whether he has been released on bond.

Those cases that advance to the stage of trial present new concerns for the victim. Victims' greatest fears are (a) will I be believed; and (b) will the lawyers ask me about my sexual activity? Although new legislation protects the victims from being questioned about their sexual activity except as it relates to the defendant, many victims still fear being questioned about their sexual behavior with other men.

II. Reactions of Victims to Sexual Assault

A. The Sexual Assault Research Project

This research and demonstration project is a joint effort of the Medical University of South Carolina and People Against Rape, a Charleston, S.C., rape crisis center. Funded by the National Center for the Prevention and Control of Rape, the Sexual Assault Research Project has two major objectives: (a) longitudinal assessment of victim reactions to a sexual assault experience; and (b) evaluation of treatment efficacy for rape-induced fear and anxiety responses. To accomplish the former objective, recent rape victims and a comparison group of nonvictims matched for age, race, and residential neighborhood were assessed at the following postrape periods: 6–21 days, 1 month, 3 months, 6 months, 1 year, 18 months, 2 years, 3 years, and 4 years. The assessment measures are objective, standardized measures of anxiety, fear, mood state, psychological complaints, self-esteem, and self-concept.

B. Biographic–Demographic Characteristics of the Research Sample

Two recent articles describe the demographic characteristics of the victim ($n = 46$) and nonvictim ($n = 35$) samples used in these studies (Kilpatrick, Veronen, & Resick, 1979a, b). All victims were at least 16 years of age and were referred by People Against Rape. The mean age of the victim sample was 25.3 years. A comparison group of nonvictimized women was selected that matched the victims with respect to age, race, and neighborhood of residence. The mean age for the nonvictims was 26.3 years. Table 7.3

TABLE 7.3

Demographic Data on Victim and Nonvictim Groups (percentages)

Variable	Victims ($N = 46$)	Nonvictims ($N = 35$)
Racial status		
Black	37.0	37.1
Caucasian	60.9	62.9
Other	2.2	—
Occupation		
Student	21.7	17.1
Housewife	13.0	14.3
Clerk–secretary	8.7	14.3
Salesperson	6.5	.0
Waitress	2.2	11.4
Teacher	2.2	5.7
Nurse	2.2	5.7
Other	37.0	22.9
Never worked	2.2	8.6
Educational Status		
Attended elementary school	.0	2.9
Completed elementary school (1–8)	10.9	8.6
Attended high school	8.7	14.3
Completed high school (9–12)	54.3	42.9
Attended college	8.6	13.0
Completed college	22.9	13.0
Business–vocational training	28.3	34.3
Attended graduate school	6.5	10.5
Completed graduate school	—	—
Marital status		
Never married and not cohabiting	39.1	25.7
Married (first marriage)	13.0	62.9
Separated	19.6	17.1
Divorced	15.2	14.3
Cohabiting	6.5	2.9
Remarried	4.3	2.9
Widowed	2.2	.0
Residence		
Apartment	34.8	11.4*
Own or rent house	32.6	65.7
Trailer	15.2	14.3
Other	17.4	8.6
Present living arrangements		
With parents	30.4	22.9
With husband	15.2	37.1
With boyfriend	8.7	6.5
With female roommate	8.7	6.5
With male roommate	4.4	—
Living alone	6.5	5.7
Living with offspring	30.4	28.6
Other	30.4	14.3

Continued

TABLE 7.3 (*Continued*)
Demographic Data on Victim and Nonvictim Groups (percentages)

Variable	Victims ($N = 46$)	Nonvictims ($N = 35$)
Religious preference		
Catholic	15.2	5.7
Protestant	54.3	65.7
Jewish	2.2	2.9
None	23.9	17.1
Other	4.3	8.6
Church attendance per month		
Never	43.5	20.0
1 or 2 times	32.6	37.1
3 or 4 times	15.2	20.0
More than 4 times	8.7	22.9
State of legal residence		
South Carolina	84.8	97.1
Other	15.2	2.9
Length of time have resided in South Carolina		
Less than 1 year	13.0	—*
1–3 years	17.4	2.9
3–5 years	4.3	2.9
5–10 years	8.7	22.9
More than 10 years	56.5	71.4

*$p < .01$

presents comparisons of the victim and nonvictim samples on a variety of biographic–demographic variables. The only significant differences between the two groups were the type of residence they lived in and the length of time they had resided in South Carolina. A greater percentage of nonvictims lived in houses, whereas victims were more likely to live in apartments. It appeared that a greater percentage of victims had lived in the state less than 1 year, whereas a greater percentage of nonvictims had lived in the state 5 years or more.

C. Summary of Research Findings: Victim Symptomatology

Five studies describe some of the results of this assessment study. Veronen *et al.* (1979) reported victim ratings of the extent to which they experienced a variety of physiological and cognitive symptoms during the rape itself and during the 2- to 3-hour period postrape. Victims experienced profound cognitive and physiological symptoms of anxiety during the rape itself and for several hours thereafter.

A second study (Kilpatrick et al., 1979a) focused on the fear, anxiety, mood state, and psychological symptomatology of victims 6–21 days, 1 month, 3 months, and 6 months postrape. When compared to nonvictims, the victims' initial response to the rape during the 6–21-day and 1-month periods was characterized by high levels of generalized distress on practically all of the assessment measures. Victims scored as significantly more disturbed on 25 of 28 assessment measures. By the 3- to 6-month postrape periods, however, victims were more distressed than nonvictims on only 7 of the 28 assessment measures, those which measured fear and anxiety.

The third study (Kilpatrick et al., 1979b) looked at specific items and situations that were rated as most disturbing by victims at each assessment period through 6 months postrape. Using the Modified Fear Survey (MFS) developed by Veronen and Kilpatrick (1980), victims and nonvictims rated the 120 MFS items on the degree of disturbance produced by each. Victims were more fearful than nonvictims, and victims' fears declined somewhat over time. Content analysis of highly feared situations revealed that most fears were rape related in that they were rape cues, rape-precipitated concerns, and/or cues signaling vulnerability to subsequent attack. Patterns of fear changed, with attack-vulnerability cues becoming most feared at the 3- and 6-month assessments.

The fourth study (Kilpatrick, Veronen, & Resick, Note 2) focused on the aftermath of rape at the 1-year postrape assessment. Victims scored as significantly more disturbed than nonvictims on 9 of the 28 assessment battery measures. In general, those measures on which the victims reported increased distress were those tapping fear, anxiety, and obsessive thinking about the rape and its aftermath. Comparison of 1-year postrape scores with those obtained at the 6-month postrape assessment suggested that the victims' distress had stabilized. Thus, victims were still more distressed than nonvictims, although their distress levels had diminished considerably from the 6–21-day and 1-month postrape assessment levels. A year after the rape, these women are still distressed.

The final study (Veronen & Kilpatrick, Note 3) dealt with the self-esteem of rape victims. In general, victims had lower self-esteem scores than nonvictims at each of the assessment intervals, including the 1-year postrape period.

D. Findings regarding Asymptomatic Victims

Rape victims as a group experience more distress and have less self-esteem at the 1-year postrape period than their nonvictimized counterparts. Given the focus of this chapter, however, it is relevant to look at individual differences among victims as well as at their responses to rape as a group. From this perspective, it would be of considerable interest to determine what percentage of rape victims appear to be functioning normally 1 year after the assault.

One of the measures is especially well suited for this purpose. The Derogatis Symptom Check List (SCL-90-R; Derogatis, 1977) is a 90-item, self-report symptom inventory designed to reflect psychological symptom patterns of psychiatric and medical patients. Each item is rated on a 5-point scale, zero indicating no discomfort and 4 indicating extreme discomfort during the past week. Scores are obtained for nine primary symptom dimensions: somatization, obsession–compulsion, interpersonal sensitivity, depression, anxiety, hostility, phobic anxiety, paranoid ideation, and psychoticism. Additionally, three global indexes of distress are scored: global severity index, positive symptom distress index, and positive symptom total. Since the test is designed as a screening instrument, excellent norms are available regarding the extent to which the general population experiences each of the symptoms. One way of identifying relatively asymptomatic victims would be to compare their SCL-90-R scores with those of the normative group. Those victims scoring at or below the mean score for normal, nondistressed women could be defined as relatively asymptomatic.

The anxiety, phobic anxiety, and global severity index scores seem particularly relevant. Therefore, the percentages of the victim and nonvictim groups that fall into the asymptomatic range for these SCL-90-R measures at the initial assessment and at 1 year are presented in Table 7.4. The fact that more nonvictims than victims are asymptomatic at both initial and 1-year postrape assessments is not surprising and reflects the significant mean differences between groups. It is also interesting to note that the percentage

TABLE 7.4

Percentage of Victim and Nonvictim Groups
Asymptomatic at Initial and One-Year Assessments

Group	Global severity index		Anxiety		Phobic anxiety	
	Initial assessment	1-year assessment	Initial assessment	1-year assessment	Initial assessment	1-year assessment
Victim	5.7	17.1	11.4	22.9	0.0	25.7
Nonvictim	28.1	40.6	25.0	43.8	50.0	65.6

of asymptomatic members of both groups increases on all three measures at the 1-year assessment.

Given our focus on asymptomatic victims, the most interesting findings were that 1 year after their rape (*a*) 17.1% of victims were asymptomatic on the global severity index; *b*) 22.9% were asymptomatic on the anxiety scale; and (*c*) 25.7% were asymptomatic on the phobic anxiety scale. Thus, these data show that some victims are relatively symptom-free a year after their assault.

III. Models for Promoting Positive Change
Subsequent to Sexual Assault

A. *Overview*

The findings on asymptomatic victims reveal that some women are functioning normally 1 year after a rape experience. This indicates that women can "recover" from the rape. Let us consider the next logical question: Can a rape experience result in some women actually functioning better after than before the rape? Our experience working with victims suggests that rape prompts some women to make positive changes in their lives. Through our work with victims, we have identified four models that describe the mechanisms by which positive changes appear to be promoted.

Before presenting these models for positive change, we must offer a few clarifications, restrictions, and generalizations to place the subsequent material in proper perspective. First, we are *not* advocating rape as a positive experience for women. Second, as we have discussed in further detail elsewhere (Kilpatrick *et al.*, 1982), there is considerable diversity among victims, among the characteristics of assaults, among the support systems available to victims after the assault, and among coping skills of victims. Therefore, any statements about how *the* rape victim responds to *the* assault must be recognized as generalizations that do not reflect important individual variability. Third, there are a variety of variables that produce change in psychological functioning, ranging from formal treatment intervention to informal support (or lack of same) from family and friends. The impact of other life changes on the victim is also important, and preliminary data from our project indicate that victims experienced a significantly greater number of life changes in the first year postrape than did nonvictims. Given the vast array of variables that can produce change, it is obvious that any model attempting to explain how change occurs is, of necessity, an over-simplification.

Recognizing that it is somewhat presumptuous of us to outline these models, we proceed in doing so because of our belief that their presentation may clarify how changes occur. We have tentatively identified four models: (a) life threat–life appreciation; (b) agency-, institution-, and system-mediated change; (c) rape as a consciousness-raising experience; and (d) rape as a challenge or test.

B. The Life Threat–Life Appreciation Model

This model is depicted in Figure 7.1. The major features of this model are as follows: First, the rape experience poses a threat to her life as perceived by the victim. Second, this threat to her life prompts the victim to imagine her death and the consequences that her death will have for important people in her life. Third, her survival prompts her (a) to appreciate the value of her life; (b) to reassess priorities in life; and (c) to see the rape experience as a significant crossroads in her life. The major aspects of this model are illustrated in the following case history.

D. P., a 22-year-old white woman, was hitchhiking on a major interstate highway when she accepted a ride with a man in a late-model car. After riding a short distance, the man exited from the interstate, pulled up in an abandoned area, threatened her with a knife, and told her that he was going to kill her. She jumped out of the car and began to run. He overtook her, threw her to the ground, forced himself on top of her, put the knife to her throat, and said, "Before I kill you, bitch, I'm going to have 'relations' with you." He raped her. During the rape, she recalls feeling like she was not in her body.

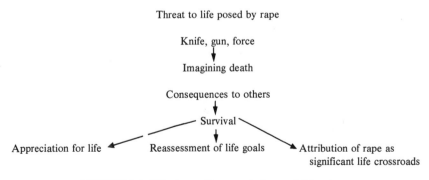

FIGURE 7.1. Life threat–life appreciation model for change.

She has little awareness of exactly what went on. She reports that her thoughts were racing. She imagined herself having her throat slit, being cut up in pieces, and floating in a swamp. She recalls that she could see the faces of her family and their reaction to her death. She remembers having images, feelings, and flashbacks about arguments and disagreements she and her family had in the past. She recalled a suicide attempt 2 years earlier in which she took an overdose of pills. As the assault progressed, she remembered thinking that she did not want to die now—not this way. She wanted to live.

After raping her, the assailant left. She ran to a nearby house; the police were called and she was taken to the Medical University of South Carolina Sexual Assault Treatment Center. She recalled that, at the time of her ride to the treatment center, she was already thanking God for sparing her and allowing her to live. She resolved to make changes in her life, to communicate and establish better relationships with her family. Within 6 weeks following the assault, she joined a church, enrolled in a technical school, stopped drinking and going to bars, started voice lessons, and broke up with her boyfriend, whom she described as a bad influence on her. At 3-month follow-up, she was making good grades in technical school, had lost weight, and reported having established significant relationships with women friends.

This victim's experience is an excellent illustration of how the threat to life of a rape experience promoted a greater appreciation of life and its value as well as considerable reassessment of goals and values. Thus, rape can serve as a crossroads in life; some women take the road leading them to a richer, more satisfying life.

C. The Agency-, Institution-, and System-Mediated Change Model

This model, illustrated in Figure 7.2, has as its key element the notion that detection of a woman as a rape victim facilitates her entry into a variety of service-delivery systems. Her contact with a rape victim advocacy counselor not only provides her with information, support, and counseling about rape-related problems but also identifies her other needs. Thus, the victim is encouraged and helped to obtain services from agencies and institutions that can deal with her other needs and problems. The amelioration of these problems helps the victim achieve a higher level of functioning.

This process is illustrated by the experience of T. C., a 24-year-old white woman of borderline intelligence and multiple social handicaps, as well as the physical handicap of a birth defect that caused her right arm and hand to

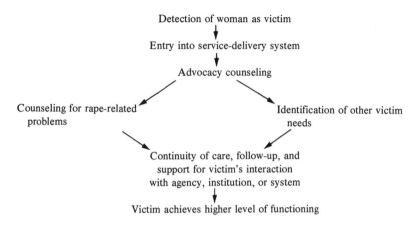

FIGURE 7.2. Agency-, institution-, and system-mediated model for change.

be minimally functional. Her social handicaps included lack of education, inadequate parenting, and living with her elderly, nearly blind father in an isolated rural setting.

T. C. was raped in March of 1978. The police took her to the emergency room of a hospital where she was met by a counselor advocate from People Against Rape. While in no way diminishing the traumatic effect of the rape, the assault, in some respects, was the least important of the conditions and problems that T. C. suffered.

At the emergency room, the gynecologist conducting the examination to gather evidence determined that T. C. had a massive pelvic infection. The source of this infection was the plastic top of a vibrator that had become lodged in her uterus. She was too embarrassed then to tell how the top had become lodged in her, but later reported that her boyfriend had placed it inside of her several months before. Two days after the rape, T. C. was operated on to remove the piece of the vibrator.

T. C. had other physical conditions warranting treatment. T. C. had never been to a dentist; her teeth were brown and rotten. Also, her arm and hand had never been checked by a physician. In fact, she had not received any professional medical care for more than 10 years.

Through the People Against Rape counseling advocate, who provided transportation to her appointments and directed her to the appropriate medical and health clinics, numerous changes were made. All her teeth were pulled and she obtained dentures. She had an operation on her right arm and subsequent physical therapy that made her hand functional. She received information regarding sexual functioning, pregnancy, and birth control. She was visited by a public health nurse who provided her with information about hygiene and nutrition.

These physical changes and the attention of caring individuals promoted an increase in self-esteem. She began to care for herself by wearing clean clothes and grooming her hair and nails. She began going out socially and regularly attending church. At her last appointment with the research project in March of 1980, T. C. brought in pictures of her wedding. She was married several months later to a man she met while attending physical therapy sessions. Latest news of her is that she is the mother of a 2-year-old son.

This case illustrates quite well how a rape experience, through placing the victim in contact with a sympathetic victim advocate, can help a victim make connections with agencies and institutions that can provide badly needed services. It is most unfortunate that some women have to be raped to bring them to the system's attention, but there is little question that some women get considerably better services after a rape experience than before.

D. Rape as a Consciousness-Raising Experience Model

This model for change is depicted in Figure 7.3. As a result of her rape experience, the victim interacts with a feminist counselor–advocate, who is almost always a woman volunteer. The grass-roots rape crisis center movement has been an extremely important force in obtaining better services for victims (Largen, 1976), and research studying the characteristics of women who serve as volunteer counselor–advocates found these women to be low in anxiety and well adjusted psychologically (Best & Kilpatrick, 1977). In addition, to suggesting methods for dealing with various rape-related problems and situations, the advocate serves as a model of a strong, independent woman. Through her analysis of rape from a feminist perspective, the advocate helps the victim realize that her victimization is not an isolated event and that many sociocultural and political factors are important antecedents of rape. Considerable emphasis is placed on the importance of obtaining support from other women as well. As a result of gaining a better understanding of these issues, the victim identifies other areas of exploitation and victimization in her life. She then makes personal and situational changes in order to take more control of her life. This model is illustrated by the following case history.

C. W. is a 30-year-old white woman who had been assaulted 7 years ago by an acquaintance. She sought to prosecute; there was a court trial; her assailant was acquitted. She felt humiliated and thought no one believed she

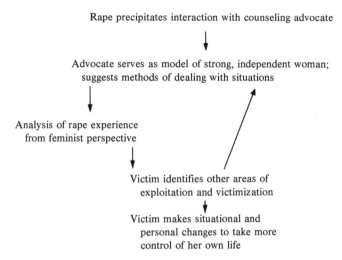

Rape precipitates interaction with counseling advocate

Advocate serves as model of strong, independent woman;
suggests methods of dealing with situations

Analysis of rape experience
from feminist perspective

Victim identifies other areas of
exploitation and victimization

Victim makes situational and
personal changes to take more
control of her own life

FIGURE 7.3. Rape as a consciousness-raising experience model for change.

had been raped. She moved to Charleston and obtained a job. C. W. came to our attention through the counselor-training program of People Against Rape where she had volunteered to become a rape crisis counselor. Because of her lack of perspective on the rape event, which was revealed through her defensiveness, anger, and inability to empathize with and listen to others, she was counseled, and it was suggested that she participate in our research treatment study.

Two years ago, she entered the peer-counseling treatment of the Sexual Assault Research Project. Among the concerns and fears for which she sought treatment were fear that her husband might sexually exploit her daughter, a child by a previous marriage, and her perceived inability to stop advances by men.

The focus of the peer-counseling treatment was exploration and investigation of societal myths and attitudes regarding rape and women's sexuality, as well as the relationships between the genders. An effort was made to break down sex-role stereotypes and to see women as sources of support, influence, and power. Suggestions for dealing with difficult situations were offered by the advocate, employing principles of assertiveness training.

While in peer-counseling treatment, C. W. identified several problem areas and situations. She felt exploited, humiliated, and intimidated by the rape that had occurred 7 years ago. She felt her husband was preoccupied with sex and her sexual functioning. He was sexually demanding of her, with little concern for her pleasure. A third problem area was division of household chores. Her husband expected her to do all the housework and child care, yet he was unemployed and home all day. Her job situation was also a source of dissatisfaction. She was working as a cosmetologist, selling an expensive line of cosmetics at a large department store. She felt that pushing expensive cosmetics on women who could purchase cheaper products was exploitive.

As a result of her participation in peer-counseling treatment, she made several changes. She has become increasingly assertive in her marriage and in her sexual interactions with her spouse. She has told him what she will do and will not do regarding sex. She has arranged a more equitable division of household duties. Additionally, she is striving to make job changes that are more consistent with her abilities and interests. She is taking night classes to move into sales management rather than direct selling. One other important change that must also be noted is how she relates to other women. She now seeks the company and support of women through groups, such as assertiveness training for women, and interpersonally by going out to lunch and shopping with women friends. She is presently a counselor–advocate with People Against Rape.

Space limitations preclude a comprehensive examination of the issues involved in consciousness-raising, feminist-oriented approaches for working with rape victims, although this topic has been reported on elsewhere (Albin, 1977; Veronen & Kilpatrick, Note 3). However, this case illustrates key elements of such approaches: A strong emphasis on helping women understand that they have the right to make important decisions about their own lives while encouraging them to seek the support of other women in their attempt to make desired changes.

E. Management of Rape Reaction as Test or Challenge Model

The key elements of this model are outlined in Figure 7.4. The rape victim has the expectation that rape is a devastating event that causes its victims to fall apart and their lives to be ruined. The victim resolves to avoid this typical reaction. Although she may experience distress, she suffers silently or alone but forces herself to behave as normally as possible. Because of her maintaining normal behavior and avoiding "typical" reactions, she appraises herself as brave, strong, and capable. Additionally, she receives support from other people for her strong behavior. Having met the challenge of her rape experience successfully, the victim is then encouraged to attempt other

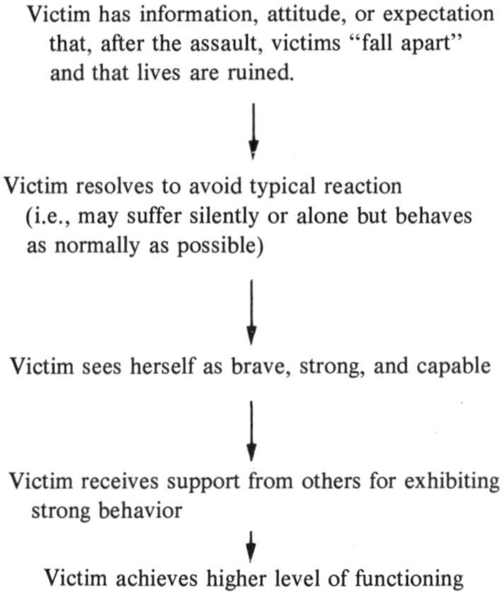

Victim has information, attitude, or expectation
that, after the assault, victims "fall apart"
and that lives are ruined.

↓

Victim resolves to avoid typical reaction
(i.e., may suffer silently or alone but behaves
as normally as possible)

↓

Victim sees herself as brave, strong, and capable

↓

Victim receives support from others for exhibiting
strong behavior

↓

Victim achieves higher level of functioning

FIGURE 7.4. Management of rape reaction as a test or challenge model for change.

difficult or challenging endeavors. This model is illustrated in the following case history.

M. S., a 28-year-old mother of three, was raped by an unknown man in midday while she was at home with her children. The assailant threatened to kill her children if she attempted to resist.

A few weeks prior to the rape, M. S. had watched a television show of an account of a rape victim. The television character's life was all but ruined as a result of the rape. The police intervention was intimidating, and the victim wished she had not reported the rape. Additionally, her husband was accusatory, and he ultimately divorced her.

This television program had a strong impact on M. S. It appeared to serve as a model for her on how *not* to behave. M. S., according to her own report, was a highly emotional person; yet, subsequent to the rape, she strived to be calm and controlled. She saw the rape as a test. She recalled that one of her friends had commented to her, "I don't know how you are holding up. I didn't think you'd be able to stay together after all you've been through." Comments of this type served to strengthen M. S.'s motivation to manage her reactions. She recalled talking to herself: "I can't fall apart; I must be strong." Her husband was also complimentary and appreciative of her strength. She reported that their relationship had improved.

At her last assessment, 6 months after the assault, she reported that she felt stronger, more capable, and more mature than she had ever felt in her life.

IV. Conclusions

In this chapter we have discussed issues surrounding definitions of rape and nonnormative life events. We have made the case that rape is a nonnormative life event that has profound effects on the victim. Data have been presented regarding psychological responses to sexual assault, both with respect to the typical responses of most victims and more atypical positive responses. Finally, we proposed four models that appear to mediate and/or explain positive changes that occur subsequent to rape.

Given the scope of material covered, the complexity of the topic, and the exploratory nature of our research, it is not surprising that several questions remain unanswered. What are the characteristics of women who make positive changes? How do they differ and how do their environments differ from women who respond more negatively? What strategies do women use to cope successfully, and can these strategies be taught to other women? The feminist movement has prompted great changes in the status of women and in the options that are open to women. It has also provided a much more accepting and supportive atmosphere for rape victims. How have these changes affected the aftermath of rape for the victim?

An extremely important question concerns the unique contribution of the volunteer advocate in promoting positive changes. Do volunteers provide something that is difficult for professionals to provide, or is the key factor the presence of someone who is sympathetic, knowledgeable about rape, and accepting?

Another important question is what are the effects of early intervention with victims on their subsequent functioning? Do victims with whom there is contact soon after the rape do better than those with whom there is no contact? There is some evidence from our research that victims who do not have the benefit of counseling experience more distress than those who have contact with advocates.

What conclusions can be drawn from the material we have presented? The first and most important one is that rape can be a precursor for positive change. A second conclusion is that the change models we have identified are probably applicable to stressful life events other than rape.

A final conclusion takes the form of some speculations about how a woman can overcome the effects of rape. To overcome the effects of such a traumatic, life-threatening event, it is necessary for her to mobilize considerable resources, both internal and external. She must discover strength within herself she did not know she had. She will benefit greatly if she can also gain the external support of women and men who understand rape and who support the right of women to be freed from attitudes and values that lock them into stereotypic, subservient roles. In this way, victims may eventually "get beyond" their rape experience and place it in proper perspective. That is, they must eventually get to the point where they do not define their identity exclusively as a rape victim.

Reference Notes

1. Veronen, L. J., Kilpatrick, D. G., & Best, C. L. *The invisible woman: Characteristics of the rape victim who does not participate in research*. Paper presented at the 24th annual convention of the Southwestern Psychological Association, New Orleans, April 1978.
2. Kilpatrick, D. G., Veronen, L. J., & Resick, P. A. *Aftermath of rape: One-year follow-up*. Paper presented at the 13th annual convention of the Association for Advancement of Behavior Therapy, San Francisco, December 1979.
3. Veronen, L. J., & Kilpatrick, D. G. *The response to rape: The impact of rape on self-esteem*. Paper presented at the 26th annual convention of the Southwestern Psychological Association, Oklahoma City, April 1980.

References

Albin, R. S. Review essay: Psychological studies of rape. *SIGNS: Journal of Women in Culture and Society*, 1977, *3*(2), 423–435.

Best, C. L., & Kilpatrick, D. G. Psychological profiles of rape crisis counselors. *Psychological Reports*, 1977, *40*, 1127–1134.

Burgess, A. W., & Holmstrom, L. L. *Rape: Victims of crisis*. Bowie, Md.: Robert J. Brady Co., 1974.

Burt, M. R. Cultural myths and supports for rape. *Journal of Personality and Social Psychology*, 1980, *38*, 217–230.

Chappell, D. Forcible rape and the criminal justice system: Surveying present practices and projecting future trends. In M. J. Walker & S. L. Brodsky (Eds.), *Sexual assault: The victim and the rapist*. Lexington, Mass.: D. C. Heath, 1976.

Derogatis, L. R. *SCL-90R manual*. Printed in U.S.A. by Leonard R. Derogatis, Ph.D., Clinical Psychometrics Research Unit, Johns Hopkins University, Baltimore, 1977.

Kilpatrick, D. G., Best, C. L., & Veronen, L. J. The adolescent rape victim: Psychological responses to sexual assault and treatment approaches. In A. K. Kreutner & D. R. Hollingsworth (Eds.), *Adolescent obstetrics and gynecology*. Chicago: Year Book Medical Publishers, 1978.

Kilpatrick, D. G., Veronen, L. J., & Resick, P. A. The aftermath of rape: Recent empirical findings. *American Journal of Orthopsychiatry*, 1979, *49*(4), 658–669. (a)

Kilpatrick, D. G., Veronen, L. J., & Resick, P. A. Assessment of the aftermath of rape: Changing patterns of fear. *Journal of Behavioral Assessment*, 1979, *1*(2), 133–148. (b)

Kilpatrick, D. G., Veronen, L. J., & Resick, P. A. Psychological sequelae to rape: Implications for treatment. In D. M. Doleys, R. L. Meredith, & A. R. Ciminero (Eds.), *Behavioral medicine: Assessment and treatment strategies*. New York: Plenum, 1982.

Kreutner, A. K., & Hollingsworth, D. R. (Eds.). *Adolescent obstetrics and gynecology*. Chicago: Year Book Medical Publishers, 1978.

Largen, M. A. History of women's movement in changing attitudes, laws, and treatment toward rape victims. In M. J. Walker & S. L. Brodsky (Eds.), *Sexual assault*. Lexington, Mass.: D. C. Heath, 1976.

Veronen, L. J., & Kilpatrick, D. G. Self-reported fears of rape victims: A preliminary investigation. *Behavior Modification*, 1980.

Veronen, L. J., Kilpatrick, D. G., & Resick, P. A. Treatment of fear and anxiety in rape victims: Implications for the criminal justice system. In W. H. Parsonage (Ed.), *Perspectives on victimology*. Beverly Hills, Calif.: Sage, 1979.

CHAPTER 8

Violence to the Family

ROBERT L. BURGESS
JAMES GARBARINO
BONNIE GILSTRAP
THE PENNSYLVANIA STATE UNIVERSITY
UNIVERSITY PARK, PENNSYLVANIA

I. Introduction

The theme of this chapter is that developmentally significant nonnormative life events can be conceptualized usefully in terms of those events that damage or do violence to the normal functioning of families. Thus, our use of the term *nonnormative* is unconventional in at least two respects. First, we have selected a functional definition of nonnormative events rather than a statistically or rule-based definition. Second, we argue that the family is the principal context in which the consequences of life events should be assessed.

We begin our analysis by providing a rationale for the use of such a functional approach and for the family as our basic unit of analysis. We next turn to a discussion of the "normative" role of the family as the central arena for individual development throughout the life span. Our analysis of families as contexts for human development also includes a discussion of those properties of families that present developmental risks for their members. The analysis then proceeds to consider external and internal threats to

LIFE-SPAN DEVELOPMENTAL PSYCHOLOGY
Nonnormative Life Events

families as well as the major consequences those threats have for the normal functioning of families.

II. Assessing the Seriousness of Nonnormative Life Events

Writing in 1974, Manis proposed three criteria for assessing the seriousness of a social problem: its "primacy," its "magnitude," and its "severity." *Primacy* refers to a problem's role in producing or precipitating other problems (e.g., poverty is a primary problem because it is implicated in a wide range of other problems). *Magnitude* refers to the frequency of the problem in a population (e.g., the number of cases of juvenile delinquency per 1000 families). *Severity* refers to the degree of damage or threat associated with a particular problem (e.g., permanent brain damage leading to profound mental retardation). We propose to use these criteria in seeking to understand the impact of nonnormative life events on the family.

Nonnormative life events have been previously defined in several ways. Most recently, life-span developmentalists (e.g., Baltes, Cornelius, & Nesselroade, 1979) have adopted a statistically based model focusing on the timing, unpredictability, and/or relatively low frequency of nonnormative life events. Other theorists (e.g., Blake & Davis, 1964) have focused on the rule-based character of social norms to define as nonnormative that which is not sanctioned by society.

Although these definitions do offer insight into some definitive characteristics of individual nonnormative events, they do not explain what makes a nonnormative event significant beyond the experience of the individual person. Our concern with violence to the family encompasses those events that potentially can do damage to the normal functioning of families. We use this challenge to normality rather than infrequency or social stigma to identify nonnormative events. Moreover, we move away from focusing strictly on individual development and use the family as our unit of analysis.

We propose this alternative, functional definition of nonnormative life events, because our interest is anchored by a concern for the human significance of events (i.e., their "seriousness" [Manis, 1974]). We suggest that events that challenge the normal functioning of families are the most serious of life events because they have multiple consequences. They affect the life of the community in which the family is embedded, as well as the lives of individual children and adults. In the terms proposed by Manis, such events have the greatest primacy. Furthermore, these problems have considerable magnitude, because families are empirically the principal contexts for the development of individuals and because individual life events (e.g., suicide) most often affect the individual's family as well. Finally, because the primary functions of families involve the basic processes of creating and maintaining human character, challenges to families are always potentially severe.

Thus, we intend to adapt the concept of nonnormative life events to explore violence to the family and its results for family life. *Violence* will be considered functionally, as damaging stress that impinges on the family as a whole. *Conflict* will be used to refer to the internal strife among family members that can result from or cause violence to the family. It should be noted that our functional definition of nonnormative events implies that "normative" or adaptive events are those that contribute to an individual's adjustment to prevailing environmental circumstances. As Cairns (1977) has aptly noted, adaptation to certain environments sometimes requires "the development of activities that may depart markedly from the norm of the species [p. 1]." It should be further noted that we will be concerned with those events that do violence by producing stress for the family as a unit, maintaining as we do that very few individual life events occur independently of an individual's family. From this perspective, any event that interferes with the normal family processes of families (marriage, childbearing, and childrearing) can be considered nonnormative. Family functioning serves as the "gold standard" upon which the currency of our social life is based.

Before turning to an examination of violence to the family, we first need to consider one other reason why the family serves as a particularly useful unit of analysis for analyzing nonnormative life events. This rationale follows from the growing application of evolutionary theory to human social relationships (Alexander, 1979; Barash, 1977; Chagnon & Irons, 1979; Wilson, 1975). From this perspective, the family is important not only because it serves as a bridge linking individuals to the larger community, nor because the family is the principal context in which most early and much later individual development takes place, but also because *homo sapiens*, as a species, has, throughout its history, solved problems of survival and adaptation by establishing close attachments to individuals related by blood (Lancaster & Whitten, 1980). Moreover, as we shall see, several of the concepts and principles of modern evolutionary biology provide us with a broader theoretical context for identifying the principal components of normal family functioning.

The most fundamental assumption of evolutionary theory is that all of life, from the beginning of time, has been subjected to a continual process of natural selection or differential reproduction. Alexander (1979), an evolutionary biologist, has cogently argued that altruistic behavior toward close relatives has played a key role in the evolution of human behavior in general, and social relationships in particular. His argument pivots around the assumption that humans evolved to be altruistic toward their offspring and other genetic relatives. Thus, altruism is not indiscriminate. Rather, by being directed principally toward our children and other relatives, such behavior has had the function of increasing the probability of our own genes being represented in succeeding generations. Consequently, and paradoxically, altruism is fundamentally selfish. As outlandish as this notion may appear to persons unfamiliar with evolutionary biology, there is a growing body of evidence drawn from interspecific comparisons as well as from historical analyses that the probability of altruistic behavior varies proportionately with the degree of relatedness (e.g., Chagnon & Irons, 1979). This process has been labeled the *principle of inclusive fitness*. However, for this principle to operate we would need to be able to make fairly accurate assessments of our genetic relationships. Without discussing the mechanisms by which we learn to make such assessments, it is quite clear that, as a species, we have seemed to be obsessed with the identification of genealogies and blood relationships. Every known human language devotes numerous terms to the recognition of individuals in terms of their genetic relationships. As the work of anthropologists indicates, even the simplest societies typically have subtle and complex kinship systems (Fox, 1972). And, sociologists such as Parsons (1964) and Buck and Jacobson (1968) have discussed the role of kinship relations in the evolution of complex human society. Thus, there is reason to suspect that much of our behavior today can ultimately be related to the contributions those behaviors make to our inclusive fitness (i.e., the transmission of our genes to succeeding generations), including the universal tendency to court potential mates, to establish relatively enduring bonds with each other, to produce and care for offspring, and to mourn the loss of loved ones.

One of the most important concepts of evolutionary theory is parental investment (Trivers, 1972; Williams, 1966). *Parental investment* refers to behavior displayed by a parent that increases the reproductive potential of the child toward whom the behavior is directed, at the cost of similar investment by the parent toward other or future offspring. Implicit in the definition is the notion that a parent has limited resources and a finite life span to expend those resources in the rearing of children. Knowing this, some basis for the preferential distribution of resources and energies would be expected simply because random behavior would not be adaptive in an evolutionary sense.

Examples of the adaptive quality of selective parental investment abound in the ethological literature. For example, the bonding of mother to infant has been reported for most species where there is any period of relative dependency of young on parental nurture for survival (Cairns, 1979). Bonding has the effect of making a parent selective with regard to the distribution of limited resources. Moreover, there is evidence that parental nurture is neither dispensed indiscriminately to all conspecific young (e.g., Hrdy, 1974) nor is it invariant over a parent's reproductive lifetime (Barash, 1977). If an individual parent's investment in his or her offspring varies adaptively, then we should expect that parental care of children would be limited by circumstances that predict a reduced probability of inclusive fitness payoffs or that involve intolerable social or psychological costs for the parent. We shall touch on each of these eventualities in later sections.

What we wish to emphasize now, however, is the fact that, from biological as well as psychological and sociological perspectives, the family historically has played a decisive role as a chief site for individual development. With these arguments in mind we can begin our examination of violence to the family. This will require a discussion of families as an essential context for individual development, normative family functioning, and external and internal threats, including conflict and other effects of nonnormative events on family functioning. We see this discussion as a useful exercise because it opens the way for a more ecologically valid and socially useful conception of nonnormative events, one that can serve as a bridge to other important areas of research and policy (cf. Bronfenbrenner, 1979).

III. Families as Contexts for Human Development

Defined as a unit of related individuals in which children are born and reared, the family is the primary context for human development. The overwhelming majority of children grow up within the confines of a family (Bane, 1976). Thus, cognitive development, social competence, academic achievement, and occupational aspirations are fundamentally affected by the quality of a child's family life (cf. Jencks, 1972). What is more, the family determines a child's socioeconomic status, with all that implies for place of residence, peer association, educational opportunities, and even the selection of potential mates. There are also significant legal implications associated with the family, ranging from rights and obligations that run the gamut from economic interdependence, to sexual access, to the use of physical force (Fraser, 1976). Consequently, the developmental significance of the family derives from a network of overlapping social forces working in concert (Bronfenbrenner, 1979).

The very quality of the children produced by a family reflects that family's place in the community. One example of this is the relationship between early developmental delay and subsequent intellectual impairment. Willerman, Broman, and Fiedler (1970) found that 12% of children from low-income families who were developmentally delayed at 8 months of age were mentally retarded at 4 years of age (i.e., their IQ was less than 79), whereas the equivalent figure for children with similar characteristics from middle- and high-income families was less than 1%. Comparable results have been found by other investigators (Drillien, 1964; Werner, Simonian, Bierman, & French, 1967). Thus, even the implications of early developmental delay seem to depend in part on the circumstances of the family in which it occurs.

There is little doubt that the influence of the family is paramount for children. They literally rise and fall on the basis of what their family offers in the way of personal and social resources (cf. Garbarino & Gilliam, 1980). What may be less clear is how adults depend on families, and how families shape adult development. We can begin with the fact that creating a family, through marriage and childbearing, is a strongly normative act—in both the statistical and cultural sense. Ideology aside, adults believe in family living and act on that belief (cf. Blake, 1979). Survey evidence documents that "the most satisfying part of life to . . . Americans today is family life. A substantial 92% of the public say this is very important to them. And 67% say they are very satisfied with the way their family life is going [Harris, 1978, p. 1]." Despite the trauma of divorce, most divorced American adults (80%) seek out opportunities for remarriage, and the rate of initial marriage remains high (Spanier & Glick, 1980). Most persons also retain a sense of normative timing of the key events in the family life course—even when their own behavior violates those norms (cf. Hill & Mattessich, 1979; Nock, 1979). The cultural status of the family endures even if its social standing is jeopardized by a variety of threatening and stressful forces.

Adopting a systems approach to human development can help us see that the family is the central "microsystem" in the lives of both children and adults (Bronfenbrenner, 1979). One way to appreciate the centrality of the family as a context for development is to examine the joint concepts of risk and opportunity as they apply to family microsystems.

Families present developmental risks when they are *structurally inadequate*, when they are *asymmetrically predictable*, and when interaction is dominated by *negative affect*. They are structurally inadequate when there are insufficient adults to perform the normative functions prescribed by expressive and instrumental roles (Parsons, 1964). This complementary diversity is an important resource for both children and adults within a family. A structurally complete family, in the sense of having multiple adults, presents many developmental opportunities. A well-connected family, one that is tied to potent prosocial support systems and social networks, is stronger still (Garbarino, 1977, 1980b). The issue is not so much one of personal characteristics as it is of social system characteristics.

As individuals, single parents may be excellent caregivers. Indeed, the ability of single parents to cope with the awesome task of rearing children alone is testimony to the strength of the human character (cf. Brandwein, 1974; Hetherington, 1979). But as microsystems, their families may be insufficient, unless they are augmented from the outside to produce a fuller, richer range of roles, activities, and relationships for the child to use in his or her development. In this respect, the single-parent family is part of a larger trend toward an "emptying" of the family microsystem. Mothers are more likely to be working outside the home in the labor force (more than one-half do); kin are less likely to be involved in the child's day-to-day life because of geographic mobility and a trend towards privacy; age segregation in housing has increased (with old and young going their separate ways); and, the many distractions of modern life pull parents away from the home and result in less time being spent in the kind of purposeful, cooperative activities that nurture child development (Garbarino, 1980c). A recent replication of the classic Middletown survey of youth done originally some 50 years ago, found that adolescents now wish their mothers could spend more time with them, where once they seemed to take it for granted that she would (Bahr, Note 1). Also, they still wish that their fathers could spend more time with them, testimony to our continuing problems with the paternal role. It is reasonable for us to worry about this emptying of the family microsystem because the available data suggest it is linked to a variety of developmental difficulties (Bronfenbrenner, 1975). It does violence to the normal family.

One of the essential features of a normal family is "reciprocity"—the give-and-take of interaction that both respects and challenges the child, that stimulates the child and responds contingently to the child's behavior. When this essential reciprocity is significantly reduced it jeopardizes development. How does this happen? It happens when the balance of power within the family microsystem becomes one-sided and patterns of interaction become asymmetrically predictable (Gottman, 1979). Typically this means that the parent or parents seize complete control of the parent–child relationship and seek to dominate the child—and thus thwart his or her development, although it could mean that a child or adolescent has assumed a dictatorial role (Patterson, 1976). More typically, however, it is a parent who assumes a tyrannical stance. With an infant this may mean extreme rigidity with respect to feeding and other aspects of caregiving. The natural way of things is for the infant to play an active role in shaping the parent's behavior, just as it is natural for the parent to influence the infant (Bell, 1968). This is a healthy family microsystem. When the parent refuses to be influenced by the infant's tempo, rhythms, cycles, and spontaneous verbal and facial gestures, the essential principle of reciprocity is violated and normal family functioning is jeopardized.

For the older child, the issue of asymmetry in interaction structure is found in the childrearing style adopted by parents. Baumrind's (1979) studies of childrearing styles and their consequences for development provide an insight to the importance of reciprocity to the family microsystem. She found that where reciprocity was upheld in day-to-day interaction (what she called an "authoritative" orientation) the child is provided with the greatest number of opportunities to develop social competence. Where it was systematically violated, the child's development suffered. An "authoritarian" style violated the principle of symmetry by lodging excessive power in the hands of the parent and thus placing the child in a passive role. A "permissive" pattern inappropriately gave carte blanche to the child and his unformed drives, and thus placed the parent in a passive role. Neither the authoritarian nor the permissive style does justice to the family.

Children's experiences in the family color their views of the world. Children incorporate these experiences into their emerging concepts of themselves, the world, and their place in that world (cf. Coopersmith, 1967). The microsystem problems of structural inadequacy and asymmetrical predictability are important, but probably of equal or greater importance is a normal affective tone—one that is positive and supportive. A negative tone can be expressed in the full range of microsystem behaviors, including what is said, or not said, and what is done or not done. A positive climate produces a kind of social momentum in the child, whereas a negative climate produces social deadweight. Positive climate contributes to success in the world because it gives the child a reservoir of self-confidence that is an important foundation for competence (McClelland, 1973). A negative climate makes the child vulnerable to being easily discouraged by everyday problems and turns the child away from full and satisfying participation in the world. As such it is part of nonnormative family functioning.

Coopersmith (1967) demonstrated that the child's microsystem plays an extremely important role in determining whether the child experiences the world and himself in positive or negative terms. A nurturing, involved, and actively contributing parent tends to produce high self-esteem in the child, whereas a passive, neglectful, and uninvolved parent produces low self-esteem. Much as the slogan "you are what you eat" conveys the notion that we become what is offered to us, so the statement "you are what you are shown about yourself by others" conveys the notion that children construct an image of themselves based on feedback from significant others. This view of personality is in the classic tradition of George Herbert Mead (1934) and others who argue that by defining the roles a person plays we go far toward defining the person. To deprive the child of positive self-regard, either by deliberately deprecating his or her accomplishments, or conveying a sense of worthlessness by neglect, is to place the child at developmental risk, and may constitute emotional abuse (Gabarino, 1978).

To develop a positive sense of self the child needs warm, responsive, and active partners. The microsystem can fail the child in two ways. One is presented by neglectful parents who starve the child of emotional sustenance. These parents are likely to exhibit what Polansky (1976) calls "the apathy–futility syndrome." The elements of this pattern are a kind of emotional deadness, an unwillingness to initiate behavior, a pervading sense of ineffectiveness, and a general unresponsiveness to the initiatives of the child. The developmental threat posed by this apathy–futility syndrome is that it characterizes adults in microsystems who are unable or unwilling to provide the intense, contingent interaction necessary to the adequate development of competence and self-esteem. Rather, these caregivers project a world view of passivity, depression, and rejection. There is little of the active encouragement needed to develop a personal reservoir of self-esteem and positive regard.

Like all personality or trait variables, the apathy–futility syndrome needs to be understood in terms of actual behavior. Burgess and his colleagues have provided such documentation (e.g., Burgess, Anderson, & Schellenbach & Conger 1980). They observed families interacting in their homes both in unstructured interaction and in pursuit of several tasks provided by the investigators. The principal conclusion of these studies was that parents who otherwise abuse and neglect their children interact with each other less often than normal families—they are less positive and more negative. They also issue commands to each other more often yet comply less, and they are more likely to reciprocate negative affect behavior than they are positive behavior. This is certainly a social system well suited to the task of producing psychologically damaged human beings.

This pattern is detrimental to children. It is part and parcel of a broader risk: rejection. Children who are rejected are in trouble (cf. Rohner & Nielson, 1978). This is the conclusion of Rohner's wide-ranging studies of the problem. Rohner (1975) examined rejection, its antecedents and consequences, in cultures all over the world. He found that across cultures rejection is a kind of emotional malignancy, a psychological cancer that eats away at the individual's capacity for self-esteem, social competence, and hope. Rohner (1975) concluded that "parental rejection in children as well as adults who were rejected as children, leads to: hostility, aggression, passive aggression, or problems with the management of hostility and aggression; dependency; probably emotional unresponsiveness and negative self-evaluation (negative self-esteem and negative self-adequacy); and probably, emotional instability as well as a negative world view [p. 168]."

Rohner also found that rejection increased when a child's caregivers were isolated from the nurture and feedback of interested others—kith and kin. The normal family is a social as well as a psychological creature. It depends on support from without as much as support from within (Rossi, 1968). It is threatened by internal conflict as well as by conflict with the community and larger society.

In brief, an effective family is one that provides: (a) a stable context for childbearing; (b) a stable context for childrearing; (c) a context that reinforces prosocial behavior and the development of competence; (d) a context that provides intimacy and sexual satisfaction; (e) a context that serves as an economic unit—for consumption and income transfers (and for production to some extent). These functions are rooted in the evolutionary history and contemporary purposes of families. The basic needs of children and adults are relatively constant across time and place. Effective families are so because they meet these needs. When conditions outside or inside the family undermine the essential functions just noted, they do violence to the family and, thereby, lower the overall adaptiveness of society.

The quality of parent–child relations is a social indicator (i.e., it marks the degree to which "all's right with the world") for a family and is associated with the social fortunes of families. Straus, Gelles, and Steinmetz (1980) found some 21 social stress factors that were associated with the use of aggressive physical force in families. Similarly, Steinberg, Catalano, and Dooley (Note 2) found that child maltreatment rates are associated with economic shifts within a community: Economic downturns produce increased rates of child abuse. Thus, parent–child relations reflect the quality of the family environment and are responsive to a variety of external and internal threats.

IV. External Threats to Family Functioning

One of the chief external threats to families is "social impoverishment" (i.e., stealing away the nurture and constructive feedback families need to cope with stress [Garbarino, 1980b]). We know that chronic economic impoverishment is bad for families; it undermines health and well-being (Kenniston, 1977; National Academy of Sciences, 1976). We know that acute economic deprivation undermines families, particularly where the marital relationship is weak (Elder & Rockwell, Note 3). Chronic poverty and acute economic deprivation do violence to families insofar as they interfere with normative functioning. Therefore, our notion of poverty is primarily a social concept. Economic forces are significant to the degree to which they produce social impoverishment. This view highlights the importance of the broader cultural and societal context of families, because it is this larger context that both spawns economic deprivation and gives significance to it by defining and implementing the social and political implications of poverty (Elder, 1977).

Economic deprivation is not the only external threat to normal family functioning, of course. Of equal or greater importance are values that are antithetical to the best interests of families and children. Families depend on a supportive context in which the weight of culture and politics stand clearly behind families, where performing family roles is given strong support (Featherstone, 1979). Where values encourage behavior incompatible with such roles (e.g., favoring materialist acquisition and career development over investment in family activities), or where they permit commercial exploitation of children, families are threatened. They are likewise threatened when the culture is suspicious of children and subordinates their needs and interests to adult convenience and political action (e.g., when children are turned against their parents by the state). A prime example of this was Nazi Germany where efforts were made "to align institutional and personal life with service to the state [Garbarino & Bronfenbrenner, 1976, p. 80]."

Political threats to normal family functioning play an important historical role. Families are the principal casualties of war and revolution. The father-absence associated with World War II and the millions of homeless children produced by the 1920s civil war in the Soviet Union are but two examples (cf., Garbarino & Bronfenbrenner, 1976). Perhaps because of its evolutionary function, the family is basically a conservative institution. It resists revolutionary change and is thus often the target of revolutionaries. It thrives in a political climate of diversity within stability. Threats to political pluralism are threats to families, whether they come from the right or the left (Garbarino & Bronfenbrenner, 1976).

The external threats of socioeconomic deprivation, antifamily values, and political disruption undermine the necessary relationship between families and support systems. They deplete the social resources on which families depend. The result is social impoverishment. In addition to external threats, threats internal to the family have an erosive effect, and are thus also nonnormative with respect to families.

V. Internal Threats to Family Functioning

A. Structural Stresses

It has been suggested that there are several structural features of family life that may contribute to the occurrence of conflict within marriages and families (Burgess, 1979; Gelles & Straus, 1979). Among these structural characteristics is the great amount of time family members spend in face-to-face contact. One consequence of spending a considerable amount of time in close contact with someone is that otherwise trivial annoyances can easily become exaggerated in importance, perhaps because of their predictability. Another consequence is the gradual overlap of interests and activities. These, in turn, become circumstances around which conflicts of interest arise, giving rise to disputes and disagreements. Contributing to these conflicts of interest is the finite nature of most family resources. Thus, parents and children may disagree, for example, about what constitutes appropriate care of family possessions or property.

Still another characteristic of family life that may set the stage for conflict is the high level of emotional involvement that typifies families and which generates its own risk, as when one spouse deceives the other or a child fails to live up to a parent's expectations. A third structural characteristic of families is that membership usually implies the right (and for parents the obligation) to influence or control other family members' behavior. Given the additional fact that, in most societies, the kinship and household structure insulates the family from the social constraints of other individuals and groups, dissatisfaction with the conduct of another family member may be exacerbated by inept or aggressive attempts to change that person's behavior. All of these structural features of families, as well as others such as the fact that membership is largely involuntary (at least for children), can easily lead to escalating disengagement and disaffection. In support of this argument there is evidence that we often tend to be less gentle, polite, and approving with members of our own families than we are with strangers (Birchler, Weiss, & Vincent, 1975; Ryder, 1968; Winter, Ferreira & Bowers, 1973).

Given such structural stresses, as well as the external threats to families discussed earlier, it is understandable that many marriages fail. Indeed, it has recently been estimated that 40–50% of all first marriages eventually end in divorce (Weed, Note 4). And, importantly, divorce turns out to be a major crisis for most people. For example, Gurin, Keroff, and Feld (1960) discovered that approximately 25% of divorced men and 40% of divorced women seek some form of professional help for personal problems. From a life-span perspective, it is interesting to note that younger people seem to have an easier time adjusting to divorce since they can more easily mix with groups of young, never-married persons. An important alternative source of support, for older divorced persons especially, are kin groups that often help out by providing companionship, lending money, offering child care services, and making their homes available (Weiss, 1975).

One of the more troublesome issues resulting from divorce is who will retain or attain custody of the children. Furthermore, even beyond the trials surrounding custody, children generally find the transition from a two-parent to a single-parent household painful (Hetherington, 1979). Common responses are anger, fear, depression, and guilt. Though this discord may, under some circumstances, wane as early as 1 year following the divorce (Hetherington, 1979), it has also been found that single parenthood in lower SES families actually contributes to the occurrence of those family interaction patterns found to be associated with child abuse and neglect (Burgess et al., 1980).

Another potential cause of stress that may do violence to families by increasing the probability of coercive styles of interaction is the sheer size of the family. Holding resources constant, increasing the membership of a family should result in fewer resources available per family member and thus increase the likelihood of conflicts of interest over those resources. Indeed, research indicates an inverse relationship between family size and a family's standard of living (Douglas & Blomfield, 1958), nutrition (U.S. Commission on Population Growth and the American Future, 1972), infant mortality (Terhune, 1974), and levels of health and physical development (Tanner, 1968). Parental time and energy are themselves limited resources, and it seems reasonable to expect that their allocation per child may decrease as family size increases. Research by Burgess and his colleagues indicates that there is a strong inverse correlation between family size and the frequency of direct verbal contacts between a parent and a child, and that the general emotional climate becomes more negative as these interactions occur less frequently (Burgess et al., 1980). Again, such a pattern would be especially likely in low-income families where resources are already relatively scarce. Thus, external and internal threats may interact to violate normative family functioning.

In the next section, we shall discuss individual characteristics of both children and adults that may function as threats to effective family relationships, but one such characteristic overlaps with family structure, and thus will be mentioned here. We are referring to the nature of the biological relationship between parents and children. According to estimates from the

U.S. Bureau of the Census (1977), 85–90% of all children live with at least one of their natural parents. Should the divorce rate continue at its present high level, the percentage would, of course, decrease. Nonetheless, what is significant about these present figures for the normative functioning of families is that data from several samples of child-abuse cases drawn from England, New Zealand, and the United States reveal that a full 50% of those cases were families with stepparent–stepchild relationships in the home (Burgess, 1980a). Such empirical findings are consistent with predictions from the evolutionary principle of inclusive fitness. What is more important, however, is the fact that a step-relationship may result in up to a fivefold increased probability of a child being abused.

B. Individual Characteristics

The effects of external and structural threats on overt conflict within the family may be mediated by the individual characteristics of children and adults. Some families consist of strong, healthy, easygoing individuals who seem to be able to withstand huge amounts of stress. Other individuals may have learned effective coping skills to deal with stress. However, there are certain attributes of individual members that can present additional threats to normative family functioning, either by independently producing stress or by reducing the individual's and the family's ability to cope with stress from other sources.

The realization that children, as well as their parents, shape the course of their development by affecting family interaction, is a fairly recent perspective in the field of child development. Articles by Milow and Lourie in 1964 and by Bell in 1968 spawned considerable research and thought on how children affect caregivers (e.g., Lerner, Spanier, & Belsky, 1980; Lewis & Rosenblum, 1974). Moreover, this perspective has led to the identification of child characteristics that threaten normal family functioning.

Many of the threats to families that children produce are a result of congenital conditions, characteristics over which they have little or no control. For example, premature babies have repeatedly been found to be overrepresented in populations of abused children (Parke & Collmer, 1975). Prematurity can place stress on infants and parents in several ways. An obvious one is the element of surprise. The infant is not developmentally ready for the many stimuli of the world outside the womb, and the parent is not completely prepared for plunging into child care sooner than expected (Goldberg, 1979). Goldberg also suggests that premature infants are less readable and predictable than normal infants in terms of their needs, and that they are less responsive to parental attempts to engage them. Coupled with findings that the preterm infant's cry is more aversive to parents (Frodi, Lamb, Leavitt, Donovan, Neff, & Sherry, 1978), it seems that premature infants require more patience and sensitivity from their parents if the reciprocity and symmetry of normal family functioning is to be created and maintained.

Other child characteristics, such as hyperactivity, "difficult" temperament, mental retardation, physical handicaps, and chronic illness have been associated with dysfunctional parent–child relationships (Gil, 1970; Johnson & Morse, 1968; Young & Kopp, Note 5). All of these conditions, like prematurity, can make it more difficult for the child to reciprocate parental involvement and thereby put more burden on the parent to maintain positive interaction with the child.

Some parents are able to adjust their actions and expectations to meet the needs of their handicapped children with a minimum of difficulty. However, there are those who seem to lack the resources to respond effectively to the care demands of even normal children. Still other parents, who are reasonably capable under most conditions or with most of their children, are unable to cope when under too much stress from nonnormative events or situations.

The causes of such individual differences are, of course, complex. However, there is one factor that seems to be common to all parents (actually all individuals) who find themselves facing escalating conflict within their own families. They lack the behavioral skills to respond in appropriate ways under stressful conditions (Burgess et al., 1980). Behavioral skill deficits can be the result of loss of control due to chemical abuse or mental illness, though such extreme disturbance probably accounts for very little of the dysfunctional family behavior in our society (Spinetta & Rigler, 1972). Another small minority of parents doing violence to their families has some physical or mental disability that can produce stress in its own right, as well as limit possible coping behaviors.

The vast majority of skill deficits can be traced to learning histories. Parents who were emotionally and socially deprived as children appear to be more likely to abuse their own children (Steele & Pollack, 1968). Teenage parents, who at their early age may not have had the opportunity to learn sufficient parenting skills, often experience difficulty adjusting to the demands of a family (Belsky, 1980). As a final example of how individual development can result in behavioral skill deficits, evidence shows that parents without adequate social networks or social experience may fail to get feedback from others about their behavior (Garbarino, 1977).

Although we have concentrated on threats to the parent–child relationship, most of the stressful characteristics discussed can do damage to marital and sibling relationships as well. Unfortunately, marital and, especially, sibling conflict have, in comparison to parent–child relationships, been somewhat neglected as research topics, so that much of our knowledge about them is incomplete and speculative.

It is evident that neither the children's nor the adults' characteristics can be looked at separately to reveal whether a *threat* of violence to the family will actually do damage to the family. Balance must be achieved in each of the dyadic relationships within the family to assure their ability to adapt to stress. It is the interactions within these dyads that offer clues to the understanding of family conflict (Burgess *et al.*, 1980).

Parental expectations, for instance, can have a large effect on that parent's reaction to her or his child. Thomas and Chess (1977) report significant differences between Puerto Rican parents' preference for active, demanding babies (particularly boys), and Caucasian parents' preference for easygoing, predictable babies. They refer to the link between parental expectations and infant temperament as parent–infant match. The better the match, they hypothesize, the less stress produced in the parent–child relationship and the fewer the number of dysfunctions in children, parents, and families. Data reported by Gannon (1978) support these hypotheses insofar as they relate to child dysfunctions. Thus, once again, we return to the family as the primary unit of analysis. The impact of nonnormative individual characteristics on the family can only be predicted when seen within the context of family relationships.

VI. Effects of Violence to the Family

There is substantial variability in how individuals (and cultures) respond to family stress, but common negative responses include depression, withdrawal, rigidity, and confusion. Each of these psychological responses has deleterious implications for family functioning. Each places the normative family in jeopardy because the normative family depends on high morale, high levels of interaction, flexibility, and consensus (cf., Burgess, 1980b). One study (Stinnett, 1979) identified six elements of "strong families": mutual affection, spending time together in purposeful activities, effective communication patterns, a high degree of mutual commitment, a high degree of spiritual orientation, and coping skills coupled with an optimistic outlook. When events do violence to the family they throw a monkey wrench into its complex social workings, producing personal difficulties for family members and the community, and even impairing individual development (seen most clearly in children). At least four consequences of violence to the family are worth noting.

1. The undermining of parental ability to provide necessary nurture and feedback to children and to each other is one such consequence. The family functions as a support system for its members. As defined by Caplan (1974), support systems are

> continuing social aggregates that provide individuals with opportunities for feedback about themselves and for validations for their expectations about others, which may offset deficiencies in these communications within the larger community context... People have a variety of specific needs that demand satisfaction through enduring interpersonal relationships, such as for love and affection, for intimacy that provides the freedom to express feelings easily and unself-consciously, or validation of personal identity and worth, for satisfaction of nurturance and dependency, for help with tasks, and for *support in handling emotion and controlling impulses* [pp. 4–5; emphasis added].

Parents should provide nurture and feedback to their children and to each other. Marital quality flows in large measure from how successful spouses are in serving these joint support system functions for each other (Burgess, 1980b). When the family is under attack, these spousal relations are challenged. Where they break down, the marital dyad breaks down, with all the problems that attend upon fragmented marriages, both for the adults and for their children (Hetherington, 1979). Similarly, when the family is functioning well, parents can provide a developmentally enhancing mixture of nurture and feedback to their children—what Baumrind (1979) calls the "authoritative" style in which love and acceptance are coupled with age-appropriate limit setting and reason-oriented discipline. When the family is besieged, this authoritative pattern tends to break down. Depression, withdrawal, rigidity, and confusion all threaten the authoritative style by distracting or incapacitating the parent.

This internal effect is compounded by an external one as well. Disrupted families tend to become estranged from the natural support systems of the larger social environment. They are thrown back on their own devices at a time when those devices are likely to be least adequate. Social isolation is a correlate of family disruption (Garbarino, 1980b; Garbarino & Sherman, 1980). Disrupted families often fall out of their social orbits or are thrown out of them. Thus, a divorce may lead to a shift in social orientation both because it is a voluntary initiative and because it is imposed by friends. This form of social isolation is a prime correlate of impaired development for children (Rutter, 1978).

Finally, social isolation reduces the potential of a family to serve as a resource for *others*. Disrupted families are a drain on their social networks and communities. Natural helping networks depend on people whose resources are not overtaxed (Collins & Pancoast, 1976), and all exchange networks depend on mutuality to some degree (cf., Stack, 1974). The disrupted family is a *social* as well as a psychological threat to its members. Violence to the family depletes the social resources on which informal helping networks depend.

2. Violence to families decreases the learning and performance of caregiving roles by parents and children. Firsthand experience remains the primary teacher of norms for caregiving behavior. Modeling (coupled with contingent positive reinforcement) is the best way to learn how to be a successful and effective parent (Bronfenbrenner, 1978). Thus, family disruption, either from within or from without, impairs basic learning of caregiving roles. What is more important, the same external conditions that do violence to the family deprive parents of the support and encouragement they need to be competent parents (Bronfenbrenner, 1978).

Family formation and the transition to parenthood are best understood as examples of the broader phenomenon of socialization and life-span development, a process of role transitions and sequences (Brim, 1959; Brim & Wheeler, 1966; Elder, 1977; Garbarino, 1977). These transitions "entail both entry and exit, some measure of rejection and acceptance, separation and integration. Their psychological effects are contingent on the nature of the change and the adaptive potential of the individual, as defined by resources, social preparation and support [Elder, 1977, p. 9]." Family disruption reduces the individual's opportunity to learn caregiving roles and thus undermines future life success. The parental role is difficult to learn in a hostile or unsupportive context.

3. Violence exposes children to physical, psychological, and social risk. Children need protection. A normal family provides that protection. It shelters children from physical danger, both from outside threats (e.g., a dangerous physical environment) and from their self-generated risks. A disrupted family is less able to provide this protection. A normal family protects the child from psychological harm by monitoring threats from the outside world (e.g., academic failure or sexual molestation) and the child's own development (e.g., mental retardation). A disrupted family is distracted and does not attend well to these sources of psychological harm. Finally, a disrupted family cannot serve as an advocate for the child in his or her contacts with institutions. The child is thus exposed to greater social risk than if the family were functioning normally.

4. Violence reduces the likelihood of reinforcement contingencies needed to facilitate child development and parental satisfaction. The family is the primary site for many vital operant behaviors that form the core of social competence. Parents may fail to respond to infant smiling and vocalization,

for example. They may ignore positive behavior and reinforce negative behavior. These behaviors are encompassed by global terms such as psychological abuse, emotional neglect, and rejection (Garbarino, 1978, 1980a). Also, disrupted families are prone to engage in physical abuse and neglect (Burgess *et al.*, 1980). The level of domestic physical assault is proportional to the level of family disruption (Straus *et al.*, 1980).

VII. Summary and Conclusions

In this chapter, we have attempted to analyze nonnormative life events as those processes that damage the normal functioning of families. Our reason for using a functional definition of nonnormative events was based on our dissatisfaction with both statistical and rule-based definitions. For example, the fact that an event occurs at low frequencies or at unpredictable times may or may not have developmental implications. Similarly, violation of a societal norm may simply indicate the presence of normative pluralism which, again, may or may not be significant developmentally. For these and other reasons discussed earlier we decided to consider events nonnormative insofar as those events increase the probability of developmental harm.

Our reasons for using the family as our central unit of analysis were severalfold. First, family relationships have played key roles in the very evolution of human nature as we presently know it. Second, the family is the primary context in which individual development takes place throughout the life span. Third, the family has historically functioned as a social bridge linking individuals to the larger community.

Given our functional definition of nonnormative life events and the three assumptions just mentioned, we proceeded to examine circumstances that can cause damaging stress or violence to families. These circumstances included structural inadequacy, asymmetry in family relationships, and a predominance of negative affect in those relationships. We also examined various external and internal threats to families that contribute to these sources of domestic stress. Among the external threats were chronic poverty, acute economic deprivation, political disruption, and societal values incompatible with the best interests of children and their families. Internal threats included structural stress such as endemic conflicts of interest, marital discord and divorce, single parenthood, step-relationships, and large family size. Other internal threats were seen to result from certain characteristics of individual family members such as deficient parenting and social skills, prematurity, mental retardation, physical abnormalities, chronic illness, and temperamental mismatches between parents and children.

One important implication of our analysis is that all or most families periodically experience varying degrees of stress that affect normal (i.e., optimal) family functioning. Not only are these internal and external threats common throughout the family cycle and the life spans of its members, but we also know that family members are sometimes faced with choosing the lesser of two evils (e.g., single parenthood versus continual conjugal conflict). The fact remains, however, that these threats—whether they occur frequently or predictably—or whether they are culturally proscribed or not, do tend to exacerbate the usual conflicts of interest within families and lead to an emphasis on coercive or negative interaction, with resultant power imbalances.

Finally, we concluded with a discussion of four major consequences of violence to families including disruption in the provision of parental nurture to children; a reduced probability of learning as well as performing caregiving roles; increased exposure of children to physical, psychological, and social risk; and breakdowns in the reinforcement contingencies necessary for child development and parental satisfaction. One important outcome of the breakdown in these contingencies is a rise in domestic conflict. In a sense, then, we have come full circle: Violence *to* the family helps bring about violence *in* the family.

Acknowledgment

We would like to thank Gunhild Hagestad, Richard M. Lerner, and Michael Smyer for their thoughtful comments on an early draft of this chapter.

Reference Notes

1. Bahr, H. *Change in family life in Middletown: 1924–1977.* Paper presented at the annual meeting of the American Sociological Association, Chicago, August 1978.
2. Steinberg, L., Catalano, R., & Dooley, D. *Economic antecedents of child abuse and neglect.* Unpublished manuscript, University of California at Irvine, 1980.
3. Elder, G., & Rockwell, R. *The life course and human development: An ecological perspective.* Unpublished manuscript, Boys Town, Neb.: Boys Town Center for the Study of Youth Development, 1977.
4. Weed, J. A. *National estimates of marriage dissolution and survivorship.* Unpublished manuscript, U.S. Department of Health, Education, and Welfare, 1980.
5. Young, M., & Kopp, C. *Handicapped children and their families: Research directions.* Unpublished manuscript, University of California, Los Angeles, 1980.

References

Alexander, R. D. Natural selection and social exchange. In R. L. Burgess & T. L. Huston (Eds.), *Social exchange in developing relationships*. New York: Academic Press, 1979.

Baltes, P. B., Cornelius, S., & Nesselroade, J. R. Cohort effects in developmental psychology. In J. R. Nesselroade & P. B. Baltes (Eds.), *Longitudinal research in the study of behavior and development*. New York: Academic Press, 1979.

Bane, M. J. *Here to stay: American families in the twentieth century*. New York: Basic Books, 1976.

Barash, D. P. *Sociobiology and behavior*. New York: Elsevier, 1977.

Baumrind, D. A dialectical materialist's perspective on knowing social reality. *New Directions in Child Development*, 1979, *2*, 61–82.

Bell, R. Q. A reinterpretation of the direction of effects in studies of socialization. *Psychological Review*, 1968, *75*, 81–95.

Belsky, J. Child maltreatment: An ecological integration. *American Psychologist*, 1980, 35, 320–335.

Birchler, G. R., Weiss, R. L., & Vincent, J. P. Multi-method analysis of social reinforcement exchange between maritally distressed and non-distressed spouse and stronger dyads. *Journal of Personality and Social Psychology*, 1975, *31*, 349–360.

Blake, J. Is zero preferred? American attitudes toward childlessness in the 1970's. *Journal of Marriage and the Family*, 1979, *41*, 245–265.

Blake, J., & Davis, J. Norms, values, and sanctions. In R.E.L. Faris (Ed.), *Handbook of modern sociology*. Chicago: Rand McNally & Co., 1964.

Brandwein, R. Women and children last: The social situation of divorced mothers and their children. *Journal of Marriage and the Family*, 1974, *36*, 498–514.

Brim, O. G. *Education for child rearing*. New York: Russell Sage Foundation, 1959.

Brim, O. G., & Wheeler, S. Socialization after childhood: Two essays. New York: John Wiley & Sons, 1966.

Bronfenbrenner, U. The origins of alienation. In U. Bronfenbrenner & M. Mahoney (Eds.), *Influences on human development*. Hinsdale, Ill.: The Dryden Press, 1975.

Bronfenbrenner, U. Who needs parent education? *Teachers College Record*, 1978, *79*, 767–787.

Bronfenbrenner, U. *The ecology of human development*. Cambridge, Mass.: Harvard University Press, 1979.

Buck, G. L., & Jacobson, A. L. Social evolution and structural-functional analysis. *American Sociological Review*, 1968, *33*, 343–355.

Burgess, R. L. Child abuse: A social interactional analysis. In B. B. Lahey & A. G. Kazdin (Eds.), *Advances in Clinical Child Psychology*, Vol. 2. New York: Plenum, 1979.

Burgess, R. L. Family violence: Some implications from evolutionary biology. In T. Hirschi (Ed.), *Understanding criminal behavior*. New York: Sage Publications, 1980. (a)

Burgess, R. L. Relationships in marriage and the family. In S. Duck and R. Gilmour (Eds.), *Personal relationships*. London: Academic Press, 1980. (b)

Burgess, R. L., Anderson, E. A., Schellenbach, C. J. & Conger, R. D. A social interactional approach to the study of abusive families. In J. P. Vincent (Ed.), *Advances in family interaction, assessment and theory: An annual compilation of research* (Vol. 2). Greenwich, Conn.: JAI Press, 1980.

Cairns, R. B. Beyond social attachment: The dynamics of interactional development. In T. Alloway, P. Pliner, & L. Krames (Eds.), *Communication and affect*. New York: Plenum, 1977.

Cairns, R. B. *Social development: The origins and plasticity of interchanges*. San Francisco: W. H. Freeman, 1979.

Caplan, G. *Support systems and community mental health*. New York: Behavioral Publications, 1974.

Chagnon, N. A., & Irons, W. *Evolutionary biology and human social behavior*. North Scituate, Mass.: Duxbury Press, 1979.

Collins, A., & Pancoast, D. *Natural helping networks*. Washington, D.C.: National Association of Social Workers, 1976.

Coopersmith, S. *The antecedents of self-esteem*. San Francisco: W. H. Freeman, 1967.

Douglas, J.W.B., & Blomfield, J. M. *Children under five*. London: George Allen & Unwin Ltd., 1958.

Drillien, C. M. *The growth and development of the prematurely born infant*. Edinborough, Scotland: Livingston, 1964.

Elder, G. H. Family history and the life course. *Journal of Family History*, 1972, *1*, 1388–152.

Featherstone, J. Family matters. *Harvard Educational Review*, 1979, *49*, 20–56.

Fox, R. Alliance and constraint: Sexual selection in the evolution of human kinship systems. In B. Campbell (Ed.), *Sexual selection and the descent of man*. Chicago: Aldine, 1972.

Fraser, B. The child and his parents: A delicate balance of rights. In R. Helfer & C. H. Kempe (Eds.), *Child abuse and neglect: The family and the community*. Cambridge, Mass.: Ballinger Publishing Company, 1976, 315–333.

Frodi, A., Lamb, M., Leavitt, C., Donovan, W., Neff, C., & Sherry, D. Father's and mother's responses to the faces and cries of normal and premature infants. *Developmental Psychology*, 1978, *14*, 490–498.

Gannon, P. *Behavioral problems and temperment in middle class and Puerto Rican five year old boys*. Unpublished masters thesis, Hunter College of the City University of New York, 1978.

Garbarino, J. The human ecology of child maltreatment: A conceptual model for research. Journal of Marriage and the Family, 1977, *39*, 721–736.

Garbarino, J. The elusive "crime" of emotional abuse. *Child Abuse and Neglect*, 1978, *2*, 89–100.

Garbarino, J. Defining emotional maltreatment: The message is the meaning. *Journal of Psychiatric Treatment and Evaluation*, 1980, *2*, 105–110. (a)

Garbarino, J. An ecological perspective on child maltreatment. In L. Pelton (Ed.), *The social context of child abuse and neglect*. New York: Human Sciences Press, 1980. (b)

Garbarino, J. The issue is human quality: In praise of children. *Children and Youth Services Review*, 1980, *1*, 353–377.

Garbarino, J., & Bronfenbrenner, U. The socialization of moral judgment and behavior in cross-cultural perspective. In T. Lickona (Ed.), *Moral development and behavior*. New York: Holt, Rinehart and Winston, 1976.

Garbarino, J., & Gilliam, G. *Understanding abusive families*. Lexington, Mass.: Lexington Books, 1980.

Garbarino, J., & Sherman, D. High-risk families and high-risk neighborhoods: Studying the ecology of child maltreatment. *Child Development*, 1980, *51*, 188–198.

Gelles, R. J., & Straus, M. A. Determinants of violence in the family: Toward a theoretical integration. In W. R. Burr, R. Hill, F. K. Nye, & I. L. Reiss (Eds.), *Contemporary theories about the family*. New York: The Free Press, 1979.

Gil, D. *Violence against children: Physical child abuse in the United States*. Cambridge, Mass.: Harvard University Press, 1970.

Goldberg, S. Premature birth: Consequences for the parent–infant relationship. *American Scientist*, 1979, *67*, 214–219.

Gottman, J. M. *Marital interaction: Experimental investigations*. New York: Academic Press, 1979.

Gurin, G., Keroff, J., & Feld, S. *America looks at its mental health*. New York: Basic Books, 1960.

Harris, L. Importance and satisfaction with factors in life. *The Harris Survey*. November 23, 1978.

Hetherington, E. Divorce: A child's perspective. *American Psychologist*, 1979, *34*, 851–858.

Hill, R., & Mattessich, P. Family development theory and life-span development. In P. B. Baltes & O. G. Brim (Eds.), *Life-span development and behavior* (Vol. 2). New York: Academic Press, 1979.

Hrdy, S. B. Male–male competition and infanticide among the langurs (*Prebytis entellus*) of Abu Rajasthan. *Folia Primatologica*, 1974, *22*, 19–58.

Jencks, C. *Inequality: A reassessment of the effect of family and schooling in America*. New York: Basic Books, 1972.

Johnson, B., & Morse, H. A. Injured children and their parents. *Children*, 1968, *15*, 147–152.

Kenniston, K. *All our children: The American family under pressure*. New York: Harcourt Brace Jovanovich, 1977.

Lancaster, J. B., & Whitten, P. Family matters. *The Sciences*, 1980, *20*, 10–15.

Lerner, R. M., Spanier, G. B., & Belsky, J. The child in the family. In C. B. Kopp & J. Krakow (Eds.), *Developmental Psychology*. Reading, Mass.: Addison-Wesley, 1980.

Lewis, M., & Rosenblum, L. A. (Eds.) *The effect of the infant on its caregiver*. New York: John Wiley & Sons, 1974.

Manis, J. Assessing the seriousness of social problems. *Social Problems*, 1974, *22*, 1–15.

McClelland, D. Testing for competence rather than for "intelligence." *American Psychologist*, 1973, *28*, 1–14.

Mead, G. H. *Mind, self and society*. Chicago: University of Chicago Press, 1934.

Milow, I., & Lourie, R. The child's role in the battered child syndrome. *Society for Pediatric Research*, 1964, *65*, 1079–1081.

National Academy of Sciences. *Toward a national policy for child and families*. Washington, D.C.: U.S. Government Printing Office, 1976.

Nock, S. The family life cycle: Empirical or conceptual tool? *Journal of Marriage and the Family*, 1979, *41*, 15–26.

Parke, R. D., & Collmer, C. Child abuse: An interdisciplinary analysis. In M. Hetherington (Ed.), *Review of child development research* (Vol. 5). Chicago: University of Chicago Press, 1975.

Parsons, T. *Social structure and personality*. New York: Macmillan, 1964.

Patterson, G. R. The aggressive child: Victim and architect of a coercive system. In L. A. Hamerlynck, L. C. Handy, & E. Mash (Eds.), *Behavior modification and families I. Theory and research*. New York: Brunner/Mazel, 1976.

Polansky, N. Analysis of research on child neglect: The social work viewpoint. In Herner & Company (Eds.), *Four perspectives on the status of child abuse and neglect research*. Washington, D.C.: National Center on Child Abuse and Neglect, 1976.

Rohner, R. *They love me, they love me not*. New Haven, Conn.: Human Relations Area Files Press, 1975.

Rohner, R., & Nielson, C. *Parental acceptance and rejection: A review of research and theory*.

New Haven, Conn.: Human Relations Area File Press, 1978.

Rossi, A. Transition to parenthood. *Journal of Marriage and the Family*, 1968, *30*, 26–39.

Rutter, M. Early sources of security and competence. In J. Bruner & A. Garton (Eds.), *Human growth and development*. Oxford, England: Clarendon Press, 1978.

Ryder, R. G. Husband–wife dyads versus married strangers. *Family Process*, 1968, *7*, 233–238.

Spanier, G., & Glick, P. The life cycle of American families: An expanded analysis. *Journal of Family History*, 1980, 5, 97–111.

Spinetta, J. J., & Rigler, D. The child-abusing parent: A psychological review. *Psychological Bulletin*, 1972, *77*, 296–304.

Stack, C. *All our kin: Strategies for survival in a black community*. New York: Harper & Row, 1974.

Steele, B. F., & Pollock, C. B. A psychiatric study of parents who abuse infants and small children. In R. E. Helfer & C. H. Hempe (Eds.), *The battered child*. Chicago: University of Chicago Press, 1968.

Stinnett, N. In search of strong families. In N. Stinnett, B. Chesser, & J. DeFrain (Eds.), *Building family strengths*. Lincoln, Neb.: University of Nebraska Press, 1979.

Straus, M., Gelles, R., & Steinmetz, S. *Behind closed doors*. New York: Doubleday, 1980.

Tanner, J. M. Earlier maturation in man. *Scientific American*, 1968, *218*, 21–27.

Thomas, A., & Chess, S. *Temperament and development*. New York: Bruner/Mazel, 1977.

Terhune, K. W. A review of the actual and expected consequences of family size. Washington, D.C.: U.S. Department of Health, Education and Welfare, Publication no. (NIH) 75-779, 1974, 1–233.

Trivers, R. L. Parental investment and sexual selection. In B. H. Campbell (Ed.), *Sexual selection and the descent of man, 1871–1971*. Chicago: Aldine, 1972.

U.S. Bureau of the Census. *Marital status and living arrangements: March 1976*. Current Population Reports p. 20, Vol. 306. Washington, D.C.: U.S. Government Printing Office, 1977.

U.S. Commission on Population Growth and the American Future. *Population and the American future*. Washington, D.C.: U.S. Government Printing Office, 1972.

Weiss, R. S. *Marital separation*. New York: Basic Books, 1975.

Werner, E., Simonian, K., Bierman, J. M., & French, F. E. Cumulative effect of perinatal complications and deprived environment on physical, intellectual and social development of preschool children. *Pediatrics*, 1967, *30*, 490–505.

Willerman, L., Broman, S. H., & Fiedler, M. Infant development, preschool I.Q. and social class. *Child Development*, 1970, *41*, 69–77.

Williams, G. C. *Adaptation and natural selection*. Princeton, N.J.: Princeton University Press, 1966.

Wilson, E. O. *Sociobiology: The new synthesis*. Cambridge, Mass.: Harvard University Press, 1975.

Winter, F., Ferreira, A., & Bowers, N. *Research in family interaction: Readings and commentary*. Palo Alto, Calif.: Science and Behavior Books, 1973.

CHAPTER 9

Marital Separation: The First Eight Months[1]

BERNARD L. BLOOM
WILLIAM F. HODGES
UNIVERSITY OF COLORADO
BOULDER, COLORADO

ROBERT A. CALDWELL
MICHIGAN STATE UNIVERSITY
E. LANSING, MICHIGAN

Increasingly, marital disruption is being acknowledged as a stressful life event of the first magnitude. Judged by Holmes and Rahe (1967) and their colleagues (e.g., Holmes & Masuda, 1974) as second only to death of a spouse in terms of its intensity and duration, marital disruption and its consequences have been the subject of several investigations (see Bloom, Asher, & White, 1978; Levinger & Moles, 1979). This research is part of the growing interest in stressful life events and in the possibility of organizing community-based preventive programs around such events.

With over 1-million divorces granted annually in the United States, and with an average of one child per divorcing couple, more than 3-million persons are directly involved in that stressful life event each year. The magnitude of that number is great: It represents 1.5% of the total

[1]This report is based on work supported by the National Institute of Mental Health through Grant No. MH26373 (Preventive Intervention for Newly Separated Persons). The authors gratefully acknowledge this support.

LIFE-SPAN DEVELOPMENTAL PSYCHOLOGY
Nonnormative Life Events

United States population. In comparison, there are only slightly more than 3-million births and slightly less than 2-million deaths annually in the United States (U.S. Department of Health, Education, and Welfare, 1979). But in contrast to births and deaths, stressful life events in their own right, it is rare that our society provides any systematic help or support to persons undergoing marital separation or divorce.

This chapter examines the developmental trends in response to marital disruption across the first 8 months of separation. Although it is commonly asserted that accommodation to this particular stressful life event requires a matter of years (Hetherington, Cox, & Cox, 1977; Wallerstein & Kelly, 1980), relatively little is known about the specific characteristics of that accommodation.

I. Marital Separation as a Stressful Life Event

An informative although limited literature exists on the impact of marital separation as distinct from divorce. In fact, divorce usually occurs significantly later than separation and is far less stressful. Ironically, there is a more substantial literature on divorce as a stressful life event than on separation (see, for example, Bane, 1979; Bloom, Asher, & White, 1978; Ferri, 1973; Hetherington, Cox, & Cox, 1976; Kessler, 1976; Kitson & Sussman, 1977; Raschke, 1977; Schlesinger, 1969; Smith, 1971; Wallerstein & Kelly, 1980; and Zautra & Beier, 1978). Weiss (1975, 1976) provided a very useful qualitative analysis of separation based on interviews with 150 self-selected newly separated persons who met in eight different group discussion seminars for the separated. Weiss (1976) found that "the disruption of marriage regularly produces emotional distress, almost irrespective of the quality of the marriage or of the desire for its dissolution [p. 135]," and identified as one basis for that distress the near-universal persistence of attachment to the spouse.

Gray (1978) analyzed questionnaire replies from 126 separated and divorced members of a self-help group in California and found that her sample scored well below average on a variety of measures of positive mental health, including self-acceptance, self-regard, and inner directedness. In addition, significant negative behavioral changes (e.g, in weight, job effectiveness, and in smoking) were reported in the time since the beginning of the separation. There was some evidence of improved adjustment in a repeat of one of two questionnaires 6 months later.

Chiriboga and Cutler (1977) and Chiriboga, Roberts, and Stein (1978) studied a sample of divorcing men and women and came to the conclusion that "the period of marital separation constitutes a time of emotional upheaval perhaps more stressful than any other point during the process of divorce [1978, p. 21]." A number of earlier studies (e.g., Goode, 1956) have come to the same conclusion.

Chiriboga and Cutler (1977) interviewed 252 men and women who were separated from their spouses and in the process of obtaining a divorce. They found that "separation is the single most traumatic phase of the divorce process [p. 98]," but that an additional time of great trauma occurred earlier, specifically before the decision to divorce. In examining the reports of relief felt in the divorce process, the authors indicated that the "majority experienced some resolution of the crisis even before the divorce actually became final [p. 101]."

In a detailed study of 50 unstructured interviews with individuals who had filed for divorce in Pennsylvania within the preceding 2 years, Spanier and Casto (1979) found it possible to distinguish between two separated but overlapping adjustment problems—the adjustment to dissolution of the marriage and the adjustment to setting up a new life style. In this qualitative study, the authors were able to identify problems respondents had with the legal system (32 of the respondents were already divorced at the time of their interviews), with children, social networks, and with personal reactions. The authors found that the intensity of the initial emotional reaction was related to the suddenness and unexpectedness of the separation. Spanier and Casto, in contrast to Weiss (1976), found that persistent attachment to the spouse was far from universal and that there was no significant relationship between the strength of that attachment and the difficulty of adjustment to separation.

As for setting up a new life style, the authors examined economic problems, child-custody issues, social adjustments, heterosexual adjustment, and personal problems. They found adjustment problems to be less severe among persons with high levels of social interaction and heterosexual behavior (see also Raschke, 1977).

Brown and Manela (1978) interviewed 253 separated women and found that among whites, women with traditional sex-role attitudes (that is, women who valued home-centeredness, child-centeredness, and who did not object to subservience to men in the world of work) experienced more distress, less personal growth and well-being, lower self-esteem, and a lower sense of personal effectiveness than women with nontraditional sex-role attitudes. This finding did not hold for black women (Brown, Perry, & Harburg, 1977).

Detailed information is lacking, but it does seem clear that profound distress surrounds the time of separation. Little is known about the rapidity and nature of the resolutions of various facets of that distress. It is not clear how to identify unusually vulnerable subgroups of separated persons. Few specific sex differences have been found, and the role played by children in the adjustment of the separating parents has not yet been established. In addition, a number of findings just reviewed have yet to be replicated.

II. Study Design

The main purpose of this chapter is to describe and analyze the impact of marital separation on various areas of functioning in a sample of 50 newly separated persons who served as a control group in a longitudinal study of a comprehensive intervention program. The overall study is important for several reasons:

1. The data form the base for a prospective longitudinal investigation beginning shortly after separation. Periodic interviews are being conducted with this sample and relatively little data depend on retrospective recall.
2. The data are more systematically quantified than in the case of previously reported studies permitting a more objective identification and analysis of problem areas.
3. The data were obtained from volunteers in a nonclinical sampling procedure avoiding the overestimates of psychopathology inherent in samples of divorcing persons who are seeking clinical assistance.
4. The data permit the analysis across time of a broad range of areas of impact, including helpseeking behavior, finances, socialization patterns, housing and homemaking, career and employment, and parenting problems.

The general plan of the study was to obtain a reasonably representative sample of newly separated persons in Boulder County, Colorado, who met a set of specific criteria, assign them at random to an intervention program and control condition, and then examine the effectiveness of the intervention program. The research design called for follow-up interviews to be conducted 6 months after entrance into the study (by which time, persons in the intervention group would have completed the program), and again 1 year and 2 years later, that is, 18 months and 30 months after entrance into the study. Details about subject selection can be found in Bloom and Hodges (1981). A total of 101 persons were assigned to the intervention program and 52 persons to the control group. Of the 52 controls, 50 persons completed the initial and 6-month follow-up interviews. These 50 initial and follow-up interviews form the basis for this report.

A. The Data Collection Instrument

The initial data collection took place by means of an in-person interview that required between 90 minutes and 2 hours to complete. Study participants were given a copy of the interview form to follow along in order to simplify the interviewing process. Except for open-ended questions, all replies were precoded. Six-month interviews were conducted in person or on the telephone and required about 30 minutes less to complete than the initial interviews.

The initial interview format consisted of 14 separate documents. These documents included forms to obtain (a) participant consent; (b) residential-tracing information to facilitate locating the participant when the time arrived for the next interview; (c) demographic information; (d) information regarding the events surrounding the separation, prior and current histories of help-seeking behavior, current life problems, and characteristics of the support network; (e) information about socialization patterns and practices; (f) information about income and expenses; (g) housing and homemaking information; (h) career and employment information; (i) a symptom checklist covering the period 6 months prior to separation; (j) information about parenting; (k) child behavior data for a maximum of three children age 18 or younger; and, in addition, (l) the Rotter Internal–External Locus of Control Scale; (m) the Male–Female Role Relationship (MAFERR) sex-role orientation scale (Steinman & Fox, 1974); and (n) a stressful life-events inventory covering the 6 months prior to separation. The Rotter and MAFERR scales were not repeated at the time of the 6-month interview. All other follow-up interview forms were oriented in terms of obtaining information regarding the 6 months since entrance into the program, and generally paralleled the initial interview in design. Data from the child-behavior schedule will be presented elsewhere, as will the results of the analyses of the Rotter and the MAFERR.

B. Characteristics of the Sample

To determine if the random assignment of study participants into control and intervention program conditions was successfully accomplished, four analyses were undertaken on 69 different major descriptive variables drawn from all of the interview forms. In these analyses, we contrasted, between the control and experiment groups, male parents, female parents, male non-parents, and female nonparents. The 276 analyses contrasting the inter-

TABLE 9.1

Demographic Characteristics of the Study Population

Variable	Study group					Significance of Differences by[a]	
	Total sample	Male parents	Male nonparents	Female parents	Female nonparents	Sex	Parent status
Number	50	11	11	15	13		
Age	31.4	30.2	30.2	37.8	25.9		.001
Length of marriage (months)	103.4	102.1	48.9	187.7	53.3		.001
Residency in county (months)	105.2	86.2	66.8	164.1	85.8	.05	.05
Length of separation (days)	57.8	59.2	42.8	70.3	55.1		
Percentage experiencing first separation	70.0	54.5	72.7	80.0	69.2		
Monthly spendable income	$795.	$1077.	$727.	$863.	$533.		
School years completed	15.6	15.4	16.5	15.3	15.4		.05
Percentage now employed	90	100	82	80	100		
Number of children	.98	1.7	—	2.0	—		
Percentage having child custody[b]	60.9	27.3	—	91.7	—	.001	

[a]Blanks indicate nonsignificant findings.
[b]Based on 11 male parents and 12 female parents with children age 18 or younger.

vention and control subgroups yielded only seven differences significant at the $p < .05$ level or better. Thus, we have reason to believe that the assignment procedure successfully divided the entire study population into two demographically similar groups.

Information describing the demographic characteristics of the sample is shown in Table 9.1. As can be seen in the table, about 50% of the study subjects were parents and 44% of the subjects were males. The age range of study participants was 22–50. The range in length of marriage was 6 months–32 years, and the range in length of residence in Boulder County was 1 month–35 years. Females in the sample were about 2 years older and had been married about 4 years longer than males. Parents, as contrasted with nonparents, were nearly 7 years older, had been married 9 years longer, and had lived in Boulder County 4.5 years longer.

At the time of the initial interview, about 50% of the sample reported that they had moved since their separations, which had occurred on the average 8 weeks earlier. Female parents were the least likely to have moved, whether they were themselves study participants or the spouses of study participants. Most moves occurred within Boulder County. At the time of the 6-month interview, nearly half of the sample reported that they had moved since entrance into the project, in fact, moving an average of nearly two times. Most moves were again within Boulder County.

Virtually all of the study participants were white. About 40% were Protestants and 20% were Catholics; nearly 25% expressed no religious preference. About 30% of the study participants indicated a significant level of participation in religious activities. There was no significant change in religious involvement reported at the time of the 6-month interview.

With regard to marital status at the time of the 6-month interview, 2 of the 50 study participants had reconciled, 24 had obtained a divorce, 23 were still separated, and 1 had already remarried. Of the 48 persons who were already divorced or still separated, 30% reported that some efforts at reconciliation had taken place, although few thought that a reconciliation was likely. Of those persons still separated, virtually all thought that divorce was almost certain.

III. The Separation: Precursors and General Reactions

Prior to the difficulties that led to the separation, respondents reported that their marriages were generally good. During the 6 months prior to their separations, however, there was clear evidence of personal disequilibrium in the study population in terms of a number of stressful life events and psychological and physical symptoms. Mentioned as stressful life events by

25% or more of the respondents were changes in sleeping habits, changes in eating habits, changes in financial state, sexual difficulties, in-law troubles, changes in work responsibilities and working hours, changes in social and recreational activities, as well as the more general changes in relationships with the spouse.

Stressful life events continued to occur after entrance into the program, and were, in fact, more numerous during the 6 months following the start of participation in the program. Only one stressful life event—in-law troubles—that more than 25% of participants experienced prior to separation did not occur to that large a proportion during the same time period after separation. Every other event mentioned by at least 25% of respondents prior to separation was mentioned by at least that same proportion following separation. But in addition, several other stressful life events were mentioned by at least 25% of the study participants as taking place during the first 6 months of program participation that were mentioned by fewer than 25% prior to separation. These events included change in residence and divorce, two events directly associated with the marital disruption, and changing to a different line of work and borrowing less than $10,000, two events indirectly associated with the marital disruption.

A. Sources of Marital Dissatisfaction

Study participants were asked to rate 18 different potential sources of marital dissatisfaction in terms of the extent to which they existed and played a role in the decision to separate. The list was expanded from the one used by Levinger (1966). The three most commonly voiced complaints, communication difficulties, differences in values, and lack of love, are a manifestation of the slow distancing that takes place within a couple as their relationship deteriorates. Contrary to what might have been expected, women did not complain about physical abuse significantly more often than men did, essentially because physical abuse was an infrequent complaint in the entire sample. But infrequent does not mean nonexistent. One of the 28 women in the study reported physical abuse to be a major factor in her decision to separate, and 3 other women reported it to be one of the most important factors. Verbal abuse was reported far more commonly and was more frequently mentioned by women than by men and by parents than nonparents.

B. Causes of Marital Disruption

Two-thirds of the study participants reported that some specific event precipitated the decision to separate. In specifying what those events were, three particular experiences were mentioned most often: (a) infidelity; (b) events impinging from outside the relationship (e.g., completing school, moving to start a new job, taking a trip without the spouse, or expiration of the lease on their home); and (c) some version of the "last straw," that is, as a consequence of an event that had occurred previously but could no longer be tolerated (e.g., second suicide attempt, continual delays on the part of the spouse in completing graduate school, and habitual drinking and staying out late).

With regard to who made the decision to separate, significant sex differences were found, with women reporting taking the role of initiator more frequently than men. Whereas 29% of women indicated that they had been primarily responsible for the decision to separate, and 39% indicated that the decision was primarily their spouse's, only 9% of men indicated that the decision to separate was primarily their's, whereas 55% indicated that the decision was primarily their spouse's. Differences were found in reported initial attitude toward the separation, with men significantly more opposed to the separation than women, and parents significantly more opposed than nonparents. At the time of the 6-month interview, attitudes toward the separation had become considerably more favorable, and differences by sex and parental status no longer existed.

C. Symptom Checklist Responses

The frequency with which 20 symptoms were reported both initially and at the time of the 6-month interview is shown in Table 9.2. At the time of the initial interview, half or more of the study participants mentioned weight loss, upset stomach, bodily aches and pains, fatigue, appetite loss, headaches, the feeling of an impending nervous breakdown, difficulty getting things done, and difficulty sleeping. Three significant differences (two by sex and one by parent status) were found. Females reported significantly more frequent headaches and weight loss than males; parents reported significantly more frequent fainting than nonparents.

As shown in Table 9.2, virtually no significant changes in symptoms were reported over the 6-month interval. About as many problems increased as

TABLE 9.2

Initial and Six-Month Interview Symptom Checklist Responses:
Mean Scores and Significance Tests[a]

Symptom	Interview		Significance[b]	
	Initial	6-month	t	p
Nervousness	2.44	2.38	.62	
Morning fatigue	2.12	2.20	.56	
Sleep difficulties	1.98	2.06	.52	
Weight change	1.92	2.14	1.56	
Upset stomach	1.92	1.86	.44	
Appetite loss	1.76	1.86	.70	
Can't get going	1.74	1.74	.00	
Impending nervous breakdown	1.72	1.76	.36	
Headaches	1.66	1.62	.40	
Aches and pains	1.64	1.48	1.38	
Nightmares	1.60	1.70	1.00	
Pounding heart	1.56	1.42	1.41	
General weakness	1.54	1.58	.53	
Sweating hands and feet	1.44	1.34	.93	
Ill health	1.44	1.60	1.59	
Shortness of breath	1.30	1.34	.63	
Trembling hands	1.28	1.20	1.07	
Dizziness	1.28	1.20	1.43	
Cold sweats	1.16	1.24	.94	
Fainting	1.10	1.02	2.06	$< .05$

[a]Participants were asked to rate the frequency of these symptoms on a 4-point scale: $1 =$ never; $2 =$ sometimes; $3 =$ pretty often; $4 =$ nearly all the time. Figures given indicate averages.

[b]Blanks indicate nonsignificant findings.

decreased in frequency. Only one overall significant difference was found, and in 20 *t* tests, one such difference would have been expected by chance. A total of 80 *t* tests were performed on the same 20 symptoms examining the four study subgroups separately—male parents, male nonparents, female parents, and female nonparents. Again, the changes were unremarkable. Only 5 significant differences were found in the 80 comparisons.

With so few significant changes in reports on the symptom checklist, and with these changes having no persuasive coherence or patterning, the most appropriate conclusion to be drawn is that no remarkable changes in reported symptoms take place when symptoms during the 6 months prior to separation are contrasted with symptoms during the 6 months following entrance into the longitudinal study.

In summary, men and women appeared to have very different attitudes toward their marriage and its ending. Men were much more satisfied with the quality of their marriage prior to separation and much more opposed to its ending than were women. During the 6 months prior to separation, women reported a somewhat greater number of physical and psychological symptoms and more often made the decision to separate. At the time of the 6-month interview, sex differences in reported symptoms were no longer in existence, although the mean symptom level had not diminished.

IV. Helpseeking and the Social Support System

A total of 19 (38%) of the study participants reported obtaining some form of couples counseling prior to their separation, mainly, but not exclusively, from mental health professionals in the private sector. Fourteen (28%) participants indicated that they had been interested in marriage counseling but their spouses had been opposed to it. Most found couples counseling mildly helpful, commenting particularly on the opportunity it gave them to clarify their own feelings and ideas, and improve their communication and problem-solving skills. It should be remembered, however, that all these persons did subsequently separate from their spouses and are not a random sample of couples in marital counseling.

A total of 25 persons (50%) obtained individual counseling prior to separation, mainly from the private sector. Of these 25 persons, 14 also reported participating in couples counseling. That is, a total of 30 different people had some form of counseling prior to separation. Respondents found these individual sessions moderately helpful, with females reporting significantly greater helpfulness than males. In the main, study participants who had had individual counseling prior to their separations reported that they were helped to deal more adequately with personal problems, found the counseling supportive, and felt that they could deal more successfully with interpersonal difficulties as well. These figures on formal helpseeking are not dissimilar to those reported by Chiriboga, Coho, Stein, and Roberts (1979) and by Kitson and Sussman (1977).

Regarding the 6-month period following entrance into the study, 28% of study participants reported either beginning psychotherapy or resuming previously interrupted psychotherapy; 30% reported continuing psychotherapy or counseling that had begun earlier, and most were finding it helpful. More than one-third of those persons not in psychotherapy reported feeling the need for some form of counseling.

Virtually every person in the study indicated that there was someone with whom they could discuss their marital problems. Nearly all mentioned friends. Most mentioned professionals, their own parents, and siblings. Many mentioned acquaintances. Friends and relatives were felt to be quite supportive, with female participants judging that degree of support to be significantly greater than male participants both initially and at the time of the 6-month interview.

Loneliness was a problem for many study participants, although for some, the problem predated the separation. Particularly in the case of women, study participants reported doing things alone—both before their separations and between the time of their separations and entrance into the study—that other people often do together (e.g., eating, going to the movies, watching TV, or going to parties). Most study participants indicated that they would have liked to have done more things with other people, both before as well as after their separations. At the time of the 6-month interview, loneliness was reported a problem as frequently as it had been originally.

A. Involvement with the Opposite Sex

At the time of entrance into the study, 19 of the study participants (38%) were closely involved with a person of the opposite sex. Just under 50% of those involvements had predated the separation. Of these 19 people, 16 were similarly involved 6 months later. At the time of the follow-up interview, 29 (58%) of the study participants were so involved. Whereas 3 persons of the original 19 had terminated their close involvements, 13 persons established such a relationship. Despite the relative stability of these relationships, study participants were generally equivocal about their interests in remarriage, both initially and at the time of the 6-month interview. Attitudes toward cohabitation were generally more favorable, particularly in the case of men and nonparents.

In summary, there was a very high level of formal and informal help seeking among the study participants that had started before the separation and continued afterward. Women seemed to feel a greater sense of support and loyalty from friends and family than did men. Despite this support, many study participants felt socially isolated, a feeling that often predated the separation. It was possible to meet new people, however, and more than 50% of the study participants were closely involved with a person of the opposite sex at the time of the 6-month interview.

V. Problems and Benefits Since Separation

Even though study participants had been separated an average of only 8 weeks at the time they entered the project, they were able to identify and

TABLE 9.3

Initial and Six-Month Interview Separation-Related Problem Reports:
Mean Scores and Significance Tests[a]

Problem	Interview		Significance[b]	
	Initial	6-month	t	p
Relationship with spouse	3.44	3.16	1.43	
Loneliness	3.16	2.76	2.19	< .05
Sense of personal failure	2.74	2.66	.50	
Mental health	2.74	2.66	.43	
Financial stress	2.68	2.90	1.42	
Self-blame	2.64	2.66	.12	
Sexual satisfaction	2.40	2.36	.18	
Feeling incompetent	2.38	2.22	1.02	
Housing	2.34	2.29	.29	
Legal matters	2.20	2.48	1.59	
New relationships	2.18	2.44	1.18	
Relationships with children	2.14	2.04	.39	
Childrearing	2.12	2.77	1.97	< .05
Career planning	2.08	2.58	2.12	< .05
Homemaking	1.96	2.26	1.36	
Physical health	1.92	2.06	1.00	
Employment	1.82	2.08	1.37	
Parental relationships	1.76	2.11	2.14	< .05

[a]Participants were asked to rate the severity of these problems on a 5-point scale: 1 = none; 2 = mild; 3 = moderate; 4 = considerable; 5 = severe. Figures given indicate averages.
[b]Blanks indicate nonsignificant findings.

judge the severity of problems that were of concern to them since their separation. The severity of separation-related problems as reported by this newly separated sample, both at the time of the initial interview and 6 months later, is shown in Table 9.3. Of the 18 problems, 4 exhibited significant changes in severity in the total group—loneliness, while still common, became less severe, although problems associated with childrearing, career planning, and parental relationships became more severe. In general, perhaps as a function of regression to the mean, initially severe problems became less severe while initially mild problems became more severe. On the other hand, there is no evidence of a general reduction in problems over the first 8 months, as might have been expected.

At the time of the initial interview, no significant differences in problem severity by sex were found. In the case of parental status, however, three significant differences were found, in each case being less severe in the case of parents. These three problems included mental health, self-blame, and feelings of incompetence. All three differences persisted at the time of the

6-month interview, but in the case of self-blame, the difference was no longer significant.

The significant changes between the initial and 6-month interview were remarkably consistent in all four subgroups. Loneliness decreased or remained constant in severity in every subgroup. Problems associated with childrearing increased in severity both for mothers and fathers, and problems associated with career planning and parental relationships increased in all four subgroups.

At the time of the 6-month interview, males reported significantly less severe problems than females in four problem areas—guilt and self-blame, feelings of incompetence, homemaking, and relationships with parents.

Study participants were asked on the initial interview sheet what they had learned about themselves as a consequence of the separation, and their responses indicated that their insights were far more often positive than negative. They felt they had experienced substantial personal growth and increase in self-knowledge, some increased happiness and sense of independence (in both cases significantly greater in the case of females than males), and a moderate sense of relief from conflict. These benefits persisted during the next 6 months for women and increased in the case of men, with the result that sex differences in perceived benefits of the separation no longer existed at the time of the 6-month interview.

A. Current Relationship with the Spouse

Study participants at the time of the initial interview continued to be in contact with their spouses, most often about once a week. By 6 months later, contact with the spouse had significantly decreased in frequency. As for the reasons for these contacts, initially about one-half of the respondents indicated that they wanted to spend time with their spouses (parents in the study mentioned this wish significantly less often than nonparents). About two-thirds of the respondents indicated that they were in contact with their spouses in order to work out details of the separation, about one-half mentioned future planning, and one-quarter mentioned legal problems (more commonly by parents than nonparents). A few respondents mentioned that they and their spouses continued to meet through mutual friends. About half of the parents in the study reported that they were in contact with their spouses because of their children. At the time of the 6-month interview, contact with spouses was largely limited to working out legal problems and separation details and because of the presence of children.

B. Financial Issues

The average study participant was responsible for the primary financial support of two people including himself or herself. As might be expected, men and parents indicated that they supported significantly more people than women and nonparents. Parents' incomes were significantly greater than those of nonparents (see Table 9.1). This income differential is undoubtedly attributable to age differences, since in the entire sample income was significantly higher in older age groups, and as has been mentioned, parents were substantially older than nonparents.

About one-third of study participants reported on the initial interview that they had to seek some form of financial assistance since their separation. More than one-half of those persons needing financial help looked to their families for this assistance. About one-quarter arranged for bank loans, with the remainder using public assistance and borrowing from friends. Males needing loans reported less difficulty obtaining them than females. At the time of the 6-month interview, 40% of study participants reported that they had sought financial help in the past 6 months—women significantly more often than men.

Most noncustodial male parents with children age 18 or younger reported paying child support at the time of the initial interview. Among male parents, nearly one-half were paying maintenance. No female parents and virtually no nonparents regardless of sex were paying maintenance. Maintenance arrangements were generally considered fairly satisfactory by all study participant groups. Child-support arrangements were judged less satisfactory, but somewhat surprisingly, there were no initial differences in the degree of expressed satisfaction regarding either maintenance or child support as a function of sex and in the case of maintenance as a function of parent status. At the time of the 6-month interview, however, males were significantly less satisfied than females regarding the arrangements for child support.

C. Housing and Homemaking Issues

In comparison with other issues, problems in the area of housing and homemaking were relatively minor. Most study participants lived in single-family homes or apartments. Monthly cost for housing was higher for parents than for nonparents, particularly, as might be expected, for female parents most of whom held custody. Few study participants had attempted to buy a home since, or in anticipation of, their separations. Women more often than men mentioned financial difficulties in maintaining their homes. Men mentioned low quality of housing more often than women. This latter finding is undoubtedly associated with the fact that men moved from their preseparation homes more often than women did. As for specific home-making difficulties, few were reported. In general, problems were minor in the areas of cooking, house cleaning, laundry, shopping, and home repairs. Parents, however, reported significantly more difficulty in keeping their homes clean than did nonparents, and females reported significantly more difficulty in making home repairs than men. At the time of the 6-month interview, while problems continued to be relatively mild, women were generally reporting more difficulties than men.

D. Educational, Career, and Employment Issues

The educational level of the study participants was relatively high, accurately reflecting the characteristics of the community. The average study participant had completed nearly 4 years of college. One-quarter of the study participants, both initially and at the time of the 6-month interview, were attending an institution of higher education, and more than one-half of those not currently in school were planning to return to school. For those study participants in school, a number of difficulties were reported, such as avoiding studying and receiving grades below those that they felt capable of earning. Many students reported occasional conflicts with teachers or other students and relatively little sense of satisfaction with school activities. By the time of the 6-month interview, the level of satisfaction with school had clearly increased.

Of all study participants, 90% were employed at the time of the initial interview and nearly that many at the time of their separations 2 months earlier. Most were employed full-time. Even though half of the employed sample were in professional-level positions, traditionally reported sex differences in type of employment were found, with males more often in professional, managerial, and skilled craftsman positions and females in clerical positions.

A total of 42 people were employed at the time of the 6-month interview, but only 57% of them were in the same job as at the time of their separation. About one-third of people who sought employment or a change in employment since their separations reported some difficulty in finding a position, both initially and at the 6-month interview. People who reported difficulty cited competition, lack of qualifications, and interest in a career change as the bases for that difficulty. At the time of the initial interview,

20% of persons who had had difficulty obtaining employment felt that their separations had contributed to that difficulty. Six months later, no one mentioned the separation as a factor.

Of employed study participants, 15–20% reported specific work-related difficulties such as missing work, loss of work quality or effectiveness, or conflict with co-workers at the time of the initial interview. More than 60% of employed study participants reported fatigue and difficulty concentrating at work at the time of the initial interview. This proportion increased to over 90% at the time of the 6-month interview. In addition to these specific work-related difficulties, there was clearly a general lack of satisfaction with the work experience. Three-quarters of the sample had plans, sometimes vague, for changing or starting employment or a career, both initially and at the time of the 6-month interview.

In summary, there was considerable disequilibrium in the areas of employment, education, and career planning. The majority of study participants were involved in effecting some change in how they derived income from gainful employment, even though most were employed at the time of their entrance into the study project. For those in school, the experience was clearly not anxiety free. For those at work, numerous and sometimes quite severe problems were reported, both initially and even more commonly 6 months later.

E. Parenting Issues

As mentioned earlier, 26 (52%) of the 50 study participants were parents. These parents had a total of 49 children, of whom 40 (82%) were age 18 or younger. Of the total of 26 parents in the study, 3 did not have minor children. Of the remaining 23 parents, 11 were male and 12 were female. The description of parenting issues is based on the analysis of these 23 parents.

At the time of the initial interview, in about 75% of the 23 couples, mothers had sole custody of their children. Fathers had custody of children in 16% of the cases, with the remaining 10% having joint or split custody. Six months later, the same proportion of mothers had custody, but fewer fathers reported having sole custody. Five (22%) of the couples were sharing custody of their children. Virtually all noncustodial parents had visitation rights and most typically saw their children about once a week. There was relatively little change in this visitation pattern between the time of the initial and 6-month interviews.

Despite who was the custodial parent, there was considerable sharing in the responsibility for childrearing. As might be expected, however, shared responsibility was often seen as a mixed blessing, and a good deal of disagreement between the spouses was reported.

Initially, about 70% of custodial parents felt there had been important changes in their children since the separation, but nearly 40% of the changes were viewed as positive ones. Changes in children's behavior at the time of the 6-month interview were more often seen as positive than as negative. Physical health problems in the children were quite rare. About 50% of custodial parents initially reported that their school-age children were having difficulties in school, mainly interpersonal in nature, but most custodial parents felt that these difficulties were unrelated to the marital disruption.

Initially, custodial parents generally felt that having children increased the difficulties associated with their marital disruption, a feeling that remained just as strong 6 months later. At first, parents generally felt that the number of problems they had with their children had increased since the separation. During the next 6 months, however, there appears to have been a slight dimunition in these problems.

In summary, some difficulties in the area of parenting were reported in this sample of newly separated people, and many parents indicated that difficulties associated with their marital disruptions seemed greater because they had children. Children provided a link between the separated parents and a reason for continued interactions, but these interactions were often unpleasant. Few changes in issues related to parenting were reported at the time of the 6-month interview.

VI. Discussion

This chapter has described the ways in which the stressful nature of marital separation manifests itself during the first 8 months of separation. Not only is there ample evidence of a generally high level of stress associated with marital disruption, but there is substantial reason to believe that this stress continues and in some areas increases during this period. The frequency and intensity of physical as well as psychological symptoms during the 6-month period prior to separation, the extraordinarily high level of help seeking both before and after separation, and the variety, duration, and generally increasing severity of postseparation difficulties are all consistent with the belief that a very large proportion of persons undergoing marital disruption find it an experience high in emotional distress.

Reconciliation occurs very rarely. By the end of the 8-month period there is a growing acceptance of the separation as a psychological reality and of the virtual inevitability of divorce, even though the level of stress associated with the marital disruption has not significantly diminished.

It is not surprising that one of the arenas in which the stressful character of marital disruption shows itself is in the work setting. Not only are there major disruptions in work performance reported throughout the first 8 months of separation, but the disruption of the marriage is generally followed by attempts to change career objectives or work settings. It is entirely possible that work-related difficulties play a causative role in marital conflict—the centrality of the work role can hardly be overestimated in a group as young and well educated as this sample (see Hageman, 1978; Handy, 1978). Furthermore, the work setting can become centrally important as a source of social support when the marital relationship comes to an end. For example, Bromet and Moos (1977), in studying the posttreatment functioning of alcoholic patients, noted that "among working patients, a more positively perceived work environment was associated with more successful post-treatment performance, but only among patients lacking marital support; for patients living with their spouses, no relationship was found [p. 326]."

Accordingly, both employees and supervisors need to be prepared for difficulties that might appear at the time of marital disruption. Employers, particularly those hiring relatively well-educated personnel, might consider the development of proactive strategies such as providing occupational counseling, reducing work responsibilities, or thoughtfully changing work assignments in the case of employees dealing with the stresses of marital disruption, and they should not minimize the duration of this source of stress.

Work-related difficulties are undoubtedly due, in addition, to the increasing financial problems that are associated with marital disruption. Financial problems appear to predate separation and become more severe very rapidly after separation. Furthermore, and particularly in the case of women, their severity continues to increase for at least the first 8 months of separation.

The presence of children in the divorcing family appears to add materially to the stressful character of the marital disruption throughout the entire time period. Less clear are the effects of parental divorce on children. Although it is commonly believed that these effects are nearly universal and nearly always negative, it can be seen in these data that this is not the case. Many parents report positive changes in their children associated with the separation, both initially and even more so 6 months after entrance into the project. Hodges, Wechsler, and Ballantine (1979) found no significant differences in behavior pathology between preschool children of divorced families and age- and sex-matched children from intact families. The critical need for appropriate age- and sex-matched intact-family controls is apparent, and studies that follow such matched children longitudinally will need to be undertaken before credible assertions as to the effects of divorce on children can be made.

Relatively coherent sex differences in initial response to marital disruption can be noted. In this sample, in comparison to men, women, prior to separation, have greater dissatisfactions with their marriages and more symptoms, and more commonly initiate the separation. They seek more help and have stronger social supports, as has also been reported by Kitson and Sussman (1977). At the time of the initial interview, women perceive more benefits from the separation. On balance, women's initial adjustments to the separation appear to be more positive and to be made more easily.

Men, who are initially generally opposed to the separation, perceive fewer separation-derived benefits at the time of the initial interview. During the first several months of separation they begin to perceive the benefits associated with that ending. By the end of the first 8 months of separation, men have virtually caught up with women in terms of their overall adjustment to the separation and tend to perceive fewer problems associated with it. In the case of both men and women, attachment bonds (Weiss, 1976) appear to undergo considerable weakening during the early months of separation.

To the extent that our data allow for interpretations of differences in response to marital disruption that can be attributed to parent status, two conclusions stand out. First, although parents are initially more opposed to the separation than nonparents, they appear to have fewer postseparation problems. In part this may be a function of the fact that they are older than nonparents. Second, reactions of parents to the disruption of their marriages are characterized by far more and longer lasting anger than in the case of nonparents. Parents, regardless of sex, tend to blame their spouses for their marital difficulties, see as little of their spouses as possible during the early postseparation period, and even when they describe increasing acceptance of the ending of their marriages, persist in their intense feelings of anger. It may well be that part of the reason why parents appear to have fewer postseparation problems is because of their tendency to displace their frustrations and hostility onto their spouses.

This chapter has described the first segment of a process that has clearly not yet run its course. Certain aspects of the process of accommodation to marital disruption seem to have been at least partially mastered, notably the acceptance of its reality and permanence. Other aspects of the marital disruption appear to be just as profoundly disturbing 8 months after separation as they were initially, as displayed by the maintenance of a wide variety of physical and psychological symptoms. Still other aspects of the separation process appear to become more disturbing as time goes on.

Notable in this category are work-related difficulties and problems with childrearing.

Two longitudinal studies that have recently been concluded indicate something of the general duration of the straining in response to this stressful life event. Hetherington, Cox, and Cox (1977) followed a sample of divorced parents for 2 years and noted that it was impossible to state whether "the re-stabilizing process in the divorced family had reached an asymptote and was largely completed at two years or whether this readjustment would continue over a longer period of time [p. 427]." Wallerstein and Kelly (1980) (see also Kelly, 1982) followed their sample of divorcing parents for 5 years and found that it took women 3.3 years and men 2.2 years after separation before their lives assumed a sense of coherence, postdivorce reorganization, and stability. Further, they found that 31% of the men and 42% of the women in their sample had not achieved a restructured postdivorce stability 5 years after separation.

Continuation of this longitudinal study will help clarify the differential development of the responses to marital disruption. While this chapter has concerned itself only with an intervention program control group, we expect that in both the intervention and control groups, changes over time will continue to take place in the process of adjustment. Continued analysis of the study data should clarify these changes in terms of content area as well as permit increased specification of how sex and parental status play a role in the development of an accommodation to the dissolution of a marriage.

References

Bane, M. J. Marital disruption and the lives of children. In G. Levinger & O. Moles (Eds.), *Divorce and separation: Context, causes, and consequences.* New York: Basic Books, 1979.

Bloom, B. L., Asher, S. J., & White, S. W. Marital disruption as a stressor: A review and analysis. *Psychological Bulletin,* 1978, *85,* 867–894.

Bloom, B. L., & Hodges, W. F. The predicament of the newly separated. *Community Mental Health Journal,* 1981, *17,* 277–293.

Bromet, E., & Moos, R. H. Environmental resources and the posttreatment functioning of alcoholic patients. *Journal of Health and Social Behavior,* 1977, *18,* 326–338.

Brown, P., & Manela, R. Changing family roles: Women and divorce. *Journal of Divorce,* 1978, *1,* 315–328.

Brown, P., Perry, L., & Harburg, E. Sex role attitudes and psychological outcomes for black and white women experiencing marital dissolution. *Journal of Marriage and the Family,* 1977, *39,* 549–561.

Chiriboga, D. A., Coho, A., Stein, J. A., & Roberts, J. Divorce, stress and social supports: A study in help seeking behavior. *Journal of Divorce*, 1979, *3*, 121–135.

Chiriboga, D. A., & Cutler, L. Stress responses among divorcing men and women. *Journal of Divorce*, 1977, *1*, 95–106.

Ferri, E. Characteristics of motherless families. *British Journal of Social Work*, 1973, *3*, 91–100.

Goode, W. J. *After divorce*. New York: Free Press, 1956.

Gray, G. M. The nature of the psychological impact of divorce upon the individual. *Journal of Divorce*, 1978, *1*, 289–301.

Hageman, M.J.C. Occupational stress and marital relationships. *Journal of Police Science and Administration*, 1978, *6*, 402–412.

Handy, C. The family: help or hindrance? In C. L. Cooper & R. Payne (Eds.), *Stress at work*. New York: Wiley, 1978.

Hetherington, E. M., Cox, M., & Cox, R. Divorced fathers. *Family Coordinator*, 1976, *25*, 417–428.

Hetherington, E. M., Cox, M., & Cox, R. The aftermath of divorce. In J. H. Stevens, Jr., & M. Matthews (Eds.), *Mother–child, father–child relations*. Washington, D.C.: National Association for the Education of Young Children, 1977.

Hodges, W. F., Wechsler, R. C., & Ballantine, C. Divorce and the preschool child: Cumulative stress. *Journal of Divorce*, 1979, *3*, 55–67.

Holmes, T. H., & Masuda, M. Life change and illness susceptibility. In B. S. Dohrenwend and B. P. Dohrenwend (Eds.), *Stressful life events: Their nature and effects*. New York: Wiley, 1974.

Holmes, T. H., & Rahe, R. H. The social readjustment rating scale. *Journal of Psychosomatic Research*, 1967, *11*, 213–218.

Kelly, J. B. Divorce: The adult perspective. In B. Wolman & G. Stricker (Eds.), *Handbook of developmental psychology*. New York: Prentice-Hall, 1982.

Kessler, R. C. A strategy for studying differential vulnerability to the psychological consequences of stress. *Journal of Health and Social Behavior*, 1979, *20*, 100–108.

Kitson, G. C., & Sussman, M. B. The impact of divorce on adults. *Conciliation Courts Review*, 1977, *15*, 20–24.

Levinger, G. Sources of marital dissatisfaction among applicants for divorce. *American Journal of Orthopsychiatry*, 1966, *36*, 803–807.

Levinger, G., & Moles, O. C. (Eds.). *Divorce and separation: Context, causes, and consequences*. New York: Basic Books, 1979.

Raschke, H. J. The role of social participation in post-separation and post-divorce adjustment. *Journal of Divorce*, 1977, *1*, 129–140.

Schlesinger, B. The one-parent family in perspective. In B. Schlesinger (Ed.), *The one-parent family*. Toronto: University of Toronto Press, 1969.

Smith, W. G. Critical life-events and prevention strategies in mental health. *Archives of General Psychiatry*, 1971, *25*, 103–109.

Spanier, G. B., & Casto, R. F. Adjustment to separation and divorce: An analysis of 50 case studies. *Journal of Divorce*, 1979, *2*, 241–253.

Steinmann, A., & Fox, D. J. *The male dilemma*. New York: Aronson, 1974.

U.S. Department of Health, Education, and Welfare. *Monthly vital statistics report: Provisional statistics. Annual summary for the United States, 1978: Births, deaths, marriages, and divorces*. DHEW Pub. No. (PHS) 79-1120. Washington, D.C.: U.S. Government Printing Office, 1979.

Wallerstein, J. S., & Kelly, J. B. *Surviving the breakup: How children and parents cope with divorce*. New York: Basic Books, 1980.

Weiss, R. S. *Marital separation*. New York: Basic Books, 1975.

Weiss, R. S. The emotional impact of marital separation. *Journal of Social Issues*, 1976, *32*, 135–145.

Zautra, A., & Beier, E. The effects of life crisis on psychological adjustment. *American Journal of Community Psychology*, 1978, *6*, 125–135.

CHAPTER 10

Children of Divorce:
Impact of Custody Disposition
on Social Development[1]

RICHARD A. WARSHAK

UNIVERSITY OF TEXAS HEALTH SCIENCE CENTER
DALLAS, TEXAS

JOHN W. SANTROCK

UNIVERSITY OF TEXAS AT DALLAS
RICHARDSON, TEXAS

I. Introduction

The award-winning motion picture *Kramer vs. Kramer* made a compelling case for a father obtaining custody of his son following divorce. Yet Ted Kramer lost the legal battle and kept his son only through the discretion of his ex-spouse. In real life, fathers do not win very often either. In 9 out of 10 cases children are placed with their mother following divorce. This reflects the legal and cultural presumption that mothers are more capable custodians of their children than are fathers.

This chapter begins by reviewing the historical background of this

---

[1] This chapter was based in part on the doctoral dissertation of the first author (Warshak, 1979). The research was funded by grants to the second author from the Hogg Foundation and the University of Texas at Dallas, although the views expressed do not necessarily reflect those of the supporting institutions. Please address correspondence concerning this chapter to the first author at: 5735 Brushy Creek Trail, Dallas, Texas 75252.

presumption as it has emerged in child-custody decisions. We then discuss what is currently known about the impact of mother custody and father custody on child development. Major findings are emphasized, as are the contributions of recent research to our conceptual and methodological sophistication in studying custody dispositions. We then report some of the findings from the Texas Custody Research Project on the impact of father-custody and mother-custody on children's social development.

II. Historical Background of Child-Custody Decisions

Child-custody decisions have a long and interesting history. Although it has been the tradition since the beginning of this century to award *mothers* custody of their children following a divorce, this has not always been the case. Had Ted Kramer lived in the nineteenth century, he would most likely have been granted custody, since U.S. courts perpetuated the English common law tradition of granting fathers near-absolute right to child custody. In England, the father's right was tempered only by a doctrine that gave the crown protective jurisdiction over those deemed to have no other protector. An interesting literary note is that it was under this doctrine that the famous poet Percy Shelley, in 1817, became one of the first fathers in history to be denied custody of his children because of his "vicious and immoral" atheistic beliefs.

In the nineteenth century few women were permitted to own property, and thus few had adequate means for financial support of children. It was believed that since the father was responsible for child support, he was entitled to custody. In fact, in the rare event when a father was deprived of custody, he was no longer considered liable for the support of the child. Bishop wrote in an 1881 legal text: "It seems to be a principle of the unwritten law, that the right to services of the child and the obligation to maintain them go together. The consequences of which would be that, if the assignment of the custody to the mother extends to divesting the father of his *title to the services of the children*, he cannot be compelled to maintain them [p. 473; emphasis added]."

Note the view of children as service-providers. From this vantage point it can be seen that, although the father's right to custody was defended on the grounds of his ability to provide support, and thus indirectly in the interests of the child, in truth it was recognized in the nineteenth century as a property right.

It was only when the father was held responsible for support—regardless of custody—that mothers, in the early 1900s, were freed from financial constraints against their receiving custody. In addition, the twentieth century brought a new interest in child welfare. The importance of maternal care in early childhood was increasingly emphasized, in part as a consequence of the development of psychoanalytic theory.

Thus, at the beginning of the twentieth century a tradition of awarding custody of children to mothers was established, a tradition that is rooted in the presumption that mothers are, by nature, uniquely suited to care for children. The child will suffer irreparable damage, so the argument goes, if separated from the mother during the formative "tender years." This "tender-years" doctrine has emerged as a legal guideline supporting the mother's growing advantage in custody decisions. This advantage was enhanced by the "best interests of the child" standard which, in spite of its literal meaning, came to be used primarily as a justification for the mother's preferential claim. Until recently, a father was awarded custody only if the mother was proved exceptionally unfit.

Recent changes are challenging the "motherhood mystique" and threatening the mother's decisive advantage. Many courts are beginning to entertain the notion that the father could provide a healthier psychological environment for his children.

A New York court crystallized a growing dissatisfaction with the tender-years presumption and recommended that it "be discarded because it is based on outdated social stereotypes rather than on rational and up-to-date consideration of the welfare of the children involved."[2] There is a small, but increasing, trend toward a genuine commitment to the actual needs and interests of the child and away from generalizations that give an a priori paramount claim to either parent. Although each case must be decided on its own merits, psychological research on the effects of different custodial arrangements will help in decreasing the reliance on cultural stereotypes and historical biases, and increasing the likelihood that decisions will be truly based on the best interests of the child.

III. Impact of Mother Custody on Children's Social Development

In the past 2 decades there has been a staggering increase in the incidence of divorce and the number of children involved in divorce. If trends since 1960 continue, by the end of the 1980s close to one-third of all children in the United States will have experienced their parents' divorce.

Given the theme of this volume, the status of divorce as a *nonnormative* life crisis may be questioned. It is possible that in the future divorce will

---

[2]Watts vs. Watts, 350 N.Y.S., 2d 285, (N.Y. 1973), p. 288.

emerge as a normal and expectable life event with which most families must contend. Then, perhaps, children will be overheard asking their friends, "Are your parents divorced . . . yet?" in a tone not very different from, "Are you going to be in Little League this year?" In fact, in the past many mothers had assumed that young children do not react significantly to a divorce (Goode, 1956; McDermott, 1968). And recently the cry is heard that researchers have focused too much on the harmful effects of divorce and not enough on the benefits.

This notion contrasts sharply with the evidence available from numerous studies of the past 30 years. These studies document the period of stress and turmoil ushered in by a family dissolution. They establish that, at least in our present culture, divorce is very much a *non*normative event. Indeed, divorce is one of the most stressful and disorganizing life events (Holmes & Rae, 1967), for which most people—adults and children—are not psychologically prepared. The following discussion of the effects of divorce refers to the mother-custody arrangement exclusively.

Virtually all children experience the period during and immediately following their parents' separation as upsetting and painful. In their longitudinal study of preschool children, Hetherington, Cox, and Cox (1978) found no "victimless" divorces. Children of divorce are significantly overrepresented in outpatient psychiatric clinic populations compared to the proportion of children in the general population who experience a divorce (Kalter, 1977; Sugar, 1970; Tuckman & Regan, 1966).

Children's responses to divorce run the gamut of emotional and behavioral disturbances (see Gardner, 1976; Tessman, 1978; for comprehensive clinical descriptions of these). Frequently noted reactions are denial, regression, depression, abandonment fears, anger, and generalized feelings of anxiety, helplessness, and lowered self-esteem. Some children, particularly younger ones, feel that they are responsible for the divorce; others become excessively preoccupied with fantasies of parental reconciliation. Even in nonclinical samples, dramatic disruptions in children's relationships with parents, teachers, and peers, and in their play behavior, have been documented (Hetherington *et al.*, 1978; Hetherington, Cox, & Cox, 1979b; McDermott, 1968; Wallerstein & Kelly, 1980). For example, compared with children in nondivorced families, preschool children of divorced parents show more oppositional, aggressive, dependent, whining, and demanding behavior and less affection. These studies leave little doubt that divorce is significantly upsetting to virtually all children. In addition to their own stress, children must cope with parents whose physical and emotional health is, in many cases, significantly deteriorated (Bloom, Asher, & White, 1978; Hetherington *et al.*, 1978).

This should not be taken as an indictment of divorce or as an implication that all children would be better off if their parents did not get divorced. On the contrary, in studies that go beyond the acute reactions to divorce, it has consistently been found that children in single-parent families show fewer problems than children in unhappy, conflict-ridden intact nuclear families (Hetherington, Cox, & Cox, 1979a; Nye, 1957; Rutter, 1978).

How then can these findings be reconciled with the knowledge that divorce is distressing to almost all children? A useful model that accommodates this apparent inconsistency is one that views divorce as a complex transitional process initially triggering acute stressful reactions, necessitating a period of recovery and adjustment, with subsequent establishment of a new pattern of equilibrium (Hetherington, 1979; Nye, 1957; Wallerstein & Kelly, 1980; Weiss, 1975). Clear indications of this restabilizing process are apparent between 1.5 and 2 years following divorce (Hetherington et al., 1978); Wallerstein & Kelly, 1980). Its hallmarks are a general improvement in parent–child relations with a concommitant reduction in conflict, strain, and negative behavior on the part of the child.

These findings could account for the apparent inconsistency between the acute stress noted at the time of divorce and the favorable comparisons of children from divorced homes with those from unhappy, unbroken homes. The stressful period of disorganization may be offset by the emergence of a new equilibrium, and the end result may be preferred to the continued atmosphere of tension and conflict present in the predivorce situation.

Nevertheless, it is important to consider that the period of disequilibrium following a divorce represents a substantial proportion of the total life experience of a child. In addition, family conflict does not invariably decline following divorce; in fact, it escalates in the first postdivorce year (Cline & Westman, 1971; Hetherington et al., 1978; Wallerstein & Kelly, 1980). Hetherington and her colleagues found that despite marked improvement 2 years postdivorce, preschool boys were still showing disturbances in social and emotional development (Hetherington et al., 1978, 1979a). Even 5 years following the parental separation, only one-third of the sample of children studied by Wallerstein & Kelly (1980) were functioning successfully with apparently unhampered development. The remaining two-thirds showed significant impairments judged to be related to the breakup. Their difficulties were manifested in diminished self-esteem, anger, depression, and loneliness.

The longer term impact of growing up in a mother-custody home following divorce, with the subsequent modifications of family structure and processes, have been extensively studied by developmental researchers. Two aspects of social development that have received much attention are sex-role typing and self-control (see Biller, 1976; Herzog & Sudia, 1970, 1973; Lamb, 1976 for comprehensive reviews of the literature).

Disruptions in sex-role development have been reported for young boys who have been separated from their fathers before the age of 5 (Biller, 1969; Biller & Bahm, 1971; Hetherington, 1966; Hetherington et al., 1979a, 1979b; Santrock & Wohlford, 1970; Sears, 1951). Preschool and elementary school boys from divorced families show self-concepts, play patterns, and preferences more typical of girls than boys. They also express their aggression verbally rather than physically which, again, is more characteristic of girls in our culture. Boys who are older than 5 years of age at the time of divorce do not show these deviations in sex-role development.

Reviewing the effects of father-absence on sex-role typing in preschool and elementary school girls, Lynn (1974) found few studies and even fewer demonstrable effects. Results from studies of older females suggest that there are effects. However, these are not manifested until adolescence in the form of anxiety and insecurity around males and precocious sexual concerns and behavior (Cohen, 1955; Glaser, 1965; Hetherington, 1972; Leonard, 1966; Neubauer, 1960; Wallerstein & Kelly, 1980; Hetherington, Cox, & Cox, Note 1).

Earlier marriages and greater incidences of pregnancy before marriage have been reported for females from divorced homes (Hetherington et al., Note 1). Also, as adults, both females and males who have experienced their parents' divorce or separation are more likely to have their own marriages end similarly (Landis, 1965; Pope & Mueller, 1976; Rohrer & Edmonson, 1960; Hetherington et al., Note 1).

Turning to the literature on self-control, we find that boys from divorced homes, when compared with boys from intact nuclear families, are more oppositional and antisocial, and less able to delay impulse gratification (Gregory, 1965; Hetherington et al., 1978, 1979a, 1979b; Mischel, 1961; Santrock & Wohlford, 1970). On the other hand, results of studies of girls from divorced homes do not consistently show disruptions in self-control.

IV. Factors Influencing Social Development in Mother-Custody Homes

For many years information about children growing up in mother-custody homes was typically accumulated by comparing a group of children from parentally intact families with a group of children from homes in which the father, for any number of reasons, was not present. Often, only a single measure of psychological adjustment was used. When differences between groups were found, what emerged were broad generalizations about the pathological effects of "father-absence."

The basic premise of these early studies was that father unavailability is the factor of overriding significance. Their conclusions failed to consider the influence of other important circumstances in the mother-custody home that might provide a more complete understanding of the observed effects or might account for the wide variability in response to divorce. Generally, this variability, apparent to the layperson using common sense, was overlooked by the investigators in their quest for statistically significant differences between groups.

With increasing methodological sophistication, some studies have explored variables that contribute to individual differences in coping with divorce. How children react to divorce depends in part on their developmental level. For example, preschool children are more likely to feel responsible for the divorce and to maintain reconciliation fantasies (Hetherington *et al.*, 1978; Tessman, 1978; Wallerstein & Kelly, 1980). Older children and adolescents are able to use a variety of coping strategies unavailable to the young child and are better equipped to make cognitive sense of the divorce. Despite different *styles* of coping, there are no consistent age differences in how *well* a child adjusts to divorce, according to Wallerstein & Kelly (1980) in their 5-year follow-up. However, there may be age-related effects on certain aspects of development. As mentioned earlier, investigators of sex-role development among children of divorce *have* found an effect of age at separation.

The personality and parenting styles of both parents are major factors mediating children's adjustment to divorce. For example, self-control is encouraged by the custodial parent's use of authoritative control and warm, attentive involvement (Hetherington *et al.*, 1979a; Santrock & Warshak, 1979; Warshak & Santrock, Note 2). A continued close relationship with the noncustodial father is critical to the child's coping and general adjustment (Hess & Camara, 1979; Hetherington *et al.*, 1978; Wallerstein & Kelly, 1980; Moore, Note 3). When the father does not maintain an active, positive involvement, his child is likely to suffer continued depressive affect and impaired self-esteem (Wallerstein & Kelly, 1980).

A. Sex Differences

One variable that is especially important to consider in studying the impact of different custodial arrangements is the sex of the child. We have already alluded to sex differences in responses to divorce. Recall that in mother-custody homes, boys are more likely than girls to show atypical sex-role typing and difficulties with self-control. These effects contribute to problems in relationships with parents, teachers, and peers.

How can these differences be explained? Psychoanalytic theory emphasizes the importance of the child's identification with the same-sex parent.
Social learning theory has continued this emphasis, but with stress on the
behavioral aspects of modeling and imitation processes. Support for this view
comes from Wallerstein and Kelly's (1980) finding that, in youngsters above
the age of 9, boys' good adjustment was correlated more highly with the
father–son relationship, whereas girls' good adjustment correlated more
highly with the mother–daughter relationship. Naturally, the identification
process may be bidirectional. For example, parents may know how to
interact more effectively and feel more comfortable with a child of the same
sex.

With regard to sex-role typing, from the beginning of the second year
children's attention becomes increasingly directed toward the same-sex
parent (Lamb, 1977). It may be difficult for a child to sustain strong
stereotypic sex-role preferences and behavior when the same-sex parent is
less available on a continuous basis. Support for this view was found in the
observation that boys in mother-custody homes who have more frequent
contact with their fathers identify more strongly with the masculine role
(Hetherington *et al.*, 1979a).

Another factor that contributes to the poorer adjustment of some children
living with the opposite-sex parent is what may be termed a "reverse
oedipal" situation. When this occurs, custodial parents seek from their
children emotional gratifications that are more appropriately provided by a
spouse. Feeling lonely, emotionally deprived, or stressed, they turn to their
children, most often a child of the opposite sex, for such needs as comfort and
nurture (Weiss, 1979).

However, most children are not capable of meeting their parents'
emotional needs. Thus, the parents are frustrated and disappointed and their
children are left with feelings of inadequacy at not being able to meet their
parents' expectations. This may then lead to the immature behaviors noted in
research findings. There is the long-range risk that, as these children grow
older, they will feel (and thus be) less competent in dealing with the opposite
sex.

Parental wishes for nurturance are not the only feelings that are
inappropriately directed toward children. At times, a custodial parent's anger
at the ex-spouse gets displaced onto a child (Wallerstein & Kelly, 1980).
This is more likely to occur toward a child of the opposite sex. It is not
uncommon to hear of a divorced mother overreacting to her son's behavior
while exclaiming in a derisive tone, "You're acting just like your father."

Still another possibility exists. Divorced parents are apt to have a less
positive attitude toward members of the opposite sex (Hetherington, 1972).
This may lead to less parental reinforcement for appropriate sex-typed

behavior in an opposite-sex child. For example, divorced mothers may be less likely to encourage masculine behaviors in their sons. Also, the custodial parent's negative attitude toward the ex-spouse may introduce a disruptive element of ambivalence in the child's attachment to, and identification with, the noncustodial parent. These explanations receive support from recent research with preschool children in the custody of their mothers (Hetherington et al., 1979a). It was found that maternal reinforcement of stereotypically masculine behavior and mothers' positive attitudes toward the father were both strongly associated with masculinity in sons.

All of the perspectives just discussed lead to the prediction that girls would have less difficulty in social development under a mother-custody arrangement and that boys would have fewer problems under a father-custody arrangement.

Alternative explanations for sex differences in children's responses to divorce have been advanced. It has been argued that disruptions in self-control in boys from mother-custody homes may be traced to the fact that boys are less compliant than girls. Hence, in order to be controlled, boys need the stronger authority image our culture ascribes to the father (Hetherington, 1979). If this factor has greater salience than those previously discussed, then similarly it would be predicted that boys would fare better in father-custody homes. Note that this does not portend greater difficulty for girls in father-custody homes.

Finally, it has been suggested that, in both intact and divorced families, boys are more likely than girls to be exposed to parental quarrels and to be negatively affected by parental conflict (Hetherington et al., 1978; 1979a; Wallerstein & Kelly, 1980; Block & Morrison, Note 4). Also, boys are viewed more negatively and receive less support from teachers and peers following a divorce (Hetherington et al., 1978, 1979b; Santrock, 1975; Santrock & Tracy, 1978; Wallerstein & Kelly, 1980). These considerations would seem to be equally applicable regardless of the custody arrangement. Thus, if this last explanation of sex-differential response to divorce is salient, then it would be predicted that boys would fare poorly even in a father-custody arrangement.

V. Summary: Impact of Mother Custody

This concludes the discussion of past research on the impact of mother-custody dispositions. In addition to providing valuable information, this research has enhanced our conceptual understanding of the divorce experience and our methodological sophistication in studying the effects of divorce.

To recapitulate, from a psychological vantage point divorce is best understood not as a discrete event but as a complex process that, over time, alters the basic nature of the family system. As is the case with most life crises, divorce initially exerts a disorganizing force on the family system. Many children recover from the crisis and regain normal developmental strides. Others have more difficulty and may experience significant disruptions in development.

Some of the factors that contribute to variability in response to divorce are the child's personality, developmental status, and sex, and the personality and parenting styles of each parent as manifested in the quality of the father–child, mother–father, and mother–child postdivorce relationships. Also important are the child's degree of access to each parent and the custodial parent's economic circumstances and reliance on extrafamilial support systems. Advances in mother-custody research have underscored the importance of exploring, or at least controlling, for these mediating variables. Turning next to the research on father custody we find, unfortunately, that the existing studies have not incorporated these methodological advances in their designs.

VI. Impact of Father Custody on Children's Social Development

A. Review of the Literature

Despite the strength of the bias in favor of mothers' preeminence, or perhaps because of it, there is surprisingly little research on how children fare when in the custody of their fathers. Gregory (1965) found a higher rate of delinquency among boys living in mother-custody homes than those living in father-custody homes. The opposite was true for girls: Girls living with their mothers were less likely to be delinquent than those living with their fathers.

Gregory believed these findings suggested that the identification model and control provided by the same-sex parent is more crucial in preventing delinquency among adolescents than any aspect of the relationship with the parent of the opposite sex. Extrapolating to elementary school children, it can be predicted that children from divorced homes living with the same-sex parent will show higher levels of socially responsible behavior than will children living with the opposite-sex parent.

There have been several studies in which a small number of fathers with custody were interviewed regarding their general life styles, psychological and social adjustment, parental attitudes, and use of compensatory services such as day care (Gasser & Taylor, 1976; George & Wilding, 1972; Gersick, 1979; Mendes, 1976; Orthner, Brown, & Ferguson, 1976; Schlesinger & Todres, 1976). Most of these studies found that fathers with custody report little difficulty in managing their households and child care responsibilities. Gersick (1979) found that fathers with custody use their extended family, professionals, and other community support services.

These limited studies yield an incomplete picture of father-custody families. In none of the investigations were children studied directly. The choice of measures was either a parental interview or questionnaire. In all but the Gersick (1979) study no additional methods or control groups were employed.[3] There is obviously a great need for systematic well-controlled, multimethod investigations of father custody and its impact on child development.

One of the main goals of the Texas Custody Research Project is to contribute to an empirical base of information about the social development of children in father-custody families. A second goal is to identify the factors associated with effective functioning of children in father-custody and mother-custody homes.

B. Design of Study

1. Subjects

The subjects of the study were 64 white, predominantly middle-class families with children ranging in age from 6 to 11 years. Half of the children were boys and half were girls. Approximately one-third of the children came from families in which the father was awarded custody following divorce, one-third came from families in which the mother was awarded custody, and one-third lived in parentally intact families with no history of separation. The three different types of families were individually matched for age of the children, family size, and socioeconomic status. The two groups of children from divorced homes were also individually matched for sibling status and for age when parents separated. In addition, all families in which there was a

---

[3]After this chapter was written, Rosen's (1979) work was brought to our attention. She studied persons ranging in age from 9 to 28 years, whose parents had divorced six to ten years prior to her investigation. Ratings based on interviews and sentence-completion tests revealed no differences between father-custody and mother-custody groups regardless of the child's sex. Unfortunately, the rater was not naive about the family structure of the children being judged and there is no assessment of the reliability of the ratings.

history of remarriage or in which the children were identified clinically as having an emotional disorder were excluded from the study. Noncustodial parents were not directly studied.

A separation period of 10 months, on the average, preceded the final divorce decree. In matching our groups we chose the child's age at the time of separation rather than the legal dissolution because we believe the former is the psychologically more significant event for children. The children's average age at separation was 5.0 years and at the time of the study 8.3 years. Thus an average of 3.3 years had elapsed since the marital breakup.

The procedure for obtaining the sample of families involved visiting various community agencies and Parents Without Partners, and following leads given by students and professors at various colleges and universities in the Dallas–Fort Worth metropolitan area. The father-custody group was selected first because it was anticipated that it would be by far the most difficult set of families to find. Then a mother-custody family was matched individually to a father-custody family, followed by the matching of the intact family group to each of the first two groups. The group means for selected demographic variables are provided in Table 10.1. Analyses of variance revealed no significant group differences on any of the matching variables. Although there were no social class differences (using Hollingshead's classification), postdivorced annual income was significantly lower in the mother-custody families. These families suffered a drastic drop in income following divorce, whereas the father-custody families did not.

TABLE 10.1
Means of Demographic Variables by Family Groups

	Family group					
	Father custody		Mother custody		Intact family	
Demographic variable	Boys	Girls	Boys	Girls	Boys	Girls
Child's current age	8.6	8.2	8.3	8.4	8.3	8.6
Number of children in family	1.8	1.8	1.7	2.0	1.8	2.1
Socioeconomic status[a]	2.5	2.2	2.5	2.4	2.0	1.9
Child's age at separation	5.8	4.5	5.2	4.7	—	—
Father's age	37	36	33	37	36	35
Mother's age	34	37	33	35	35	34
Annual income[b]	25	22	13	13	30	37

[a]Lower values indicate higher socioeconomic status.
[b]Income reported in thousands of dollars.

Since, when there is a custody dispute, it has been the practice of courts in America to award custody to fathers only when the mother is proven grossly unfit, we think it important to note that, in our sample, this did not appear to be the case. There were no differences between the father- and mother-custody groups in the number of custody decisions that had been reached by a court in a contested case. Nor was there any difference in the general reasons for custody assignment. By and large, in both groups custody was agreed upon before a court hearing, and most ex-spouses relinquished custody because they did not want custody or had no preference. More detailed descriptions of the selection and characteristics of our sample and of methodology have been presented elsewhere (Warshak, 1979).

2. Measures and Procedures[4]

A multimethod approach to studying social development was followed in this study. Parents and children were videotaped interacting in a laboratory situation; structured interviews and self-report scales were given to parents and children; parents and children responded to projective tasks; and teachers reported their perceptions of the children on rating forms.

a. Parent–Child Interaction. When the family came to the laboratory, the parent with custody and the child were videotaped in a structured interaction situation. In the intact family group, the mother and the father participated in the laboratory sessions on different days. During two 10-min laboratory sessions, the parent and the child were asked to (*a*) plan an activity together; and (*b*) discuss the main problems of the family.

The videotaped interactions were rated by an advanced graduate student in psychology with a clinical background. In addition, another graduate student independently rated one-fourth of the interactions. Both raters were kept naive about the group membership of the participants, although occasional comments during the interaction provided clues about family structure. Children were rated on 9-point scales in nine categories: warmth, self-esteem, anxiety, anger, demandingness, maturity, sociability, social conformity, and independence. The interrater reliabilities, based on Pearson r correlations, ranged from $+.54$ for anxiety to $+.92$ for social conformity.

b. Parent Interview. All parents were interviewed in their home using a structured interview schedule with open-ended and multiple-choice format questions. Divorced parents were asked about the circumstances leading up

---

[4]Copies of the interview schedules and rating scales are available in Warshak (1979).

to the divorce, the reasons for assignment of custody, the child's acute reactions to the separation and longer term adjustment since the divorce, and the parent's own adjustment since the divorce. We also learned about the child's visits with the noncustodial parent and the reliance on extrafamilial support systems. All interviews were audiorecorded.

 c. Child Interview. To obtain the children's perspectives on their parents' divorce, we examined their responses to a structured interview with open-ended and multiple-choice format questions. The questions addressed the children's understanding of the divorce, their attitudes about the divorce, postdivorce changes in family functioning, and their attitudes toward remarriage. The child interviews were conducted in our laboratory by graduate psychology students who had previous or current professional experience with children. The sex of the interviewer was counterbalanced within groups so that half of the girls and half of the boys from each family structure were interviewed by men and half by women. The interviewers coded children's responses during the interview and, in addition, all interviews were audiorecorded.

After the interview was completed, the interviewer rated the child on a series of personality categories. These 5-point scales were: self-esteem, anxiety, honesty, mood (happy–sad), ease of establishing rapport, cooperativeness, and overall appeal. One-fourth of the sample, stratified with respect to family structure and sex of child, was independently rated based on audiotapes of the interview. The interrater reliabilities, consisting of Pearson r intercorrelations, ranged from .06 to .67 with a mean of .44. It is difficult to interpret this relatively weak agreement because the data are not equivalent. An audiorecording does not provide the important visual cues that can be expected to influence inferential judgments of the type invoked in these ratings. However, a conservative approach would place less confidence in the ratings of self-esteem, anxiety, and honesty (reliability below +.50), and more confidence in the ratings of mood, ease of establishing rapport, cooperativeness, and overall appeal (reliability above +.50).

C. Results and Discussion[5]

1. Parent–Child Interaction

Results from the videotaped observations of parent–child interaction have

---

[5]Additional findings from this study, available after this chapter was written, can be found in Santrock, Warshak, & Elliott (1982), and Warshak and Santrock (in press).

been reported previously (Santrock & Warshak, 1979; Warshak & Santrock, Note 2). We found that boys in father-custody homes performed in a more socially competent manner than did intact-family boys, whereas girls in father-custody homes fared more poorly than girls from intact homes. When children from mother-custody families were compared with children from intact families, few differences emerged.

The comparisons of father-custody and mother-custody children revealed intriguing findings. Children living with the same-sex parent fared better than children living with the opposite-sex parent. On each of the observational measures, the mean score for boys in father-custody homes was higher than for girls, whereas the children's scores were reversed in mother-custody homes. Significant differences were found on four of the dimensions—boys whose fathers have custody were less demanding than girls in this type of family structure, whereas girls were less demanding than boys in mother-custody families. A similar, significantly positive same-sex child and parent effect was shown in the children's maturity, sociability, and independence.

We also found that the quality of the ongoing relationship between the custodial parent and the child was related to the child's behavior. Regardless of the custodial arrangement, authoritative parenting (warmth, clear setting of rules and regulations, and extensive verbal give-and-take) was significantly correlated with six of the nine child observation scales: self-esteem, maturity, sociability, social conformity, anger, and demandingness.

To cope with the demands of single parenting, divorced parents were enlisting the aid of additional caretakers, such as the noncustodial parent, babysitters, relatives, day-care centers, and friends. Overall, support systems were being used more by fathers with custody than mothers with custody (24 hr per week versus 11 hr per week). Father-custody children also had more contact with the noncustodial parent than their counterparts in mother-custody homes. In both types of custody dispositions, total contact with adult caretakers was positively related to the child's warmth, sociability, and social conformity as observed in the laboratory.

2. Children's Reactions to Divorce in Father-Custody and Mother-Custody Homes

Before discussing the children's reactions to the divorce, we would like to offer this qualification. Since we did not initiate our study of a family at the time of the initial breakup, we had to rely on the recollections of custodial parents for an account of their children's acute reactions to the divorce. We well appreciate that distortions are likely to occur in retrospective reports. However, we believe that the difficulty in acquiring a father-custody sample dictated our making an attempt to learn as much as possible about the course of divorce in these homes. With respect to the retrospective data, we place most confidence in those findings that concur with results from studies in which children were assessed at the time of the initial breakup (Hetherington *et al.*, 1978, 1979a, 1979b; McDermott, 1968; Wallerstein & Kelly, 1980). We are less confident when our retrospective data diverge from previous work, and we ask that such findings be regarded as material for hypotheses worthy of future study.

The initial event of the separation was distressing for youngsters regardless of whether it was father or mother who left the house. All parents recalled some reactions of their children in the weeks and months immediately following the breakup. The most frequently reported changes were increases in demands for parental attention and fear of abandonment and separation, as well as generalized anxiety. Other important reactions were (in decreasing order of frequency) increases in crying and expression of anger toward the custodial parent, irritability, physical complaints, sleep disturbances, withdrawn behavior, and anger with the noncustodial parent.

Although virtually all parents reported adverse reactions in some of these areas, not all the changes they told us about were negative. Approximately one-third thought their child showed *more* mature and self-controlled behavior at the time of the divorce. We must remind the reader that we are dealing here with parental perceptions and recollections. Wallerstein and Kelly (1980) commented on how parents' own needs biased their perceptions of their child's reactions to divorce; parents who opposed the divorce tended to emphasize the distress of the child, whereas parents who were eager to dissolve the marriage minimized the adverse impact on the child. In this context we note that 50% of the parents we studied said their child did not react to the separation as much as they expected and that 25% downplayed the strength and significance of the child's feelings and reactions, wondering whether they were even related to the divorce.

Type of custody was not associated with any of the children's acute reactions to the divorce except changes in their relationship with the noncustodial parent. Mothers with custody reported a deterioration in the father–child relationship in the weeks and months just following the divorce. In contrast, half of the custodial father group who noticed changes in their child's relationship with their mother viewed these changes as positive.

This finding held up when we asked parents about how things were now compared to the way they were before the divorce. Custodial mothers, with girls especially, reported a deterioration in the father–child dyad, whereas even more fathers with custody indicated improvements in mother–child relations. A parallel finding was that custodial mothers with girls more often indicated that their *own* relationship with their ex-husband was worse now than before the divorce. In contrast, custodial fathers rated their relationship with their ex-wife as better. These differences may be associated with the fact that, in our sample, noncustodial mothers were significantly more accessible to their ex-spouses and children than were noncustodial fathers. We have no way of knowing if this is an artifact of our sample or is representative of the father-custody population at large.

Though a majority of parents viewed their youngsters as more demanding, aggressive, and angry since the divorce, 72% felt their relationship with their child improved in the postdivorce atmosphere. By and large the children agreed with their parents on this point. There were some interesting discrepancies, though, between what parents told us about their child's divorce-related feelings and what the children told us themselves.

Eighty percent of the parents thought their child had *initially* harbored wishes for parental reconciliation, but half of these, 40% of the sample, did not believe in the staying power of this desire. No doubt they would be surprised to learn that their children, along with most of the children we interviewed, 84% in all, expressed ongoing reconciliation wishes, most of these intense longings. Perhaps it is even more noteworthy that over two-thirds of the children would prefer to go back in time to the predivorce family even with all its troubled circumstances.

We asked children to tell us the good and bad things about their parents being divorced. Thirty percent saw no advantages, but, of those who did see benefits from the divorce, most pointed to the reduction in parental conflict. There were no significant differences between the two custody groups, but girls were 2½ times more likely than boys to mention reduction in conflict as an advantage. The most frequent drawback cited by the children, with no significant differences between groups, was the reduced availability of the noncustodial parent.

The children were quite positive about their visits with the out-of-home parent; not one child reported an unpleasant experience on the last visit, and 62% said they would prefer more frequent visits. There was a nonsignificant trend for a greater percentage of children living with the opposite-sex parent (75% of mother-custody boys and father-custody girls) to express a wish for increased visitation than children living with the same-sex parent (50%).

Most children (62%) expressed positive feelings about the possibility of their custodial parent remarrying. Taken together—the focus on parental loss, the reconciliation wishes, and the remarriage endorsement—these findings suggest that children of divorce want to live in two-parent homes, despite the conflict, turmoil, and failure of the predivorce family.

Except where noted, in none of the results just mentioned were there differences between father-custody and mother-custody families, or between boys and girls. Divorce was uniformly upsetting to the children; most did not experience the postdivorce family structure as an improvement, and they continued to long for the days when they were part of an intact family.

3. Interviewers' Perceptions of Children in Father-Custody and Mother-Custody Homes

The interviewers' ratings were evaluated using two-way analyses of variance, with family structure and sex of child as the main factors. The results are presented in the following order: First we will look at the comparisons between children from intact homes and children from divorced homes. These analyses will shed light on the issue of whether differences in divorced and intact families based on data collected only on mother-custody families hold when father-custody families are included in the divorce sample.

Then, we focus on comparisons between children in father-custody and mother-custody families.

a. Comparison of Children from Divorced and Intact Families. The pattern of results in the interviewers' ratings parallel the findings from the laboratory parent–child interaction. Boys in father custody performed in a much more socially competent manner during the interview than did boys from intact family: They were rated as more honest, more appealing, and as having higher levels of self-esteem. There was a trend for boys in father custody to be in a more positive mood ($p < .08$) and to be easier to establish a rapport with ($p < .09$). Girls in the father-custody arrangement, by contrast, were observed to be less honest, less appealing, and have lower levels of self-esteem than girls from intact families.

When children from mother-custody families were compared with children from intact families, no significant differences emerged. Much of the divorce literature predicts that children of divorce will be less well adjusted than children from intact homes. We did not find this to be the case. Fathers who obtain custody may be very different from other fathers on a number of parenting attitudes and behaviors. The nature of these differences and the reasons why girls and boys living with fathers seem to behave so differently from their intact-family counterparts are topics we will explore in the future.

b. Comparison of Children from Father-Custody and Mother-Custody Families. In comparisons of children from father-custody and mother-custody families, children living with the same-sex parent uniformly showed more competent social development than children living with the opposite-sex parent. On each of the interviewers' ratings the mean score for boys in father-custody homes was higher than the mean score for girls in father-custody homes, whereas the children's scores were reversed when mothers had custody.

Significant differences were found on four of the seven dimensions. The interviewers found it easier to establish rapport with boys from father-custody homes than with girls in this type of family structure, whereas it was easier to establish a rapport with girls than with boys in mother-custody families. A similar, significantly positive same-sex child and parent effect was evidenced in the children's cooperativeness, honesty, and overall appeal. A similar pattern for ratings of anxiety and mood barely failed to reach significance at the conventional .05 level ($p < .067$ and $< .088$, respectively).

These comparisons provide further support for the importance of the same-sex parent in the child's life. Whether psychoanalytic, social learning, or other theories are used to explain these results, it does appear from our data from both the parent–child interaction and the child interview that there is something very important about the ongoing, continuous relationship of a child with the same-sex parent.

For these comparisons there are no main effects in the outcomes of observed children that could be attributed either to the child's sex or to the custodial family structure alone. It is clearly the particular combination of the child's gender and the parent's gender that leads to these results, and that is consistent with the predictions of a number of developmental theories.

VII. Conclusion

Traditionally, custody decisions have been based on cultural stereotypes and historical biases giving mothers preferential claim to their children following divorce. What implications does our research have for future custody decisions? Here we need to offer a note of caution.

Custody dispositions and their impact are enormously complex issues in which the optimal solution often is not clear. One of the finer points of the film *Kramer vs. Kramer* was that there was no simple resolution of the central dilemma. It is no longer tenable to support a mystique that specifies mothers as uniquely suited to care for children. We strongly hope that the old mystiques are not replaced with new ones. Although we have found strong evidence favoring a match between the sex of the child and the sex of the custodial parent, we certainly do not recommend that custody of girls should always be awarded to the mother and custody of boys awarded to the father.

The results of the present investigation argue against reliance on generalizations that give a priori claims to either parent. Instead, it is clear that the impact of custody disposition is mediated by a host of factors that include the sex of the child, aspects of the custodial parent–child relationship, and the availability of, and reliance on, extrafamilial support systems.

Naturally, any application of the present findings should be made with due recognition of the various limitations of this study. Scientific research such as this produces probabilities rather than absolute generalizations, and each custody case should be decided on its own merits. There may be unique circumstances in an individual family that warrant attention and consideration in custody decisions. Since the sample studied here was composed of elementary school children from predominantly middle- and upper middle-class backgrounds, generalizations to children of a different age or socio-economic status may be inappropriate. Further, none of the findings reported here should be used to infer the desirability of dividing custody of siblings between parents along sex-related lines. The contribution of the sibling system to a child's postdivorce adjustment is, at present, uncharted territory. In addition, the results of the present study may not apply to cases in which a reversal of a previous custody disposition is being considered. In those cases, the advantages of continuity and consistency of caretaking arrangements may override other concerns. Finally, we know little about the long-term effects of different family environments. Future changes, such as the remarriage of one or both parents, will have a definite impact on children's emotional development, and the pattern of these effects may differ in father-custody and mother-custody families. These issues are currently being explored in our step-family research project.

It is clear that generalizations about the effects of divorce, father custody, or mother custody are inadequate. Future research efforts should concentrate on sorting out the complex factors influencing a child's ability to cope with a significant alteration in family structure. As we gain a better understanding of these factors, such information can be integrated with the circumstances of each individual case and with clinical judgment in order to arrive at decisions truly in the best interests of the child.

Acknowledgments

The authors would like to thank Alvin North for his invaluable consultation in statistical methods and Karen Sitterle, Wendy Gorman, Richard Fulbright, and Sandra Burgess for their help in the data-processing phases of this project.

Reference Notes

1. Hetherington, E. M., Cox, R., & Cox, M. *My heart belongs to daddy: A study of the marriages of daughters of divorcees and widows*. Unpublished manuscript, University of Virginia, 1977.
2. Warshak, R. A., & Santrock, J. W. *The effects of father and mother custody on children's social development*. Paper presented at the biennial meeting of the Society for Research in Child Development, San Francisco, March 1979.
3. Moore, N. V. *Custody and visitations: A study of parents and children of divorce*. Paper presented at the biennial meeting of the Society for Research in Child Development, San Francisco, March 1979.
4. Block, J. H., & Morrison, A. L. *The relationship of parental agreement on child rearing orientations to children's personality characteristics*. Paper presented at the biennial meeting of the Society for Research in Child Development, San Francisco, March 1979.

References

Biller, H. B. Father dominance and sex-role development in kindergarten age boys. *Developmental Psychology*, 1969, *1*, 87–94.

Biller, H. B. The father and personality development: Paternal deprivation and sex-role development. In M. E. Lamb (Ed.), *The role of the father in child development*. New York: Wiley, 1976.

Biller, H. B., & Bahm, R. M. Father absence, perceived maternal behavior, and masculinity of self-control among junior high school boys. *Developmental Psychology*, 1971, *4*, 178–181.

Bishop, J. P. *Commentaries on the law of marriage and divorce* (Vol. 2). Boston: Little, Brown and Co., 1881.

Bloom, B. L., Asher, S. J., & White, S. W. Marital disruption as a stressor: A review and analysis. *Psychological Bulletin*, 1978, *85*, 867–894.

Cline, D., & Westman, J. The impact of divorce in the family. *Child Psychiatry Human Development*, 1971, *2*, 78–83.

Cohen, A. K. *Delinquent boys: The culture of the gang*. Glencoe, Ill.: Free Press, 1955.

Gardner, R. A. *Psychotherapy with children of divorce*. New York: Jason Aronson, Inc., 1976.

Gasser, R. D., & Taylor, C. M. Role adjustment of single parent fathers with dependent children. *The Family Coordinator*, 1976, *25*, 397–401.

George, V., & Wilding, P. *Motherless families*. London: Routledge and Kegan Paul, 1972.

Gersick, K. Fathers by choice: Divorced men who receive custody of their children. In G. Levinger, & O. Moles (Eds.), *Divorce and Separation*. New York: Basic Books, 1979.

Glaser, D. Social disorganization and delinquent subcultures. In H. C. Quay (Ed.), *Juvenile delinquency*. New York: Van Nostrand, 1965.

Goode, W. J. *After divorce*. New York: Free Press, 1956.

Gregory, I. Anterospective data following childhood loss of a parent: I. Delinquency and high school dropout. *Archives of General Psychiatry*, 1965, *13*, 99–109.

Herzog, E., & Sudia, C. E. *Boys in fatherless families*. Washington, D.C.: Office of Child Development, 1970.

Herzog, E., & Sudia, C. E. Children in fatherless families. In B. M. Caldwell & H. N. Ricciuti (Eds.), *Review of child development research* (Vol. 3). Chicago: University of Chicago Press, 1973.

Hess, R. D., & Camara, K. A. Post-divorce family relationships as mediating factors in the consequences of divorce for children. *Journal of Social Issues*, 1979, *35*(4), 79–96.

Hetherington, E. M. Effects of paternal absence on sex-typed behaviors in Negro and white preadolescent males. *Journal of Personality and Social Psychology*, 1966, *4*, 87–91.

Hetherington, E. M. Effects of father-absence on personality development in adolescent daughters. *Developmental Psychology*, 1972, *7*, 313–326.

Hetherington, E. M. Divorce: A child's perspective. *American Psychologist*, 1979, *34*, 851–858.

Hetherington, E. M., Cox, M., & Cox, R. The aftermath of divorce. In J. H. Stevens, Jr., & M. Matthews (Eds.) *Mother–child, father–child relations*. Washington, D.C.: National Association for the Education of Young Children, 1978.

Hetherington, E. M., Cox, M., & Cox, R. Family interactions and the social, emotional, and cognitive development of children following divorce. In V. C. Vaughan & T. B. Brazelton (Eds.), *The Family: Setting Priorities*. New York: Science and Medicine Publishers, 1979. (a)

Hetherington, E. M., Cox, M., & Cox, R. Play and social interaction in children following divorce. *Journal of Social Issues*, 1979, *35*(4), 26–49. (b)

Holmes, T. H., & Rae, R. H. The social readjustment rating scale. *Journal of Psychosomatic Research*, 1967, *11*, 213–218.

Kalter, N. Children of divorce in an outpatient psychiatric population. *American Journal of Orthopsychiatry*, 1977, *47*, 40–51.

Lamb, M. E. The role of the father: An overview. In M. E. Lamb (Ed.), *The role of the father in child development*. New York: Wiley, 1976.

Lamb, M. E. The development of parental preferences in the first two years of life. *Sex Roles*, 1977, *3*, 495–497.

Landis, P. H. *Making the most of marriage*. New York: Appleton-Century-Crofts, 1965.

Leonard, M. Fathers and daughters. *International Journal of Psychoanalysis*, 1966, *47*, 325–334.

Lynn, D. B. *The father: His role in child development*. Monterey, Calif.: Brooks/Cole, 1974.

McDermott, J. F. Parental divorce in early childhood. *American Journal* of Psychiatry, 1968, *124*, 118–126.

Mendes, H. A. Single fathers. *The Family Coordinator*, 1976, *25*, 439–444.

Mischel, W. Father-absence and delay of gratification. *Journal of Abnormal and Social Psychology*, 1961, *62*, 116–124.

Neubauer, P. B. The one-parent child and his oedipal development. *Psychoanalytic Study of the Child*, 1960, *15*, 286–309.

Nye, F. I. Child adjustment in broken and unbroken homes. *Marriage and Family Living*, 1957, *19*, 356–361.

Orthner, D., Brown, T., & Ferguson, D. Single-parent fatherhood: An emerging life style. *The Family Coordinator*, 1976, *25*, 429–437.

Pope, H., & Mueller, C. W. The intergenerational transmission of marital instability: Comparisons by race and sex. *Journal of Social Issues*, 1976, *32*, 49–66.

Rohrer, H. H., & Edmonson, M. S. *The eighth generation*. New York: Harper, 1960.

Rosen, R. Children of divorce: An evaluation of two common assumptions. *Journal of Family Law*, 1979, *2*, 403–415.

Rutter, M. Protective factors in children's responses to stress and disadvantage. In M. W. Kent & J. E. Rolf (Eds.), *Primary prevention of psychopathology: Vol. 3. Promoting social competence and coping in children.* Hanover, N.H.: University Press of New England, 1978.

Santrock, J. W. Father absence, perceived maternal behavior, and moral development in boys. *Child Development*, 1975, *46*, 753–757.

Santrock, J. W., & Tracy, R. L. Effect of children's family structure status on the development of stereotypes by children. *Journal of Educational Psychology*, 1978, *70*, 754–757.

Santrock, J. W., & Warshak, R. A. Father custody and social development in boys and girls. *Journal of Social Issues*. 1979, *35*, 112–125.

Santrock, J. W., Warshak, R. A., Lindbergh, C., & Meadows, L. Children's and parents' observed social behavior in stepfather families. *Child Development*, 1982, *53*, 472–480.

Santrock, J. W., & Wohlford, P. Effects of father absence: Influences of reason for and onset of absence. *Proceedings of the 78th Annual Convention of the American Psychological Association*, 1970, 5, 265–266.

Schlesinger, B., & Todres, R. Motherless families: An increasing societal pattern. *Child Welfare*, 1976, *55*, 553–558.

Sears, P. S. Doll play aggression in normal young children: Influence of sex, age, sibling status, father's absence. *Psychological Monographs*, 1951, *65*, No. 6.

Sugar, M. Children of divorce. *Pediatrics*, 1970, *46*, 588–595.

Tessman, L. H. *Children of parting parents*. New York: Aronson, 1978.

Tuckman, J., & Regan, R. A. Intactness of the home and behavioural problems in children. *Journal of Child Psychology and Psychiatry*, 1966, *7*, 225–233.

Wallerstein, J. S., & Kelly, J. B. *Surviving the break-up: How children and parents cope with divorce*. New York: Basic Books, 1980.

Warshak, R. A. The effects of father-custody and mother-custody on children's personality development (Doctoral dissertation, University of Texas Health Science Center at Dallas, 1978). *Dissertation Abstracts International*, 1979, *40*, 940B. (University Microfilms No. 7918709).

Warshak, R. A., & Santrock, J. W. The impact of divorce in father-custody and mother-custody homes: The child's perspective. In L. A. Kurdek (Ed.), *Children and Divorce*. San Francisco: Jossey-Bass, in press.

Weiss, R. S. *Marital separation*. New York: Basic Books, 1975.

Weiss, R. S. Growing up a little faster: The experience of growing up in a single-parent household. *Journal of Social Issues*, 1979, *35*(4), 97–111.

CHAPTER 11

Traumatic Injury in Midlife

JON E. KRAPFL

WEST VIRGINIA UNIVERSITY
MORGANTOWN, WEST VIRGINIA

I have begun this chapter on numerous occasions and have used numerous excuses to keep from writing it. I frankly do not know if my reluctance to write on this topic is controlled by the aversive stimuli associated with the experience described here, or by my limited experience writing from a first-person perspective; or perhaps I simply have little to say on the matter. Others have told me that the accident had a significant effect on me, but I have not been impressed by such comments. It has been my opinion that the accident had less effect on me than almost anyone else seems to believe. In any case, what follows is basically a chronology and interpretation of events related to the automobile accident in which I was involved several years ago. A chronology has the advantage of providing a sequential view of the setting or context in which my behavior occurred. Further, it can assist the reader in supporting or challenging the credibility of my interpretation of my behavior in context.

I. The Accident

In early November of 1975, a colleague at West Virginia University and I were driving to southern West Virginia. Early that evening, on the West

LIFE-SPAN DEVELOPMENTAL PSYCHOLOGY
Nonnormative Life Events

Virginia Turnpike, statistically the second-worst highway for fatalities in the United States, we were struck head-on by a semitruck that had lost control coming down a mountain. The truck struck a car in front of us head-on. In terms of those grisly remembrances of accidents, the other car and driver are what I remember most. It is not strange that I can still visualize that part of the accident better than our own crash, since I was a third-person observer of that event and its immediate aftermath. Of our crash itself, I can recall only pointing out to my colleague that there was going to be an accident in front of us. It did not occur to me, at first, that the accident was going to include us. Then I recall what seemed to be an interminably long period in which the truck seemed to keep coming down the hill. I shall report on the accident itself in some detail because at that time I not only observed what was going on around me but also made the first of many observations of my own reactions as they occurred, or immediately after they occurred.

I recall very clearly, prior to impact, thinking that time really does slow down. Apparently what I was describing was my focused attention on an aversive state of affairs accompanied by the heightened state of arousal of my autonomic nervous system in the face of powerful warning stimuli. All I can recall at the time is making the observation to myself that time seemed to slow down and that I was surprised. I had, of course, heard others make the claim that time slows down in the face of impending disaster, but I had never paid much attention to such claims. I had considered such verbal behavior to be prompted more by the special effects it might have on the audience than by time actually slowing down for the observer.

This phenomenon of time slowing down is interesting because, of course, time does not slow down at all, even in a world of space–time relativity. What I see now, as I look back on that accident, are few and simple stimuli— a truck rushing toward me out of control, a car in front of me being mangled. My view is that the feeling of time slowing down results from inordinately strong stimulus control prompted by powerful and salient warning stimuli, at which time all other stimuli or setting factors become irrelevant. Controlling stimuli usually occur in the context of complex settings, and thus we are most likely interacting in or responding to a complex stimulus environment when they occur. We might speculate that species that do not focus almost exclusively on salient warning stimuli under extreme circumstances may not survive.

In any case, this was the first of a number of events related to this accident in which I, having observed the events themselves from the vantage point of of the first person, found it necessary to reassess the verbal behavior of others. Let me now caution the reader concerning my observations. I do not claim that my first-person observations of these events are superior to third-person observations of the same phenomenon. What I claim is only that, with respect to accidents, I have now made both third-person and first-person observations, and they are different. I recognize that my first-person observations may be products of idiosyncratic features of my history and my environment. They may, therefore, have less general applicability than third-person observations, but they may also prove provocative and suggest possible lines for future research.

Returning to the scene of the accident: My neck was broken on impact, though I did not realize it at the time. It hurt, but it seemed far more important to me that I was unable to move my lower torso, legs, and feet, that I could not see very well, and that the rain seemed to be coming into the car.

Although there were some lights on outside the car, I could not see in the car. I could not move and felt that the dashboard must have been shoved against my legs. I could not move my head, but glancing down with my eyes, I realized that the dash was in place and that I was paralyzed from the waist down. It dawned on me that I was seriously hurt. I was bleeding profusely from the head. I placed my right hand on my head and stuck two fingers into the width of the cut. Head cuts bleed profusely, I knew. The blood was running into my eyes, my face, onto my clothes. It struck me then that I might be in real trouble, and at that moment I realized that imminent death was a distinct possibility. That realization evoked, or was at least immediately followed by, another emotional response. I would describe the change taking place at that moment as the onset of a moderate fear response, in contrast to terror. I emitted an expletive, the sort of thing I might have done had I missed a bus or hammered my thumb. The point is, the experience was not overly intense. I recall making another comment to myself at that point. The observation was to the effect that "there seems to be a real possibility that you're going to die, and you don't seem as upset by it as you thought you would be." I had contemplated death before, and I had never expected to face it calmly. The fact that I experienced only a moderate level of tension at that point was of considerable interest to me later in the hospital. Why was that the case? I suspect it might be related to the fact that I had been taught from an early age to deal with adversity in a constructive way.

For the next 15–20 minutes, I spent the time feeling my head, trying to calculate the likelihood that an ambulance would arrive and get me to a hospital before I bled to death. I searched my history repeatedly for information concerning head injuries, the amount of blood loss that could be sustained without death ensuing, and trying to estimate how much blood I was losing, estimating how far we were from Charleston, from a hospital, from an ambulance. Such behavior served no useful purpose under those conditions. Repeated review of the possibilities and information I had revealed nothing new to me at all, and I knew it. Probably such escape planning is often successful under similar circumstances, but in this case it was not productive.

I could not view much of the accident scene because paralysis prevented me from doing much with my lower body. The broken neck prevented me from turning my head. The blood kept running into my eyes and I could not see well. There were few external stimuli to control my behavior at that point, so I had time to contemplate my own possible death.

Perhaps the most influential event for me, directly resulting from the accident but not an inherent part of it, was the thinking I did about death at that point. I thought that the probability of my surviving this accident was not very high. The great loss of blood, the remoteness of the accident site, my fears about the competence of those who would work on me if there were to be any chance at all for me, all mitigated against survival in my opinion.

Under such conditions, lives are reviewed and evaluated. Mine was at any rate. My review and conclusion were most reassuring, and my view of death was significantly and perhaps permanently altered by the experience.

I would like to review some of my thinking at that time. I do not know whether that thinking changed me or was itself simply another set of factors related to the accident. In any case, I clearly thought that if I was dying, I did not resent its happening. I evaluated my 34 years as far more rich than most of the lives I had known. I truly felt that I had been fortunate in life. I found no objection to my life. I did not feel shortchanged. I was happy with what I had done with my life to that point. Recognizing how fortunate I had been compared with others in my physical and social environment and concluding that life had been complete have been of major importance to me since that time. Of course, some of these observations might not have been supportable from the vantage point of third-party observers, but that is irrelevant. I believed them and they comforted me. I would not accept death gladly, but I would accept it, grateful for the life I had been able to live. True or not, that is one of the more important observations I have made on myself. Since that time, I have viewed all of my life as postscript. Everything after that accident has been extra, a bonus. There was nothing left I had to do after the accident, whereas I think there was something I had to do prior to the accident, though I do not know precisely what it was. Something controlled my behavior prior to that accident that did not exert the same control later. In any case, not having anything that must be done in your life is a freeing experience. I would still work for resources and for social approval, of course. Somehow, though, there was a change in some of my behavior in that some reinforcers that had strongly controlled me lost their effect. I was no longer going to do things as much as I had previously for social, scientific, or peer approval. That approval would now be judged in a larger context of my reassessment of a worthwhile life. Basically, I think I learned to see life differently as I was facing death at that moment. I would not tell myself everything was going to be all right. What everything was going to be was unknown. I had come to know empirically that our hold on life is tenuous and that imminent death is not terrifying. I not only accepted that, but I found myself looking to the future with renewed interest.

A few other things did happen while waiting for the ambulance. Several of them illustrate the basically constructional approach I took toward the accident. First, as an undergraduate I recalled rooming with a student who worked part-time as an ambulance driver. From stories he had told me, I recalled his claim that many victims of accidents died while being rescued because of the lack of training given rescuers. Here I was in the middle of rural West Virginia. Who was going to rescue me? I realized that my side of the car was badly damaged and my colleague had gotten out of the car shortly after impact. His door would open. Rather than let someone cut me out of the car or try to get me out in some contorted way, I decided to try to move myself to the passenger seat. I did manage to move myself, using my hands as leverage, across the center console into the passenger seat, clearly reflecting the poorest judgment of the entire episode because of the high risk it involved.

The other external intrusion that interfered with my autistic calculations was my colleague. He exited the car shortly after the accident occurred and stayed out in the dark. It was still raining mixed with some snow, I believe. He would occasionally return to the car and say, "Krapfl, what the _____ happpened!" I would then recount for him what had occurred. Each time he returned to the car, he asked me what happened. Once he came to tell me that an ambulance had been ordered, and once to bring a shirt to place in the gash on my head. Once he returned to the car to get inside. That was no longer possible since I had moved to the passenger seat, and I felt badly that he was forced to stay in the rain. I had not anticipated he would return to the car to stay.

The emergency medical squad then arrived. I saw their leader running around the perimeter of the accident and then start barking orders. There is no need to chronicle this work in detail, but I was extremely impressed with their efficiency and professionalism. They placed a cervical collar around my neck and moved me to a stretcher, then to an ambulance. The pain, when I was moved at any time during the accident, was the most excruciating that I had ever experienced. I was to feel much more before this was over.

In the ambulance there were tests of vital signs, recordings made on paper, and phone conversations with the emergency room at the hospital. My behavior, I felt, was pitted against theirs. I sought to intervene to save myself, and, therefore, I sought information. They sought to keep me from jumping to inappropriate conclusions to keep me fighting for life. Their general demeanor suggested they were thoroughly interested in my case so, whatever their performance, it suggested that my well-being was their reinforcer as well. Nevertheless, the confrontation began and took something of the following form:

"Am I going to make it?"
"We can't say anything yet."
Ah, a general question was going to get me nowhere. Try specifics.
"What's my blood pressure."
No answer.
"What are my vital signs."
No answer.

I recall thinking about what I should do. I wanted information badly, but I did not know how to get it. Perhaps I should become agitated and they would decide that not telling me was worse than telling me. On the other hand, not knowing my condition, I thought that bluffing agitation might be bad for me. I would try another tactic. I decided to tell them exactly how I was feeling.

"Look, I'm really concerned. I don't know if I'm going to live or die. I don't think keeping me in the dark is good for me." The words are paraphrased, but the tone of this comment was calculated, and I remember it well.

That tone also reflected my feeling of vulnerability. At that time I had control of virtually nothing related to my life. Everything was someone else's problem. That was a drastic change for me. The response: "We're not sure what condition you're in. We're trying to get you stable. We're in contact with the hospital. We don't know the nature of your injuries, your neck or anything internal. We've slowed the head bleeding. That's really all we can tell you."

A calm simple straightforward response had resulted in what I found the first useful verbal behavior on their part. I believe that this reinforced trial had an effect on the rest of my behavior in this experience. I could at least generate information by behaving as the compliant but strong patient.

The emergency room at Charleston Memorial Hospital was the most nightmarish part of the entire experience. The EMS squad had had a calming effect. In the hospital things were frantic, and at least in part because of me. Moving from stretcher to emergency room table brought pain beyond knowing. Doctors, orderlies, nurses, whoever they were—and I never knew—were yelling , fidgeting with me, then, for unknown reasons, pulling back, working on someone else, or waiting and discussing me. They would tell me nothing. Every once in a while someone would yell something about my blood pressure and people would rush and, as far as I could tell, do nothing. Then I heard them discussing the fact that they could not deal with me. I was in the wrong hospital. Back on the stretcher, out into the cold, I still didn't know if I was going to live, and I was beginning to have more doubts. These people would not tell me anything and were behaving strangely—an analysis of the settings and their immediate effect on behavior would be appropriate, but there is no room for that in this chapter except for a few comments.

At Charleston General Hospital there was an interminable wait for a neurologist who had been called in. Everything there was more calm, however, allowing time for some very hard thinking.

Who was going to call my wife? How was she going to take this? What was she to be told? What was going to happen to the children? I was 200 miles from home. How was she to get to Charleston? Should she get to Charleston? Since she had no income, what would be my family's financial condition if I died? What would happen if I lived, but remained bedridden? What would happen in the immediate future for family income? Surely all of this was going to take a few weeks or a month, even if things worked out for the best. What proportion of these astronomical bills was I going to have to pay myself? I recall that the questions just kept coming and I had no time to answer or to think how I would find the answer before the next question came. The same questions recurred but I was in no condition to deal with them in detail. The neurosurgeon came, pronounced me stable for the moment, not having a broken neck, or at least he did not think so, but he placed me in traction for the night as a precaution, and then a resident started sewing me up. It took a long time, but he was pleasant. I was finally wheeled to a hospital room and a friend spent some time with me. I was poor company for they had allowed me to take nothing for pain, as I was needed to report on my own condition for diagnostic purposes. I fell asleep exhausted from pain and the events of the last 7 hours.

II. Hospitalization

The first day in the hospital was perhaps the most difficult of the entire experience. Shortly after awakening, I was told that my wife was in the hospital and would be in to see me after she saw the physician. In many ways I was more frightened for her than I was for me because there was nothing for me to do. Not only did she have to worry about me but she would also have to deal with our finances and with caring for our four children. I frankly did not know whether she was strong enough to pull it off. This was not the first but it was certainly the clearest instance in which I was confronted with my sexist beliefs and found them wanting. My wife and I had both learned our sex roles in the 1950s and 1960s when sex roles were clearly defined. She and I had both worked to change these roles, but the accident put everything to a serious test. I quickly learned that all that was required for her to behave authoritatively and independently was an opportunity. Her visible strength under these circumstances was a second benefit resulting from the accident, but that was to become clearer over time, not something I knew the first day in the hospital.

Before I saw my wife that first day, I was wheeled to the X-ray Department where numerous x-rays taken over a 2-hour period revealed multiple fractures. Of course the x-ray technician and the orderly were not supposed to describe anything to me—or I assumed that they were not—but my first x-rays were being developed even as later ones were being taken, and while I was still in the x-ray room, an orderly or assistant said, "Man, I've seen the pictures and it's broke as hell!" Well, that was depressing because the night before I had interpreted the physician's remarks to mean that I had likely sustained only serious whiplash. I assumed, though I had not been told, that they now expected me to live since they were moving me all around on an x-ray table, but no one had told me anything more reassuring than the very guarded comments of the previous night. Now I was confronted with the possibility of living with paralysis in both legs and with anesthesia in my right arm and hand. I wondered for a moment whether, given these alternatives, death was not the better option, but I thought that only for a fleeting moment. I also thought that I should take a note on hospital procedure. The orderly had not harmed me by informing me of my condition. Quite the contrary, he had helped me by not making me wait for 3 hours, when a physician would discuss my case with me. On the other hand, I could imagine many other conditions in which discussing or revealing diagnostic information in this way might be seriously harmful. I made numerous observations of this sort while in the hospital, thinking that I could help the hospital staff by providing them with some feedback. However, I never reported a single observation to them either during the time I was hospitalized or later.

I was wheeled back to the hospital room and waited another 20 minutes or so until my wife came in to see me. We talked for awhile about my condition. I discussed with her the fact that my neck was broken and that I was going to be hospitalized for some time. Her response was to claim that I was jumping to conclusions and did not know my own condition. I had assumed that the physician had told her that my neck was broken, and she had assumed that I could not know since she had not been informed in the conversation she had just had with the physician. I thought she was engaging in denial, and she thought I was becoming hysterical. There is a great deal of momentary control over information and its dispersal that is necessary in a hospital to prevent this kind of occurrence. My wife and I worked out a number of practical matters, and later that morning I asked my department chairman to inquire into conditions about the continuation or termination of my pay at the university, a matter of much concern to me at that moment.

A physician then came in and told me that I had a compound cervical fracture and that a neurosurgeon had been called in on my case. He also told me that there were only two possibilities for repair, one involving the use of weights and tongs—a very protracted procedure lasting months—and a second option involving surgery. Surgery would be much shorter, but it was 'extremely dangerous since the nature of the fracture required entry from the front of the neck. The entire situation was dealt with in such a matter-of-fact way that in a period of only a few minutes the neurosurgeon was placing tongs in my head. Fortunately, I was unable to see what the neurosurgeon was doing since he had given me large amounts of local anesthetic in preparation for inserting the tongs. The tongs were a huge half halolike contraption anchored to the cranium by quarter-inch bolts that had sharp points in them. I never felt anything except intense pressure on the cranium when the tongs were being placed in position. There was never any pain. It was interesting for me to observe others who, when they saw me for the first time, looked away in horror, sometimes almost wretching, and assuming that whatever pain I was experiencing was coming from the tongs. Visible signs in unfamiliar environments are quite misleading, however. In fact I never felt any pain from them for as long as I wore them.

Pain was not to be averted, however, and during the next several weeks I was to have a set of experiences that were clearly the most bizarre of my life up to that point or since. I was placed on a hospital bed lying perfectly flat except that my head was hung off the end of the mattress and lowered about ten degrees below my body. Weights, sometimes as much as 30 pounds, were hung off the end of the bed in order to stretch my spine. The combination of the pain from my neck and from being exposed for a period of more than 2 months to the slight edge or lip that is found on the edge of a mattress caused excruciating pain.

For a period of about 3 to 4 weeks pain was the most salient feature of my environment. Pain was pretty much all I thought about and all I felt. I was not angry and I was not depressed, and I was not lonely and I was not bored. I was simply in pain or not in pain, or, later, anticipating pain. Had I been in a condition to keep better records, I believe I could have clearly shown the effects of certain kinds of temporal conditioning. The conditioning effects for drug administration and alleviation of pain present a highly concentrated conditioning experience, with frequent trials, readily established deprivation conditions, and very powerful reinforcers. During my first full day at the hospital and during my x-rays, I had not been given any pain medication because it was necessary for me to assist in the assessment of my own case.

Following the insertion of the tongs, I was given Demarol IM and 10 mg of Valium twice a day. The Demarol was originally provided on a 4-hour and later on a 3-hour cycle. In only a few days it had completely taken over my life. Humans live in a diurnal cycle, by and large, and we come to assume that it is some sort of natural or biological arrangement. In fact, during my time on heavy pain medication, my view of existence moved from a diurnal to a 3-hour cycle. The 3-hour cycle began with two components and later developed into three. The first component began with the shot of Demarol IM. Demarol, given IM, works extremely fast. In less than a minute one begins to feel its soothing effects and the departure of pain. There were side effects of course, but they were clearly secondary and unimportant to me. To others the view of those side effects on my behavior must have made me seem more debilitated than, in fact, I was. Perhaps I *was* that debilitated, but what people were seeing was the effect of the drug more than my condition, had I been free of the drug. The drug would work for awhile, for a period of as much as 2 hours. After I first began receiving the drug and feeling no pain, I would lie there for a short time and then I would find myself commenting to myself that I was hurting. There would then be a long period, perhaps as much as 2 hours when I was in the kind of agony that I did not think I could bear. I did not scream out or do anything else because nothing was effective. Others commented on my bravery, but that has nothing to do with it. Such attributions are inappropriate when there is simply and absolutely nothing to do except to endure the pain. I believe that when pain stimuli are extremely intense, there is also nothing you can do to divert your attention from the pain. During that 3-week period my most lucid moments for visitors occurred when I was not under the momentary effects of Demarol. However, I was significantly more under the control of pain stimuli than I was under the control of the verbal behavior of my visitors. I would talk to visitors, and I was grateful for their coming. I felt that I would have liked to have been more responsive and attentive, but what I was focusing on during their visits was my pain.

The conditioning effect of the Demarol was quite notable. Very quickly, in 2 days, no more than 3, the 3-hour cycle switched from a two-component to a three-component cycle. The first component was nirvana. I felt no pain. I would sleep and feel rested and have pleasant dreams. This period would last for approximately 1 hour. The second period might be called the period of anticipation. This new period, which lasted for approximately 1 hour, was a period of transition from no pain to pain. During this period there was an increase in self-observations related to pain. They began by commenting to myself that the pain was coming back. The other thing I began to do during this time was to ask myself how I felt.

The neurosurgeon had switched me from a 4-hour to a 3-hour cycle when I explained to him that the pain seemed to be exhausting me. The 3-hour cycle, then, began as a two-component cycle that could be described as a pain and no-pain condition. With the maintained intensity of the pain and the continued administration of the drug to alleviate the pain, the third anticipatory condition was introduced. In terms of absolute time they were roughly equivalent. Thus, there was an hour of no pain, an hour of the anticipation of pain in which, at the beginning of the hour there was no pain but by the end of the hour the pain was real, and a third hour of searing, agonizing, pain. The middle period, which grew with repeated administration of the drug, is the interesting one, of course. It clearly did not exist when I began to take the drug but was something that I began to notice only after a few days and, even then, I am uncertain how much I would have noticed it had I not been discussing it with visitors. The anticipatory period, when I was not feeling intense pain but expecting it to return soon—knowing that it would return soon—kept getting longer and longer. My feeling at the time was that this anticipatory period, which was not nearly so comfortable a period as the hour immediately following the administration of the drug, seemed to be cutting into that "mellow" time. It seemed that the anticipatory period that got to be a full hour in length did not cut into the period of time of pain at all but only shortened the no-pain period. I questioned the advisability of allowing a pain period to alternate with a no-pain period. To me, the conditions were conducive to the development of addiction. In my judgment, it would have been better to keep me in the no-pain condition for a period of time.

One of the things that was seriously distorted during that first month was my perspective on time. The account and the explanation seem relatively straightforward. My no-pain time, subjectively, seemed to get shorter and shorter, seemed to go faster and faster. I would look at my watch thinking that perhaps 5 minutes had passed and I would discover that 25 minutes had passed. I would start to do something and, seemingly, before I had gotten anywhere, I would find myself in the anticipatory period. The temporal distortions and the pain conditions were incredible to me. I could not believe that distortion of that kind was possible, and perhaps it would not have been possible except under the conditions of the use of some natural or synthetic opiate. Under the pain condition when I was waiting for the next shot, and when that period was at least an hour long, I would sometimes look at my watch thinking that 20 minutes had passed and I would discover that no more than 60 seconds had passed. I checked this out a number of times. I would look at my watch and then I would try to focus on the amount of time passing. That process did affect the distortion somewhat, but even my concentrated attention did not change the distortion in a profound way. For me the combination of drugs and pain had profoundly disoriented me.

The strangest experience related to the accident occurred on the fifth day of hospitalization. I am mentioning it now because it was probably related to the drug experience, although I do not know that for certain. My sleep pattern also followed the 3-hour cycle and was directly related to the administration of the drug. Typically I would sleep during at least half of the first hour after the drug administration, and typically I would always be awake during the hour when I was experiencing pain. On the night of the fifth day of hospitalization, I awakened in the middle of the night. I awakened startled because I had been dreaming about a choir singing Christmas carols and was particularly startled when, seeing that I was awake, I realized that I was still hearing the carols. It was a particularly eerie feeling because I began to wonder if I had been unconscious for a month and a half and if it was now Christmas time. I tried to figure out whether or not I was hallucinating. Neither I nor anyone else in the room had a radio, unless of course I had been unconscious for a long period of time and had managed to pick up some new roommates during that time. I decided it was not a radio, however, because the music was coming from my right and my bed was located next to the window on my right. The only other two possibilities were that the nurses' intercom was playing the music or that there were carolers outside the hospital. I rang for a nurse, and an aide came to answer the call. I asked her if she heard any Christmas carols and she reported that she did not. When she left the room, I made an effort to try to turn off the sound by thinking my way through it, by analyzing it, or by doing anything I could to upset what I assumed was an hallucinatory experience. This was a particularly frightening experience, since I had never thought of myself as being anywhere close to capable of psychotic performance. It had never occurred to me that I was capable of anything like that loss of control. I found that I could do absolutely nothing about it, and I pushed the button for the aide again. She returned, a bit more irritated this time, and when I asked her if she would leave the light on in the room, she replied that that was not possible because of the three people staying in the room with me. She left and I was there with my auditory hallucinations. At that point, I came as close to panic as at any time during the entire experience. I thought to myself that I had been through a lot of experiences in only a few days, none of which were even remotely familiar to me. My world was in extreme disorder, I was highly distressed, I was taking drugs, and I was totally dependent on others for my care. I could see that under such extreme feelings of helplessness, I might be subject to all sorts of things that would be indicative of a loss of personal control. I rang for the aide again, and she came back, this time rather angry. I told her that I was sorry but that I felt that I was in some difficulty and needed to see a nurse. Fortunately for me there was a very competent nurse on duty who came in to see me and who completely understood my situation. She turned the light on, quickly finished whatever other work she had to do on her shift, and came back to stay with me for the rest of the night. She was a native Peruvian, with a name that I do not remember, but I do recall spending the entire evening discussing her childhood in Peru and the characteristics of ancient Indian cultures in Peru. I do not know what the nature of this experience was, whether it was drug induced or drug related or something else. It was certainly the most frightening experience of my hospitalization. And, true or not, I felt that this nurse had saved me. Once again I had been confronted with what, for me, was a totally novel state of affairs from a first-person perspective.

As the weeks wore on in the hospital, my environment settled into routine. One of the notable characteristics of hospitalization, especially when you are unable to move your body, is that you become extremely bored. The importance of the relativity issue when identifying effective reinforcers and when discerning salient stimuli becomes very clear. I developed some close relationships with the staff. The personnel on the ward were pleasant, attentive, and personable. They made me feel that I was getting a lot of special attention. I believe, still, that I did. Were there time, I believe I could provide instruction on being an effective patient. I found a number of things to be important during my hospitalization that were never important before and have not been important since. For example, I was able to watch TV through the use of a pair of glasses that contained triangular lenses. When you look through these glasses, they convert your vision by 90 degrees. Thus, while I was confined to my bed and looking straight at the hospital ceiling, I was able to see the same things I would see if I looked straight ahead from a vertical position. The TV was at approximately a 45-degree angle to my left, but by holding the lens in a particular way I could bring the TV into view in my left visual area. I spent many hours watching TV, developing favorite TV game shows and soap operas, and watching the Dinah Shore Show. Even then I knew this was a total waste of my time, but I found myself slowly being drawn into the world of daytime television. There was little else to do.

I had tried to write some professional papers after first entering the hospital, but I found that exhausting since I had to hold what I was writing up over my head and, in effect, write on the bottom of the page. I found that this took too much effort and was too distracting. A friend gave me the complete works of F. Scott Fitzgerald, and I found that to be just the right sort of light reading I needed, but that, too, got tiresome because of the necessity of holding the book over my head to read. So, what one finds is that boredom, too, is a relative state of affairs. Whatever the nature of the available stimuli, certain of these stimuli become salient, and, while one might remember that there were better things to do with one's time, one can become absorbed in what would at other times appear to be totally inane activity.

Friendships are an interesting phenomenon to view during the course of hospitalization. But I am not talking so much of those long-lasting and enduring friendships that existed prior to hospitalization. A number of friends did visit me in the hospital, and one graduate student took a particular interest in me during that time and we later became close friends. A psychologist on the staff at the hospital was also helpful and considerate in befriending me and discussing with me some of the things that were happening to me. But I think the more interesting friendships from a psychological point of view are those made with fellow patients. When I was first placed in the hospital, I was placed in a room with three other people, and later when they asked me to take a private room, I declined because of the financial costs involved. I was not certain that my insurance would pick up the entire cost of a private or semiprivate room. Later, I was to be grateful for the companionship provided by those hospitalized with me. My long hospitalization resulted in the acquaintance of many other people who were in for periods ranging from a few days to as much as a few weeks, or in one instance a month. One person, a businessman from Charleston, was particularly solicitous and friendly, to the point that as his recovery proceeded, he would often slip out and buy a bottle of wine, and he and I would share wine, cheese, and good late-night conversation. This man proved to be such a good friend that he drove me the 200 miles from Charleston to Morgantown when I was finally released from the hospital. He did this so that I would not have to stay in the hospital 24 hours longer than necessary while my wife was informed and made plans to pick me up. Many plans were made for posthospitalization gatherings of those people who were solicitous and caring for each other during their time of difficulty. In fact, the social relationships established in hospitals are probably not very strong, and when one moves back into one's typical social environment, the social control of the hospital contact is lost. In fact, virtually none of those contacts were maintained except that the businessman and I did get together for lunch on a couple of occasions at later times. We seemed very close friends in the hospital, yet after hospitalization it seemed clear that while he was bright and interesting in his own right, his interests and mine overlapped little except in the hospital situation.

There was humor in the friendships and in the social relations in the hospital room as well. There was also the usual kind of teasing. For example, my roommates might suggest that I sit up and take notice of something. But I remember a particular instance in which a man, whom I was to later discover was an alcoholic from skid row in Charleston, was admitted to the bed across from mine. He was a rather coarse individual, but very pleasant and likeable. As with so many other roommates, after a few days, I found him being solicitous of my welfare and helpful in finding or getting things for me. His hospitalization was based on complaints of back pain, and it was clear from nurses' and physicians' conversations with him and with each other that they believed him to be malingering. He was taking the same kind of pain medication that I was taking and kept screaming for shots. He then commented on how much he enjoyed them and discussed the experience with me. I found him to be a delightful companion who exposed me to an interesting life that I had not contemplated in more than a very casual way before. Of course, I believe that many of his accounts were exaggerated, possibly even fabricated, but in some ways that didn't matter since he was very entertaining. On his first night in the hospital when they brought dinner, he looked down at his dinner plate and I heard him exclaim, "Well, I'll be a son-of-a-bitch!" I asked him what was the matter. He replied, "Would you just look at this shit! Would you just look at this! This place is so goddamn cheap they put my jello on the same plate as my lettuce." I laughed so hard I was literally afraid of injuring my neck.

There were other occurrences that I cannot report in detail, such things as learning to walk again. This is traumatic because, while you are lying in the bed, you do not realize that you have no control over the use of your legs and that they will no longer bear weight. The length of hospitalization did not bother me, but the last couple of days when I found out that I might be able to go home very soon was a difficult time for me and I found myself becoming impatient. Not only hospital patients, but hospital staff became friends of mine and were always extremely good to me. Often they would come and talk to me when they had no specific assignment to complete. I felt extremely grateful to these people for their company and for their solicitous care. Yet, I have not been back to that hospital floor since the time of my release nor have I visited any of the people who were working in the hospital. Since I thought at the time, that I would return, if only to express my gratitude, I have been surprised by my own behavior. The entire situation must have been relatively aversive for me since I do not return to Charleston unless it is absolutely necessary, since I do not return to the hospital, and since I have contact with virtually no one or nothing associated with the hospitalization experience.

III. Epilogue

Are there important effects, long-lasting effects, that accrue from experiencing a critical accident and a long period of hospitalization? I do not think that question can be answered clearly, even in the individual case. There are, however, several observations that may be worthy of note.

Such an experience changed everything for me in that my analysis of what was worthwhile in my life, and life in general, influenced all my later behavior. This event considerably altered the relative effectiveness of certain reinforcers on my behavior, and also altered each of my later assessments of what was important and not important in my life.

Hospitals, ambulances, emergency rooms, etc., as settings for emergency treatment, have a great impact on the behavior of clients that they serve. Early interaction in such environments have a great deal to do with how a patient adjusts to that environment and to later life adjustment.

The behavior of physicians, nurses, orderlies, roommates, and other persons who offer support remain basically unanalyzed in terms of its impact on patient behavior, and the social impact is seriously underestimated. Hospital environments are so different from the physical and social environments in which we usually find ourselves. We, all of us, think we can simply generalize from our ordinary everyday environments to the hospital environment. However, only those very familiar with such environments actually know what is occurring. I was amazed at the basic distortions and misperception of many hospital visitors. Most of my visitors I would consider generally bright and observant people, but I can only conclude that the degree of environmental control over our behavior and our thinking is seriously underestimated by all of us.

This lesson and the many other lessons resulting from this injury, even the painful ones, have proven, in the final analysis, to have been of value to me. They enriched my life.

CHAPTER 12

Dialysis: A Unique Challenge?

RICHARD J. SEIME
JEFFREY ZIMMERMAN
WEST VIRGINIA UNIVERSITY SCHOOL OF MEDICINE
MORGANTOWN, WEST VIRGINIA

Dialysis technology developed into a clinically feasible intervention for end-stage renal failure in the early 1960s. The development of this technological advancement for maintaining life prompted researchers to examine the psychological and emotional ramifications of dialysis. Within the last 15 years, a great deal of literature has appeared describing the adjustment of patients to dialysis and describing the effects of this medical treatment on family, health care staff, and society. The maintenance of life by a machine certainly seems to be a nonnormative life event that could have serious developmental, behavioral, and psychological consequences.

The purpose of this chapter is to assess the impact of chronic hemodialysis treatment on the patient, family, health care staff, and society. The literature on the psychological, developmental, and behavioral ramifications of dialysis will also be reviewed. This literature will be critically examined to highlight the unique aspects associated with dialysis treatment. The chapter will conclude with a discussion of current psychological interventions and a call for a reformulation of how we view the experience of dialysis. Finally, suggestions for further research endeavors will be presented throughout the chapter.

LIFE-SPAN DEVELOPMENTAL PSYCHOLOGY
Nonnormative Life Events

I. The Impact of Dialysis Treatment

The impact of dialysis treatment appears to be wide reaching. The patient, family, health care staff, and society, in general, all experience effects associated with chronic dialysis. These effects are multifaceted, ranging from economic to psychological or from tangible (and easily measurable) to intangible (and difficult to measure). This section of the chapter will focus on those effects that are more readily observable (e.g., time, expense, and medical complications) in the various segments of the population just mentioned.

A. The Impact of Dialysis on the Patient

Maintenance dialysis is a time-consuming treatment. The dialysis patient must be on a dialysis machine for a minimum of 12–15 hours a week. He or she must also be present at a treatment facility 3 days a week. Even for patients who are on home dialysis, there is still a tremendous cost in terms of the time needed to set up and maintain the machine and to dialyze. In spite of the time-consuming, life-saving treatment, the patient may never again feel as good as he or she did before the onset of their kidney disease (Levy, 1978).

The end-stage renal disease patient experiences significant losses that may affect the quality of his or her life. In an early study, Wright, Sand, and Livingston (1966) documented the actual and threatened losses faced by the dialysis patient. They listed the loss of bodily function, loss of membership in groups, failures of plans or ventures, loss of feelings of health, loss of financial status, and loss of employment as significant for the patient. Abram (1978) also emphasized loss of health, independence, and family stability when describing the ramifications of dialysis.

One of the more important aftereffects of chronic dialysis is the loss of well feelings or of health. Many patients suffer from uremia at the outset, as well as from symptoms of physical and neurological dysfunction. Stewart and Stewart (1979) summarized the typical neurological disturbances confronted in the dialysis patient as ranging from subdural hematomas to dialysis disequilibrium and dialysis dementia. Hagberg (1974) found cerebral dysfunction in all patients tested before the initiation of dialysis. Another author (Levy, 1978) has emphasized the dialysis patient's difficulties of low energy and easy fatigability. In our own experience, the loss of energy and easy fatigability are the most profound physical symptoms encountered.

Loss of financial status and employment are documented through much of the literature. The dialysis patient has difficulty (even if feeling well) in maintaining a previous level of employment or involvement in the vocational sphere. In one study, dialysis occupied 25–38% of the work week (Friedman, Goodwin, & Chaudhry, 1970). McKevitt and Koppel (1978) found that 83% of their patients were not working because of the kidney disease and the treatment. However, Pendras and Pollard (1970) reported that 73% of the patients they followed over an 8-year period continued to function at the level established prior to their illness. This optimistic report is counterbalanced by another report in which only about 25% of patients demonstrated good vocational adjustment (Calsyn, Sherrard, Freeman, Hyerstay, & Curtis, 1978). Levy and Wynbrandt (1975) reported that the patients they studied suffered a 31–88% reduction in their income compared to the period prior to the onset of kidney disease. Obviously, the illness has a significant impact on vocational adjustment. Further data on employment are provided by Friedman et al. (1970), who found that only 11 of 20 patients studied were employed. Levy and Wyndbrandt (1975) found only one-third of the patients they studied to have good adjustment in the work and social sphere. These data highlight the tremendous challenge faced by the dialysis patient in maintaining "normal" vocational adjustment.

The loss of income caused by the need for and time associated with dialysis treatment is compounded by the literal cost of treatment for the individual. The federal government has assumed much of the expense for dialysis through legislation passed in 1973: Public Law 92-603 provides Medicare coverage to end-stage renal disease patients.

Although the patient is not responsible for purchasing the dialysis machine or paying all treatment expenses, he or she must still pay 20% of the cost. This can be a tremendous financial drain on financial resources at a time when the patient may not be able to work. These costs not only include the expense of dialysis treatment (estimated at between $12,000 to $24,000 per year) but also the expense of drugs and transportation.

Another significant problem for the patient on dialysis is the loss of or impairment of sexual function, a prevalent sequel. De-Nour (1978), in a review of studies of sexual problems, noted that the incidence of impotence is 50–80%. Similarly, Abram, Hester, Sheridan, and Epstein (1975) found that 80% of the patients interviewed had experienced a decrease in sexual activity following initiation of treatment. In the most comprehensive study of this issue, Levy (1973b) found that 59% of male patients reported partial or total impotence. Even more disturbing was the finding that 35% of the males and 25% of the females experienced worse sexual functioning after the initiation of dialysis.

The patient on dialysis not only experiences losses but he or she is also subject to a rather rigorous treatment regimen. The time-consuming aspects of the treatment have been emphasized, but it should also be noted that the dialysis patient must follow a rather strict diet. There are restrictions on the kind and quantity of food that may be eaten, especially restrictions on salt and fluid intake. It is not surprising that noncompliance with the dietary regimen is a significant problem in dialysis (De-Nour and Czaczkes, 1972; De-Nour & Czaczkes, 1976; Friedman et al., 1970; Levy, 1973a). However, compliance with the dietary aspects of the dialysis regimen is crucial since it is correlated with survival (Czaczkes & De-Nour, 1978).

The dietary restrictions and a progressive deterioration in physical health (Roger, 1975) leads to the difficult realization that being on dialysis is not only a chronic condition but also a condition that requires daily focus and participation. In spite of the dialysis treatment, the patient may experience complications and not feel well. In fact, a number of writers have stated that dialysis patients have difficulty predicting when they will feel well (Freyberger, 1973; Halper, 1971; Roger, 1975; Wright et al., 1966). Consequently, the patients face daily reminders of their condition and the necessity for daily care (e.g., in terms of diet), even though they are not being dialyzed on a daily basis.

In short, the dialysis patient has three options: death, dialysis, or transplantation. For the patient who does receive a transplant, the chronic treatment may cease. However, because many patients reject the transplanted kidney (Friedman, Delano, & Butt, 1978), the patient who receives a transplant may ultimately face a return to the chronic dialysis regimen.

B. The Impact of Dialysis on the Family

The family of the dialysis patient faces many of the same challenges that the patient faces. The time-consuming nature of the treatment usually has an effect on the family's schedule. The family is typically responsible for transportation of the patient. Furthermore, in many centers, the family is trained to set up the dialysis machine and dialyze the patient. Thus, the family member responsible for home dialysis treatment must be on the unit for a number of hours comparable to that of the patient. In our experience, the amount of time necessary for dialysis often seems more overwhelming for the healthy family members than for the patient.

The family members are also faced with new responsibilities. The spouse, in particular, may be faced with new challenges and roles. Levy (1973a, 1978) points out that about two to three times more males than females are on dialysis. Often, the traditional provider is the patient. Many women are thrust into new roles as head of household and provider. In addition to these new roles, the losses that the patient experiences are felt by the family as well. The family, like the patient, attempts to adjust to these losses in addition to taking on the responsibility of caring for the dialysis patient.

In home dialysis, a preferred method for maintenance (Friedman et al., 1978), the family becomes totally responsible for the patient's care even when complications are encountered.

The family can be disrupted by the changes or losses experienced because of dialysis. In addition, the sexual problems encountered by the patient obviously affect the spouse (e.g., Brown, Craick, Davies, Johnson, Dawborn, & Heale, 1978). The family may also encounter a change in life style as the dialysis patient becomes the focus of family concern and as income decreases. Though these same problems can be encountered in any family whose member is chronically ill, the magnitude of change appears greater when home dialysis is the treatment of choice. And like the patient, the family must live with the fact that dialysis is permanent.

C. The Impact of Dialysis on the Health Care Staff

The most apparent difference in the dialysis setting as opposed to other medical settings is that the nurses, technicians, and physicians have a long-term relationship with the patient (Czaczkes & De-Nour, 1978). The dialysis unit, thus, becomes analogous to a closely knit yet conflict-ridden family.

The nurses, in particular, are often cast in the roles of teacher, caregiver, and expert (Kress, 1975). This means that the unpredictability of the dialysis patient's physical well-being is felt by the entire health care staff. The staff has to deal with frequent hypotensive episodes, "blown sticks," and nauseated patients. They are also cast in the role of punisher and scolding parent when patients face the consequences of noncompliance through vigorous ultrafiltration and the distress experienced as a result. Because of the intensity of the relationship between the staff and the patient, much of the patient's frustration and anger may be projected onto the health care staff (e.g., Abram, 1969, Halper, 1971).

The projected anger and emotional intensity may be produced by the health care staff accepting and being held responsible for the total well-being of the in-center dialysis patient. This responsibility may lead to significant stress as the staff is often (in spite of their best efforts) not successful in maintaining the patient. This may be caused by medical conditions not related to dialysis.

The dialysis staff has considerable autonomy to make decisions about treatment and intervention (Mabry, Acchiardo, & Trapp, 1977). This can be a source of great satisfaction for the staff, yet it seems to add to the intensity of the relationship among the health care staff, patient, and family. The patient and family may strongly disapprove of schedule changes and variations in treatment. The health care staff may become particularly frustrated when they feel that their responsible actions and decisions are not being reciprocated by similarly responsible actions on the patient's part (Mabry et al., 1977; McKegney & Lange, 1971).

In short, the staff may feel misunderstood and thwarted. This situation then becomes ideal for communication to break down and for double-binding communication to develop (Alexander, 1976). Double-bind communication is typified by an overt message being negated by a more covert message. For example, the nursing staff may take responsibility for the patient's well-being and yet be covertly angry because the patient appears helpless and totally dependent on the unit and the staff. As a result, efficiency (and perhaps patient health) as well as quality of life (for patient and staff) may suffer.

D. The Impact of Dialysis on Society

Society has a role to play in dialysis treatment. Since 1973, Medicare has covered 80% of the cost of treating end-stage uremia by hemodialysis or transplantation. In 1977, it was estimated that $902 million was spent for treatment of 37,100 patients and that $2.3 billion would be spent for 55,900 patients in 1982 (Friedman et al., 1978). In 1977, the annual cost for in-center dialysis was $23,400 and for home dialysis, $12,480 per patient. Thus, dialysis has a significant and direct cost to the public. Certainly, the advent of public financing has enabled many people to live who would otherwise have died; however, the treatment has become exorbitantly expensive.

Society also loses productive wage earners. The data cited earlier indicate that many people are not able to maintain their vocational productivity after the onset of treatment. However, society expects that patients be gainfully employed (e.g., Sullivan, 1973). Simultaneously, considerable disincentives operate that make employment difficult. Campbell and Campbell (1978) describe the tremendous difficulties faced by middle-income dialysis patients whose income is only high enough to make them ineligible to receive aid. Thus, society has certain expectations for dialysis patients to remain productive; yet, maintaining employment may cost them financially. The result for society is a continued decrease in wage earners and an increase in welfare and total (rather than partial) disability payments.

II. The Psychological Ramifications of Dialysis

As stated earlier, the financial and time stress of dialysis has psychological ramifications for the patient, family, and health care staff. This section of the chapter will focus on a description of those effects.

A. The Patient

1. Machine Dependence

The most striking aspect of dialysis is the fact that a person's life is dependent on a machine. As Levy (1978) pointed out, not since the treatment of bulbar poliomyelitis with an iron lung has a group of patients been so dependent on a machine, a procedure, and a health care system for the maintenance of life. The analogies between dialysis treatment and the iron lung have also been pointed out by Abram (1969), who noted similar reactions in the two sets of patients. Since machine dependence sets the dialysis patient apart from other medical patients, it has attracted much attention.

De-Nour and her colleagues have suggested that the patient's dependence on the machine and the resultant psychological reactions are the major stressors of dialysis (De-Nour & Czaczkes, 1976; De-Nour, Shaltiel, & Czaczkes, 1968). Abram (1969) further indicated that some patients do not feel entirely human as a result of the need for dialysis treatment. In this context, Abram introduced the concept of the "semi-artificial man." It is interesting, however, that machine dependence per se is not clearly the major stressor of dialysis. In fact, in one of the earlier articles on psychological adjustment to dialysis (Wright et al., 1966) not one patient mentioned "being hooked to the machine" as stressful. The authors pointed out that familiarity with the procedure may have reduced the stress. In a now classic study on suicide in the dialysis population, Abram, Moore, and Westervelt (1971) stated that "the assault on the patient's independence, self-esteem, body image, and sense of well-being is significant to the point of intolerance [p. 1202]." However, one should not conclude that this is simply due to machine dependence. The issue seems more complex than that. Machine dependence appears to be but one aspect of the dependence–independence issues faced by the dialysis patient.

2. Dependence versus Independence

The issue of dependence versus independence is addressed by a number of authors and is described as one of the most consistent conflicts experienced by dialysis patients (Abram, 1968; Abram et al., 1975; De-Nour & Czaczkes, 1976; Halper, 1971; Levy, 1978). Abram (1969, 1978) viewed the conflict of necessary dependence with the process of striving toward independence as the central concept to understanding the stresses of life on maintenance dialysis.

The double-binding (Alexander, 1976) aspects of the independence–dependence conflict are particularly troublesome for the dialysis patient. Landsman (1975) described the dilemma of the dialysis patient in her theory of the "marginal man." The dialysis patient is expected not to be sick, yet to be sick enough to need dialysis. He or she is expected to perform routine life tasks and yet need repetitive and intrusive treatment. In short, almost every aspect of his or her life seems altered by the need for and dependence on dialysis. The dialysis patient must walk a difficult course that balances independence and well behaviors with dependence on dialysis and illness behaviors in that setting. In some sense, the dialysis patient is neither sick nor well. In the sense that the patient is dependent on dialysis, that individual is sick and chronically in need of treatment. However, as a stabilized dialysis patient, he or she is expected to be healthy (Landsman, 1975). Thus, the dialysis patient, in the double-bind of dialysis, is typified by his or her enforced dependency on a machine, health care staff, family, and society, and the concurrent expectancy that during "off hours" he or she is to be well, productive, responsible, and independent. Landsman (1978) suggested that this conflict is heightened by society's preoccupation with the importance of being a totally independent and competent person. She terms this preoccupation the "John Wayne myth." Thus, it would seem particularly difficult for male dialysis patients to live up to the "John Wayne myth" when they are confronted by the difficulties they experience on dialysis. In fact, there is evidence that the dependence–independence conflict is more difficult for male patients (Levy, 1973a). Clark, Hailstone, and Slade (1979) reported that females accept dependence on dialysis much more readily than do males. In some respects women may be more able to weather the double-bind of sickness and health.

In short, we believe this dilemma of being both dependent and independent, as well as healthy and sick, is one of the greater challenges facing the dialysis patient. As Landsman (1975) pointed out, dialysis is "perpetual treatment without cure [p. 268]."

3. Defense Mechanisms

The challenge of living on dialysis has led authors to examine the way patients handle this challenge. Denial, as a defense, is most frequently mentioned. Levy (1973a, 1977) stated that denial is more common in dialysis patients than in any other patient population with physical illness.

He suggested that it protects the dialysis patient from feeling helpless. Lefebvre, Norbert, and Crombez (1972) indicated the presence of denial in dialysis patients is a defense against fear of death and despair. Short and Wilson (1969) singled out denial as a necessary mechanism for coping with the dependence dialysis patients experience. They stated that patients minimize their limitations in order to deal with their dependence. Other authors have also singled out denial as the foremost defense among dialysis patients (Abram, 1978; Cramond, Knight, & Lawrence, 1967; De-Nour et al., 1968; Halper, 1971; Wright et al., 1966).

Denial can be a means by which the patient is able to carry on a semblance of independent healthy existence in the face of dialysis treatment (Short & Wilson, 1969). It can help the patient cope with changes in their self-image (Wright et al., 1966) and maintain an optimistic perspective (Abram, 1978).

Denial only becomes a deficit when the patient becomes uncooperative and fails to comply with the necessary dietary restrictions (Levy, 1978; Sand, Livingston, & Wright, 1966). An even more dramatic manifestation of denial is when the patient decides that he or she no longer needs treatment (e.g., Levy, 1978). Another problem with denial is that it can lead the health care staff to underestimate the impact of dialysis on the patient's life (e.g., Flannery, 1978; Wright et al., 1966). However, it is often difficult to assess whether a patient is denying illness and is actually overwhelmed or dysfunctional, or whether the patient has come to accept and adjust to the dialysis setting. Such acceptance of the dialysis regimen was pointed out by a group of authors (Greenberg, Weltz, Spitz, & Bizzozero, 1975) who found little evidence for denial in their patients.

A number of other psychological defense mechanisms have been observed in dialysis patients. Levy (1977) observed displacement, isolation of affect, projection, and reaction formation in his patients. De-Nour et al (1968) noted displacement, isolation of affect, reaction formation, and projection. In fact, these authors believe that these defenses are related to aggression stemming from dependence on maintenance dialysis. This theme is reiterated in a later study by the same group (De-Nour and Czaczkes, 1976). These defenses seem to serve to block aggression effectively. Other authors have mentioned projection as particularly common as a way of placing blame on others for the illness and resulting treatment (Lefebvre et al., 1972; Wright et al., 1966).

In summary, psychological defenses employed by dialysis patients have been related to dependence on a rigorous treatment regimen and attendant stresses. There is some agreement that these defenses are adaptive for the dialysis patient. However, in long-term adaptation, some defenses may lead to brittle adjustment (De-Nour et al., 1968) or despair (Abram, 1978) when the patient cannot deny the illness any longer or the patient jeopardizes his or her health.

4. Psychological Reactions to Dialysis

Previous sections have referred to the losses incurred by the dialysis patient and the stress imposed by the treatment. It is not surprising that the emotional reaction of the dialysis patients has been rather extensively studied.

The most commonly mentioned emotional reaction of dialysis patients is depression (e.g., Cramond et al., 1967; Lefebvre et al., 1972; Reichsman & Levy, 1972). Levy (1977, 1978) has also underscored the presence of depression in the dialysis patient. Abram (1978) described depression as a "universal problem" in dialysis patients.

It is also commonly thought that the incidence of suicide is far higher in the dialysis patient group than in the general population. Based on their survey that included 3478 patients, Abram et al. (1971) concluded that the suicide rate was at least 100 times that of the general population. Abram (1978), in a review of his earlier study, reported that the general population's suicide rate is .01%, whereas the dialysis suicide rate is 1.21%. If deaths attributable to noncompliance were included, the suicide rate would be 4.6% among dialysis patients. Thus, it is commonly stated that the suicide rate is 400 times higher in the dialysis patients than in the general population. Unfortunately, this is the only systematic study of suicide in the dialysis literature.

De-Nour and Czaczkes (1976) documented the incidence of various psychological problems in 100 patients treated for 4 years. Fifty-three percent of the patients suffered moderate to severe depression, 27% suffered anxiety, and 18% displayed psychotic symptoms. Other researchers have also reported anxiety as a frequent problem for dialysis patients, particularly in the early phases of treatment (Abram, 1978; Shea, Bogdan, Freeman, & Schreiner, 1965). Some anxiety has been accounted for by the patient's fears of complications (Freyberger, 1973) and death (De-Nour & Czaczkes, 1976). Since dialysis patients are often treated simultaneously in the same room, it is common for patients to identify with each other when one is suffering from some distress. Our staff have noticed a high incidence of what they call "sympathetic illness" whereby patients develop symptoms mediated by anxiety upon seeing someone else suffer. Fears are also heightened when a patient dies, especially when he or she is on the dialysis machine.

It appears that serious psychopathology (i.e., a psychotic reaction) is uncommon in the dialysis setting. Psychotic reactions seem to be most often related to neurological dysfunction (Stewart & Stewart, 1979). The incidence of cerebral dysfunction is particularly common in the early stages of treatment (Hagberg, 1974). Armstrong (1978), in his review of recent dialysis literature, reported that the overall incidence of poorly adjusted patients is about 46%. However, these data are affected by different operational definitions of adjustment and varied means of assessing patients. Unfortunately, many of our impressions about the psychological reactions of patients on dialysis are anecdotal. A more telling criticism of the studies of emotional reactions is that the research literature consists of approximately 130 adult patients out of the many thousands of patients who have been treated on dialysis (Armstrong, 1978).

5. Phases of Adaptation

In an attempt to account for the emotional reactions of dialysis patients and to better understand the defense mechanisms, Abram (1969) proposed a four-phase process of adaptation to dialysis. During Phase I, termed the "uremic syndrome," the dialysis patient is not yet on dialysis. This is a time when cognitive disruption may be apparent and occasional psychotic features associated with uremia are displayed. The patient is also fatigued and generally suffers malaise. In Phase II, marked by "the shift to psychological equilibrium," dialysis is initiated. The first few weeks of dialysis may be marked by apathy followed by euphoria, but followed by the development of subsequent anxiety. During Phase III, entitled "convalescence" (lasting 3 weeks to 3 months), the patient may develop symptoms of depression, and the conflicts of dependence versus independence become prominent. In Phase IV, which Abram called the "struggle for normalcy" (lasting 3–12 months), the patient struggles with adjusting to the chronic nature of the treatment and the "problem of living rather than dying." Abram's model helps us conceptualize the changes that take place over time in the dialysis patient. However, there seem to be individual response differences; one should not view these phases as absolute.

Reichsman and Levy (1972) also proposed a time sequence or stages model in understanding the adjustment of dialysis patients. The first stage, which they labeled the "honeymoon," begins after the initiation of dialysis and lasts from 6 weeks to 6 months. The patient shows physical improvement and seems to accept being dependent on the treatment. The next stage was labeled "disenchantment and discouragement." During this stage, lasting from 3 to 12 months, the patient is confronted by the double-bind of dependence–independence. It is also the time when the patient's sadness and sense of helplessness results in depression. In the third stage, or the "long-term adaptation" period, the patient "comes to grips with" the chronic nature of his or her treatment. During this time, the patient either returns to work or settles down to do nothing. The authors suggested that while denial or acceptance develop during this third stage, many patients also develop anger and resentment over the chronic treatment.

Levenberg and Campbell (1977) suggest that the conflicts and reactions displayed by dialysis patients can be conceptualized in an Ericksonian model of development. They suggest that the dialysis patient must re-examine some of the stages in Erickson's eight stages of development. In a sense, the patient has to resolve "conflicts" twice. Thus, in their opinion, the stress of dialysis is partly accounted for by the patient's need to resolve conflicts that for many years have been resolved but that are now important again as a result of the experience of dialysis.

It is easy to understand how dialysis patients can display so many different responses. It should be mentioned that little is known about how patients of various ages respond to dialysis. Czaczkes and De-Nour (1978) indicated that psychiatric complications increase with age, and Clark *et al.* (1979), who had dialysis patients characterize themselves on a Sematic Differential, observed the most negative self-perceptions in the 30–44-year-old age group. These data suggest some relationship between adjustment and age, although age was not found to be related to emotional adjustment in another study (Fischman & Schneider, 1972).

6. Psychological Interpretation of Dietary Noncompliance and Sexual Dysfunction

As a result of the prevalence of dietary noncompliance among dialysis patients noted previously, it is not surprising that authors have attempted to explain this noncompliance. Explanations commonly refer to the patient's use of defense mechanisms (e.g., Greenburg, 1977; Sand *et al.*, 1966). Conversely, compliance has been thought to represent acceptance of dependency (Greenberg *et al.*, 1975). De-Nour and Czaczkes (1972) suggested that noncompliance relates to low frustration tolerance and psychological gains from the sick role. They also suggested noncompliance may be an expression of aggression. These same authors (De-Nour and Czaczkes, 1976) found that depressed patients did not comply as well to the dietary program. Interestingly, in a well-designed study, intelligence per se was not found to affect compliance (Winokur, Czaczkes, & De-Nour, 1973).

Two authors have refrained from explaining noncompliance as a defense mechanism of denial or the result of psychological upset. Landsman (1975) suggested that the patient may be noncompliant in an attempt to clarify whether he or she is sick or well. Foster, Cohn, and McKegney (1973) suggested that the dialysis patient may noncomply with the dietary restrictions to improve their body image through weight gain.

Emotional reactions of dialysis patients have also been cited as contributing to sexual dysfunction. Depressive symptoms are implicated in heightening sexual problems in these patients (De-Nour, 1978; Levy, 1978; Steele, Finkelstein, & Finkelstein, 1976). Levy (1973b) argued that emotional factors must play a role in sexual dysfunction. He stated that patients experience an improvement in physical condition but an increase in sexual dysfunction after the initiation of treatment.

7. Indications of Positive Adjustment in Dialysis Patients

In assessing the impact of dialysis on the patient, the negative consequences have been emphasized. Common reactions to dialysis have been discussed along with the interactions among these reactions, sexual dysfunction and compliance. However, it also seems important to assess the previously reviewed literature critically because it seems more equivocal than is first apparent. Dialysis patients are not uniformly distressed, and they do not cope with dialysis in uniform ways. The impact of dialysis treatment on the patient as reported by numerous studies appears to be overwhelmingly negative. However, in these next two sections, some of this evidence will be re-examined to look for factors related to positive outcomes and to determine whether or not dialysis patients may be more "normal" than is commonly believed.

In general, dialysis patients have not been compared to patient groups with other medical problems, or non-patient groups. When these comparisons are made, the dialysis patients are not found to be more maladjusted. Clark et al. (1979), in a study discussed previously, concluded that dialysis patients perceive themselves much like other individuals. Patients, in their self-ratings, do not stand out as more disturbed or as having a more disturbed body image when compared to a non-patient group. Two other studies have also pointed out that dialysis patients may not be more disturbed or emotionally maladjusted than other medical patients. Farmer, Snowden, and Parsons (1979) reported that 10 of the 32 dialysis patients they studied displayed some psychiatric morbidity, but they pointed out that this was comparable to the rate of psychiatric morbidity in a general practitioner's office in England. In a larger, more intensive study of 85 dialysis patients based on questionnaire data, Livesley (1979) concluded that the prevalence of psychiatric symptomatology in hemodialysis patients is similar to general practice patients.

It may be that unhappiness, irritability, moodiness, and low energy are being overinterpreted as representing severe emotional maladjustment. In fact, the dialysis patient may be mourning or grieving, a normal response to loss (Cramond et al., 1967). Pritchard (1979) compared cardiac and dialysis patients on a "response to illness" questionnaire. He found that cardiac patients were more preoccupied with their illness and had more feelings of surrender than dialysis patients. The dialysis patients seemed to feel more helpless and resented dependence more than cardiac patients. Overall, it would seem that both of these groups were dealing with illness in a way that made sense, but neither group was maladjusted in a psychiatric sense.

It is interesting that many articles reported emotional maladjustment, but the data in the studies are unconvincing. Halper (1971), after describing the emotional problems faced by the dialysis patient, reported that patients in his setting manifested few psychiatric problems. A close examination of data from a now classic study by Shea et al. (1965) shows that patients were able to cope with the dialysis regimen in spite of some emotional upset. Calsyn et al. (1978) found 25% of their 107 dialysis patients to have Minnesota Multiphasic Personality Inventory (MMPI) profiles within normal limits. Another 45% displayed profiles that represented a preoccupation with physical concerns and/or denial. Only 29% of the profiles revealed evidence of depression, anxiety, or schizoid personality. This study certainly does not support the notion that most dialysis patients are psychopathologically upset. Further, Wright et al. (1966) reported the mean MMPI scores of patients to be within normal limits. In a disturbing study, Glassman and Siegal (1970) dismissed normal California Psychological Inventory Scores obtained by dialysis patients. They stated these scores were the result of a "massive" use of denial. Such interpretations of data are not uncommon. It is as if researchers are convinced that dialysis patients are disturbed; regardless of empirical findings, the patients are labeled as psychologically upset. Flannery (1978) typified such a tendency by stating that "serious emotional difficulties can be present in patients who appear to be coping very well [p. 787]." This is a truism that can apply to any clinical group, but it biases our view of dialysis patients. Dialysis patients are not considered emotionally asymptomatic in spite of their presentation. Such attitudes are unfortunate, as they may hinder our understanding of the reactions of dialysis patients and how they cope with the experience of dialysis.

8. Factors Associated with Positive Outcome

In reviewing the literature, it becomes apparent that there a considerable number of patients who adjust fairly well to dialysis. Typically, "adjustment" is operationalized as full vocational rehabilitation (Malmquist, 1973b), emotional adjustment (Sand et al., 1966), or compliance as indicated by average weight gains (Winokur *et al.*, 1973). Another (and perhaps problematic) criterion of how successful patients are in adjusting to dialysis is their length of survival (Calsyn *et al.*, 1978).

Some authors have concluded that the best predictor of adjustment is the individual's predialysis level of functioning (Malmquist, 1973a, 1973b; Winokur *et al.*, 1973). Others have indicated that more intelligent patients adjust better to dialysis (Ebra & Toth, 1972; Sand *et al.*, 1966); however, Winokur *et al.* (1973) did not find a relationship between adjustment and intelligence. However, persons who have the ability to form relationships with other people have been found to adjust better to dialysis (Beard, 1969; Hagberg & Malmquist, 1974).

The patient's attitude toward his or her treatment also seems to be important. Persons who do not gain satisfaction from the sick role are more likely to live a productive life (Armstrong, 1978; Sand *et al.*, 1966). Hagberg and Malmquist (1974) found that the patient's expectation of rapid rehabilitation was quite important in predicting vocational rehabilitation. Overall, Armstrong's (1978) review found that pre-illness employment, employment satisfaction and dissatisfaction with being sick most often predicted a positive outcome. The importance of maintaining some employment is confirmed by two studies that found length of survival correlated positively with the ability to work and being employed (Calsyn *et al.*, 1978; Farmer, Bewick, Parsons, & Snowden, 1979).

The patient's ability to cope with his or her illness, and to cope with the dependency on the dialysis system, seem intuitively important to the patient's quality of life. This is a factor that has not received much attention in the literature. One study indicates that patients whose quality of life during treatment was good described some sense of "mastery" over the illness (Levy & Wynbrandt, 1975). This area deserves more intensive study.

B. The Family

The family is obviously an important part of the dialysis treatment system. The family takes on particular responsibilities for the patient's well-being when a patient is transferred from in-center dialysis to home dialysis. In this section, the ramifications of dialysis on the family will be discussed with special emphasis on home dialysis.

1. Psychological Reactions in the Family

The family faces the same dilemma of chronic treatment with no cure that the patient faces. The patient's family must, at times, assume responsibilities formerly assumed by the patient. Streltzer, Finkelstein, Feigenbaum, Kitsen, and Cohn (1976) have pointed out that home dialysis offers flexibility, mobility, and feelings of accomplishment and control for the patient. However, the spouse and the family are faced with less free time, decreased mobility, and increased responsibility. Even in those cases in which the patient is not on home dialysis, it is important to note that in most settings the patient and family both participate actively in the dialysis regimen and related training procedures. The family assists in setting up the machine and helping initiate the treatment. Thus, the partner or family is cast into a very responsible role. At times, the family may be forced into a situation in which they must take the patient home for dialysis and assume responsibility regardless of whether they believe they are qualified (cf. Czaczkes & De-Nour, 1978). Our own observations are that most family members are initially overwhelmed and particularly fearful that the patient will suffer harm. Other families are very concerned about the effect of home dialysis on their own family life. Generally, families fear that they will not have the ability to handle dialysis or that the equipment will fail and they will not be able to deal with the situation. It is not surprising that the stress affects family members.

The stress of dialysis and home dialysis for the spouse has been documented in a number of studies. In one of the earliest papers on the effects of dialysis on the spouse, Shambaugh and Kanter (1969) emphasized the "enormous stress" on the spouse. In another study, significant psychological problems were found in spouses of dialysis patients (Smith, Curtis, McDonald, & DeWardener, 1969). There is evidence that spouses experience depression and anxiety that is similar to the patient's (Malmquist & Hagberg, 1974). One study suggested that spouses are more "consciously" anxious than patients and more concerned about depression, frustration, and anxiety than the patients, who are more concerned about their health (Holcolm & McDonald, 1973). Similar data are provided in a more comprehensive study of 40 dialysis families in Australia (Brown et al., 1978). They found that more partners (80%) than patients (17%) reported dialysis as a great strain, and that more partners (90%) than patients (55%) reported being anxious sometimes to very often. However, a cautionary note has to be added. Alexander and MacElveen (1977) found no significant differences in health status or stress between spouses of dialysis patients and a general sample of people in the community.

The incidence of sexual-potency problems in dialysis patients was documented earlier. This is another source of stress for partners. Brown et al. (1978) reported that 64% of couples reported that sexual relationships suffered. In another study, sexual functioning was the lowest area of satisfaction for couples (Holcolm & McDonald, 1973).

2. Role Changes in the Family

The kidney patient's dependence on dialysis treatment necessitates that roles change within a family. These role changes are often especially severe for the male head of a household who is employed. After initiation of dialysis, he may not be able to work or to maintain his role as head of the house (Abram, 1978). Levy (1973a) suggested that the male patient cannot maintain his previous emotional involvement with spouse and children. Streltzer et al. (1976) suggested that the realignment of roles adds stress beyond that imposed by renal failure and dialysis. They found that in couples where spouses were most dependent on the dialyzed patient for decision making, there was increased likelihood of failure in the home dialysis treatment. However, it can also be the case that the male partner is not comfortable in a more nurturing role and therefore is not comfortable caring for his partner. Such was the case in a study by Atcherson (1978). Short and Wilson (1969) pointed out how hostile feelings can develop as role changes take place. The family can then be in a position to rationalize their hostility and begin to think that "the patient is better off dead." This can be a particularly troublesome situation once it has developed.

Dialysis treatment can also affect children of the patient. The most dramatic situation may be the case in which the young person feels so responsible for his parent that he or she is unable to leave home. The child may feel guilt at abandoning the parent (MacElveen & Alexander, 1977) and, in our own unit, we have observed how adult children are sometimes given the responsibility for caring for their sick parent. In most of these cases, the son or daughter has little say in the situation. This can be tremendously stressful for the child (as well as the parent), and is a classic example of role reversal in which the child's role becomes that of the parent and the parent's role becomes that of the child.

Czaczkes and De-Nour (1978) have noted that two family reactions are particularly harmful: one is the double-bind communication system and the other is what they call a "switching attitude." They stated that, in the double-bind communication system, an overt pattern of support, consideration, and optimism is conveyed, while on a covert level the family may communicate the wish that the parent die. The switching attitude is one in which an overdevoted spouse suddenly breaks down into an attitude of "I can't take it anymore [p. 162]." In such situations, the responsibility for the care of the dialysis patient becomes very troublesome.

The emphasis on role changes sensitizes us to the dilemma faced by the patient and his family. In some respects, the patient remains a productive and responsible member of the family. Often, however, the patient is sporadically sick and dysfunctional. Therefore, the family may play an important part in hindering or enhancing the dialysis patient's (and its own) quality of life.

3. Family Factors and Positive Outcomes

The most frequently cited factors that promote positive outcome are family cohesiveness (Dimond, 1979), support, and encouragement (Greenberg et al., 1975; Levy & Wynbrandt, 1975). In one of the better studies of outcome, Pentecost, Zwirenz, and Manuel (1976) found that in families where individuals were able to express their own identity, which other family members accepted, patient survival was enhanced. Farmer, Bewick, Parsons, and Snowden (1979) found that a coping spouse was an important factor in longer survival in dialysis patients.

Sometimes the family, in spite of its cohesion and support, is not able to modify the outcome. However, cooperation among the family, patient, and hospital staff seems particularly important. The family is the primary caregiver once the patient leaves the hospital. There is evidence to suggest that maximum cooperation among the family, patient and staff enhances compliance, patient morale, and the patient's activity level (MacElveen, 1972). Further efforts need to be directed toward enhancing the ability of patients and families to cope with the rigors of dialysis (cf. Halper, 1971).

C. The Health Care Staff

The characteristics of the dialysis treatment setting are such that the health care staff develops a long-term relationship with the patient and his or her family. It is a setting in which patients initially enter treatment being very sick and ideally progress with treatment toward more normal functioning (cf. Abram, 1969). The dependence–independence problems of the dialysis patient and his or status as neither entirely sick nor entirely well (as discussed earlier) have a bearing on the staff's reactions to these patients. Dealing with chronic treatment and the intensity of the relationships that develop provides unique challenges for the health care staff.

1. Emotional Reactions of Staff

The prolonged and intense relationship with patients is reported to be one of the most stressful aspects of dialysis for the staff (Abram, 1969; Halper, 1971; Czaczkes & De-Nour, 1978). This situation is unlike most other nursing situations in which intensive care is usually more limited. De-Nour and Czaczkes (1968) noted emotional reactions among staff including feelings of guilt, overpossessiveness, and overprotectiveness toward the dialysis patients. Other authors have reported the presence of disturbing dreams about dialysis (Abram, 1978; Mabry *et al.*, 1977). In general, there is agreement that the staff experiences stress in the dialysis setting (Czaczkes & De-Nour, 1978).

2. Reactions to the Dialysis Patient

There is some evidence that withdrawing from patients is a very common reaction among staff (Czaczkes & De-Nour, 1978; De-Nour and Czaczkes, 1968). These authors cited evidence of high dropout rates for nurses and other personnel as an example of withdrawal. A more common type of withdrawal is that shown when the staff simply withdraws its attention from patients and seems to retreat from patient care. It is not uncommon for the health care team to become angry with patients—particularly for not cooperating or complying (McKegney & Lange, 1971). It is particularly common for noncompliant patients to be scolded and cajoled about noncompliance. The staff also must deal with patients who project blame for their problems. This can lead to mutual feelings of aggression and anger (Czaczkes & De-Nour, 1978). It is common for some of this anger to be displaced on other members of the health care team, thus leading to increased staff tension.

The health care staff deals continually with issues of chronic illness and death in the dialysis setting. It is not surprising that staff denial is mentioned as a way of coping with these stressful factors (De-Nour and Czaczkes, 1968; Short & Wilson, 1969). Unfortunately, such denial can interfere with patient care. The team may demand and expect behaviors from some patients (such as a return to work) that are impossible. Sullivan (1973) has pointed out that unrealistic demands for a return to work or for the patient to live a more productive life may actually be harmful. The staff may experience particular difficulty in understanding the patient's attitude toward life on dialysis—especially when the patient appears to have given up hope. The staff may also tend to deny the seriousness of the patient's condition and then may deny feelings of hopelessness experienced by the patient. McKegney and Lange (1971) discussed the common communication gap that may develop, which they label a "dissonance of values" (i.e., the staff believes that no matter how bad it is, it is worth going on). In some cases, dialysis staff members feel as if they care more about their patients than the patients (and their families) care about themselves (Mabry *et al.*, 1977).

De-Nour and Czaczkes (1971) conducted an interesting study in which they compared patients' perception of their illness and staff's perception. It is interesting that a staff member perceived all patients as suffering or alternatively perceived none of the patients as suffering. The staff's assessment of a patient's adjustment in specific areas was the same across all areas regardless of the particular type of adjustment difficulty described in a questionnaire item. Patients and staff tended to agree about the physical condition of the patient, but there was little agreement about the difficulty with diet and the patient's emotional feelings. The authors noted that most staff viewed compliance as a matter of willpower and not particularly difficult for the patient. Thus, problems develop when staff expectations do not coincide with how patients actually respond.

Since the health care staff must provide care for the dialysis patient, expectations tend to play an important role. In general, the expectations for the patients to comply with the treatment and to be "good patients" may make the staff feel wanted and appreciated (Abram, 1978). If a patient is not living up to the expectations of the staff, the staff may feel responsible for this "failure." After a number of disappointments, the staff may shift blame onto the patient. In such a situation, the team may lose sight of its own role and the patient's well-being. The relationship between staff behavior and expectations of patients is a complex one that deserves further study.

3. Health Care Staff and the Double-Bind

In an earlier section of this chapter, it was suggested that the dialysis patient is dependent on a system that includes dialysis treatment, the family, and the staff. The concept of the double-bind was introduced previously in describing the experience of the dialysis patient. In this section, the focus will be on the health care staff's role in the double-bind and the effects this has on both the patients and the staff.

Alexander (1976) has applied the concept of the double-bind to the dialysis setting. She describes the criteria that must be met to label a relationship as a double-bind: (a) an ongoing complimentary relationship; (b) a primary injunction; (c) a secondary injunction negating the primary one; (d) nonescape from the field; (e) repeated experience; and (f) learned perception. An example she provides is an injunction that the patient be "independent" negated by the injunction to be "dependent" on the staff and dialysis. Second, the dialysis patient is told by staff to live a "normal life" yet everything about the situation tells the patient that "you are not normal." Finally, the patient is expected to be "grateful" for the help he or she receives, and at the same time is given the message that it is not possible to be healthy. Although the double-bind applies to many systems, we believe it is particularly salient in understanding relationships in the dialysis arena. The dialysis patient has to live chronically in a setting where he or she is dependent yet independent—in a setting from which one cannot simply escape.

In our experience, this double-bind becomes apparent when the staff seems to appeal to medical necessity for making decisions that are related more to interpersonal or emotional issues. For example, the noncompliant patient may be the first person asked to shift to a less desirable time when schedule changes are made. The overt message is that he or she should be a "good" patient and help someone else in medical need. The covert message is that this individual has been a "bad" patient; this patient has angered the staff and does not deserve the consideration afforded to a more compliant patient. Thus, if the patient agrees to the schedule change he or she admits to being a "bad" patient, and if the individual does not agree he or she surely is a "bad" patient. It is also common for the staff to pressure a patient to comply. This is often done in the name of the patient's own "good" and to facilitate personal responsibility. The overt message is that the staff member is trying to help the patient be more responsible. The covert negating message is that the patient is not capable of being responsible. Thus, the patient who *complies* with the demands is not acting responsibly, and the patient who *does not* comply is also presenting further evidence of irresponsibility.

The staff is also caught in a double-bind with respect to the reactions and demands of the patients on time. Some patients may demand attention and insist that the staff make them well. The overt message is that the staff can and should do something to make the patient well. The covert message may be that the staff is incapable of helping because the patient cannot be made well. Thus, if the staff "helps" by agreeing to make the patient well they will not succeed, and if they do not "help" the patient will certainly not be made well. Of course, the individual staff members always have the option of fleeing the field. This may be a reason for the staff turnover and withdrawal. Perhaps the most troublesome bind the staff finds itself in is the expectation by family and society that the patient should be cured, and if not cured at least helped to feel better or be more productive. The more covert message on the part of society (as evidenced by lack of support for part-time employment) is that nothing can really be done to cure dialysis patients.

This emphasis on the nature of the double-bind is the result of our conviction that this is an important factor in the dialysis setting. We concur with Alexander (1976) when she suggests that we must account for relationships in dialysis—their nature, structure, and consequences—if we are to understand fully the unique challenge of dialysis.

4. Health Care Staff and Positive Outcome

The relationship of staff behavior and attitudes to patient adjustment is unclear. Czaczkes and De-Nour (1978) concluded that "realistic expectations" on the part of the staff were correlated with better patient adjustment. Beyond that, little is known about the impact of staff attitudes on patient outcome.

We would like to suggest that part of the problem in assessing the impact of staff attitudes on patient behavior is that researchers have tended to ignore the effects of attention on patient behavior. There is certainly ample evidence to suggest that differential reinforcement of patient behavior by staff would show a profound effect. However, well-designed studies of this factor have yet to be conducted. This is a theme that will be discussed in the next section of this chapter.

III. Psychological and Behavioral Interventions in Dialysis

Most of the research literature in dialysis emphasizes the impact, distress, and incapacity resulting from treatment. Thus, the literature on psychological reactions and adjustment difficulties in dialysis patients is extensive compared to the literature describing psychological or behavioral interventions in the dialysis setting. This is a situation that is certainly not unique to dialysis (Turk, Sobel, Follick, & Youkilis, 1980). It would be useful in this section to trichotomize interventions into those directed at patient problems, family difficulties, and the reactions of health care staff; however, the intervention studies are so few that it is best to discuss them simply categorized as traditional psychotherapeutic interventions and behavioral interventions.

A. Traditional Psychotherapeutic Interventions

A number of authors suggest that psychological interventions are useful in the dialysis setting (e.g., Abram, 1969; Levy, 1977; Wright et al., 1966). Czaczkes and De-Nour (1978) recommended goal-limited psychotherapy. Efforts directed toward resolving patient conflicts about dependence–independence, problems of aggression, body-image problems, and issues of ambivalence about continuation of life were all mentioned as particularly pertinent topics for psychotherapeutic interventions. However, these same authors (Czaczkes & De-Nour, 1978) pessimistically concluded that psychotherapeutic success with patients in dialysis is limited and that the "psychiatrist" is often of little help in direct services to patients.

Many of the psychotherapeutic efforts directed toward patients' adjustment problems have been in the form of group meetings with patients (Cole, Stelzer, & Bayersdorfer, 1979; Marshall, 1974; Wilson, Muzekari, Schneps, & Wilson, 1974). Group interventions have also been used with families of patients and spouses (Cole *et al.*, 1979; Holcolm & McDonald, 1973; Marshall, 1974). One of the earliest reports of an intervention with spouses (Shambaugh & Kanter, 1969) described a group in which the hostility of the members eventually led to dismantling the group. In general, the results of the interventions with both patients and families have been difficult to evaluate because of the anecdotal nature of most of the studies.

Psychotherapeutic efforts directed toward staff attitudes and staff adjustment have frequently been recommended. Some indicated that regular team conferences are important to help staff deal with their problems (e.g., Halper, 1971; Lefebvre *et al.*, 1972; Roger, 1975; Shea *et al.*, 1965). However, these recommendations were not supported by empirical evidence on their effect on staff behavior. Certainly, the rationale for these meetings is excellent but the data are anecdotal (e.g., Cole *et al.*, 1979).

B. *Behavioral Interventions*

Some studies have used behavioral methods to modify particular areas of patient adjustment. Springer (1976) developed a program to increase activity levels of dialysis patients. He found that patients acquired new skills, and that both patients and staff reported the time on dialysis was spent more productively than before intervention. Patients also reported feeling less depressed. In a similar vein, Lira and Mlott (1976) developed a behavioral home dialysis training program. The experimental group followed a program sequence of learning about the machine with feedback provided by a progress chart. The group provided with this type of training took fewer days than the control group to learn the techniques of home dialysis, and they reported feeling more confident in their abilities.

Behavioral interventions have been used to address a number of other problems in the dialysis arena. This methodology has been used to modify fluid intake (Barnes, 1976), improve compliance with a blood-drawing procedure (Wenerowicz, 1979), improve the dietary compliance of children on dialysis (Magrab & Papadopoulou, 1977), and to treat a hemodialysis phobia (Katz, 1974).

Studies of the incidence of noncompliance with dietary restrictions in dialysis indicate that this is a significant problem in dialysis. Behavioral interventions seem well suited to modify noncompliant behavior. We have had some success using self-control procedures such as self-monitoring (Nelson, 1977) to improve compliance. In addition, social attention on the part of the nursing staff could be effective in modifying noncompliance. It is our opinion that in dialysis more attention is given to the noncompliant patient in the form of scolding and suggestions for improvement than is given to the more compliant patient (Seime, 1980). It would seem that further behavioral interventions (such as those used in other medical arenas [i.e., Sand, Treischmann, Fordyce, & Fowler, 1975]) using contingent staff attention are warranted.

IV. Adjustment to Dialysis: A Reformulation

The emphasis in the dialysis literature has been on the description of the tremendous adjustment problems faced by the patient. Very little attention has been directed toward understanding how these patients restructure their lives, how some develop effective ways of responding to the illness while others do not, and how patients meet the challenges of dialysis (cf. Turk et al., 1980; Turk & Follick, Note 1).

As stated earlier in this chapter, adjustment is difficult to define. What is clear is that adjustment is not a static outcome but a process of adaptation (Turk & Follick, Note 1). This is a particularly pertinent consideration when we assess the ways in which dialysis patients respond to the treatment regimen. Dialysis patients may adjust to certain aspects of treatment and yet be dysfunctional in other aspects of their lives. Most studies do not take into account the complex nature of adjustment. In fact, the presence of emotional upset in patients may be a necessary component of adjusting to the treatment and not an indication of maladjustment (cf. the "work of worrying," Janis, 1958). Ignored in almost all of the studies reviewed has been the patient who is apparently accommodating successfully to dialysis. It would seem particularly useful to assess how these patients adapt to dialysis and not simply report on the responses of dysfunctional individuals (Turk & Follick, Note 1).

Sobel and Worden (1979), in their extensive studies of psychological adaptation to cancer, have noted how generalized notions about the plight of cancer patients have hindered understanding of how cancer patients cope. This same problem exists in our understanding of the dialysis patient. At the present time, dialysis patients are considered to be a highly stressed group of individuals who respond similarly to the dialysis regimen. In the process of describing the adjustment of patients to dialysis, we have assumed coping homogeneity (Sobel & Worden, 1979) among dialysis patients. It seems clear from a careful reading of the dialysis literature that patients cope in different ways, and that some patients are more effective in coping than others. We believe that it is important for an emphasis to develop in the dialysis literature on understanding the demands for adjustment and adaptive responses (Turk & Follick, Note 1) of dialysis patients.

A behavior-analytic approach (Goldfried & D'Zurilla, 1969), termed sequential criterion analysis (Turk *et al.*, 1980, Turk & Follick, Note 1), has recently been applied to the area of chronic illness. Such an analysis is particularly useful in determining the predominant concerns and variations in what is required of a patient to cope with an illness (Turk & Follick, Note 1). It is not our purpose to elaborate on the specifics of the sequential criterion model, but we suggest that it may be a fruitful model for assessing the impact of dialysis treatment and designing effective interventions. The emphasis in a behavior-analytic approach is on careful identification of problems, identification of covert and overt coping responses to the illness, and evaluation of the relative efficacy of these responses. A secondary stage in the process is to develop instruments to assess competency in coping and to identify patients "at risk" (Turk & Follick, Note 1). Such an approach to the understanding of coping also provides content for intervention strategies (Turk *et al.*, 1980). A sequential criterion analysis requires that patients be studied both longitudinally and cross-sectionally. As is apparent from reviewing the dialysis literature, the bulk of current studies are cross-sectional and do not permit us to evaluate how patients adjust over time.

The methods being developed to understand how individuals cope with chronic illness must be applied to the dialysis setting. It is our opinion that the general notions of emotional upset in dialysis patients and the emphasis on psychodynamic defenses have hindered our understanding of the response of the dialysis patient, his or her family, and the health care staff. It was our contention earlier in this chapter that the unique challenge of dialysis was the patient's dependence on the family and health care staff and the problems of being both sick and well. An emphasis on adjustment and coping rather than maladjustment would enhance the dialysis patient's quality of life. The predominant emphasis in the literature is that patients are maladjusted. Patients are not expected to cope or to behave in adaptive fashions. At the present time, there is little to offer in the way of interventions because so little is known about the coping strategies required in the dialysis setting. We believe that this lack of knowledge implicitly reinforces the double-bind in a situation that is covertly (but perhaps inappropriately) viewed as hopeless.

The potential of a careful sequential criterion analysis of coping in the dialysis setting would assist the staff in recognizing those patients at risk for developing problems. These same patients could then be instructed in how to cope more effectively. Similar interventions could be directed at families at risk. Finally, and perhaps most importantly, such an approach would underscore adjustment to dialysis as an adaptive process in which coping responses are possible.

V. Conclusions

The impact of dialysis on the patient, family, health care staff, and society has been reviewed. The challenge of dialysis is that of living a satisfying life in the face of chronic treatment and dependence. The importance of machine dependence itself may not be as pronounced as the dependence of the dialysis patient on a system that includes the family and the health care staff.

The dialysis patient is thought to be particularly stressed and subject to psychological maladjustment. Unfortunately, a mythology has developed about the adjustment difficulties of the dialysis patient that seems to hinder our understanding of the adaptive responses in this population. Our understanding of the dialysis patient is based on studies that have focused on the "maladjustment" of dialysis patients. Many of these studies lack significant findings of psychopathology (e.g., on psychological tests), yet the majority of the patients are considered emotionally upset.

The patient who accommodates successfully to dialysis has not been studied as intensively. We believe that the dialysis patient, his or her family, and the health care staff will be better served by an approach that systematically examines how successful patients adapt to and cope with dialysis treatment. Such an approach will ideally facilitate a more complete understanding of those factors that contribute to adjustment. Consequently, methods may develop by which a preventative approach might be used to avoid some of the complications and stressors associated with chronic hemodialysis.

Reference Note

1. Turk, D. C. & Follick, M. J. Coping with covert illness. A proposal for a preventative model of intervention. In E. Blinchik (Chair), *Cognitive-behavioral intervention in pain and chronic illness*. Symposium presented at the meeting of the American Psychological Association, New York, November 1979.

References

Abram, H. S. The psychiatrist, the treatment of chronic renal failure, and the prolongation of life: I. *American Journal of Psychiatry*, 1968, *124*, 1351–1358.

Abram, H. S. The psychiatrist, the treatment of chronic renal failure, and the prolongation of life: II. *American Journal of Psychiatry*, 1969, *126*, 157–166.

Abram, H. S. Repetitive dialysis. In T. P. Hackett & N. H. Cassem (Eds.), *Massachusetts General Hospital: Handbook of general hospital psychiatry*. St. Louis: C. V. Mosby Co., 1978.

Abram, H. S., Hester, L. R., Sheridan, W. F., & Epstein, G. M. Sexual functioning in patients with chronic renal failure. *Journal of Nervous and Mental Disease*, 1975, *160*, 220–226.

Abram, H. S., Moore, G. L., & Westervelt, F. B. Suicidal behavior in chronic dialysis patients. *American Journal of Psychiatry*, 1971, *127*, 1199–1204.

Alexander, L. The double-bind theory and hemodialysis. *Archives of General Psychiatry,* 1976, *33*, 1353–1356.

Alexander, R. A., & MacElveen, P. M. Are we assessing the needs of home dialysis partners? *Journal of the American Association of Nephrology Nurses and Technicians*, 1977, *4*, (supplementary edition), 23–29.

Armstrong, S. H. Psychological maladjustment in renal dialysis patients. *Psychosomatics*, 1978, *19*, 169–171.

Atcherson, E. The quality of life: A study of hemodialysis patients. *Health and Social Work*, 1978, *3*, 54–69.

Barnes, M. R. Token economy control of fluid overload in a patient receiving hemodialysis. *Journal of Behavioral Therapy and Experimental Psychiatry*, 1976, *7*, 305–306.

Beard, B. H. Fear of death and fear of life. *Archives of General Psychiatry*, 1969, *21*, 373–380.

Brown, D. J., Craick, C. C., Davies, S. E., Johnson, M. L., Dawborn, J. K., & Heale, W. F. Physical, emotional and social adjustments to home dialysis. *Medical Journal of Australia*, 1978, *1*, 245–247.

Calsyn, D. A., Sherrard, D. J., Freeman, C. W., Hyerstay, B. J., & Curtis, F. K. Vocational adjustment, psychological assessment and survival on hemodialysis. *Transactions American Society for Artificial Internal Organs*, 1978, *24*, 125–126.

Campbell, J. D., & Campbell, A. R. The social and economic costs of end-stage renal disease. *The New England Journal of Medicine*, 1978, *299*, 386–392.

Clark, R., Hailstone, J. D., & Slade, P. D. Psychological aspects of dialysis: A Sementic Differential study. *Psychological Medicine*, 1979, *9*, 55–62.

Cole, B. H., Stelzer, S., & Bayersdorfer, M. V. Development of a psychological program on a dialysis unit. *Professional Psychology*, 1979, *10*, 200–206.

Cramond, W. A., Knight, P. R., & Lawrence, J. R. The psychiatric contribution to a renal unit undertaking chronic haemodialysis and renal homotransplantation. *British Journal of Psychiatry*, 1967, *13*, 1201–1212.

Czaczkes, J. W., & De-Nour, A. K. *Chronic Hemodialysis as a Way of Life*. New York: Brunner/Mazel, 1978.

De-Nour, A. K. Hemodialysis: Sexual functioning. *Psychosomatics*, 1978, *19*, 229–235.

De-Nour, A. K., & Czaczkes, J. W. Emotional problems and reactions of the medical fear in a chronic hemodialysis unit. *The Lancet*, 1968, *2*, 987–991.

De-Nour, A. K., & Czaczkes, J. W. Professional team opinion and personal bias—A study of a chronic hemodialysis unit team. *Journal of Chronic Diseases*, 1971, *24*, 533–541.

De-Nour, A. K., & Czaczkes, J. W. Personality factors in chronic hemodialysis patients causing noncompliance with medical regimen. *Psychosomatic Medicine*, 1972, *34*, 333–344.

De-Nour, A. K., & Czaczkes, J. W. The influence of patient's personality on adjustment to chronic dialysis: A predictive study. *The Journal of Nervous and Mental Disease*, 1976, *162*, 323–333.

De-Nour, A. K., Shaltiel, J., & Czaczkes, J. W. Emotional reactions of patients on chronic hemodialysis. *Psychosomatic Medicine*, 1968, *30*, 521–533.

Dimond, M. Social support and adaptation to chronic illness: The case of maintenance hemodialysis. *Research in Nursing and Health*, 1979, *2*, 101–108.

Ebra, G., & Toth, J. C. Chronic hemodialysis: Some psychological and rehabilitative considerations. *Rehabilitation Literature*, 1972, *33*, 2–10.

Farmer, C. J., Bewick, M., Parsons, V., & Snowden, S. A. Survival on home haemodialysis: Its relationship with physical symptomatology, psychosocial background and psychiatric morbidity. *Psychological Medicine*, 1979, *9*, 515–523.

Farmer, C. J., Snowden, S. A., & Parsons, V. The prevalence of psychiatric illness among patients on home haemodialysis. *Psychological Medicine*, 1979, *9*, 509–514.

Fishman, D. B., & Schneider, C. J. Predicting emotional adjustment in home dialysis patients and their relatives. *Journal of Chronic Diseases*, 1972, *25*, 99–109.

Flannery, J. G. Adaptation to chronic renal failure. *Psychosomatics*, 1978, *19*, 784–787.

Foster, F. G., Cohn, G. C., & McKegney, F. P. Psychobiologic factors and individual survival on chronic renal hemodialysis—A two year follow-up: Part I. *Psychosomatic Medicine*, 1973, *35*, 64–82.

Freyberger, H. Six years' experience as a psychosomaticist in a hemodialysis unit. *Psychotherapy and Psychosomatics*, 1973, *22*, 226–232.

Friedman, E. A., Delano, B. G., & Butt, K.M.H. Pragmatic realities in uremia therapy. *The New England Journal of Medicine*, 1978, *298*, 368–371.

Friedman, E. A., Goodwin, N. J., & Chaudhry, L. Psychosocial adjustment to maintenance hemodialysis: Part I. *New York State Journal of Medicine*, 1970, *70*, 629–637.

Glassman, B. M., & Siegel, A. Personality correlates of survival in long-term hemodialysis program. *Archives of General Psychiatry*, 1970, *22*, 566–574.

Goldfried, M. R., & D'Zurilla, T. J. A behavorial analytic model for assessing competence. In C. D. Spielberger (Ed.), *Current topics in clinical and community psychology* (Vol. 1). New York: Academic Press, 1969.

Greenberg, I. M., Weltz, S., Spitz, C., & Bizzozero, J. Factors of adjustment in chronic hemodialysis patients. *Psychosomatics*, 1975, *16*, 178–184.

Greenberg, M. D. Personality and adjustment in hemodialysis patients. *Dialysis and Transplantation*, 1977, *6*, 9–10, 12–13, 89.

Hagberg, B. A prospective study of patients in chronic hemodialysis—III. Predictive value of intelligence, cognitive deficit, and ego defense structures in rehabilitation. *Journal of Psychosomatic Research*, 1974, *18*, 151–160.

Hagberg, B., & Malmquist, A. A prospective study of patients in chronic hemodialysis—IV. Pretreatment psychiatric and psychological variables predicting outcome. *Journal of Psychosomatic Research*, 1974, *18*, 315–319.

Halper, I. S. Psychiatric observations in a chronic hemodialysis program. *Medical Clinics of North America*, 1971, *55*, 177–191.

Holcomb, J. L., & MacDonald, R. W. Social functioning of artificial kidney patients. *Social Science and Medicine*, 1973, *7*, 109–119.

Janis, I. *Psychological Stress*. New York: Wiley, 1958.

Katz, Roger C. Single session recovery from a hemodialysis phobia: A case study. *Behavior Therapy and Experimental Psychiatry*, 1974, *5*, 205–206.

Kress, H. Adaptation to chronic dialysis: A two-way street. *Social Work in Health Care*, 1975, *1*, 41–46.

Landsman, M. K. The patient with chronic renal failure: A marginal man. *Annals of Internal Medicine*, 1975, *82*, 268–270.

Landsman, M. Adjustment to dialysis: The middle years. *Dialysis and Transplantation*, 1978, *7*, 433–434.

Lefebvre, P., Nobert, A., & Crombez, J. C. Psychological and psychopathological reactions in relation to chronic hemodialysis. *Canadian Psychiatric Association Journal*, 1972, *17*, 9–13.

Levenberg, S. B., & Campbell, L. M. An Ericksonian approach to long-term adjustment to hemodialysis. *Journal of the American Association of Nephrology Nurses and Technicians*, 1977, *4*, 19–23.

Levy, N. B. The psychology and care of the maintenance hemodialysis patient. *Heart and Lung*, 1973, *2*, 400–405. (a)

Levy, N. B. Sexual adjustment to maintenance hemodialysis and renal transplantation; national survey by questionnaire: Preliminary report. *Transactions American Society for Artificial Internal Organs*, 1973, *19*, 138–143. (b)

Levy, N. B. Psychological studies at the downstate medical center of patients on hemodialysis. *Medical Clinics of North America*, 1977, *61*, 759–769.

Levy, N. B. Psychological sequelae to hemodialysis. *Psychosomatics*, 1978, *19*, 329–331.

Levy, N. B., & Wynbrandt, G. D. The quality of life on maintenance hemodialysis. *The Lancet*, 1975, *1*, 1328–1330.

Lira, F. T., & Mlott, S. R. A behavioral approach to hemodialysis training. *Journal of the American Association of Nephrology Nurses and Technicians*, 1976, *3*, 180–188.

Livesley, W. J. Psychiatric disturbance and chronic haemodialysis. *British Medical Journal*, 1979, *4*, 509–514.

Mabry, T., Acchiardo, S. F., & Trapp, G. Psychological aspects of dialysis from the personnel viewpoint. *Dialysis and Transplantation*, 1977, *6*, 38–39.

MacElveen, P. M. Cooperative triad in home dialysis care and patient outcomes. *Communicating Nursing Research*, 1972, *5*, 134–147.

MacElveen, P. M., & Alexander, R. A. How does home dialysis fit into the family life cycle? *Journal of the American Association of Nephrology Nurses and Technicians*, 1977, *4* (supplementary edition), 14–22.

Magrab, P. R., & Papadopoulou, Z. L. The effect of a token economy on dietary compliance for children on hemodialysis. *Journal of Applied Behavior Analysis*, 1977, *10*, 573–578.

Malmquist, A. A prospective study of patients in chronic hemodialysis—I. Method and characteristics of the patient group. *Journal of Psychosomatic Research*, 1973, *17*, 333–337. (a)

Malmquist, A. A prospective study of patients in chronic hemodialysis—II. Predicting factors regarding rehabilitation. *Journal of Psychosomatic Research*, 1973, *17*, 339–344. (b)

Malmquist, A., & Hagberg, B. A prospective study of patients in chronic hemodialysis— V. A follow-up study of thirteen in home dialysis. *Journal of Psychosomatic Research*, 1974, *18*, 321–326.

Marshall, J. R. Effective use of a psychiatric consultant on a dialysis unit. *Postgraduate Medicine*, 1974, 55(2), 121–125.

McKegney, F. P., & Lange, P. The decision to no longer live on chronic hemodialysis. American Journal of Psychiatry, 1971, *128*, 267–274.

McKevitt, P., & Koppel, D. Psychosocial needs and concerns of the elderly on dialysis. *Dialysis and Transplantation*, 1978, *7*, 435–441.

Nelson, R. O. Assessment and therapeutic functions of self-monitoring. In M. Hersen, R. M. Eiseler, & P. M. Miller (Eds.), *Progress in behavior modification* (Vol. 5). New York: Academic Press, 1977.

Pendras, J. P., Pollard, T. L. Eight years' experience with a community dialysis center: The

Northwest Kidney Center. *Transactions American Society for Artificial Internal Organs*, 1970, *16*, 77–84.

Pentecost, R. L., Zwirenz, B., & Manuel, J. W. Intrafamily identity and home dialysis success. *Nephron*, 1976, *17*, 88–103.

Pritchard, M. J. Measurement of illness behavior in patients on haemodialysis and awaiting cardiac surgery. *Journal of Psychosomatic Research*, 1979, *23*, 117–130.

Reichsman, F., & Levy, N. B. Problems in adaptation to maintenance hemodialysis: A four year study of 25 patients. *Archives of Internal Medicine*, 1972, *130*, 859–865.

Roger, B. The role of the psychiatrist in the renal dialysis unit. In R. O. Pasnau (Ed.), *Consultation-liaison psychiatry*. New York: Grune & Stratton, 1975.

Sand, P., Livingston, G., & Wright, R. G. Psychological assessment of candidates for a hemodialysis program. *Annals of Internal Medicine*, 1966, *64*, 602–610.

Sand, P. L., Treischmann, R. B., Fordyce, W. E., & Fowler, R. S. Behavioral modification in the medical rehabilitation setting: Rationale and some applications. In R. C. Katz & S. Zlutnick (Eds.), *Behavior therapy and health care: Principles and applications*. New York: Pergamon Press, Inc., 1975.

Seime, R. J. The relationship of compliance, self-reported feelings and symptoms, and staff attention in dialysis: A pilot study. In D. J. Withersty, J. M. Stevenson, & R. H. Waldman (Eds.), *Communication and compliance in a hospital setting*. Springfield, Ill.: Charles C Thomas, 1980.

Shambaugh, P. W., & Kanter, S. S. Spouses under stress: Group meetings with spouses of patients on hemodialysis. *American Journal of Psychiatry*, 1969, *125*, 928–935.

Shea, E. J., Bogden, D. F., Freeman, R. B., & Schreiner, G. E. Hemodialysis for chronic renal failure: IV. Psychological considerations. *Annals of Internal Medicine*, 1965, *62*, 558–563.

Short, M. J., & Wilson, W. P. Roles of denial in chronic hemodialysis. *Archives of General Psychiatry*, 1969, *20*, 433–437.

Smith, E. K., Curtis, J. R., McDonald, S. J., & DeWardener, H. E. Haemodialysis in the home: Problems and frustrations. *The Lancet*, 1969, *1*, 614–617.

Sobel, H. J., & Worden, J. W. The MMPI as a predictor of psychosocial adaptation to cancer. *Journal of Consulting and Clinical Psychology*, 1979, *47*, 716–724.

Springer, J. R. A preventive mental health program for dialysis patients: A preliminary report. *Journal of the American Association of Nephrology Nurses and Technicians*, 1976, *3*, 65–73.

Steele, T. E., Finkelstein, S. H., & Finkelstein, F. D. Hemodialysis, patients and spouses. Journal of Nervous and Mental Diseases, 1976, *162*, 225–237.

Stewart, R. S., & Stewart, R. M. Neuropsychiatric aspects of chronic renal disease. *Psychosomatics*, 1979, *20*, 524–537.

Streltzer, J., Finkelstein, F., Feigenbaum, H., Kitsen, J., & Cohn, G. The spouse's role in home hemodialysis. *Archives of General Psychiatry*, 1976, *33*, 55–58.

Sullivan, M. F. The dialysis patient and attitude towards work. *Psychiatry in Medicine*, 1973, *4*, 213–219.

Turk, D. C., Sobel, H. J., Follick, M. J., & Youkilis, H. D. A sequential criterion analysis for assessing coping with chronic illness. *Journal of Human Stress*, 1980, *2*, 35–40.

Wenerowicz, W. J. The use of behavior modification techniques for the treatment of hemodialysis patient noncompliance: A case study. *Journal of Dialysis*, 1979, *3*, 41–50.

Wilson, C. J., Muzekari, L. H., Schneps, S. A., & Wilson, D. M. Time-limited group counseling for chronic home hemodialysis patients. *Journal of Counseling Psychology*, 1974, *21*, 376–379.

Winokur, M. Z., Czaczkes, J. W., & De-Nour, A. K. Intelligence and adjustment to chronic hemodialysis. *Journal of Psychosomatic Research*, 1973, *17*, 29–34.

Wright, R. G., Sand, P., & Livingston, G. Psychological stress during hemodialysis for chronic renal failure. *Annals of Internal Medicine*, 1966, *64*, 611–621.

Epilogue

As the finishing touches are placed on this book, events continue to touch our lives. The conference on which this volume is based came to a close as one of our mothers, Mary Callahan, neared the end of her fight against cancer. A phone call as the conference ended revealed that she was near death and it was time to join her. Only on reaching her bedside was a note written 2 days earlier revealed. It said simply: "I must stay alive until Ed gets home." She lived through the Saturday night that the conference ended; she died at the end of the next day, Mother's Day, 1980, with her husband and children around her.

Her cancer had been a crisis for the family; it presented both a problem and an opportunity. The problem, of course, was to learn to deal with 13 years of fearing cancer, fearing her death, and needing to provide a comfortable environment for her final bout with illness and death. Cancer is still a nonnormative event in an individual's life; its increasing frequency is making it a normative event for families in America. Keeping a parent at home, to die away from the hospital, is assuredly a nonnormative crisis. Its problems are obvious: Could you keep an ill parent alive longer with hospital intervention? When do you stop trying to do painful suctioning of phlegm from the throat of a dying woman? How do you deal with the desire to call an

313

LIFE-SPAN DEVELOPMENTAL PSYCHOLOGY
Nonnormative Life Events

ambulance when breath fades slowly away? And after death, how does a family deal with a police investigation because death occurred at home instead of in the socially sanctioned hospital?

The opportunity in the process is obvious as well. At first, the opportunity for a cancer patient comes out of the problem of likely death: It is the freedom to live all available time fully, to express love fully, to establish stronger ties before death. For the family, the opportunity lies in having the chance to work out relationship issues, to say goodbye and to say I love you. Death at home offers the chance to make death more real: an acceptable friend who comes gradually, not rapidly, who ends suffering, not prolongs it. Death at home offers the family the chance to bond closely as they experience the throes of death. The pain is no less real, but the opportunity exists for strong mutual support in the shared experience with death. Accepting loss never fully ends the longing for the loved one, but it does allow building new bonds over time.

Those new bonds are symbolized for us by birth: obviously the most normative life event, but also the first step in a process that will assuredly provide some unexpected quirks and pains. At the time of this writing, a new child is expected momentarily. Perhaps it will be a redheaded girl like the grandmother lost to cancer, or brown-haired like the other grandmother lost suddenly to a heart attack; regardless, the child will present its family with crises: problems and opportunities enough for a lifetime of growth.

And as developmental psychologists we will study these processes; as clinical psychologists we will try to help participants adjust and grow; and as people, we will feel with and for those about whom this book is written: the human family.

Postscript: And a redheaded girl was born; she was named Shavahn. Her birth was caesarian and thus nonnormative; because caesarian technology exists, the nonnormative event of fetal and maternal death was avoided. Once again, a crisis provided a problem and an opportunity.

Author Index

315

Subject Index